MARGARET STORM JAM
Yorkshire, on 8 January 1891. H
then a small fishing and shipbuildir
her grandfather was a shipowner,
educated at a private school, follo
School in Scarborough. Awarde
Scholarships available in the North Riding of Yorkshire at that time,
she took an honours degree in English Language and Literature at
Leeds University in 1912 and was given a one-year research
scholarship, to be held at University College, London: she found
University College dull, and transferred herself to King's College.
Her thesis, on Modern Drama in Europe, finally approved by Leeds
University, was rewarded by the Degree of Master of Arts; it was
published in 1920, by the firm of William Collins. In the meantime
she had married and had a son.

In 1919 she returned to London, becoming for a year a copy-
writer in a large advertising agency. She published her first novel, and
began a two-year editorship of an obscure weekly magazine, *New
Commonwealth*. From 1923 to 1925 she acted as the English representative of the American publisher Alfred A. Knopf, and later, for
two and a half years, was co-manager, with her second husband, Guy
Patterson Chapman, of the short-lived publishing house of Alfred A.
Knopf in London. She married Guy Chapman in 1925, a
deeply happy marriage, broken in 1972 by his death, after
a distinguished career beginning with the publication in 1933 of
A Passionate Prodigality, his classic account of trench warfare in
France, and ending in a study of the politics and history of the Third
Republic of France.

Between the years of 1919 and 1979 Storm Jameson published a
total of forty-five novels. She has also written short stories, literary
essays, criticism, and a two-volume autobiography. In 1939 she
became the first woman president of the British section of International
PEN, where she was an outspoken liberal and anti-Nazi, and a friend
and helper of refugee writers. In 1952 she was a delegate to the
UNESCO Congress of the Arts, held in Venice. She was awarded a
D.Litt. from Leeds University in 1943, and is a member of the
American Academy and Institute of Arts and Letters. With her
husband, she has been an inveterate traveller, mostly in Europe. She
now lives in Cambridge.

If you would like to know more about Virago books, write to us at 41 William IV Street, London WC2N 4DB for a full catalogue.

Please send a stamped addressed envelope

Autobiography of Storm Jameson

JOURNEY FROM THE NORTH

Volume I

Published by Virago Press Limited 1984
41 William IV Street, London WC2N 4DB

Journey From the North Volume I first published 1969
This edition of Journey From the North Volume I offset
from the Collins & Harvill Press
edition of 1969

Printed in Great Britain by
The Anchor Press at Tiptree, Essex

British Library Cataloguing in Publication data

Jameson, Storm
  Journey from the north.
  Vol. 1
  1. Jameson, Storm   2. Authors,
  English – 20th century – Biography
  I. Title
  823′.912   PR6019.A67Z/
  ISBN 0-86068-501-2

The cover shows a detail from 'Entering Whitby' by Henry Redmore, reproduced by
kind permission of Freeman Fine Arts, Whitby.

Written for my judges

the forgotten men and women who made me

If a man has the temerity to write the story of his life, he should have a double aim: first, to show it and his little ego in relation to the time and place in which he lived his life, to the procession of historical events, even to the absurd metaphysics of the universe; secondly, to describe as simply and clearly as he can, his personal life, his relation, not to history and the universe, but to persons and himself, his record in the trivial, difficult, fascinating art of living from day to day, hour to hour, minute to minute.

LEONARD WOOLF: *Downhill All The Way*

Contents

Illustrations between pp 226 and 227

The author, 1923

The author's youngest sister, 1938

Lilo

The author and Marina Pauliny in Bratislava, 1938

Part I: Avoid this Spring

So soon as ever your mazed spirit descends
From daylight into darkness, Man, remember
What you have suffered here in Samothrace
What you have suffered . . .
To the left hand there bubbles a black spring
Overshadowed with a great white cypress.
Avoid this spring, which is Forgetfulness;
Though all the common rout rush down to drink,
Avoid this spring!

ROBERT GRAVES

Chapter 1

There are people, there are even writers, whose lives were worth recording because they were passed in strange or exciting ways, or involved famous persons, or could be written as the story of a great mind in search of its beliefs. I have a good but not a great mind; my chances of meeting great men have been few and I have not sought them: the men and women who have come nearest slaking my curiosity about human nature have been obscure as well as alive with humours. The humours of the great are usually too well groomed.

What is a record of my life worth—the life of a writer treated with justice in circles where *camaraderie, cette plaie mortelle de la littérature,* is the merciful rule?

Perhaps little, except that as a life it spans three distinct ages: the middle class heyday before 1914, the *entre deux guerres,* and the present; three ages so disparate that to a person who knows only the third the others are unimaginable. Anyone born before 1900 can examine one civilization as if it were done with—as it is, but for noticing that a few of its ideas and traditions are still feebly active. Indeed, I can excavate two finished stages in society, since I remember sharply the one I rebelled against while continuing to live blindly by more than one of its rooted assumptions: that people of my class do not starve, that reticence in speech, and clean linen, are bare necessities, that books exist to be read. I ought to be able to describe them both.

Possibly I lack the coolness to give a dependable account of them to the ignorant. I can try.

That arrogant half-sarcastic phrase, *it can be tried,* is one I heard so often in my North Riding childhood that it has become an instinct. I seldom know when I am being led astray by it. It was a servant's saying, but a northern servant.

The span of my life is even longer than it seems, since its roots are twisted round hundreds of lives passed in the same place. Only a life starting from centuries of familiarity with the same few fields and streets is better than fragmentary. If there is any tenacity in me, any constancy, if there is an I under all the dissimilar I's seen by those who know or knew me as daughter, as young woman, undisciplined, confident, absurd, as wife, as friend, the debt is owed to obscure men and women born and dying in the same isolated place during hundreds of years.

All I could do to destroy the pattern, I have done.

What Pascal, writing about Montaigne, called '*le sot projet qu'il a de se peindre*' is, after all, a book like any other. If it is dull, it will quickly be forgotten. Or, if it is not readable now, when there are people alive able to compare the portrait with the original and find it distorted or a lie, it may become readable when neither they nor I are here to protest.

How far can I hope to give a true account of an animal I know only from the inside? Nothing would have been easier for me than to write one of those charming poetic memoirs which offend no one and leave a pleasant impression of the author. I am trying to do something entirely different. Trying, in short, to eat away a double illusion: the face I show other people, and the illusion I have of myself—by which I live. Can I?

It is true that what one sees from the inside is the seams, the dark tangled roots of feeling and action, which may be just as misleading, as partial, as the charming poeticized version I am trying to reject. But it is *a* truth—known only to me.

I feel an ineffaceable repugnance to writing about close friends. Of the few people, men and women, I know intimately, I can bring myself to write down only the least intimate facts. This falsifies the record at once. But what can I do? Nothing.

'The real story of a life would consist in a recital of the experiences, few or many, in which the whole self was engaged. The greater part of such a book would be very dull, since as often as not our whole self turns its back contemptuously on the so-called great moments and emotions and engages itself in trivialities, the shape of a particular hill, a road known in infancy, the movement of the wind through grass. The things we shall take with us at the last will all be small.'

I wrote this, or something very like it, in a novel published thirty years ago. It is probably true. The pain and ecstasy of youth, the brief happiness, the long uncharted decline, can be summed up in the tune of a once popular waltz, of no merit, or the point in a country lane where the violence and hopelessness of a passion suddenly became obvious, or the moment when a word, a gesture, nothing in themselves, gave the most acute sensual pleasure. None of these can be written about.

It will be easy, too, to lose one's way in an underworld where time is no longer a succession of events, one damned thing after another, but a continuous present in which the dead, and the little I know about them, jostle the ghosts of the living. And where the antique chorus of frogs listened to in March 1935 in Spain is—at the same moment—distending the darkness above a lake in northern New York State fourteen years later.

The first thing I remember is the deck of a ship in sunlight. A lady, her face hidden from me by the parasol in her hand, is there in a low chair. My head, which does not reach above the arm of the chair, aches. I must just have told her so. Without turning her own, she answers, 'Nonsense. Children don't have headaches.'

She must have been mistaken. Some indefinite time later I am lying peaceably at the bottom of a crevasse, its walls densely white; two persons, indistinct, are looking over the edge, and one of them says, 'She's sinking.' The ship, I think. That the ship is sinking *out there* is no business of mine, and doesn't ruffle me.

My third memory is of a field of marguerites, so long-stemmed, or I at the time so short, that they and I were face to face, eye against incandescent eye. The whiteness seared, dazzled, blinded, a naked seething radiance, whiter than all whiteness, running out of sight.

Since beginning this book—that is, yesterday, Friday, the 11th of August 1961, the day of the new moon—I have realized what most intelligent people doubtless knew already: in any life a few, very few, key images turn up again and again, recognizable even though deformed by the changed light or the angle at which they reappear. This fierce whiteness is one of mine.

Another is the sound, a middling deep note, of the Whitby bell-buoy, ringing a mile off-shore, clearly audible at night or at any time when the wind blew off the sea.

And another sound, made, this one, by the fishermen's children when I was very young: it was like the screech of gulls—*Ah–wa–a–ah!*—piercing, barely human, half summons, half warning. You could believe that every ship in the world was casting off at once. It was years before I knew enough to interpret it as *Away*!

In due course I shall come on the other two or three of these primitive or underworld images, voices out of sleep, out of a lost harbour, which are mine. They may indeed be the only things I ever, in the positive sense of the word, hear or see.

The voyage on which I so nearly died was one of my earliest, if not the first. It was certainly not my mother's first: in those days before human existence got out of hand, a sea-captain had the right to take his wife with him on any voyage, even as far as the River Plate or the Far East. She knew one or two older women, childless, who had no shore home; all they possessed, their clothes, family photographs, curling-tongs, shared the captain's cabin next the chart-room with his clothing and the ship's papers. She, I believe, envied these freed women while barely approving of them: life in a house of her own often bored her.

So long as she had only one child, she could go away easily, joining the ship in an English port or at Le Havre or Flushing. The first of these departures that I remember was in the early light; I see clearly the half-dark kitchen and taste the end crust of the loaf, soaked in scaldingly hot tea, she had given me: it was yeasty and exquisite. Were we going to Greenock, Harwich for Antwerp, Swansea? Once, in the last port, directed to it by the man in the ticket-office of the dock station, she and I found ourselves in a small hotel, in a bedroom immediately behind the bar, which was full of lascars. It was too late to seek farther, and while I slept in my clothes my mother spent the night sitting on the trunk she had dragged across the door.

The days at sea in a less than 3,000-ton ship were crushingly long and boring—it would not have entered anyone's head to amuse me —but the ports . . . ah!

Antwerp: tall yellow-faced houses behind a quay; the Place Verte with its flower-women; the rue de la Meir; the open trams; the zoo gardens at night, a band playing to sedately strolling families, the tall schoolboys in girlish socks and blouses, ridiculously bare-legged; the superb glove shop; the rough knife-edged grass of the ramparts; the open carriage clip-clopping us back to the docks.

It was Antwerp that gave me my first notion of an art. In a shop-window of the rue de la Meir there was a large painting of a garden, with two half-embraced figures in the foreground. It seized on my imagination and became for a few weeks my idea of sensual bliss. This had nothing to do with its merits as a painting, which doubtless did not exist.

One day when we came ashore—off the *Saxon Prince*?—the wharf was strewn with black brittle husks from some outlandish cargo; a man waiting to come aboard told us that Queen Victoria had died, news that made my mother pull a sorrowful face. So far as I knew, I had never heard of the woman, but a sense of her importance and the strange husks underfoot started up in me such a crazy excitement that to this day voyages and death resemble each other in my mind as one harbour is like another in another island.

So many journeys, begun before memory, so many half-obliterated departures, how could they fail to ruin my life?

Its pattern, if the word can be used of such a coil, was set by them at the start.

The impulse to go away has disturbed, delighted, mocked me, and is to blame for my failure to settle anywhere. I left one place with anguish, leaving behind half my soul, the less indifferent half: none of the many others I have lived in keep more than a thin paring of it, thinner and less persistent than the shadow I catch sight of in Bordeaux or Antwerp of my mother, pausing to stare in a shop-window at a hat she would buy if she could barely afford it, and were less arrogantly afraid of the foreign saleswoman: in those days she was an elegante—the word is not used now, but it fitted her—coveting finely simple dresses and beautiful gloves. I doubt whether she was content anywhere—any more than I am. I even doubt whether she felt the pleasure I rate higher than any other, that of being in a foreign town for the first time, free of its probably mediocre streets and cafés, its sounds, and the silence which encloses the stranger walking about in it, obliged to no one for her happiness.

The restlessness in my nerves and senses comes to me through her. Where did she get it? From sea-going ancestors, from the North Sea, from the stones themselves of the little port (already able in the seventh century to build a parish church and an Abbey to which the body of St Edwin, first Christian king of Northumbria, was brought at the end of the century: in the ninth, the Danes burned both church and Abbey), with its memories of loss, flight, violence?

Restless, adrift from the start, spiritually clumsy and imprudent, can I make sense of my life? Has it a meaning? If I can find the courage to stare coldly at its ghosts (including my own past selves, clumsy ungovernable young idiots), and as coldly at the moments of happiness as at griefs, blunders, sins, humiliating failures, will the meaning, if there is a meaning, emerge?

It can be tried. I am too old to be mortified by a failure.

And in a world so sharply menaced by destruction as ours, there is something friendly in the idea of going on gossiping to the last minute—if it is no more than to call a friend's attention to the exquisite yellow of a dying leaf or to ask for news of a child, the one who came last year to stay, and tethered an imaginary horse in every room in the house.

Chapter 2

I have a trick, when forced to make a speech—a folly I commit as seldom as possible—of repeating mentally: I am the last voice on earth of my grandfather George Gallilee and my mother Hannah Margaret Jameson.

This—call it what you like—this invocation has usually eased the ordeal. Once, on the 14th of December, 1943, it had an odd sequel. I had been speaking to the French Chamber of Commerce, at a luncheon, to please a friend, Pierre Maisonneuve, one of de Gaulle's Free French. Heaven knows what I talked about, and has mercifully erased the memory, but what happened afterwards is still entirely clear in my mind. An insignificant-looking Frenchman came up to me, smiling, and said: 'I have been sent to tell you that everything is all right. An old gentleman, very upright, with a great deal of white hair, was standing behind your chair when you spoke, and everything is all right.'

Taken completely aback, I made a stupid and ill-bred reply: 'That was George Gallilee, my grandfather; he was a severe man, with a bad temper.'

I don't pretend to explain the incident.

Possibly, when we talk of ourselves as being the only foothold the dead keep, the only channel for their voices, it is not nonsense or a sort of poetry (I distrust poetic prose). They insist on living in us. They deflect our voices. They dictate our first choices, those which further or ruin our lives.

My grandfather, my mother's father, had the reputation of a hard stubborn man, arbitrary, incorruptibly honest, with a violent temper kept, for the most part, under control. I did not know him. How could I? By the time I might have made something of him he had begun his long death, and all I felt for him was the shocking aversion I feel from illness and sickrooms. I suspect him of strong feelings, brutally repressed: an egoist by instinct and training, he could not help regarding women as inferior creatures, mentally and morally. He had a degree of respect for my mother, the only one of his children who was at all like him in looks and temper. He believed with cold ferocity that Lloyd George should be hanged and the lower classes kept in their place: a workman repairing the roof was all but startled into falling off when my grandfather shouted at him from the nearest window to stop whistling or go home.

When I knew him, and until he died, he was handsome in a forbidding way: a head of hair as white as silk, springing strongly back from his forehead and temples, a thick white goatee, the long upper lip of his hard fine mouth clean-shaven, a splendid nose, and the formidably clear cold pale blue eyes he passed on to my mother and she to her last-born. (Not to me: mine are a darker clouded greyblue: I fit badly into my skull, and while my eyes are taking you in my brain is trying to guess what you are thinking and what will keep you at a safe distance.)

He was bookish and extremely fastidious. He took daily ice-cold baths, dressed formally, and until his stroke held himself as straight as a bolt.

He had been a ship-owner. He sold out of shipping too early in life, and before it began to make money again. He married twice: his second wife was the one I knew as my grandmother: he married her to look after his seven children (seven living, out of I forget how many born) and entertain his friends; she was a middle-aged widow with three sons of her own; a rascally solicitor had bolted to Australia with the money left her by her husband: whenever, in street or church aisle, she saw one of his relatives she would ask loudly: 'Ha' ye heard from t' thief lately?'

It turned out that a fondness for fine old port unfitted her both as stepmother and hostess. My grandfather at once rearranged his life to conceal the blunder he had made. He put his children, five girls and two boys, into another house and visited them morning and evening: what social life he had was carried on outside his own house.

All his children were afraid of him, my mother, the youngest but one, less than the others: she had spirit and a hot temper, though at fifteen she was discovered to be 'in a decline,' that commonest of Victorian illnesses. The treatment ordered for her was the raw cod-liver oil brought by the whaling boats, and cold baths: she faithfully took both, carrying the cold water up every night to a hip-bath in her room, and lived.

Her father was no gentler with her than with the others; she had orders to be practising the piano when he arrived at eight in the morning, and he beat time by clapping his hands loudly within an inch of her ear: in winter, since he refused to allow fires to be lit in the house in daylight, her fingers stiffened immovably on the keys (as mine did at the end of the icy train journey to Scarborough to take a music examination in the Imperial Hotel. In spite of having less music in me than a crow, I passed three of these before my mother resigned herself to the certainty that I should never, being now fourteen, acquire the ghost of an ear). He disapproved of pampering anyone, of any age or sex. During the years when he was only half alive, his youngest unmarried daughter, now in her fifties, dutifully sat with him an hour every day. Even on the bitterest days he refused to allow her near the fire—'Back, girl, back!'

Except under his eye, it was a lively household: the youngest two, my mother and my aunt Jenny, laughed at everything, at their sisters, at each other, even, under the name of Mr Bultitude, at their terrible father.

My aunt, who was actively pious—she was a deacon of the Congregational Church—with none of my mother's profound indifference (masked by habit), had the irrepressible laugh of a very young child. I remember an afternoon when they talked about graves. Neither of them can have been less than sixty-five, and my mother was sharply vexed that she had not been able to find out from my father how many people had been buried in the grave belonging to him.

'I told him, "We can't expect to stay very much longer," and he said, "But I *will*." I have no patience with him, Jenny! Let me think: his father was lost at sea, but there's his mother and her father and mother, and a child. I believe there will be nine to a grave. So there should be plenty of room for him.' Her eyes started with anger. 'I won't go into *his* grave, not on any account.'

'Ours has Mr Bultitude and our mother, and sister Ann and sister

Mary, yes, and two children, Emily and Amy—I think they count as one.'

'And of course there's you to go in,' my mother said calmly. She frowned. 'It would be maddening to have to buy more land at the last minute.'

The absurdity of this conversation struck them both in the same instant and they went off into a fit of laughter; it lasted for minutes and was the gayest sound in the world.

As a very young child, I was mortally afraid of my grandfather. Yet the one time I had anything to do with him then, he behaved with great gentleness. My mother had been thrashing me. Made reckless by my fear of pain, I ran wildly round my bedroom, howling, trying to dodge the cane. Exhausted, she told me, 'I must bring your grandfather to deal with you.'

She left the house and I waited, in the state of self-induced apathy, a sort of stupor made up of dislike of showing distress, fear of being pitied, and a purely instinctive animal immobility, in which—so far —I have always been able to sink myself at will. Crouched on the landing outside my room, I watched my grandfather between the balusters as he came up the last flight: he halted half way up, stared at me for a moment and, to my great astonishment, said only, 'You shouldn't wear your mother out,' then turned and went down.

In those days it was the custom to thrash children. Few people imagined that they could be trained by any methods except those used on savagely unbroken horses. Whitby may have been backward in this respect (as in some others), still early Victorian, but not, I think, a great deal. My mother herself was impatient, easily bored, and perhaps more determined to bring her children up well than were some few of her contemporaries.

The cruelty of the method lay in its deliberateness. *I shall thrash you when we get home* had the ring of a death sentence. Any act of carelessness or disobedience outside the house merited it. If other people were present, the offender might get only a terrible glance, a warning what to expect. The pupil of my mother's eye seemed to send out a flash of light, like the discharge from a gun: I have never seen another such glance. The walk home might be short or long; no delay was long enough to ward off the assault on bared flesh and stretched nerves. And the business of forgiveness, which came hours later, was as emotionally racking as the punishment itself.

Only at this moment, as I write, sixty years after the event, I realize that when my grandfather halted and looked up, he saw a desperate little animal behind bars.

His second wife was my father's mother. The two familes were kept apart. My mother cannot have had even the most short-lived sense that she was marrying a stepbrother. Certainly she never regarded her mother-in-law as a stepmother. She disliked her. One day when she was an old woman herself, she spoke to me about her with all the bitterness of a high-spirited young girl.

'She was a wicked woman, malicious, a wilful liar, quite unscrupulous, and she had the tongue of a viper. I remember her saying to a servant who had just married, "I hope you'll ha' ten bairns and not a bite to put in their mouths." She was capable of any trick.'

She played evil tricks on her young daughter-in-law, and an amusing one. As a gesture of independence, my mother and her youngest sister had joined the Congregationalists, a sect the second Mrs George Gallilee considered not merely heretical but vulgar: she begged my mother to let me be decently baptized into the Church of England, promising to give 'the poor innocent bairn' a handsome christening present. The ceremony over, she presented an egg, a pinch of salt, and the smallest possible piece of silver, a threepenny bit.

I had no feeling for her, hardly even distaste. She handed out port and Christmas cake once a year, and pennies when we were taken to visit her on Sunday morning—'You'll ha' been to t'chapel,' she would say contemptuously—and occasionally begged one of us off a beating. She was then quince-yellow and shrunken, wearing lace caps over the sparse remains of black hair. In the end she, too, had a stroke and lay in the room next her husband's, speechless. The stroke paralysed her tongue.

My mother had one word for this. Justice.

Chapter 3

Of the uncounted places I have lived in, for years or months, only one haunts me. Since I left it for good, I have been adrift, and shall drift to my death. Yet I cannot go back there—any more than a tree, cut down, could return to its roots left in the ground.

I cannot be sure that everything I remember about a now vanished Whitby is my own memory or my mother's. The most grotesque memories are probably hers. Isolation—before the opening of a railway line through the valley to Pickering in 1836—bred, in counterweight to its benefits, a crop of eccentrics, harmless fools, misers, house devils, despots, male and some female, who behaved towards their families with a severity even George Gallilee would never have allowed himself.

Talking to me about those obscure Catos, my mother's tone implied a certain respect. Later, when I came to study the Russian dramatist Ostrovski, I thought I recognized them in his plays of crushed lives and meaningless cruelties inflicted behind the bolted doors of provincial merchants' houses. Bitter tears must have been shed, decently, in strict secrecy, by the families of well-to-do men (and a few matriarchs), some of them only hard and miserly, some laughable, but all egotistical to the verge of madness, or so rigid with principles that they might as well have been lunatics.

In the early years of my childhood Whitby was still beautiful. It no longer built ships—sailing-ships, whalers, and, later, small steam-ships which had to be towed to Middlesborough or Newcastle to fit their engines—but the skeletons of two of the old yards were rotting placidly, weeds thrusting between the stones and iron rings, on the edge of the upper harbour. I have a confused memory of a launching—the last?

I should admit at once that, for me, Yorkshire is Whitby—but not the town you will see if you go there now in search of a happiness which depends on a place.

Since my fortunate infancy, the high-hedged lanes and fields, the bare cliff-tops covered with short springing grass, have been disfigured by a brick rash, the ancient pier intolerably tawdrified, the splendid subscription library thrown away, and heaven knows what other outrage and perversion. Something remains. Impossible—unless there are no limits to insensitivity and contempt for what is only charming and dignified—to spoil the ruined Benedictine Abbey on the East cliff, or the quiet waters of the estuary. Or the Norman church crouched, pressed into the ground by the wind, between abbey and cliff-edge, and reached by a hundred and ninety-nine wide shallow stone steps from the harbour. The soul of an old ship inhabits this church and its three-decker pulpit: ships' carpenters put up the present roof, and the windows under it are so like cabin windows that on the rare Sundays when we occupied my grandfather's pew in one of the galleries I could only dream of voyages. Outside, the dust of Saxons, Danes, monks, ship-builders, master mariners, lies deep under the rank grass between wrinkled gravestones eaten by the salt.

Standing on the cliff-edge, three hundred or more feet above the sea, and looking north past the mouth of the harbour and the West cliff, you see a gently-curving coast-line, which moves me as music moves people who understand it.

In the narrow streets on both sides of the harbour, you may come on a child with the wiry reddish-gold hair of the Norsemen, harriers of this coast, driving their murderously beaked black boats into the sandy mouths of streams, and landing to kill, burn and, as they did at the mouth of the Esk, settle. (The first name I saw in Norway was *Storm*, on a doorway in Horten, a small town in the Oslo Fjord.)

Looking back, I seem to see the first step towards an inevitable deterioration in the re-naming—to please an enfeebled taste—of the Saloon. This was—you could not call it a cliff-garden, since there was only grass and paths or steps twisting half way down the West cliff to a theatre and a small reading-room and, built out above the sands some fifty feet below, a broad asphalted walk, with a bandstand in the open air: ticket-holders walked up and down during the concerts (as in Antwerp) or sat about on benches and iron chairs listening to Berlioz, Auber, Rossini, Weber, Strauss, and looking at the sea. It was re-named the Spa. Then the end of the walk was glassed in, to shelter orchestra and audience from the often cold sea wind; then . . . but why go on?

Or, perhaps, mark the beginning of the end by the humblest of graves—that of the last of the old fishwives who came round singing *vessel*(wassail)-*cups* in December. They carried a box lined with evergreens, holding a little cheap doll, and sang in quavering voices, as harsh as gulls,

God a-rest you, merry merry gentlemen . . .

The oldest of them died well before 1914.

Before 1914, too, the pier and the narrow street under the East cliff had superb jet-shops. If you own one of the elaborate necklaces cut by Whitby jet-workers, cherish it; there will be no more: a craft started in the Bronze Age no longer pays.

Not a great way beyond the upper harbour, the hills begin to fold in; a few miles inland they rise to a wide stretch of moor, by turns fox-red, purple, bone-grey, seamed by runnels of peaty water and narrow valleys filled with foxgloves, gorse, dog-roses, thyme, bracken, and a few self-possessed villages. In my childhood the moor road from Pickering to Whitby said all there is to say about the instinct for solitude, sharper than the impulse to herd: peewits, sea-gulls, a few grouse and, at a certain point, the first sight, piercing the heart, of the church and the Abbey clinging to the East cliff.

Eleven years ago, an unexpected glimpse of them from a lonely road running east brought tears to my eyes before I could check them, and I had to turn away to hide from my two companions my ridiculous anguish.

If I think of anything at the end of my life it will probably be the sea, the North Sea: the milky blue of summer, harmless ripples caressing the ankles of trippers and drawing slowly out to an air of Rossini's; the savagery of winter, waves rearing thirty feet to break against the pier lighthouse; suave, icy, gentle, enticing, treacherous, charging the air with splinters of light and the houses with exotic junk, shells from Vera Cruz, enormous dried seeds like the shrunken trophies of head-hunters, boxes and silk screens from Japan, egg-shell china, elaborate French clocks, an African necklace, ostrich eggs on which I copied in oil-paint the birds and flowers from a great book of foreign birds.

Bringing in, too, a fever, a bacillus of restlessness and violence to creep into the veins. Not all veins; only those liable to catch the fever.

Chapter 4

There is a sense in which it is true that we only live in one house, one street, one town, all our lives. I have no memory of the first house I lived in, though I ought to be able to remember an afternoon in my sixth month when I began climbing its dangerously steep staircase on hands and knees: I set off six times, and was fetched back and whipped six times.

Have I been doing anything ever since except setting off again up those infernal stairs?

The first departure I remember was from our next house.

Whether reflected from the sea, or filtered as it crosses the moors, the light on this strip of the north-east coast has an unusual clarity. It may be this light—it could be flattered by the hand like a young horse—which sets 5 Park Terrace apart from the unnumbered houses I have lived in since. It was a terrace of Victorian houses, facing another on a lower level; from its end a very steep road, North Bank, dropped to Esk Terrace which faced, across a slope of rank grass, the upper harbour. Of what other house can I recall the satin-striped wallpaper in the upper sitting-room, the textures of its saddle-bag chairs, the exact shape of the horsehair sofa in the dining-room, and the position, relative to each other, of bedrooms and attics? There was no bathroom: a wide hip-bath was filled for us in front of the kitchen range; I should be glad to forget a horrible night when I upset it.

At the farther end of the terrace, a cul-de-sac of four dull houses, moss and short fine grass pushing between its cobblestones, filled me, however often I entered it, with a voluptuous sense of strange-ness—*le Pays sans Nom*.

This nameless country is now a few narrow streets, a harbour divided into upper and outer by a vanished swing-bridge, a naked cliff-top, the whole small enough to fit into a tiny flaw in my skull.

Do not believe that the earliest memories are anything but disguised choices. My first memory of injustice is attached to this house and this time: next door a family called Corney kept a school for very young children, to which I was sent a week after my fifth birthday: one morning I was accused of breaking a window and my truthful and passionate denials not believed. And my first memory of guilt and shame: I filled my infant brother's shoes with water from the yard tap and waited for him to be accused of the crime; my treachery must have been perfectly obvious, and, confronted with it, I could only take my whipping. And my first memory of lust, evil: two children my age, brother and sister, giving themselves up to some scandalous joining together of their bodies (I knew it was scandalous because they told me so, and made me swear not to talk about it).

Infantile eroticism is a very curious affair. It involves no sexual knowledge at all, and needs none. My ignorance was as complete as my want of curiosity. I was nine or ten before I learned—through watching a boy on the stern of a barge on the Scheldt—that male and female bodies are anatomically different. The discovery made an impression on me and led to day-dreams of childish indecency, savagely naïve and absurd; I wove them round a story about two heroes of the Indian Mutiny, Generals Havelock and Outram—an innocent source, one would think, but there is no protecting the imagination from its power to corrupt itself.

Attached to this first house, too, are a handful of night dreams, the earliest one of pure fear: there were evil dwarfs in the streets; one touch from them would horribly twist your body, if not kill you. How did those chthonic gods, the Cabiri, get into a northern child's dream?

My so-called school taught a few children to write, count on their fingers, read, and learn by heart so many paragraphs a day of history, geography, grammar, poetry, the best method in the world, since it leaves the child's imagination severely alone. I could read before I went to this school; I taught myself, probably driven to it by boredom. No special books were given me, I read everything in the house. One evening my mother mocked me sharply for spelling out the word tobacco in Samuel Baker's *Albert N'yanza, Great Basin of the Nile*. I was sitting in the circle of light from the lamp in the centre of the red chenille cloth, absorbed in the hideous and fascinating journey shared by the devoted Mrs Baker. I was seven, or at most a year older. It was like my mother to expect me to recognize in print an object I had seen.

I still have the two volumes, published in 1886: the engravings are superb.

Forbidden to read before breakfast, I hid books under the mattress of my bed. They were discovered at once—I was either too young or too stupid to reflect that they would be—and I was thrashed, and did it again, and was thrashed again.

The year after her third child was born my mother went off on a long voyage. She put me to board with the Misses Corney. During the day I was unconcerned, but the moment I had been put to bed in the room I shared with the eldest Miss Corney, my tears started of themselves and flowed torrentially for more than an hour. This happened every night for three or four months. I could not explain my despair to the poor woman, and she had to let me cry myself into the sleep of exhaustion.

It was my first experience of loss, and my grief was as atrocious as any I have felt since.

I knew, with absolute certainty, that my mother would die at sea and I should not see her again—except in a way I could not imagine: before leaving she had said, 'If I'm drowned in a storm I'll come to you.'

This incomprehensible promise was the only hope I had.

My sister, three years old, and my brother, who was still in petticoats, had been left with a magnificent woman known as Mammy Fisher. I never saw them. With her husband and sons, she kept a greengrocer's shop: when a family in the neighbourhood was in trouble—sickness, a death, a hard birth—she was sent for. Fat and strong, with a voice ripened by years of advising, cajoling, soothing, seeing people into the world and seeing them out, she was sixteen stone of hard stubborn Yorkshire flesh, and a saint.

The second time my mother left on a long voyage I felt nothing. But at the station I pretended to cry, for fear she should be disappointed. Already, at the age of eight, I was an accomplished hypocrite.

This time my sister stayed at the school with me. It was nearly the death of her. The Misses Corney were young marriageable women, and after school hours left us with a servant: she let us do as we pleased, and one afternoon we walked into the country as far as the village of Ruswarp, two miles. The Esk was in spring flood, with a strong, fast current, and we amused ourselves on its bank until my sister lost her footing on a loose stone, and sank. I snatched at her desperately from the same jutting stone and dragged her out, drenched and shivering. We ran to a cottage, where a woman stripped her and dried her clothes.

For a week after this, to bring home to her the depth of her wickedness in coming within a hair's-breadth of drowning, she was made to stand on a stool before the roomful of grinning children, every morning for an hour. She was five, a little less.

I was not punished. Why? I had no idea, and a child does not try to understand the behaviour of his masters. The truth is, he does not think of himself as a child and of his elders as adults; he thinks in terms of rulers and ruled, helpless and powerful. Very much, I suppose, as the inhabitants of an occupied country feel towards an occupier, however benevolent.

Our brother had been sent to Mammy Fisher; she loved him fondly and gave him anything he asked for. When my mother fetched him home he refused to believe she was his mother, and rushed back scowling to his *real* mother. He was a singularly fierce child, with a frown that made people call him a 'black bairn.' A woman came one day to complain that he had torn her son's cap off his head and thrown it into the harbour. 'How old is your son?' my mother demanded. —'Nine.'—'My son is not yet five. I think little of a nine-year-old boy who lets a little child of four master him.'

My mother never allowed anyone, friend or stranger, to criticize her children.

Her passionate loyalty and devotion—she would without hesitation have stepped between one of us and an enraged tigress—and her severity (the merciless thrashings) sprang from one and the same impulse: we were to have everything she could get for us, and be everything she admired, upright, truthful, well-mannered, clever, quick, sincere.

How could it have entered her head that insincerity was one of the lessons I learned early and thoroughly, very early, very thoroughly?

Chapter 5

For several years I had a recurring dream in which I was living with her in a badly-lit room: I knew that I should be forced to wake up and leave her there. I wept bitterly, I assured her over and over again that she, not *the other one*, was the mother I loved. I'll come back, I repeated, all the time struggling to stay asleep, but the room, the figure of my mother, became shadowy, wavered, vanished . . .

It seemed that a nerve led direct from my young mind to hers: I knew instantly what she wanted me to say, what it would please her to hear, what she wanted. She was curiously reluctant to say frankly: I want this, I want to do that. (I see, now, that she hated as I do *to be seen caring*.) When she coveted something she could not afford, I encouraged her to buy it. This habit became fixed: to the end of her life I encouraged her in extravagances, and spent recklessly on her. Even as children we somehow scraped up the money to give her a birthday present she would value. Once my brother refused to hand over his small savings, and gave her his own choice of present, a penny loaf with a tulip stuck in it. She did not thank him.

What she wanted she wanted blindly, unable for the time to see anything else in the world. I, too . . .

My terrible anxiety for her to be happy took in the most trivial events; playing bezique with her, I tried not to win; when she planned a day in the country I prayed feverishly for sun: a fiasco made me feel guilty.

I cannot remember a time when I was not aware, and with what helpless pity, that her life had disappointed her.

Those seeds of guilt and responsibility, sown in me at the beginning, were not able to strangle an egotism as involuntary as George Gallilee's, but they have given it an atrociously uneasy life.

In those days, how gay she could be! A fine day made her madly happy: she hurried us out of the house to walk the four or five miles to the moors, the road climbing, slowly, between stone fences; or, when my aunt Mary was still alive, to Carr Hill. (This aunt, the best-looking of the five Gallilee sisters, had married a small landowner who went mad, not violently, but tiresomely for his family: he used to turn his wife and my four cousins, two of whom went mad in their turn, out of the house at night, so that they had to take shelter in the nearest farm.) But she was rarely contented. How, given what she was, could she be? Take a young attractive woman, with a passion for change and movement, and shut her up with three un-predictably lively children in a house in a small town—even before the birth in 1906 of her fourth child she had given up long voyages—and what could come of it but boredom, an agonizing boredom?

I only understood years later, at a time when I was tempted to knock my own head against the wall, the fits of rage in which she jerked the venetian blinds in her room up and down, up and down, for the relief of hearing the crash.

She had married—to get away from a house full of her sisters?—too young, a man inferior to her in breeding, sensitivity, warmth of heart and force of character. He had his own courage, tenacity, dreams, but she was too young, too uncompromising, to forgive him traits that vexed her and roused her contempt. She never understood or forgave him a habit of lying about himself—if you can call lies the instinct to appear clever or cunning, or to defend himself from her scathing tongue. She baffled and tormented him (and herself) for the disappointments and revulsions he made her suffer. Her passion for perfection—in everything she owned, a dress, the furni-ture of her room—scandalized him. No Whitby sea-captain's wife clothed herself and her children as she did, or bought Dresden china, costly rugs, Hepplewhite chairs, searching antique shops for bar-gains, bidding at auction sales. She spent on these things every penny that came into her hands, saving only in order to spend.

He did not like it any better when, on one of their first voyages, an old captain took her to be his daughter, though he was not more than nine years the elder. She was slender, with the complexion of a young child.

When they married he was not yet a captain, and they were pinched for money. I have her account book for that year, a little thin book with an olive-green cover. The first item runs: Cab and fare to Newport, and it ends on the 31st of December with the note that she had a Balance in Hand of £6 10s 6d. I doubt if she ever kept accounts again.

Before their marriage, she told me, he had begged her to correct his clumsiness and ignorance. (Of his mother's three sons, he was the one who suffered from the poverty into which the defaulting solicitor threw her; at the age of thirteen he was taken from school and sent as apprentice in a sailing-ship, to be schooled in bitter hardship and cruelty.) An eager haphazard reader, he mis-saw words —a geranium became a genarium on his tongue, and the like. His manners, unless he were able to condescend, were rough or too familiar. He made a cult of shabbiness and would let a new uniform moulder in his cabin, unworn, for years. (Like his mother with her dozens of boned silk bodices.) After their marriage, he would have nothing to do with her attempts to teach him a few graces. He was neither humble nor generous enough. Nor, I'll be bound, she adroit.

Used, in his ship, to the absolute authority of a captain, he might have bullied her and us if she had not, from the very start, been too much for him, too quick-witted, too lively, too stubborn and over-bearing. He would have done better for himself to marry a stupider or an easy-going young woman. My mother's contempt for devious ways, her fastidiousness, her wilfulness and impatience, her (in his eyes) insane ambitions for her children, her love of beautiful things, vexed him, but he did not know how to deal with them. He was no match for her unconscious arrogance, the echo in hers of George Gallilee's intimidating voice.

Only in physical courage and a deep obstinacy was he her equal. Their long separations—months long—stretched the gap between them to an abyss. Before he had been home longer than a week they were quarrelling, bitterly. The bitterness, the impatience, were on her side, the stubborn incomprehension and lack of generosity his. But she was fully as stubborn as he; a quarrel might last days, and be followed by a reconciliation that must once have been eager, the passionate repentances of a quick-hearted young woman, but with the years became mere dry exhaustion.

The first years, of voyages to South America, France, Belgium, Norway, Vera Cruz, Odessa, must have been the least disappointing of her life: she loved strange cities, and from all of them her curiosity picked up new ideas, new recipes, new ways of setting a dinner-table, a new elegance. No doubt she was sometimes bored, shut up at sea for slow weeks with a husband whose ways jarred on her. But the one thing she respected in him was his seamanship.

In whatever else he fell short, as a sea-captain he had *aretê*— excellence in the highest degree. To the marrow of his bones and the smallest cell in his brain he was a good seaman. Not that this made him a just man: towards his officers he was neither considerate nor impartial.

On one voyage to the River Plate they ran into a storm, a *pampero*, of more than common violence, and were fourteen days overdue at Buenos Aires. 'We'd given you up, Captain,' the agent waiting on the wharf told him.

The ship lay on her side for three days and nights, and on the last of these nights he came down off the bridge to tell her, 'I daresay we s'll go down, she's lying right over, and the sea's very high now.' He would try, he added mildly, to get back to her, 'before aught happens.'

I try, and fail, to imagine the thoughts of the young woman waiting, alone, in the crazily-tilted cabin, in darkness.

Left to him—if we had been left to him—his children would have been poorly off. Years later, but only then, I understood his indifference to our education, his resentment of the money spent on us. The child who at thirteen was forced to endure, as if he were a man, cold, indifference, brutality, could not find in himself either the tenderness or the warmth to forgive other children, his own, their softer lives. He never spoke about his boyhood except when he was muttering over some—as he saw it—wicked extravagance. His wife could not bear him to pity himself, and cut such mutterings ruthlessly short.

'If I allowed it, he would ride roughshod over us,' she said to me.

It was true.

Not until he died did I see that he, too, was to be pitied and respected. He was brave, tortuous, full of mean resentments, grudging, naïvely vain, and patient. He had a streak of fantasy that in other circumstances might have changed his life. He kept a commonplace book into which he copied verses and anecdotes that impressed him. When he could, he took long solitary walks: I have a photograph he sent me when I was living in London in the thirties--he was then eighty—of a stretch of moorland with one signpost: on the back he had written: *Place for dreams*.

What dreams?

Chapter 6

One evening when my mother was leaving the house in anger after a quarrel, I asked her when she would be back.

'Never!' she said drily.

I was much too young to reflect that one does not leave home for ever on foot, without so much as a dressing-case. In despair, I followed her. She took a road that after four miles or so would bring her to Aisalby moor, and we walked for an hour or longer, I keeping myself, as I imagined, out of sight. At last she turned round, took my hand, and we went back together, in the gathering darkness, in silence.

I shudder now when I think what unhappiness that silence of hers hid.

She had a terrible need to be in the right. It was impossible for her to admit that she had made a mistake, or been clumsy, or had acted from any but the highest motive. This was one of the traits that made living with her hazardous. But, as well as repeating itself in me, it taught me tact.

Is this really a benefit? I doubt it.

My anxiety to please, and my nakedness to all the winds blowing from other people's minds, start here. What a Frenchman who mistrusted me called '*la bouche fleurie de Madame Storm Jameson*' is nothing whatever but a gesture of propitiation, such as savages make to their gods. And a defence. To be noticed suffering, or even rejoicing too much—how frightful!

Some time between the wars, when I read *Souvenirs d'egotisme* for the first time, and came on the sentence which ends, 'with one idea in my mind: *not to be seen into (avec une seule idée; n'être pas deviné)* . . .' my heart leaped with joy, a stray dog recognizing its master.

That *nothing whatever* is too shallow. I fear punishment, I fear the pain of mockery, but I fear also to give pain. Too often, I see a naked quivering little creature behind the eyes of the person I am talking to, and cannot bring myself to disappoint it; I want passionately to give it the joy and reassurance of being approved. Anger can blind me to it and make me forget everything but the pleasure of striking. Or, if I feel a reasonable trust in the other person, I may risk frankness.

There are a few people, four or five, I feel no need to guard myself from—and no need to handle them as if they were fragile. One of these speaks, kindly, of 'your flunkey's tongue, dear Margaret.'

I see now that this double-stranded fear has been the strongest impulse in my life for as long as I remember.

Something that happened during my eighth year shows both her children's fear (in the Biblical sense) of my mother, and my own weak dislike of making myself unpleasant. The three of us had gone into the fields near Park Terrace and were playing there when a poorly-dressed boy, perhaps sixteen, came up and offered to teach us a new game. I did not like the look of him, he was obviously a low fellow, but I did not know how to get rid of him without hurting his feelings, the feelings of a wretchedly poor boy. I let him take us into the avenue of trees between one field and the next, and here he kneeled down and squeezed his hands round my throat; I was paralysed by astonishment, but the other two flung themselves on him, beating him with their fists, screaming. There was a group of picknickers in the next field: these must have shown signs of interest, because the lout made off in one direction and we in another, hoping fervently that no one would give us away.

It did not enter my head that my mother would not punish me if she found out. I hardly believed my luck when—the picnickers must have told her—she took me on her knee and in her gentlest voice asked me to tell her what had happened before ordering us in future to turn away if a stranger spoke to us.

She had two voices, the harsh penetrating one she used in anger— it could sharpen to a cruel mockery—and the other, her singing voice, strong and untrained but clear and perfectly true—

It's nothing but a shower
Just a quarter of·an hour
Don't you think you'd better shelter 'neath the chestnut tree,
For the wind is blowing sweet
And there are daisies at your feet
And if you'd like to dance I will pipe for you . . .

Here the voice breaks off, I strain after it, it swells on a note, falters, dies.

She had a third voice she used very rarely. No—it used her. It was the voice of a saucy smiling child. It echoes in my ears, which have forgotten the others.

When she sang hymns we bawled them with her. If anyone were to sing *God be with you till we meet again*, in my hearing, I should die of grief.

Another incident of that time when, fearing a scene, I behaved as I still instinctively do: just before leaving the house to go to school, I opened the *Daily Mail* and read a paragraph saying that the *Saxon Prince*, captain William Storm Jameson, had been seized by the Japanese—a war in which no one took any interest was going on—carrying contraband steel rails, and towed into Sasebo. I pushed the paper under the cushions of a chair, and hurried out. The letter from Newcastle, from the firm, came during the day. I pretended astonishment and concern.

My father spent several pleasant weeks in Japan and brought back a magnificent fold-fold silk screen (which, when he was an old man living alone, he destroyed), the antique God of Plenty I have, and various oddments. These included a photograph of himself in Japanese dress, with parasol and fan, at which my mother smiled drily.

Have I succeeded in drawing a portrait, however faint, of this warm passionate generous young woman, whose face I catch sight of only in sleep, and then uncertainly?

She expected and wanted so much and had so little.

She gave me more than my ludicrous conviction of being responsible for other people, and of being a laughing-stock. I have her bottomless weight of boredom, a never-appeased restlessness, which becomes torture in surroundings I dislike, and the jeering violence I keep out of sight. And, too, a deep, deeper than everything else, indifference—which may only be fear. My working patience and stubbornness I owe to that master mariner with the clouded blue eyes and a mind full of bits and pieces like a sea-chest.

The Yorkshire character has a monolithic appearance which in fact is a lie. Under that air of shrewd hard horse-sense it is complex in the extreme, even neurotic, one edge of its violence and irony turned inward. I have my full share of both, but some other strain in me mocks and bedevils the Yorkshireman—those Gallilees, perhaps? My grandfather, who felt a keen interest in his ancestors, never traced them farther back than their appearance, during the early eighteenth century, in a village on the coast a few miles north of

Whitby. (In a document of that time, recording the births of six members of the family, the name is spelled *Gallaley*, and *Galliley*. Galileo?) It vexed him not to know certainly whether he came from gentlemen or a common stock . . .

Do not imagine that as children we were unhappy. Far from it. We were storing up sensuous wealth for a lifetime. We had everything that children brought up in large towns and cities, or with mechanical amusements, miss. Perhaps because my mother did not like having other people in her house, we had no friends of our own age. A closed society, we played endless ingenious games together. We sometimes fought; I was unkind and arbitrary, and the other two rebelled: my most powerful hold on them at this time was a trick of story-telling I found I had, week-long versions of books I had read, and fairy-tales—the trick deserted me when I was twelve and beginning to be serious about my future.

And we had the sea—endless days on the shore in summer, from nine in the morning until six or seven at night, by which hour we were alone, three children on the edge of an infinity of sand and water—enclosed in a boundless blue world, steeped in light, in a radiance of sun and salt, sauntering in and out of gently-breathing waves or racing in front of them, bare wet legs smarting from the sand-grains driven into the skin.

In spring and winter we went to the end of the pier to watch heavy seas breaking over the lighthouse—this was before extensions were built on to the ancient stone piers with their old mooring-posts, making the bar safe for fishing-boats and spoiling the storms. We stood close under the lighthouse, waiting, listening, for the next wave, and when it reared hissing and fuming overhead ran madly to be out of reach of the deluge; now and then one of us was caught and drenched; then it was a matter of drying off in the icy wind before daring to go home.

With my mother we learned a rhythm of country walks: in February the snowdrops in the woods of Mulgrave Castle, the pale yellow of primroses, scattered across the fields above the Carrs in April, thick oozing yellow of bog-buttercups, and an enormous bird-cherry, a dazzling cloud of white, in May, wild roses, orchids, fox-gloves in the hot narrow June lanes below the moor; and in August and September the moors themselves, the intoxicating scent, the humming of flies and bees, the great cloud-shapes passing over-head—all, all belong to years before I knew the meaning of time, or that it was more than a word: time to leave the sands, already empty, the rock-pools darkened by the lengthening shadow of the cliffs, time to rush out of the house to school, to start for the Saloon before every sheltered bench has been filled, for the Saturday morning market before the scores of pounds of yellow butter vanish off the stalls, time to expect the reindeer tongues and small barrel of cranberries sent to my grandfather every year's end from Archangel, time to pick brambles in the abandoned quarry, time to look for mushrooms, wild daffodils, broom, time to dye the Easter eggs, to buy holly, time, time, time, a bell tolling to the beat of the deep-sea current, time gone.

I can live in it for a moment. For less than a moment—after that I only imagine, inventing echoes.

We kept anniversaries with religious happiness, from rolling Easter eggs down the steepest fields, through Whitsun and birthdays to Christmas, New Year and Twelfth Night. Birthdays began formally, with a tray known as the birthday tray, heaped with presents: it was large and square, with high edges, of gold and black lacquer from Sasebo. It must still be somewhere, it was strong as well as beautiful. Why—I have saved other things—did I not keep it?

One can't save everything.

Chapter 7

In the spring of 1903 we were living in a newly-built house on the West cliff, at that time two miles of fine turf, naked to the North Sea wind. The move brought us within hearing of the sea, close to the cliff-top and the zig-zag path leading to the sands. Not that we used it, preferring to climb down and up two hundred feet of slippery red clay and rocks. There was a very large yard at the back of the house, and my mother let me keep a young white rabbit a friend of hers offered me. She detested animals; when, in a week or two, I grew bored with looking after it, she was thankful to give it away. No sooner had it gone than I was filled with remorse, imagining its grief at being unwanted, and weeping bitter tears which started again each time I recalled its trick of springing from the ground upright, like a dancer.

'You should have cared when you had it,' my mother said, with dry justice.

This house was two miles from our new school; we did the walk four times a day, always late and always running. We became known for the habit. We ran to dancing-class, to the Spa fireworks and concerts, even, when we were alone, to church. No one was surprised to see us racing through the streets to my eldest aunt's funeral. She and my aunt Jane, eldest and youngest of the Gallilees, were the only ones not married, still living in the same house. My mother had gone early, leaving us to dress and follow. In the end we had to run like hares.

As it turned out, we need not have run. The funeral had been held up by the refusal of the undertaker's men to nail the coffin. Dr Mitchell had to be called to assure them that the old lady was dead: her gleaming white hair, rosy cheeks and wide-open blue eyes frightened them. Pray God she really was dead.

My mother this summer was out of all patience with her life, herself, us. She was going to have a child in November; she had not wanted another child, eight years after her son's birth, and her exasperation and weariness drove her to violent rages, which were really fits of despair.

During these weeks I went through a crisis of anxiety about her. Farther back than I can remember, this irrational anxiety had been growing in me: it now reached a desperate climax. It woke me at night and sent me creeping downstairs from my room on the top floor to crouch outside the door of her bedroom: I sat there for two, three, four hours, until I was chilled to the bone, then went back to bed and fell asleep. During the days, too, when she locked herself in her room, to endure, out of our sight, the unhappiness we did not —how could we?—understand, I couldn't bring myself to carry away the tray of food she refused, but waited outside with it uselessly for an hour before giving up.

After this summer, my anxiety diminished slowly, overlaid by the energies and ambitions which, at the age of thirteen or earlier, began to take savage possession of me. Perhaps what is more nearly true is that I became able to ignore it, at least in its acute form.

My youngest sister, Dorothy, was born on the 13th of November, and became my mother's last and overwhelming passion. They were laughably alike.

I can fix the month, almost to the day, when I ceased to be a child. Soon after we moved to the new house, my mother went on the last of her long voyages. She went to Buenos Aires (pronounced by every Whitby sea-captain's family Bonnus-airs), leaving us as boarders in the private school we had been going to daily for a year. She was at sea when we went down with scarlet fever, all three of us. Rather than send us to the fever hospital, it was decided to open up the house and put us in it on the top floor, in charge of a nurse and an old woman called Nightingale. We spent six or seven weeks shut up here, we were not ill, and had nothing to amuse us except a number of cardboard dress-boxes that we turned into a fleet of liners and sailed in them about the rooms. On the fourth or fifth day when I woke, I glanced down at the ship moored alongside my bed, and realised in the same instant that I was an adult shut up with two children.

From this moment until we were released I endured an excruciating boredom, the worst of my life until I had to live in a house of my own—which was infinitely worse.

I had two books, no more—the nurse, a fool, had a theory that reading was bad for fever patients—*Kenilworth* and a copy of the *Arabian Nights* from which she had torn the opening pages as unfit for a child to read. Neither was left in my hands for longer than half an hour. Every evening I prayed avidly that God would kill her in the night. A black mamba secretes less venom than a child's impotent hate.

The gap that separated me from the others widened at the speed of a galloping horse. I could no longer invent fairy-tales for them, I began to dream feverishly of *getting away*—away from Whitby, from a barren life without excitement or a chance to show that I was an exception.

Where did my ambition come from? The devil knows. Long before I spoke about it to anyone I was determined to get myself to a university. No pupil of the Misses Ingham had done such a thing; I doubt whether, at that time, there were more than two persons in the town attending any university. It was not the custom, even among the rich. There were several very rich shipping families, at some of whom my mother laughed because they spoke with a strong Whitby accent.

Many years later, J. B. Priestley laughed at me for having forgotten my Yorkshire accent: I took care not to tell him (because he would not have believed me) that I never had one; my voice is a thin poor echo of my mother's and George Gallilee's.

Each year from my thirteenth I took one of the Cambridge examinations, Preliminary, Junior, Senior. I prepared for them by learning enormously by heart: at that time I memorized a page of print by reading it through, and so long as I had a use for it, could summon it to appear in my mind as a printed page: after that I forgot it forever. I read extraordinarily fast, taking in three or four lines at a glance— as I still do. I learned the whole of *The Lady of the Lake, Marmion, Henry V,* the first book of *Paradise Lost,* pages of Macaulay, of Biblical commentary . . . On the long walk to and from school, I kept a book open, reading and muttering. For that matter, I read everything that came under my eye, from perniciously bad novels— pernicious to anyone, poison to a future writer—to the Encyclopaedia I stole paragraphs from for my essays. I did not know bad writing from good—then, nor for many a year.

When I look now at children of the age at which I began to be ambitious, I seem to myself never to have had a childhood. Not true: I had all the pleasures a child born between sea and moor could have. But already at this age I knew that I was responsible for myself, that the future existed, and depended on me alone.

I was ambitious without understanding, without even knowing it: it seemed perfectly natural that I should want to get away. So it was—*my* nature. I was a small cauldron of desires and longings, and ignorance. Infinitely more naïve than a normal child of my age now —or indeed then. And—I see this only today—my ambition was sharpened to an unknown degree by my social failure.

To say that I was not a success with children of my age is to say very little: there are no sharper mental torments in life than those endured by the child marked out to be ridiculed, left out of games— at which I was awkward and useless—and convinced of inferiority in the one field which matters at that age. It began, my sense of being different and inferior, when I started at Miss Ingham's. Here for the first time I was in a community of children a little older than I was. No doubt I am exaggerating the number of times when I drew on myself—without having the faintest notion why—the mockery of girls who at fourteen and fifteen were in my eyes self-assured and sophisticated adults.

I cannot see myself as I appeared to them. I try vainly to catch a glimpse of that child, so well-meaning and friendly, to detect what quality in her, what eccentricity, roused others to make her their hare, their mimic prey. I cannot see her, because the eyes with which I look at her are those of the child I was, and still, when I stumble over one of these derisive memories, am.

I shall die without understanding it. Thank goodness, there are no freaks in the grave.

I remember one occasion when mockery turned into a more savage form of baiting. I am in the yard behind the school (where one day a week a coastguard drills us), and four or five older girls have twisted the skipping-rope round me below my knees; they have only to tighten the coils a fraction and I shall fall headlong on the flag-stones. I recall their jeering laughter at my helplessness, and my terror of falling, and terror that they would notice it. How did it end? I don't know. The image does not tell me.

On the first day we moved to the new house, I stood in the large, extravagantly large scullery, cutting slices of bread on the table under the window, and listening with excitement to the voices of children playing on the other side of the seven-foot high wall dividing their garden from our yard. I did not know them, they went to a different private school. A new life, new friends who did not know that I was in some way ridiculous, were within reach. I had a few minutes of pure confidence.

They were two families of children, cousins, living side by side in houses which shared a very long garden. The larger family had four or five girls: the eldest, my age, was the best-looking, with yellow hair, blue eyes, a deliciously fresh skin. She had only one fault, she was bow-legged. She was amiable, perhaps stupid, and when we were alone together very friendly, and each time I believed that now, at last, I had been accepted.

This was an illusion.

I was never accepted. As soon as others joined us she abandoned me to them. (My experience of treachery, my own and others', is, as you see, very old.)

It was one of her cousins, a fat sharp-witted boy, who first spoke of me as 'a freak.' I pretended not to care, I was already able to give myself an air of stolid indifference.

What mark, invisible to the victim, appears on the forehead of the child who is a freak? Had I been naïve enough to talk about myself and my absurd ambitions and opinions? I am certain not. I was naïve, but not a complete fool.

It took me a long time to realize that my case was hopeless: any gesture of friendliness gave me fresh hope. Yet, from the time I was eight or nine I began assiduously, began or continued, to practise all kinds of reticences, evasions, hypocrisies and, above all, indifference.

This habit of indifference, painfully acquired, was extraordinarily useful later on. It was during these years that I began to teach myself a shallow stoicism: nothing lasts, the bitterest disappointment is endurable if kept at a reasonable distance. Tricks for keeping it at its distance can be learned as easily as other evasions.

It would be only natural if these humiliating scenes and the tears shed in secret were clearer than my other memories of that time. But I remember as sharply, and with a quivering happiness, the yellow sprays of broom, dazzling, sprinkling us with a cold dew, gathered on an embankment near the house; the exquisite smoky taste of peat-cakes (flat currant scones baked on a peat fire) in a moor farmhouse; the triumph of finding a bee orchis. And the sea, colours of deep sea, calm twittering of waves inshore, glittering salt-sharp air, returning then, now, and at the hour of my death.

The legacy my failure left me was a rooted mistrust. My lack of trust in human beings is as deep and ineradicable as any of my instincts, deeper than feeling, and I can trace its movements everywhere in my life.

I do not believe that human beings are evil; to not a few I owe an immense debt for kindness and happiness received. I cannot believe that they are to be depended on.

This has nothing to do with whether they are or are not trustworthy. It is a geological fault in me to be unable to trust people, and to expect them, if given the chance, to turn out malicious.

The other day a friend showed me a letter from that intolerant incorrigibly un-venal and uncompromising French writer, Ignace Legrand, in which he said: '*Ah, elle connaît le monde, Margaret. Elle est trop intelligente pour ne pas voir que la plupart des gens sont cons.*'

This is barely just. I don't despise people, I crave their approval. Yet I am indifferent, too—which is a sin, *the* sin.

Chapter 8

My mother was zealous for my future. Was it she or I who discovered that three County Scholarships—worth sixty pounds—were
awarded yearly, in each Riding, on the results of the Matriculation
examination? Only three—and every school in the Riding would
enter its scholars. It was my one chance. Sixty pounds would cover
the fees at a provincial university—to our innocence all universities
were equal—and she could, she said, find another pound or thirty
shillings a week for my living expenses.

It occurred to neither of us to ask my father for help.

I had already passed the three Cambridge examinations: to take
the third, the Senior, I had to spend the week in Scarborough, with
two pupil-teachers who were sitting for it. I was in a fever of excitement and insisted on taking a hansom cab from the station to our
lodging—the two young women thought me nearly insane. I can
smell now the warm musty scent of vegetables from the shop under
my bedroom, and feel the hard knot of blood rising to the back of
my head when I came out of the hot examination room into the icy
December street.

Miss Lily Ingham could not prepare me for Matriculation. My
mother told her so, bluntly. I must leave at the end of the term, to go
to the Municipal School at Scarborough. It meant a daily train
journey of one hour and ten minutes, but neither of us thought that
excessive. Only remained to arrange with the school to take me. My
mother wrote to the headmaster to say that we should be calling
on him on such and such a day: it did not enter her head that I might
be refused.

A day in Scarborough was nothing new. We went five or six
times a year, she and I, on the early train, ritual visits that began with
coffee in Rowntree's, after which we combed every floor of the shop,
from top to bottom; we went more cursorily through two other
large shops; we sauntered along every one of the better streets,

visited every antique dealer—my mother was known to them all—
and the Valley and South Cliff gardens.

This day, except for the interview with Mr Tetley, was like any
other. I have tried since to imagine his feelings when, after a sentence
or two, my mother said coldly, 'My daughter will come to the school
in September to take Matriculation next June, and get a County
Scholarship.'

He glanced from her face to mine: at that time—I was sixteen—
and for years after, I had a childishly round face and a habit of staring
fixedly from wide-open unclear eyes. He must have thought us both
a little mad.

'There are only three of them,' he said.

'Yes. She must take one of them.'

'I hope she will,' he said gently.

Smiling, my mother rose, and we went out into the bright day, to
go through the ritual. As we went she said, 'Well, now you're
started, my little dear.'

In Rowntree's, a young assistant in the fur department persuaded
her to try on a sable coat. There was no question of her buying it, it
was far beyond her purse, but she held its collar under her chin and
looked at herself in the long glass with an intent fixed gaze, her
invariable expression when she was trying on a dress or hat: it was
as though she were seeking in her reflection someone not herself,
some image the mirror held and, if she looked closely enough, would
surrender. So, now, I seek her in a glass she used.

'One of these days,' I said to her, 'I'll buy you a fur coat.'

My ambition was personal and selfish but, twisted through it, a
living nerve, was the anguished wish to please her by getting myself
success and praise. Now that she is dead it no longer frets me to be
without honours (in the plural).

A day in Scarborough like any other? No. We did all the proper
things, without meeting a single failure; the sun shone, and a light
wind lifted the Valley trees. A few words she said in the train marked
the difference.

'I've taken many journeys with you, very long some of them.'

'We'll go many more journeys,' I answered.

'No. My time is over. You will go journeys, my little love, you're
a Thursday's child—far to go.'

There was no trace of bitterness in her voice, yet she knew then—
knew as the body knows these things, with a mute grief—that already I had my back to her.

'Vor daughters ha' mornen when mothers ha' night . . .'

For two terms, autumn, winter, spring, I travelled to and from
school by train. A gleam of light out of these journeys will not vanish until I do. There was a moment in spring when, as we left Robin
Hood's Bay, the just-risen sun passed behind a dark bank of cloud,
and its rays descending stretched a thin silver line along the rim of
the sea. (I saw it again—for the last time?—in 1965, in Portugal—
looking across a sea as grey and lively as the North Sea in March
but fuller of light, towards an horizon sweeping from east-south-
east through south—a great hoop of silver let down below livid
clouds from the sun behind them. Old image, old miracle, and infinitely moving.) And there was a moment in winter on the return
journey when the train rounded a curve, and the little town sprang
below it as a scatter of glittering points in the thick of darkness, the
narrow streets invisible, only their gas-lamps and a few uncurtained
windows alive. I have no idea why so ordinary a sight made my heart
beat against my ribs like a fist, nor what name to give the pleasure
that suffocated me.

A foretaste of voyages?

In my third and last term my mother allowed me to spend five
days of the week in Scarborough. It was the first time I had lived
alone in lodgings. I took to freedom like a duck to water, or a monk
to his cell. There was nothing monkly about the turbulence of my
secret life.

Apart from the accident—no one's fault—that the habits and
tastes of a vagabond and a solitary rooted themselves in me firmly,
below a superficial neatness, I count my years in what its pupils
called The Muni as good. At that time it was co-educational, girls'
classrooms on one side of the great hall in which the whole school
assembled for prayers and to bawl a hymn, boys' on the other. On
the boys' side, a single class, the headstrong 5b, was mixed, boys
and girls of fifteen and sixteen. After a brief try-out, I was sent to
that.

Train scholars from Whitby were a quarter of an hour late in the
morning. A short time ago a friend, my oldest, told me,

'The first day you came into 5b, I looked up when the door
opened, and saw a country-faced lass walk in, taking her time about
it, and staring round as though she owned the blooming place. Ha, I
thought, thinks better than well of herself!'

I was a cold knot of fears and insane hopes. And able already to
hide both.

None of my fears was realized. In 5b—a class approached with misgivings by a timid master—no one looked on me as a freak. I made my first friends, among them the two I think about as my other selves, with the blessed carelessness, ease, irresponsibility, that implies. One of the Harland brothers, the elder, became a famous geneticist: as a schoolboy he was taken to be the more eccentric of the two, he tumbled from scrape to scrape, once accidentally setting fire to a moor, at other times suspected of insolence, blasphemy, genius, heaven knows what. The eccentricity of the younger, Oswald, went deeper: he had, has, a strong arbitrary mind, a delight in the grotesque, the singular, a bigoted disdain of bigots, and a total inability to play tricks to get an audience: hence the unjust neglect of his few novels, and the reason why a man who would have been a great headmaster was not allowed the chance.

At the time—so ready was I to accept miracles as part of my new life—it did not surprise me that the Harlands chose to make a friend of a raw naïvely ignorant girl, no match for them in any way.

What did they see in me? An empty channel into which they could turn the torrent of ideas—socialism, atheism, anarchy—pouring through their restless brains? A willing disciple? A creature so obviously untamed that someone ought to put a hand on her?

None of us knew our luck in having A. S. Tetley as headmaster, a well-bred man and a humanist, with a genius for awakening enthusiasm in the minds of the barbarians he was condemned to teach. The afternoon he read *Lycidas* to us blinded me with the light that met Saul on the Damascus road: to this day I cannot read it without a shock of pleasure.

This year I fell in love for the first time—that is, with a living person, not with a hero of the Indian Mutiny or a character in one of the novels my mother brought, three at a time, from the subscription library on the pier. H.C. was a handsome, gentle, not at all intelligent boy of my own age: we took two or three silent walks together, but the affair, to call it that, took place in my imagination. *Le diable au corps*, mine, has always been the dupe of my imagination. Until the habit began to bore me, dreaming about a passion I might at any moment feel, or even rouse, gave me infinitely greater pleasure than the reality.

I see, but only now, that I have always fallen in love in the same way, by catching sight of a face which, for some inexplicable reason —since it was never even the same type of face—abruptly blotted out every other within sight and became, for a day, a month, an hour, the centre of an obsession. The duration of the folly was fixed by circumstances—a straw was enough to turn fervour to contempt. Nor could I go on admiring a person who showed no reciprocal interest: hence—after devoting myself silently for five days to a Swedish poet with the face of a Gothic gargoyle, tall, bony, really horribly unattractive, taking pains to sit where I could watch him unobserved, making careful written notes of his features—I lost all interest within five minutes of leaving Stockholm, and filed the notes for use in a novel.

I was never seriously in love, that is, for a stretch of months or years, except a few times, let us say three, in my life.

Each time the process was the same. I spent entire hours day-dreaming, recalling every detail of voice, gestures, looks, incapable of settling to any other occupation, contrived to be in places where I might catch sight of the obsessive object, schemed to hear his name spoken, to get news of him indirectly, without giving away my silliness, trembled when I caught a word connected with him, the name of his birthplace or of a writer he admired—in short, behind an apparent calm, behaved like a lunatic or a fever patient.

These fevers, fortunately, are rarely caught in their acute form. No harm is done by slight infections. In my thirty-third year, when I fell in love seriously for the last time, I became immunized, to all but the mildest disorders.

Alas, now that I no longer catch fevers, I find writing a love-scene intolerably boring.

What seems to me strange is that—with my inconceivable ignorance, no one having breathed a syllable to me about sex—I could experience, as it were in skeletal form, and for a rather stupid boy of sixteen, all the emotions that later on devastated my life . . .

I sat for the Matriculation in June, supremely confident with every paper except the mathematics. Figures baffle me—to this day my brain swoons in my head when it comes on a mathematical formula on the page of a book.

The County Scholarships were not announced until September: I was relieved to get one of them, but not much surprised. Why else had I come to Scarborough?

It had been decided that I should go to Leeds University, and I had already had an interview, of which I remember nothing. It was later that Professor C. E. Vaughan, who disliked female students, interviewed me: he asked what I had read, and I gave him in what I thought ampressive list of authors.

'Have you read Burke?' he asked drily.
'No.'
He frowned. 'None of you reads Burke, it's disgraceful.'

A Miss Douthwaite, who taught drawing in Whitby, an uncommonly cultivated woman, begged my mother to send me to Newnham. It was out of the question—even in 1910 sixty pounds was a pittance. We did not give Newnham a thought. But Cambridge might have steadied me and taught me to make better use of my mind. Or I might—why not?—have fulfilled my first and strongest ambition—to become a don.

Chapter 9

As the day of my leaving for Leeds came near and nearer, my mother began to regret that I was going away. To console her—fool!—I bought her one of the gilt mesh purses fashionable that year. 'For you to have when I'm not here,' I told her.

'That won't comfort me in my lonely round.'

The day I left, she came as far as Scarborough with me. I see her, standing beside the Leeds train, looking up at me as it moved out: I was too well-trained to show more than a flicker of my pleasure in beginning a new life, but I did not, God forgive me, realize that the train was carrying off the last rag of her youth and its banners. For the first time in my life I hardened my heart, refusing to let myself feel her unhappiness.

I tell myself now that it is forbidden, on pain of death, to creep back to the mother. But the rejection, the victory, is a poor cold business at best. The hands I drew from hers were maimed.

When, years later, I read *Sinister Street*, I realized that in Leeds I had lived in another world and age. The difference did not lie in the disenchanting grime, the ring of steel furnaces and mills belching smoke by day and flames by night, the ceaseless beat of industry in our ears, the total lack of everything implied in talk of dreaming spires and punts idling between fields yellow with buttercups. It lay deeper—in a thin thread of spirit joining us tenuously to the mediaeval universities and their asperities, rough freedom, immersion in a harsh reality. For most of us, a degree was the only gateway to a tolerable life: an undergraduate who did not have this urgency biting him was a rare bird, probably the son of a steel or wool firm training in one of the admirable technical departments.

The rain of State scholarships that set in for good after the last war tamed the provincial universities, and opened the way to the rise of the meritocracy. I notice one trivial but curious effect. The Harlands and I emerged from our three starveling years with a lighthearted confidence that we were conquerors; we had none of the slightly sour grudge against society which today is usual: not only did we want nothing it could give us, but we felt certain of being equals in any social class. In those early years I had no *consciousness* of being shabby, I thought I could go anywhere, into any company. What paralysed me, and still does, is to know that I am an intellectual inferior. It was only later that I began to covet an elegance I had discovered I lacked—and that, after all, may have been a craving handed down to me.

Perhaps I am speaking only for myself and the Harlands. A pity that so few of a lively self-reliant sanguine generation lived to speak for itself. With one exception, the young men who were my friends at Leeds were all dead—Ypres, Loos, Passchendaele—within three or four years after they went down.

As did all undergraduates except those unfortunates who were able to live at home, I had to find rooms. There were then no hostels for women, and only one, I think, for men. The rest lived as near the university as they could, in streets that formed a graceless sooty Latin Quarter, without benefit of cafés, without a rag of charm. But there were few rules, and if you could get into the house without disturbing your landlady no reason why you should come in before three or four in the morning.

In my first two years I moved four times—until I had got myself near enough the university not to have to run for more than five minutes to my first lecture. Then I settled down; my mother began to send me each week thirty shillings instead of a pound and I could pay eighteen shillings for the tolerable discomfort of a sitting-room and dingy bedroom, with breakfast and a meagre supper. My landlady paid me the highest compliment in her power when she told me, 'You're as little trouble as a man.' She was deaf as well as amiable, which allowed me more freedom than—given my total lack of sense —was good for me.

Very soon, partly because of the time I spent idling in full sight, and partly because a charming senior with a reputation for being what then was called fast invited me to dine with her and two handsome and notoriously wild medicals in the Queen's Hotel—why? I had a round face and nothing to say for myself—I began to be thought irresponsible. I had no reverence for authority as such, and a manner that hid my profound uncertainty.

In my third year I was judged to have become responsible—this at a time when I was committing secretly my worst follies—and elected Secretary of the Women's Representative Council of the Union. This must have been the first incident in my life when I impressed people by what dear Michael Sadleir later called 'your specious air of competence.' (If I had had no aptitude for business, how much simpler my life would have been. I had enough to induce hard-headed people to employ me in jobs with which, after a few months, I became acutely bored.)

The Women's Representative Council had no funds, and our rooms, in a terrace of grey houses, were sordidly shabby. I decided to order a new carpet, and did, knowing that the Union would be forced to pay for it. The professor of classics who was the Union Treasurer said that in his long experience no undergraduate, male or female, had acted in so unprincipled and profligate a way.

He was wrong in one particular. I had acted on principle—no doubt a rash principle, one which has bedevilled my life.

A life without ties suits me better than any. In spite of being poor —a misfortune at any age—I was madly happy, even during times when I was living through one of the ridiculous, unfeigned and groundless miseries proper to my age and nature, which even then was moody, passionately in love with gaiety and change, intolerant, horribly afraid of being mocked . . . that *n'être pas deviné* . . . impatient of control, nervously kind and deeply scoffing and pigheaded, fatally quickly bored and fatally certain in company to make the one remark that would damn me for ever in the eyes of sober right-thinking persons.

I was too young, even for my age, too deficient in prudence, in the most ordinary worldly sense, to realize that I was playing ducks and drakes with my whole life. Any sane person would expect that, with

ambition biting me, I should take care not to waste a minute, or lose
sight for a minute of the figure I might be cutting in the eyes of my
world. Not a bit of it. I threw away hours every day, in delicious
reveries, in lounging on the tennis-court watching a game I cannot
play, in reading outside the curriculum, and dodging prescribed
work. In those days I found it utterly impossible to hold my mind
down to a book that bored me. The ferment of so-called advanced
ideas in my brain came from many sources, none of them of any
use to a scholar. Even my ambition was chaotic, and except for the
idea of becoming a don, had neither direction nor singleness of
mind. Nor did anyone attempt to direct it.

After the first weeks I began to cut lectures. I never cut Professor
Vaughan's. For that severe woman-hating humanist, who must have
found me pretentious and detestable, I had too much respect, not to
say fear. The other honours students in my school—what a fool I
was to choose to read English, with all its temptations to pass off
ideas and invention as scholarship, but I had no one to give me advice—waited to see me come a cropper at the end of the first year.
But I was working harder than they knew: in those days I could
read until six in the morning, have a bath (in my wash-basin: there
was no bathroom in the house) and breakfast, and go off to the university with the lightness of a young animal, as though my body
had no weight. And I was a born examinee, a Napoleon in the mar-
shalling of any facts I happened to have on hand, and—over ground
that gave my imagination room to gallop—all but unbeatable. To
their frank surprise and disappointment, I passed the Intermediate in
the first three.

Two years later, in the Finals, I triumphed again, coming out at
the top of the honours class. Much good this triumph did me.

If a ship that has slipped its moorings could think, it might have
the illusion that it was free at the very moment when it was at the
mercy of every wind and current. I did not even notice what, to
make myself safe, I ought to be doing. It never crossed my mind that
the erratic way I worked was unlikely to earn me the reputation I
might have got by being overtly studious, attending every lecture,
and slaving at Anglo-Saxon and the duller subjects of a course which
was more of an endurance test than an education: it swept us from
Beowulf as far as Keats, past Langland, past Chaucer, past Shakespeare and his forerunners to Sheridan and through a score or two
of divines, essayists, pamphleteers, novelists, besides the history and
theory of criticism, starting off in the *Poetics* and Longinus and

marching through Sidney, Johnson, Dante, Dryden, Boileau, Pope, Wordsworth, Shelley and I forget what more. Oddly, this part of the course fascinated me, I read avidly, without acquiring the feeblest trace of self-criticism.

Years later, reviewing my third novel, Rebecca West noted that I had no taste, which, she went on, 'is incurable.' She was right about my lack of taste. I did, painfully, cure it, but not for several more years.

Chapter 10

Honours students were required to write a thesis, and I wrote eighty thousand words on William Blake, working in Leeds, in the admirable Public Library, all through a stiflingly hot July and August and a fortnight's feverish attack of some sort. At home, in Whitby, I copied it in my round hand. During the last week of the vacation, I worked on it most of the night, keeping myself awake with green tea my mother bought for me. She put it in a little silver caddy I kept with my manuscript, and about three in the morning made myself a cup of the bitter stuff and went on copying.

I had no notion how to write, and the thesis was written in immensely long involved sentences. Moreover, I did not understand Blake. I supposed I did, but it was an illusion.

The manuscript had to be typed for the university authorities, and, later, two or three other persons read it. J. G. Wilson of Bumpus's bookshop, kind and zealous friend of young writers, was one: it is in my mind that he showed it to a publisher, but I forget. I kept the original handwritten manuscript for some years, in the corner of a shelf in my first house, then at the bottom of a trunk; it became shabbier and dustier, and at some point I must have torn it up.

The typescript I lost sight of, and after a time forgot what I had done with it, or when I had seen it last. My indifference to such things wiped it out of my mind. If asked, I should have said I had destroyed it. Only many years later, in 1941, did I discover that this would have been a lie.

I cannot see myself as my professors must have seen me. A photograph of that time shows a placid-faced schoolgirl. I must have seemed much more like an unbroken colt, with no manners.

In my first year I fell in love with a charming theological student. It was a safe thing to do, since these young men from the College of the Resurrection at Mirfield were dedicated to poverty, chastity and obedience, and I doubt if any one of them ever transgressed his vows. Apart from boring my closest female friend of that time by talking about him, the obsession did no damage. The one I fell into the following year was fatal.

After so long, can I tell the truth about it? From this distance I see much too clearly—in outline, not in the living tormenting detail— how disastrous it was, how unlucky. But I do not see how, given the circumstances and my own character, I could have avoided the trap laid for me by my senses and total lack of commonsense.

K., whom I later married, was in his third year, studying classics. He was very tall, with a narrow face and finely shaped mouth: his least attractive feature was a snub nose, which gave him a slightly impudent air, very marked when he was in a self-assertive or jaunty mood. Short-sighted, he disliked glasses and wore a pince-nez for reading: without it, his glance was kinder and less assured. He had, in my eyes, a maturity which was, I daresay, the effect of his quick tongue and the pleasure he took in supporting the unpopular side in any debate. I saw his self-assurance, his volubility, as enviable virtues, and was overwhelmingly flattered when he took notice of me during the journey of a delegation from the Debating Society to Liverpool University. My infatuation developed through all its stages. This time I said nothing about it, aware, without knowing why, that my friends disapproved of him. We took three or four long walks, during which I listened, tongue-tied, without a coherent idea in my head. At last, one February evening, the affair came to a head. I remember, exactly, the words K. used, because they were doubly revealing—of him, his comparative clearsight (compared with my immaturity and emotional imbecility), his lack of shyness, and of my dumb self-surrender.

'Poor Miss Jim,' he said calmly, 'you love me, don't you?'

'Why poor?' I stammered.

'Because I shall make you unhappy.'

Did he know what he was saying?

I was sensually and imaginatively obsessed, and as imprudent as possible. Several times, during the short nights of May and June, we walked far into the country, then closer to Leeds than it is now, and did not get back until after sunrise.

Some time during this year a friend who discovered my ignorance felt it a duty to instruct me, and did, astonished that she had to explain the most elementary facts of sexual life. The only effect on me of enlightenment was like the effect on a mill-race of stirring up the mud at the bottom. There was never anything sober or untroubled about the affair, I was often unhappy, without understanding why a slight argument turned almost at once into a quarrel, followed by fevered reconciliation, in which everything that had driven me near despair was resolved—or forced underground.

At the end of my second year K. went down, with a not very good degree. He went, I believe, to Cambridge, to take a diploma of some sort—in education?

Without him, I wasted less time. And—naturally without telling him, or feeling less involved with him, and without reflecting for a moment on the shocking ambiguity and bad faith it showed—I fell in love with yet another Mirfield student. Together we trudged about the slums beyond the filthy River Aire during a strike which had been going on for several weeks or months—what strike was it?—carrying tins of cocoa and other oddments given us by the Charity Organisation Society. We walked about all day, and took back written reports to the Society: 'Room bare, all movable objects pawned, wife pregnant, needs bed linen, food.' What in decency's name can these half-starved women, sometimes lying in bed within a few hours of their time, have felt about the awkward smiling girl and the young man with a charmingly ascetic face who came in, set down the tin of cocoa and asked politely,

'Do you need anything at once? Have you pawned all you can pawn? Will this be your first, second, seventh child?'

As with the earlier infatuation, this broke down on the young man's unshakable probity and purpose.

I had forgotten—until this moment—another theological student, with an improbably Russian name, and money of his own, who proposed to me in form, five times, in my first year, embarrassing me: he was kind and good, and, to me, unattractive and a terrible bore.

I don't remember that I felt any disappointment that my nearest rival in the English Honours school, a man, was given a lectureship and I fobbed off with the John Rutson research scholarship, to be held at London University. My expectations had been too indefinite. Nor did I realize that this was a clear snub to my hopes, vague as these were, of an academic career.

No doubt the authorities knew me better than I knew myself. To these sensible experienced men I must have seemed thoroughly unstable, quite unfitted to be a don. But to this day I regret that life. Under direction, I should probably have grown to it. And certainly I should have been a great deal happier than as a novelist, an occupation for which I am even less suited.

When I left Leeds I was in debt to a bookseller. The temptation to buy books I could not afford was too strong. It took me four years to pay off a debt of less than fifteen pounds.

Chapter 11

When I come to stand, as they say—used to say—before my Maker, the judgement on me will run: She did not love enough.

Every unforgivable act in my life may be explained by that flaw. Explained, not forgiven. For such a fault, no forgiveness.

During the years when I was living my self-absorbed and undisciplined life at the university, my young brother was stumbling about, trying to find his way. The 'black bairn' had grown into a clumsy silent boy, who disliked school, never opened a book for pleasure, spent all his time out of the house, where he was often sullen and disobedient, and never told anyone what he had been doing. Pressed, he might say, 'I went with some boys for a walk.' On one of these walks he let the others lower him over the cliff on a thin frayed rope they had, to take a gull's eggs.

I knew very little about him, and thought less. What room was there in my life for an inarticulate awkward boy, five years younger than I was?

Immediately after his fourteenth birthday he refused to go back to school, it was a waste of time—he wanted to get away. Encouraged to it by my father, he went off in another Prince Line ship as an apprentice, since there was no other way.

My mother tried to dissuade him, she knew too well what sort of life a boy had on tramp steamers. She knew, too, that he would dislike it for other reasons than its hardness: for all his fourteen years, he was still a child, with a child's blurred face and unmanageable body: the mind behind his clouded eyes was groping for something he would never find in that life. Utterly silent as he was about himself and his wishes, not able to explain anything, she knew that much about him.

'Your father,' she told me, with barely controlled savagery, 'maunders about his own misery at that age. Then why, I said, condemn your son to the same life? and he said: A hard life never did anyone any harm. Very well, let us hear a little less about yours, I told him.'

The first letter from my brother, and every succeeding letter, from New York, Santos, Rio, Victoria, Montevideo, Trinidad, gave away his disillusion and cruel loneliness. In his sprawling hand, he—who hated writing—wrote long letters, telling her all the details of his life, at sea and in port, and asking for news. 'Please write often and long, it is letters like yours which keep one going.'

She saw him distinctly, sitting on the edge of his berth, his hand moving slowly over the sheets of thin foreign paper, the clouded eyes downcast. To sit writing and writing his little news, he must, she knew, be lonely past all.

At last, after five months, he wrote at the end of a letter about Rio and Bahia: 'If it is possible I want to get something on shore, I know what you must feel about having me back after the life I led you before, but I think I have learned a few of the lessons of life, here where we all have to help one another and everyone is civil. If you think it better for me to stop out here I will, but I do want to come back and see if I can't do better. Now that we are only eight days' run from New York, I am wondering what it is going to be for me, for I do not want to make another trip down here if I can help it, so when you write will you tell me what you think about it. I miss you and everyone more every day now, and I would be glad to do anything. Your loving son, Harold.'

She felt an atrocious dismay. Never since he was born had he asked her, or anyone, for help. She could not afford to bring him home half way through the voyage, but she wrote promising to do what she could when he came back, and wrote at the same time to her husband, asking him not to discourage the boy. After another two months she had a letter ten pages long. Embedded in a laboriously detailed account of the museum in Buenos Aires, she read sentences that, when she repeated them to me, choked her.

'I had a letter from Father yesterday from Santos. He said I would be no good on shore, and that whatever I went to I would not stick at it. And that I would have no chance for anything except for an engineer or motor driver. Taking all together he made it clear that now I am at sea I have got to stop there. Perhaps he is right, there is very little in England for me, and nothing at all in Whitby. I have been wondering if it would not be better if it is possible to get work out of England somewhere, in the Colonies or the States. But I will think for a couple of months yet, for I find that the longer you let anything lie, the better are one's views on it . . .'

I saw her despair—not my brother's. In the blindness of my heart I did not see him. It never entered my head that he was as restless and ambitious as I was, and as profoundly uncertain. And even more desperate *not to be seen into*.

The ship was trading between New York and South American ports, and this, his first voyage, lasted nineteen months. His hands, when he came home, sickened my mother, they were shapeless lumps of scarred raw flesh.

She had no plan ready for him. At this time George Gallilee was still alive, a half-paralysed invalid. It was some years before her share of his money, severely diminished by the scoundrel Lloyd George, and by neglected investments, came to her. She had no money to train my brother for another career. It was useless—worse than useless—to ask his father for help. And, too, she was ill at the time, in pain.

Knowing that she had failed him—since he must have come home hoping against hope that he need not go back—she let his father arrange for him to be transferred to his own ship.

Her misgivings were cruelly justified. He came back again in October 1913, a week ahead of his father, thinner, and more silent than ever. During his first meal he dropped and broke a cup. She exclaimed, and he horrified her by bursting into a dreadful strangled sobbing. It went on and on. Since he had wept with rage as an infant she had never known him cry. In his sleep that night, he shouted horribly. Next day she called the doctor, a hard unsentimental Scotsman she liked and trusted. After looking my brother over, he told her that no boy of sixteen ought to be in so violently nervous a state. 'He has had a bad time, or a bad shock.'

'Did you,' she asked him that evening, 'have a hard time on this trip?'

He avoided her eyes. 'No. But I don't want to go back. Or perhaps I could get another ship.'

'You didn't like your father's ship?'

'No, not much,' he mumbled.

'Why not?'

'Well, I don't know. I didn't care for it.' He turned red. 'I'm not lazy, I'll work, I'm not a good-for-nothing, there must be *something* I can do.'

She got nothing more out of him, at any time.

I do not remember whether, even after this, I took any serious interest in his difficulties. I was not then at home, I did not see him, and my life which that autumn had run into a blind alley divorced me from my family as casually as if I had been living on the moon. What I remember is my mother's voice, cold and implacable, when, three months later, she told me about it.

'I don't know what his father did. But this finishes him with me.'

The words fell like a guillotine on the whole of her married life, its memories, and what gentleness, a mere sediment, remained.

Chapter 12

I was to hold my research scholarship at University College, working under W. P. Ker.

It did not surprise me at the time, but it has surprised me a little since that my mother raised no objection to my sharing rooms with the two Harlands, who were at King's College in the Strand. The elder, Sydney, my closest friend at that time, had taken his degree in geology, but he was still in London, and it was he who invited me to join them.

Nothing better could have happened to me, but why—in September 1912—did my conventionally-bred mother see nothing out of the way in letting me live in rooms with two young men she barely knew?

There were in fact three: the third was another Yorkshireman whom the Harlands had met at King's, Archie White.

The London I lived in as a poor scholar is as unlikely to rise again as Nineveh. Where is Appenrodt's Lager Hall, where is Maxim's? Where is the sixpenny gallery in the Coliseum from which we watched Reinhardt's *Scheherazade*, Polaire of the fifteen-inch waist, Florrie Forde, the ageing Bernhardt, the ageless Marie Lloyd? And those ladies with magnificent poops, navigating, with a wake of powerful scent, a far less crowded Leicester Square and Piccadilly? Where is the Vienna Café? At Maxim's, near the corner of Gerrard Street, the five-course dinner cost half-a-crown, at the smaller Boulogne next door, one and sixpence. The Vienna Café, in New Oxford Street, with its red plush benches and incomparable coffee and brioches, pleasures of a poor intellectual, has been replaced by a bank. A bank, God help us all!

I shall be accused of telling nostalgic lies if I write that those were the last years in which London was a town where young men could live happily on a pittance. Why let that abash me? It is true.

To enjoy all we four *poure scolers* enjoyed easily, a young man today will need the income of, say, a bank manager.

Even at that he is forced to put up with streets so overcrowded that to walk in them he will have to overcome the nausea induced by the nearness of so many swarming bodies, eat worse meals at higher cost, and endure the intolerable boredom of having to *organize* his amusements, since every café, theatre, and even the Reading Room of the British Museum, is fuller of people than it will hold decently.

Under the simplicity and gaiety of this London lay an even simpler town, known to me as a child. My mother and I left my father's ship —lying where? Tidal Basin?—in the early morning, and went by train to Fenchurch Street and from there (Mark Lane Station) by underground to Hyde Park, Bond Street, Piccadilly, Regent Street, and all the squares and smaller more exquisite streets between, admiring the window-boxes and striped awnings of private houses— the eighteenth century had not yet been demolished—and shop windows filled with hats, gloves, jewels, fur coats, antiques. My pretence of interest in these was word-perfect.

The only thing my two Londons had in common was the endless walking I did in both. We four lodged in a small house in Herne Hill, and after breakfast walked over Denmark Hill to Camberwell, to get a bus: on days when it was a question of riding or eating, we walked the whole way—along the respectable squalor of Walworth Road, past the Elephant and Castle (now vanished) and over Waterloo Bridge to the Strand. Walking long distances, even on pavements, was no hardship to our country-bred muscles: on a few fine Sundays we spent the entire day walking about Epping Forest.

Half consciously, we remained a foreign body in this swarming city which did not know we existed. Did not recognize an occupying force sauntering in its streets, eating in the cheapest restaurants, waiting outside a music-hall for the early doors, and talking, my God, talking. A passer-by would sometimes look twice at Oswald Harland, but that was his hair, a flaming bush of the brightest possible red. His, too, was the most intractable tongue, he never gave way in an argument, and argued for the love of it and because any accepted belief, and most human beings, presented themselves to him at an angle.

His brother, Sydney, was intractable in another way. He was black-haired, with the face of a young smiling gargoyle: his mind was an active volcano of ideas and speculations—the label fixed to him at the time: *Brilliant but probably unsound,* turned out to be a lie when, after stumbling round for a year or two, he found his way into genetics. His brilliance had the soundest of bases. Emotionally, he was as irresponsible as I was, with fewer hesitations. He landed himself easily in impossible situations, and encouraged his brother, and me, to help him out of them. We did it with a comforting sense of our own greater steadiness and mother-wit.

Where I was concerned, this was an illusion.

The only one of us who was self-possessed, knew what he wanted, and had coolness, tenacity, and judgement to match his self-possession, was Archie. He had a passion for military history and spent more time on it than he should. Even that, as it turned out, had been the right thing. He kept his ambitions to himself: his tongue—he had his share and more of the jeering northern irony— was less loosely-hung than ours. Joining the O.T.C. struck us as an eccentricity, but to be eccentric was, after all, normal behaviour, and when he was given his first stripe I sewed it on for him, taking immense pains.

He had stronger nerves than the rest of us. Some time in December, a terrified landlady woke us in the dead of night, her husband, an old man, had had an internal haemorrhage: while Oswald and I, sickened by it and by the wretched man's groans, cowered on the staircase, Archie took charge calmly, quietening the poor woman and looking after the dying man until doctor and ambulance arrived.

A rehearsal . . .

Half way through my first term, I abandoned University College. I had taken a dislike to it, almost at sight: to my conceited ignorance it seemed to be a factory for turning out pedants; the two or three lectures I attended bored me, and after a few weeks, except for two visits to Professor Ker, I did not go near it. Instead, I registered myself at King's, which at that time had less than a dozen women students, and followed one of Israel Gollancz's brilliant and fantastic courses. It was no use to me, but then nothing I did at this time was useful, or even sensible.

When I allow myself the folly of thinking about it, a door opens on timeless limitless space, filled like an ash-can with bright scraps of sound, worthless songs, the noise of an orchestra tuning up, and with bat-flittering images, the Thames seen from Waterloo Bridge in early sunlight, a street now torn down or unrecognizable, vanished cafés, the first Cézannes shown in London, a fire blazing in the grate of shabby lodgings, in front of it the four of us eating—long after midnight—toasted muffins, split and filled with sardines: once, I think only once, we added a one-and-ninepenny bottle of Australian burgundy.

And talk—my God, how we talked. Generations since ours have talked as feverishly, but not with our confidence, or our illusions. The difference between them and us is that we *knew* we were at the frontier of a new age . . . of social justice, freedom, perpetual peace. *Because* of us—and the millions like us we felt on our heels—the world was facing towards it; there was really nothing much we need do, except think, talk, exist.

We were socialists of a sort—we disliked and distrusted Fabians, partly because those we saw and heard were middle-aged, even elderly, an order of brahmins. And, worse, smelled of a bureaucracy. We carried our Yorkshire distaste for officials into all our beliefs; a whiff of dogma drove us from the room.

I remain obstinately sure that if, thousand by thousand, our lot had not been slaughtered like animals and pushed quickly into the earth, there would now be fewer bureaucratic noses asking to be tweaked. Or more fingers able to tweak them.

About a year ago a young man wrote asking me to tell him when I had ceased to be a Communist, and why. Ceasing to be a Communist is, or was, a great opportunity, and since I was never one, I missed it. I told him so. He protested acidly at what he took to be a lie, and quoted a sentence from an essay written at a time when all but the most prudent or most astute English writers were violently anti-Fascist.

I may have told him about the Eikonoklasts.

A dozen or so young men, calling themselves by this name, met once a week in the men's common room at King's, to talk. By Sydney's insistence, I was allowed to join them. (I have since wondered what would have happened if the authorities had found me there.) I rarely opened my mouth. I had—have—no quickness in argument, unless I am angry. A serious social misfortune.

The Eikonoklasts—the spelling was an affectation, but a harmless one—were sceptics, unavowed anarchists, self-dedicated to the unmasking of hypocrites, politicians, clericals, reactionaries, bigots, and dogmatists of all ages and conditions. How the devil, after this fighting-cock start, could I have chosen to become a Communist and stomach the most rigid dogma the world has ever known? Anything, but not the dogma.

We admired certain people—Orage, H. G. Wells, Freud, the writer of *La Révolte des Anges*—so sincerely and blindly that we adopted their enemies. One of the very few moments when I found my tongue was to add an insolent phrase—well-received—to the jeering letter we were writing to the founders of the *New Statesman*: we had our philosophical reasons for rejecting this paper, but our real one was that Bernard Shaw, whom we suspected of having the mind of a puritanical rate-payer and no passions, supported it.

After these meetings, the four of us walked home across the bridge and through half-lit streets foreshortened by cold and darkness, still talking, I a little less tongue-tied now that we were again a foreign body with four heads. Four northern voices in a South London street, sounding, at this distance, like a single broken phrase of music, caught as it dies away. Now, as I write, after so many years, so many deaths, the echo brings tears to my eyes.

Our freedom intoxicated us; there was nothing we should not be able to attempt, no road not open to us, no barriers in the world that we children of farmers and seamen were going to walk about in as equals. Our certainty, our optimism, our illusions, are what mark our difference from every other generation which has talked its tongue off its roots since. No generation has ever been so naturally idealistic. Nor, perhaps, so happy, since of all the illusions on which young men get drunk the illusion of a future, a road running towards infinity, breeds happiness more surely and quickly than even a successful love-affair.

Chapter 13

Some time during these months I read (where?) an appeal for someone to give free tutoring to the students of a newly-founded Working Women's College in the Victorian limbo of Earl's Court. I went there, and found a large house in one of those solid yellow terraces built in not the worst manner in the world, its rooms almost bare of furniture, unheated, and with two or perhaps three young women living on heaven knows what scratched-up food, almost without books, and without other help in their random studies.

The founder of this generous, courageously hopeful, preposterous and foredoomed scheme for picking young women out of mills and factories and giving them two or three months' education was Mrs Bridges Adams, then elderly. She lived as Spartan a life as her protégées, in a room of which I recall only the bed and a chest of drawers with a spirit lamp on which she made tea for herself, and fried kippers: I doubt if she troubled to eat meals.

I went there on and off for a year. She told me a great many stories of her young married life in a small community of other young well-bred social revolutionaries living near London—I forget where, but the husbands travelled to London to work (not as conspirators) and the wives met the evening train, hoping to hear that the revolution they expected daily had broken out.

In 1913, too, I had a moment of triumph. Orage's *New Age* was our Bible, the source of half our ideas—the less anarchical half. On the 20th of March it published an essay by an unknown writer, Storm Jameson, on George Bernard Shaw, a joyous exercise in iconoclasm. After saying that his work contained only one living character (Andrew Undershaft), it ended:

'In Mr Shaw's work there are no others—from the annoying Candida to the futile Tanner they belong to an age that is passing and will pass with it. To create them their author has spent much wit and little humour, much mockery and little irony; much in-

tellectual sky-rocketing and little truth; no beauty, and hardly anything of inspiration.'

The other two—Sydney was by now in the West Indies—took my
elated jump-ahead well and coolly. They neither discouraged nor
took me seriously. On the other hand, they saw to it, kindly, that I
did not get above myself—as we say in Yorkshire. Was I in any
danger? I doubt it. Even in those days I did not expect to succeed
without being whipped for it.

The impudent essay was an extract from the thesis I was writing.
Before I left Leeds, with my research scholarship in my pocket, I
had agreed to write on pantheism in French and German literature.
Even today I cannot feel that the subject was anything but academic
flummery. But it was what had been laid down for me, and I made
another of my light-headed blunders in not submitting.

I cannot remember when I decided that it was quite impossible to
waste time and energy on a boring exercise, but certainly before my
first interview with W. P. Ker. I told him frankly how little the
official subject appealed to me.

'Then what would you like to work on?' he asked.

I had my answer ready. 'Modern European drama.'

He smiled and said, gently and drily, 'I hardly think you're old
enough—or wicked enough.'

He told me to go to the British Museum Reading Room and look
at what I should have to read: having done that, to prepare him a
synopsis. Much later I realized that he had been certain I should
hand him in something so confused that he would be able to turn me
painlessly back to the safe path.

Little he knew me. If there is one thing I do easily it is to lay out
the ground-plan of a piece of work; I do it with method, enthusiasm,
and the purest enjoyment.

I worked for two months, and produced a synopsis, ten thousand
words long, of a critical study of European drama from before Ibsen
to the latest—latest in 1913—Russian (German, Spanish, French,
English, Belgian, Scandinavian, Italian) dramatist, lined up by
nations, influences, heaven knows what. It formed an exact chart of
all I did not know about the subject.

I left this document with Professor Ker at the end of December,
and waited confidently.

He sent for me as soon as the term opened again in January, and
with the same dry kindness said,

'It's better than I expected. And now don't you think you had

better let your professors in Leeds know what you've been doing?
You've rather neglected pantheism, haven't you?'

With no lessening of my green confidence I wrote to Leeds—and
was astonished by the rebuke I had so thoroughly deserved.

Since it was too late for me to start again, they let me go on. I
daresay, though I heard nothing about it, that Professor Ker also
wrote to them. I appreciated neither their forbearance nor my own
blindness and levity. I had not the wit to see that I had simply con-
firmed them in their opinion of my irresponsibility and unfitness for
any position.

I worked in feverish bouts followed by a day or days wasted in
running about London.

Wasted? Nonsense. The waste time in a life is the days, weeks,
years, spent living against the grain—all the social and domestic life,
the thousand masks, the wearisome copybook filled even to the
margins with unnecessary words. Dust in the mouth.

The gaiety and insouciance with which I wrote that thesis is unimaginable. Since I could read easily only French and English, the
bulk of the dramatists who came within reach of my claws were
translations, and all or almost all the dramatists I found worth
praise were foreign—Ibsen, Strindberg, Hofmannsthal, Chekhov—
I have not the courage to re-read the book and make a list. For the
rest, I mocked, censured, rebuked, tore down, with reckless delight,
Shaw, Yeats, Masefield, I forget who else.

It was the first—and last—time my natural violence and jeering
northern malice was given its head. The shyness that paralysed me in
the common room at King's disappeared as soon as I was seated in
the Reading Room with a pen and a sheet of foolscap. I had no
sense that my victims were flesh and blood.

Will anyone believe that I was imbecile enough to imagine I should
be praised for my severity?

Some time before the end of that year, 1912, Sydney Harland
made one of his sudden, apparently eccentric decisions, and applied
for a post as schoolmaster in Santa Cruz. We went down to the docks
to see him off on a Danish ship, and came home feeling that we had
had a limb amputated. Morally speaking, we had. With him went
part of the warmth and vivacity of our lives; none of the rest of us
had his trick of conjuring exciting ideas out of the air, or his mer-
curial brilliance. Without him we were more sober, but not—or I
was not—wiser.

We left Herne Hill, and in January went to live in Shepherd's

Bush, in rooms I found for us. They were as freakish as Herne Hill had been dull and orderly. At first slightly dismayed by being expected to share the dusty sitting-room with ten canaries and two Spaniards, the others quickly took to them. The canaries belonged to our landlady, a thin bright-eyed, falsely yellow-haired and tolerant woman who had been a dresser in Sir Herbert Tree's company. It was for her sake I took the rooms. As soon as I set eyes on her, I knew we belonged to the same vagabond race.

As well as the canaries, she kept three dogs and an elderly wrinkled gnome of a German husband, who had once played the cat in *Dick Whittington*, and now mended clocks. (Later, during the war, he was interned: it broke his gentle heart and killed him.)

The Spaniards were an odd pair. They were travelling the world collecting the signatures of famous people; they had several hundreds already and expected to sell the haul for a vast sum. Now middle-aged, they began this strange life as young men. One of them was ill; he lay shivering, coughing, grumbling, on the shabby couch, nursed by the other with patient delicacy and gentleness. What became of their book of signatures? It may exist somewhere, a useless curiosity, though the two pairs of brown-fingered thin hands which held it jealously, turning the pages for our indifferent eyes, must long have vanished.

From that house, when our restless energy drove us out at night, Oswald and I could walk across Ealing Common as far as Kew without feeling that we were in a city: it was partly an illusion of the darkness, but partly, too, that the country had not yet been defeated in London; there were still rearguards holding out, where now all is lost.

I have forgotten too many details of my life then, but not the poverty and happiness.

No life I have led since has come so close to satisfying me—a life, that is, without possessions, above all without responsibility, to things or people. I was offended, sometimes, by the extreme shabbiness of my surroundings—they were pleasant compared with the house and street to which I sank a little later—but these moments of queasiness only roughened the surface. A little more money would have cured them.

I was completely unconscious, then, of the benefit to my mental and spiritual condition of living with intelligent boys rather than with girls or women. Even when they ignored some display of female silliness—or laughed only among themselves—the sense of their disapproval reached me sooner or later. Within reason, they treated me like a younger brother, with as much unconcern and good-temper. I don't recall being damned in any stronger words than: Don't be a calf. It was enough. Later in life I found attentions paid to me surprising and boring. I did not—do not—expect to have allowances made for me.

14th of January, 1963

The disadvantages of having been a member of Class 5b, and an Eikonoklast, were brought home to me today. I found myself the only person in the room not in ecstasies over a copy of *The Private Eye*. It was the second I had tried to read, almost sobbing with boredom, hardly able to believe that jokes so old and puerile were meant to be read by adults. All these irreverences, the rude nose-thumbing at middle-class idols, at religion, royalty, all manner of *idées reçues*, were going the rounds in 5b. We had not learned to talk of the Establishment, but that did not prevent us from being side-splittingly funny about the thing itself. I am stupefied, not by the titter of Kensington-bred ladies over a lewd joke . . . after all, poor dears . . . but by my worldly intelligent friends. How can they find these aged witticisms startling? Do they? Or are they afraid of seeming to have pieties? Or did they all, all, lead such sheltered lives in their youth that these jeers and mild blasphemies shake them?

I felt out of things, but took heart: it is not my fault, it is the fault of 5b and the Eikonoklasts.

Chapter 14

I have forgotten what K. was doing during this time: he came only once or twice to see us in London. The boys did not like him. They were less than frank with me about the reasons for their dislike, but I knew them too well to miss seeing it: I looked the other way and hoped that K. would not notice that he was being judged. I am sure he did not.

His visits had an unpleasantly disturbing effect on me. For a time, when he was with us, I saw through his eyes that we were an uncouth lot, slovenly provincials. I wished we had more elegance, a nicer knowledge of the world. When he left, my discontent and disquietude went with him.

I was still helplessly in love, but something, some submerged current, had begun to set against him in my mind, at a great depth. I knew, vaguely, that it was there. Given time, I should have become critical of him, and in the end my obsession would have died and I should have been free . . .

At some time in 1913 my mother read letters K. had written, which I had left in my room at home. Their language made her feel that the sooner I was married the better for my soul. She came up to London determined to save me.

So there I was, back where I had so often stood, cowered, as a child crushed by guilt for a half-realized crime. I was neither hard enough, nor adroit or singleminded enough, to withstand the force of her anger and grief. I had nothing to set against it except my deep inarticulate reluctance to be married, my profound instinct to keep my freedom. She swept this contemptuously aside. The strange thing —no, not strange; given her age and breeding, perfectly natural— was that she knew she was saving my moral being at the expense of my future, that future in which she had sunk so many of her own hopes: its collapse into a mere marriage was the cruellest of disappointments to her. But she knew she was right.

She is not to be blamed. *I* was responsible; the choice, after all, was mine.

Letting others trap me, I trapped myself.

I had made blunders before this, plenty. This was the first crippling choice. All that can be said is that it harmed no one but myself—and K.

My memory for the details I ought in decency or politeness to remember is shockingly vague. I remember the names of Whitby shopkeepers long since dead, and the exact number of steps from the gate to the front door of a house left behind more than fifty years ago, and the exquisite taste of crusts soaked in warm tea, and the turnings to be taken from the Hôtel de France in Nevers to reach the baker selling the finest bread, but I do not know whether K. and I began living together at once after our marriage, or if I went back for a time to my room above the sitting-room with the canaries and the ailing Spaniard.

I believe I did. But certainly in the late summer I was living with him in another room in Shepherd's Bush, a dreadfully dingy shabby room in a street of sordid little houses (in 1941 bombed to a pile of rubble) on the north side of the green—Caxton Street.

I cannot remember what we had to live on, unless my scholarship money still had a month or so to run. K. must have had a little money—from his parents? We paid six shillings each *a week* for bed and breakfast in this squalid room. I was still working on my thesis, of which I had written about two-thirds.

Every morning I walked from Shepherd's Bush to the British Museum, starting at half-past eight. When, in 1956, I went to live in a flat looking across Hyde Park near Marble Arch (before this edge of the park was barbarously and uselessly mutilated), I tried to catch sight of a carelessly-dressed girl walking past lightly, carrying an attaché case and a paper bag holding a half-pound of plums. I bought the plums in Shepherd's Bush to eat in the cloakroom of the Museum at midday. And there were little cafés in the streets near the Museum where, if I am not dreaming, in those innocent unorganised days the food, simple, tasted of itself.

For the evening meal there was a coffee stall at the Wood Lane end of Shepherd's Bush Green, where the man in charge was obliging enough to make me a ham sandwich without the pungent mustard he used. For the rest, I lived largely on energy and illusions of future greatness.

I was happier and unhappier here than seems possible—and not bored. London made my happiness. At that time I had a passion for it which neither poverty nor despair could dim.

For the life of me I cannot remember what K. did during the day. A little journalism? My egotistical absorption in my thesis made anything he may have been doing of little interest. It did not enter my head to rely on his earning anything.

The sum of two egoisms, two green vanities, does not add up to a placid life. Used to the boys' amiable wrangling, I was disconcerted by K.'s readiness to take offence. The discomforts of our way of living—neither of us noticed them except as one notices bad weather —cannot have helped. The young rarely have any mercy on each other—not that we thought of ourselves as young. We were two egoisms face to face, and incapable of seeing through each other's greeds, self-absorption, illusions, to the naked inner creature in need of kindness. I must too often have been madly stubborn. We quarrelled over trifles, bitter quarrels in which neither wanted to give way: I knew I was right and waited in anguish for K. to recognize it: then, only then, I could admit to being in the wrong.

One night, in despair and a reckless wish to be anywhere but where I was, I swallowed all the phenacetin tablets in a bottle I had just bought—in those days I knew only two remedies for any ailment, the ones my mother used: phenacetin and Eno's. I expected so much phenacetin to kill me. Feeling cold, I became afraid and told K. what I had done: to my grieved astonishment he flew into a sour rage, threatened to fetch the police to me, and did fetch a doctor who was anything but kind.

I begged him not to tell anyone what I had done. But he told the boys, who listened to him without comment.

At some time during this poverty-stricken autumn and winter his parents made him an offer. They were religious people, American Quakers, and before the marriage had made one or two gestures of lukewarm friendliness towards me: they could not like me, I was young, penniless, and not of their religion, but I think they saw my faults too clearly to notice that I had a virtue or two—among these, an eager goodwill; I responded to kindness like a puppy, licking hands, wagging my tail. I forget what they offered K., except that it was further training of some sort, I think at Cambridge. The condition, of course, was that he must give up the wretched wastrel life he was living with me.

I can sympathize, now, with their anxiety about their son, an only child. At the time, I rejected coldly the part of the offer which concerned me: they were willing, they said, to pay for a room in a women's hostel until I had finished my thesis. After that . . . probably they did not look further. The important thing was to save K. and separate him from a wife who was no good to him. Given enough rope, they may have reflected, I should hang myself. (Running off with an Italian organ-grinder was one of the things my father-in-law suggested I was likely to do at any minute.)

Did they expect me to oppose their plan? Far from that, I urged K. to seize the offer. When he had gone my only feeling was of excitement. I was alone, the world open to me. Later that afternoon, I went into a small café near Caxton Street (it is still there), to drink coffee and think what I had better do at once. Glancing up, I saw K. striding past, towards our lodgings. My heart leaped with surprise and disappointment.

Chance had brought him back. When he reached his parents' house in North London, they were both out, and he had time to regret leaving me. He left the house again at once, before they returned. As his mother wrote to him, 'If I had been at home, you would never have gone away.'

What a ridiculous accident, lighter than a touch on the shoulder, to alter the whole of my life.

Later that autumn my mother was in London with the ship, and came to see where I was living. She gave few signs that the place horrified her. Scarcely able to speak, she sat in the window, looking out on the sordid little street with its choked gutters and flea-bitten cats, her back turned to the room overfilled by the brass-knobbed bed, a chest of drawers, and the minute table covered by my books and papers, the whole an indeterminate rusty brown, the colour of age and grime. This room was scrupulously tidy—I hate disorder: any room I live in is properly ship-shape—but neatness did not hide its ingrained squalor and the musty smell of poverty. By now I was so used to it, and to washing from head to foot night and morning in a bowl of cold water (I have never dared ask a survivor of Ravensbrueck what, apart from torture and hunger, was worse than not being able to keep a clean body), that I did not guess what she felt. I brought out the two cups and the spirit lamp, and made tea for her, and she drank it, trying to smile.

Years later, with a shudder of disgust, she told me, 'It made my heart ache to see you in that horrible room. I thought you were done for.'

At the end of the year I fell ill in this room: there was nothing wrong with me except semi-starvation and a touch of fever, but I did not recover and at last thought of going home for a time. My thesis was all but finished; there was only the summing-up to write, and the labour of copying it on the secondhand typewriter I had bought with my first money from the university.

I hung on until the first days of January. I had no money at all now, and arrived in Whitby with a single ha'penny in my purse.

K., too, went home. He had begun applying for a post as schoolmaster, in London.

Chapter 15

'Thank goodness you've come,' my mother said, 'I'm going to be lonely.'

My middle sister was away, and a few days after I came my brother went off to Manchester, to a place calling itself the Northern School of Wireless: he knew nothing about it, but wireless was a new thing, and the fees at the school so low that my mother could afford it. She did not ask him how he was lodged: she expected all her children (except the youngest) to be able to survive anything.

The dominating person in the family now was this youngest, my sister Dorothy. She was eight, a very beautiful little creature, quick and graceful, warm-natured except in cross-grained moods when she was furiously intractable. My mother pretended to believe that these devilish moods could be traced back to a nearly fatal illness when she was six months old: an all but lifeless little skeleton, she had been given a glass of fresh blood, pressed from hunks of raw beef, every day for a long time. They gave it to her in a green Venetian glass and she drank it greedily, smacking colourless little lips over it.

In the middle of February my brother telegraphed: Have joined the Flying Corps, letter follows.

The letter next morning was almost as laconic: the Royal Flying Corps wanted wireless operators, he was eligible, it was a splendid chance, better than he had hoped for. But, since he was only seventeen, my mother must give her permission. Terribly agitated, she sent me to Manchester to stop him.

The imposingly-named Northern School turned out to be two small attics at the top of a shabby building. The thin young man who was running it talked with smiling enthusiasm about the Flying Corps: it was the coming thing, there were six squadrons, and there might soon be thirty, even more. 'It's a great piece of luck for your brother that they want men—by going in now he'll do very well for himself.'

Men! I thought, looking at my brother's short red childish hands. He was clenching them, and said, 'It's the only way I can get into the Flying Corps. If I had money I could go in for being a pilot, but——'

'What will you be?' I asked him.

'A Second-class Air Mechanic,' he said, scowling. 'But it's my chance. I *must* take it. You can tell her that.'

I don't think that, even now, I had the grace to take his ambitions wholly seriously. He was awkward and unformed—that I was both myself did not occur to me. Only his eyes, with their steady clouded stare, reflected an anxiety I recognized. The three of us in that shabby room were all young, seventeen, twenty-two, twenty-six, and at this distance from her my mother's fears seemed those of an old woman who knew nothing about the world.

I left promising to make her agree, and, without much trouble—after all, what else had she to offer him?—did.

Before this, I had missed a chance of my own. When I was in London, I had written two pieces of dramatic criticism for *The Egoist*, and met its founder, Harriet Shaw Weaver, and that remarkable woman, her friend Dora Marsden. I was not much given to respect in my first youth, but I knew enough to revere pure intellect when I met it. A small delicately-boned woman, Dora Marsden had a subtle and powerful mind and a passion for philosophy, I believe her only passion. She treated me with the most unmerited kindness and friendliness. and gave me the manuscript of her first book. I understood it only in the cloudiest way.

Soon after I went home, Harriet Shaw Weaver wrote offering me work on *The Egoist*, at a weekly salary of two pounds. My excitement when I was reading her letter is indescribable. I had not the wit to realize that she was inventing the job with the sole idea of giving a young provincial nobody the chance to make something of herself. The prospect of setting foot in a world of brilliantly clever and advanced men and women, who would, I thought, cure my worldly timidity and ignorance, made me wildly happy. I was a long way from knowing just how green and uncouth I was, and had no doubt at all that I should make my literary fortune.

It no more came into my head to refuse the offer than to cut my throat, and I wrote to Miss Weaver that I would come to London at once.

When I told my mother, she looked at me from eyes so remotely fixed that they appeared colourless. 'I thought you would be here at least until April,' she said; 'I shall be very sad and sorry without you.'

'But I should have had to go some time.'

'The money is very little.'

'It is a start. And I shall be in London.'

She said nothing more for the moment. I saw her pressing her lips together over her bitter sense of my eagerness to get away. A too familiar anxiety seized me, but I hardened my heart. Later in the day she said,

'This time next week you will be gone. I was planning a day in Scarborough, but not alone.'

'I shall be coming back.'

'That doesn't comfort me now, my little dear. It's dull here by myself. And no kind girl to go the round with me. It's not,' she added, smiling, 'as if you had a husband to go to. When K. has found work and sends for you, it will be a different affair altogether.'

The round was a walk we had taken so many times from this house that its rough flagstones and grass are sunk in my other life, the one in which I am innocent.

I might still have held out if she had not told me calmly, 'My body is not right, you know. Since Dorothy was born. It can't be put right.'

I did not know what she meant, but I had already noticed, and avoided thinking about it, that she had become, suddenly, older and heavier.

My heart dropped under its weight of regret, pity, despair. 'I needn't go,' I said, 'I can refuse.'

Her face changed slightly. 'I thought you had written accepting.'

'Yes. But I can write again.'

I wrote the next day, a clumsy letter of apology and refusal.

Cruelly disappointed as I was, I yet did not realize clearly what I had done. *Don't be to tell twice* is a sentence I heard so many times in my childhood that it ceased to make sense. Before experience teaches me anything, the lesson has had to be repeated not twice but a score of times. My whole life, if I had seized this offer, would have been different. When she got my second letter Miss Weaver passed the offer to another young woman, Rebecca West, who accepted it. Believe me, who should know, *The Egoist* and the world of letters got a better bargain.

At twenty-two, one expects to meet a chance round every corner. There was still my great work on European drama, from which I expected at least a living, if not fame. I worked on it, with no interruptions except my mother's demands on me, until April, then sent it, with a formal apology for the time it had taken me, to Leeds.

I had better finish with this at once. It was approved by the university, and I rewarded with the degree of Master of Arts. By this time I had other things on my mind, and we were in the middle of a war. I put my carbon copy away, and did not look at it again until the end of the war: then I added to it briefly, leaving my three-year-old son with my mother for a fortnight while I read feverishly in the British Museum, and sent it to a publisher. I did not confide to him —or anyone—what my hopes were.

I doubt whether Messrs Collins were less startled than I by what happened. The dramatic critics took me seriously and very hard. In a majestic column in *The Times*, A. B. Walkley spoke of 'a female Nietzsche': at even greater length, under the title 'The Young Person in Print', Mr St John Ervine dismembered the book with Ulster savagery; for good measure he said I ought to be spanked.

I was never more astonished in my life, and terribly mortified, feelings I hid from everybody—without exception. I felt that, even though they could not have known about all those pounds of plums eaten in vain, the brutes should at least have realized how hard I had worked.

For Mr Ervine I felt a violent dislike. Some months later I was standing in a crowded room where I knew nobody—one of Naomi Royde-Smith's Thursday evenings—when my hostess came up to me, and taking me by the arm said, 'St John Ervine is here, I think you ought to speak to him.' Nervously, but not at all unwilling—the idea of single combat did not alarm me—I went with her into the next room. The brute was not what I had expected:

leaning on a stick, tired and hot, he appeared as tongue-tied as I was. Possibly he had not expected my too obvious simplicity and harmless looks.

A short time afterwards, hearing that I had written a novel, he offered to send it to an American publisher and, more usefully still, invited me to lunch. During the meal, he did all he could to advise me.

'What you need most,' he said emphatically, 'is discipline.'

To me then, discipline implied thrashings, hunger, poverty. I considered that I knew more than enough of all three, and saw no meaning whatever in his words.

His kindly-meant and fruitless advice, a small sum in royalties, and a critical article by Austin Harrison in the *English Review*—why did I not keep it?—were all the good that came of the book. Except an absurd memory of Austin Harrison himself. I see myself in his room at the offices of the review, my body hard with suppressed laughter. 'Look down,' he had said, 'now look up . . . Yes, I was right, you have perfect Oriental throwback!' What can he mean? I think: the man's daft . . . Daft or not, he was kind to me: he allowed me to write for the review an essay on Walter de la Mare which pleased that incomparable man, and two or more articles on, of all things, the United States, which must, since I was as ignorant as a calf, have been very queer.

I think I was before my time—before a time when impudence is a merit. Yet I really knew more about European drama than anyone but A. B. Walkley himself, and if I had been offered the chance should have made, softened by age and authority, an admirable dramatic critic.

This would, I am certain, have saved me from being tempted to write a novel.

Chapter 16

In April 1914 I sealed and posted the package addressed to Leeds
University, containing a great weight of confidence and ambition.
I was without money, without a job, and I had heard from K. that,
rejected for every London post he had applied for, he had taken
one in a town in the Midlands. All I knew about Kettering was that
it made boots and shoes. I was dismayed. There was no hope of my
finding any work there, I should be dependent on K. This idea
deeply offended me.

It did not come into my head that I could refuse to go.

At this time I was still bound to K. by ties which loosened only
slowly, over the next four or five years and, if we had lived a retired
life in the dead of the country—this supposes what is not true, that
I was willing to live in such a way—would probably have needed half
a lifetime to wear out completely: they were sensual and imaginative,
like the grief I felt, as soon as I had abandoned it, for the white
rabbit.

I meant to behave well, and set off with as many resolutions as
misgivings.

At my first sight of Kettering I made a vow not to stay a day
longer than I must. I refused to look for a house. We lived in a small
commercial hotel near the station. No one else *lived* in it: no one
except me would have dreamed of living there. We paid 16/6 a week
each, for a bedroom, a small sitting-room and all our meals: I had a
perpetual grudge against our landlady for her habit of mixing potato
peelings with the little coal she allowed us; she did it to damp down
the fire, but the smell was insidious and abominable. Had I complained she would gladly have got rid of us.

Shocked by what seemed to them my inexcusably disorderly life,
the wives of other masters in the school were always telling me about
small houses I could rent. I evaded them. Not only because of my
secret determination not to stay in Kettering, and not even because

of a loathing for these rows of human rabbit hutches without a
shred of charm, to say nothing of dignity. My hatred of a settled
domestic life was, is, an instinct, and borders on mania.

With my large ideas of what was barely necessary for life on a
salary of less than fifty shillings a week, I took out a subscription to
The Times Book Club. The discovery of Allen Upward's *The Divine
Mystery*, and J. A. Symonds's *History of the Renaissance in Italy*, read
volume by volume in that shabby room smelling of decayed vegetables, gave me the greatest pleasure I have ever had from books. I
read in a fever of excitement, my cheeks burning, my mind in ferment.

These hours when I was alone, reading, sunk, were purely happy.
Apart from them I was neither happy nor sensible. My mind behaved
like a newly-trapped wild animal, throwing itself at the sides of its
cage with undirected fury. I did not know where to turn to escape
from a life which, the instant I shut my book, became an intolerable
waste of energy and time. I must have been an uncomfortable companion, irritating K. as often as he disheartened and affronted me. I
was changing as helplessly as a tadpole, and K. hardly at all. He was
exactly as he had been in London, amiable and fond when he was
pleased with me, rancorously ill-tempered when I vexed him, which
I did too easily: I had only to be incautious enough to begin a
sentence with the words: One of these days we'll buy . . . we'll go
abroad . . . we'll see Greece . . .

I daresay that what he resented in me were changes he could not
put his finger on but suspected. Under the features of the undeveloped
girl, the tadpole, who had succumbed readily to his involuntary skill
in playing on his own and her sensual curiosity, was faintly visible
the confused outline of a young woman he could only see as detestable, foolishly unreasonable and splenetic. I was at times all
these.

And no doubt I judged too harshly faults, a naïve vanity and self-
importance, at which a kinder or more sophisticated woman would
have smiled.

All this is shocking egoism . . .

My only amusement was walking. No moors, no sea, only bird
cries and the muffled sigh of wind in long grass, and, in the month of
May, hedges full out in hawthorn, an unbroken torrent of whiteness
reaching me along the same level as the marguerites of my infancy.

Twice I enticed K. farther afield. We spent a Saturday in Leicester.
In a shop-window my eye was caught by a long green sofa: it re-

minded me of one at home, and the idea of buying it entered into me like a devil. I have never been able to see round or past what I want. Like my mother when she coveted something, I was *possessed*. But I was worse than she, stubborner and more cunning. There was room in our ugly sitting-room for the sofa and I persuaded K. to buy it on the never-never—13/6 a week for eighteen months. That evening when we got back, our landlady told us she would have to raise her weekly charges to 19/6 each—thirty-nine shillings. K. behaved nobly, leaving me to reproach myself.

My second extravagance was a day in London at half-term. Somehow we had saved thirty shillings and I could see no better use for it. The thought of even one day there made me insanely happy.

My brother was stationed near London, and my conscience, rather than any wish to see him, made me write and invite him to lunch with us in Soho. He came, a clumsy childish figure in his Air Mechanic's uniform. He had little to say, and that little had to be dragged out of him. Perhaps—I have just seen this—K. had on him the effect he had had on me when I saw him as a man of the world. After lunch, he mumbled something about 'going back now'. I knew he had the day off until evening, but, impatient to run about London, I made no attempt to keep him. We left him in Coventry Street and crossed the road. I glanced back. He was walking slowly, head down, and I saw—thank God for my long sight—that his face had turned red and he was struggling not to cry.

I rushed back across the road. Pretending not to see that there were tears in his eyes, I took hold of his arm.

'Can't you possibly stay longer? We only came up to see you, you know, and you're spoiling it by going off. Isn't there *something* we could do that would amuse you, a theatre, anything?'

Was he taken in? I shall never be certain. He muttered something about his frightful boots.

'What do your boots matter?' I said. 'In a theatre no one will see them, and we'll go to some small café for tea. Do stay.'

'Very well.'

Each time I recall this incident, I thank God for an uncovenanted mercy. Of all the escapes I have been allowed, all the deserved punishments I have been let off, this is the one I shall be as thankful for on the day I die as I am at this moment—after more than half a century.

Chapter 17

Since there was nothing else I could do, I began to write a novel.

It was a gloriously bad novel—perhaps not the worst I have written. It had no theme, only a riot of scenes and emotions, new characters brought on the whole time (and only one living breathing character among them), a great deal of talk, lively, cynical, jeering, images and ideas borrowed from the *New Age*, Anatole France, Upward, Symonds, thrown down in a style that dodged between curtness and the purest (most impure) Wardour Street. But the energy, the delighted playing with phrases and ideas, the irreverence, the reckless gaiety and enthusiasm of this frightful book—what happened to me to suppress them? I know. The double error of a settled life and the decline into writing for a living.

It is laughably clear that Nature was no more eager to make me a novelist than the university authorities to make a don of me. What did it intend me to be? What conceivable life would have satisfied my instincts of a *vagus* and my crying need of a sort of discipline I had no idea of?

I had emerged from an ill-found ill-considered academic course completely ignorant of contemporary writing, nothing in my head but echoes. I have a strong patient brain, but it is myopic and slightly mad. It reminds me of a young horse I once rode, which was blind in one eye and under the delusion that it could jump walls.

I suppose that this first book had an awkward cleverness, mine at the time. No publisher or reviewer but took it for a young man's book. This suggests that at its worst it was crudely energetic.

With all the reading I did for pleasure, and my habit of day-dreaming, and the outbreaks of restlessness when to sit in a room became unendurable, not much of it had been written when we left Kettering. Our leaving was my doing entirely. It was, I think, the first time I took on myself to manoeuvre another person's life. I discovered that I had a talent for *managing*. True, I only used it when my own life was involved.

Every week since we came to Kettering I had been going into the public library to read an educational journal, searching for a London school in need of a man to teach Latin. At last, at the end of May, a school in Liverpool advertised the post of junior classics master, and, Liverpool being at least a city, I used all my cunning to persuade K. to apply. He applied and was chosen.

Not long after, he caught a vicious form of influenza. My savage loathing of illness and sickrooms might have been the end of him if his mother had not travelled from London to nurse him. Reminding herself to be kind, she said gently, 'Don't feel that I want to push you aside.'

'Oh, but do!' I cried.

Not until he was recovering did I begin to feel anxious about him, and to think: Let us only get to Whitby and he will be safe. As soon as—at the end of July—he could travel, I took him there. All I did by way of preparing our future was to send the green sofa to a Liverpool warehouse.

My brother was at home on leave. For the first time, my mother caught a glimpse of his secret ambition. Sitting in her room, red short-fingered hands sprawled on his knees, feet in clumsy boots widely apart, he told her,

'I'm in the right thing. In the Corps you're not ordered about as if you were nothing, like we were in the ship. The officers talk to you, I've been up several times with one pilot; he said I ought to learn to fly, and he would help me if there was a chance for me learning.'

'How would there be a chance?' she asked.

His clouded eyes did not meet hers: he was ashamed of his ambitions. 'There's always changes. That's why it's lucky I went in now, when everything's possible.'

She felt the anguish of having no money, and under it a colder anguish, the fear that he would be disappointed. At other moments, she believed that he would distinguish himself in some way: she no longer expected anything of me, and placed all the hopes she had on this son who, for the first time, looking, with his round blurred face, an unformed boy, talked like a young man.

Suddenly—the suddenness was an illusion—the talk of a crisis in Europe leaped on to the front page of the newspaper. The telegram recalling my brother excited him so fiercely that he forgot to be ashamed.

'If there's a war,' he said, 'I might get a chance. It might be the very thing for me. You'll see, they'll be taking in new men, but us old ones will have the start. That officer I was telling you about said so to me—well, something of that.'

Us old ones . . . On the day war was declared my mother comforted herself with the certainty that *they* would not send him out of the country until he was eighteen. But he flew to France with the first English squadrons, on the 10th of August, and had his eighteenth birthday there.

He made his first stroke very early in November. My mother heard about it in a pencilled letter from him. He still wrote like a child, in sprawling uneven lines almost without stops.

'You will be pleased to hear that I got the medal which is called in France the Médaille Militaire, Medal Military, and seems to be very highly prized by them. I got it for working the wireless in a aeroplane over the German lines, a shell from one of their anti-aircraft guns exploded near us and blew part of our inlet valve away and cut the pilot's hand. This was on our great retreat of which you have read so much. The medal was given by the French government and presented by General Henderson. The war seems to be getting on slowly much slower than I expected. There is a heavy fog hanging about today and things are very quiet. I am still in the best of health and I am surprised to see how quickly we have got used to this kind of life. There is one thing when we do get back we will get a nice long holiday so let us hope it will be in the Spring. Looking at my pay book today I noticed I had over ten pounds to draw already . . .'

She noticed without surprise that he had not told her what he had done for the French army to deserve their medal. It was like him to say little. And she was not even faintly surprised that he had done well already. It was what she expected.

Chapter 18

I had no intention, not the least in the world, when I urged K. to try for Liverpool, of becoming a householder and ratepayer—my term then for all that is dull, base, petty, in a word *Prudhommesque*. It came about inch by stumbling inch.

I took the first of these ill-judged steps before we left Whitby, when I accepted my mother's offer to lend me a hundred pounds to buy furniture. What she thought of as my disorderly life shocked and worried her; she was convinced that I must want a house of my own (accursed and nauseating phrase), it was what every decent normal young woman wanted. If it had crossed her mind that on this point I was neither decent nor normal, she would have been all the more anxious to whip the devil out of me. When I told her that I preferred living in rooms, with a landlady to keep them clean and cook, the flash of rage in her eyes reminded a child of an old terror. It had less effect on me now than my reluctance to disappoint her.

I might still have dodged but for the birth in me of a new guilty feeling—born since his illness—that I ought to look better after K. And the germ of another notion, one that went a very little way to justify my mother in her belief that I could not be entirely out of my mind: a weak stirring of greed to possess things I should not dislike looking at.

In the instant of saying, 'Thank you very much, you're being awfully kind,' I was seized by panic: I *knew* I had done the wrong thing. The sensation was familiar, but more piercing than I had ever known it; I felt emptied of all except panic.

There was still time to draw back. I was not morally brave enough.

A flat, I considered, would be a lighter burden than a house. I had not reckoned with the provincial barbarity of Liverpool. After two and a half months of living as paying guests in a respectable run-down house, and rejecting one unsavoury pseudo-flat after

another in street after sallow dingy Victorian street, I was driven to
rent a new house in the Garden Suburb, an estate, to my eyes raw
and graceless, on the edge of Liverpool, in an unmade road of
identical pairs of little houses, two small living-rooms and narrow
kitchen downstairs, and two cramped bedrooms above. If I had been
ordered to describe the kind of house which most nauseated me, I
could not have found a more exact image.

We took this clean loathsome place from the 1st of December,
handing the estate twenty-five pounds, to be given back to us when
we left.

My mother came to Liverpool for a week, to help me to buy the
furniture: she was delighted with the house, and even more delighted by the end of my disorderly life. In order not to hurt her, I
kept up a pretence of happiness.

The evening before she left it broke down when I was face to face
with the prospect of moving into the house as soon as its floors had
been scrubbed. (Not that I object to scrubbing floors: I prefer it to a
great many things—for instance, to speaking at a luncheon.)

The panic I had felt in Whitby was nothing compared with the
mortal abhorrence I felt now, as much physical as moral, the sen-
sations of a trapped human animal—a maelstrom of irrational disgust, despair, revolt. It was ridiculously out of proportion with its
cause—I could not have felt a worse dread on my way to be hanged.

I tried to hide my demented state from my mother behind a stolid
face. But I suppose that it was sullen as well as calm, and when I said
that I would get the house ready but not live in it until January, her
anger at what seemed my ingratitude and folly got the better of
her. She spoke to me in her harshest voice, with violent contempt.
After a minute I began to cry, and cried uncontrollably. My mother
went up to bed, leaving me to my inexcusable misery. K., who had
not said a word, was unexpectedly gentle with me. Neither of them
had the faintest conception of my state of mind. I daresay I had none
myself, all I knew was that I was trapped.

I cannot explain my pathological hatred of domestic life and
frantic need to be free. Not free to write, or to be amused, or famous.
To be free. To call it a spiritual nausea only pushes it farther out of
reach. A crazily violent character, a tramp or a lunatic, shares my
skin with a Yorkshire housewife.

In any event, in 1915 I was, all else apart, biologically trapped.

I kept the house dreadfully clean, washing, scrubbing, dusting,
with feverish energy. I had forgotten, until the other day I opened a

novel written in 1932, how K.'s shockingly meagre salary was spent. I cut and sewed a strip of while calico into four tiny bags, writing on each its name and the sum it was supposed to receive, and every Monday morning divided the week's money (£2 15s 6d, minus 13s 6d for the green sofa) between them. The Rent and Rates bag was remorseless in swallowing its 12s 9d, but the Coal, Light and Gas bag (4s 6d) and the one marked Food (25s) borrowed from each other with reckless optimism; there were many weeks when the miserable Coal, Light and Gas held nothing but a scrap of paper on which I had written: Owed by Food, 7s 8d. K. took ten shillings of the total to pay tram fares and his six two-course luncheons at school.

I had no skill in the knacks by which poor women make ends meet, and when the wife of one of K.'s older colleagues offered me a recipe for cooking an ox-heart I shuddered. In London I had contentedly eaten or gone without the cheapest meal, but now that I was cooking my own the only food I thought worth buying were things I had eaten as a child, smoked bacon, sirloin, fillet steak, English lamb, the finest country butter: each Saturday I bought a joint for the next day, and stretched it to make supper for K. during the week, pretending to eat midday dinner—not to spare him discomfort, but from an instinct to keep my clumsy shifts to myself.

Another young schoolmaster and his wife lived in the suburb. He was the first pacifist I had met. I hated the war, and swore with my tongue that I approved of his refusal to fight, but in fact I had neither sympathy nor respect for him. A letter from Archie, though heaven knows I did not understand it—he might as well have been writing to me in a foreign language, from a non-existent country ('I'm writing this in a field near a farm. We were relieved two days ago and brought back to this village for a rest. The men were dog-tired when they came in. For the last mile or so I was carrying three rifles and trying to encourage the weary. I was too tired to take my things off and the bed looked clean, a delusion, so I lay down on the floor and slept. We're all right now, as fresh as May. A small French child, about nine, is hanging round me as I write. I'm bound to say she's not attractive. I don't think war agrees with children.')—swung me violently round the compass. Without reflecting about it, I was on his side, and not on the side of the Fellowship of Reconciliation, which in theory I supported.

Chapter 19

During these early months of 1915, I tried in various childishly clumsy ways to find out what giving birth is like. Desperately unwilling to let K. see I was anxious, I waited several weeks before asking him what he knew about it—after all, he was a doctor's son. He advised me amiably to read *Anna Karenina*. The account of the birth of Levin's son terrified me. I became convinced that I was going to be tortured. Is anyone now so ignorant? In my first youth, these things were not talked of, no more than the sexual act, or abortion, or any of the body's daily habits.

What on earth would today's young novelists do if they were without these staples of their interest?

K. dealt drily with my awkwardly put questions. It may have been the instinct of a schoolmaster. And since I did not say I was afraid . . .

I did not think it strange that I was not treated gently: I had been well-taught in my first years that illness is nothing to make a fuss about. Looking back, I think that K. carried his lack of concern too far. Certain memories of those months are so bitter that the scars are alive. The young do not pity each other—or themselves. But the child who knew it had behaved badly *because* it was punished was too near me in time not to expect the consoling forgiveness that had always, sooner or later, followed the beating. It was usually I who consoled K., but that is irrelevant. His repentances were sincere. And I have never been able to prevent myself melting like butter in hot sun the instant an enemy shows the faintest sign of remorse. It is a fault.

K. was not, or not consciously, my enemy. Neither was he my friend . . .

I had leisure during these months to write, and tried to finish my novel. I failed completely. My mind had lost its power to concentrate: the energy was still there, but the sap did not run. Surprised, I thought: It must be the child.

I loathed the deformation and heaviness of my body, and envied every thin young girl I saw, the poorest and plainest.

In spite of all this, in spite of everything, I never thought that I was done for. I would rather have died than tell K.—or anyone— that I still hoped. Hoped what? To escape, to become famous? Ashamed when I remembered my insane hopes and ambitions at the university and in London, I did not dare to make plans.

I had moments—when I was alone—of gaiety and confidence, when the life I was living seemed no worse than marking time, an interval to be got through. Miraculous mornings when, however exhausted I had been the night before, however unhappy or anxious, I woke, like a child or an animal, knowing instantly where I was, to a pure bubbling spring of energy, worth a fortune.

I had so much lightness of heart (or head) that it could not always be kept out of sight. Nor did I take myself seriously. But I should have liked others—K. especially—to do this.

Until I wrote them down, in 1932, in *That Was Yesterday*, I re-membered almost every incident of the two and a quarter years I spent in that house. Writing them down freed me of the memory, but not of the lessons in distrust, dryness, patience.

My son was born in Whitby, in my mother's house, a little after eleven o'clock on the morning of Sunday the 20th of June, 1915. Two of my mother's friends looked in on their way from church (chapel, Mrs George Gallilee corrects me tartly) to enquire, and were shown a child whose eyes were able to focus on them steadily and directly, with none of the wavering vacancy of a new-born child's glance—blue eyes with long black lashes, and a smooth clear skin, not red or wrinkled.

The strangest things about the underworld through which I am travelling, trying to move backwards against the current, towards the sun of my setting-out, is that the darkness is not dark. None the less, there are areas, centres of total blackness, where my groping hands touch a reality I cannot understand. These centres attach themselves to an actual experience—so that I cannot recall it without running my head violently against the blackness, against a blackness filled with masks I do not understand, messages I cannot read. This happens to me when I remember my son's birth. I was unlucky, it is true; I had the misfortune to fall into the hands of a conceited midwife whose boast was that she needed neither anaesthetics nor a doctor to bring 'her' children into the world.

The moment I stumble into the blackness which streams away on all sides from this experience, my hands touch the masks. They cover the mystery which has haunted my life, and haunts it—the mystery of cruelty. During my day and night of agony I could not know that, in less than twenty years, torture would be in use again in Germany, and a little later in other countries of Western Europe: I did not know that the people I believed to be the most civilized in the world—they bore names like Molière, Stendhal, Mallarmé, Valéry, Giraudoux—would be not only enduring torture but inflicting it. The one thing I know is the moment when *I* should have broken down and blabbed all I knew—after only twelve hours of the extremes of pain.

What I do not know and cannot even hope to understand before I die, is why human beings are wilfully, coldly, matter-of-factly cruel to each other. What moves in the nerves of the men who bend over another man they have strapped to a table so that they can more easily make him suffer the most atrocious pain? In the nerves of concentration camp guards hurrying men, children, women carrying their smallest children, into gas-filled rooms to die of suffocation in agony and terror? In the nerves of men, soldiers, who are cutting the throats of children on the edge of the ditch into which their little bodies will be thrown ('*Sir, you're hurting me!*')? The ways to be cruel, to inflict pain, are countless: all have been or will be tried. Why? Why? What nerve has atrophied in the torturer, or—worse—is sensually moved?

I don't understand the masks, I don't understand them.

I am not, as are some of my closest friends, a believing and practising atheist. I should be very glad to believe that God is. But I cannot believe in a Creator who created man. Nor can I believe in the possibility of redemption for a race of beings capable of inventing gas-chambers for each other. When I remember these and the children lifting their hands to protect their throats, or in blind terror as they drown in their torpedoed ship, I think that the human kind is *damned*, it must, will and ought to perish. If there were a just God he could not forgive it. But what just God would have allowed it? Then who damned us? Ourselves, we damned ourselves.

Then perhaps we should forgive ourselves? Never, never.

Let everything be wiped out, the columns of the Parthenon in white sunlight, the foreign harbours, the plays of Sophocles and

Shakespeare, the love of mothers for their young children, bird song, the stones of Chartres, vines, olive trees, the music of Mozart, the honeysuckle, the green tree, the rose, rather than keep alive a race without pity for itself.

Here must end a chapter which got out of hand. I shall hope, at the last second, to remember other things. What? The curve of a coast-line, of a gull's wing, the whiteness of a white petal, the sea, voyages.

Chapter 20

Today, the 4th of November, 1961, in Eric Linklater's *Roll of Honour*, I reached the phrase: 'The life he knew had blossomed like a great garden with brave young men.' Anyone, I thought, of our generation, his and mine, could write it. But, forty-six years ago, when I took my six-weeks-old son to the Liverpool house, I gave few thoughts, and those ignorant, to the young men of my age who were dying, thousands of them in one day, in another country.

If I try to find a way back to that absorbed self-willed young woman I see her, a thin gesticulating figure, half rubbed out, at the centre of an impalpable web of nerves stretched between her and her child.

Never have I worked harder. From the moment, before six, when I tore my eyelids open on another day, to the moment of dropping headlong into sleep as my head touched the pillow, it went on: I cleaned, washed linen and clothes, prepared the child's barley water, fed him, pushed him in his carriage the long walk to the shops or out into the flat country without horizons, two fields and a lane wide, beyond the Suburb, made bread from an old recipe I had, polished chairs, toiled angrily in that desert of a garden, filled with weeds, a disgrace, a menace to the gardens on either side of it.

That first autumn I planted it with potatoes, except for a square of grass under the window: when, in June, I lifted a root I found them covered with a black scum. Blight, the man next door said, pleased. Sorry for me, in spite of the weeds, he advised me to eat them at once, while I could still rub the blight off. 'You work hard, don't you', he said queerly.

I ate new potatoes three times a day for three weeks.

By this time I should have learned how to spend sensibly what little money I had. I never did and never have. Because of my upbringing, or from a shred of prudence, I pay as I go. But I have never been able to take money seriously, as a decent bourgeoise ought. I give it away or spend it—one folly equals the other—with reckless indifference. I have always lived, and still live, from my sixpence to my mouth, as a young German refugee said to me in 1934 of herself. I have saved nothing, and shall die on straw.

Not long before her death—before she let herself die, deliberately, out of disgust with life—I was with I. A. R. Wylie in her large handsome house near Princeton. We had been friendly for many years, and she asked me how much I had put aside against an imminent old age.

'Not a penny,' I told her.

She was sincerely horrified. Having made a great deal of money, far more than I have ever earned, she had a terrible fear of losing it. My imprudence saddened and irritated her. I might have dispelled the irritation at least if I had told her that, sometimes, between two and four in the morning, I endure an hour or more of sheer panic. Its effect never persists long enough to prevent my drawing my last pounds out of the bank.

In the days when I was truly poor, my only notion of saving was to go without inessentials such as dress and food. It was no hardship. When the middle of the week found me ashore for food, I lived on bread and tea, soaking the bread in the tea, delighted to find myself for a few minutes in the half-dark kitchen, safe, and on the edge of setting off.

Hunger did me no harm. I am so strong that if I had not persistently overworked and ill-used my body, the poor ass would have served me for a century—at least. Certainly I ill-used it then: one of the risks I made it run was a miscarriage I brought on myself, by inconceivable means: I remember sharply what I did, but I am not going to tell: I don't want either to harm some other young woman, as desperate as I was, who may read this book, or to pass for insane.

Always on the edge of nothing, I never for an instant thought that I could starve in real earnest. This was partly that I had been born in a class which did not—and, in spite of having seen its like in other countries wiped out like a weak pencil mark by inflation or revolution, still does not—expect to starve. But it was more my energy and blind hunger for living.

My only reason for hoping was hope, which, in those years, was a habit with me. Or an instinct, a memory in my body itself of voyages.

During the first months after I went back to Liverpool, I had no purpose more avid than my will, ferocious, to get my son the best of everything. No conscious purpose. Like my thesis on modern drama and the unfinished manuscript of my novel (both gathering dust on a shelf behind a coal-scuttle), my restlessness, my insane ambition, had been pushed out of sight. But they had sharp teeth and had sunk these into my stubborn mind below intention, below sense. While I ran from room to room, running the flesh off my bones, they waited their time, Eumenides watching a future victim—or a slow poison in my veins. After a few months they began to prick me. I became less stupefied by work and my new responsibilities, more impatient —and a more exasperating companion.

It is only by reflecting that I see K. as he might at the time have looked to older people or to anybody less close to him than I was. I was too close, and I suffered from his touchiness as often as he from my maddening need to be in the right and my moods of perfectly groundless gaiety. These were sure to earn me an irritable dressing-down. Then, raging against myself because I had been so idiotic as to talk to him about something that excited me, I became sullen or recklessly sarcastic.

One icy night in the winter of 1916 I exasperated him into throwing me out of the house. I had nothing over my sleeveless cotton overall, and I crouched against a hedge, shivering, raging helplessly, for two or three hours before the cold drove me back to the door he had now unlocked. He took no notice of me when I came in, not lifting his nose from his book.

Would I, if it had been possible, have left him after one of these mortifying incidents? I doubt it. I belong to a species of animal which endures a little death if it has to tear up roots it has put down in a human relationship. I have not a great deal of courage or will-power, and my confidence was not of the lasting indestructible kind, but I had the grip on life of a savage beast. Nothing subdued it for long.

And K. had moods when he was simple and pleasant. I could not count on them.

Today I see that he was trapped as much as I was. He could not have felt any sympathy with my unbearable sense of personal failure. It was not a disease he understood. He was only two years older than I was.

Too often I was little better than childish; I went on behaving badly—that is, grumbling and making useless plans—as a child persists in doing what it is told not to do, from the same puerile defiance. To make matters worse, when I was punished I cried with a child's maddening convulsive grief.

I had no dignity. I have little now, my character is no less awkward, but I put a much better face on it.

Chapter 21

Restless as I was, my life had its fixed centre. In the first instant I set eyes on him, held out to me by my mother—before whom I took care to seem calm and stolid—my son became its only complete passion, its final meaning.

He was strong, and faultlessly beautiful. I brought him up on a strict method, learned, since I was totally ignorant, from the latest book, and because the book said that a missed meal was as dangerous as a brick pulled out of a wall, I roused him from sound sleep to drink his milk and barley water. (A cynical old woman told me: 'No mother ever woke her *second* child to make certain it had not died in its sleep.') I bought the most expensive baby soap and powder, the finest oranges, Jersey milk. As prices rose, I pinched in other ways. Possibly K. resented my silliness—to an unbeliever a religion must always seem grotesque. When the censorship department in Liverpool needed staff, he was infuriated by my refusal to apply. Baffled, too—here I was, detesting housework, strong as a horse, with better degrees than his own, and refusing a chance to earn money. I pointed out that the salary, about two pounds a week—though it would add seventy per cent to our income—was precisely what I should have to pay a woman to do my work: financially, we should be no better off. This argument was irrefutable. It was not, and he knew it, my reason for refusal. At that time I would have cut my hand off rather than give my son over to a woman who might—how could I know?—neglect or fumble one of the rites . . .

Curiously, I had no feeling of authority over my son—or not more than an older child has over the infant handed her to look after for an hour. When he laughed, I was filled by a hard light joy. If he cried, I tore myself in half to amuse him. My happiest moments were those between five and six, when I bathed him in front of the fire before putting him down for the night. He adored the warmth and the movement of the water on his body, and so long as I sang did not mind what I did with him. I have a thin voice and no ear. It is not that I am deaf, I hear as I see, acutely; my ear picks up the lightest sounds, shiver of a blade of grass on its fellow, distant voices, separate drops of rain. At some point between the nerves of my ear and my voice there is a barrier, uncrossable. A familiar tune, even complicated phrases of music, trace themselves in my brain with exquisite clarity, but I cannot turn the lines into sounds: I feel and see them, and hear nothing, except between the walls of my skull. The only notes I can sing are those I heard repeatedly as a child.

Over and over again, in my toneless voice, I sang O *dem golden slippers, In old Madrid,* and *By the blue Alsatian mountains,* ending with the air that obviously he liked best—

> There was an old woman
> Went up in a basket
> Ninety times as high as the moon
> And where she was going I couldn't but ask it
> For in her hand she carried a broom.
> Old woman, old woman, old woman, said I,
> Whither O whither away so high?
> To swe-e-ep the cowbebs out of the sky
> And I shall come back again bye and bye.

Sleep glazing his eyes, he forced his eyelids apart, pursing his small lips in the stubborn line which meant: Again.

Evening after evening I went through my brief act, enclosed in a bubble of light and warmth as clear as a wine-glass, and no stronger.

At the end of the year I took him—I have forgotten to say he was given three Christian names, Charles William Storm—to Whitby. At the last minute, when I was closing my suitcase, I picked up the manuscript of the novel and pushed it in, out of sight, at the bottom. (It may have been one of the moments when something heavy moved in me at a great depth and my mind formed words I had not even thought. *They think I'm finished, but I'm not, I'll do something.*)

The journey from Liverpool to Whitby passes through the corroded valleys of Lancashire and the West Riding of Yorkshire, vast troughs of solid grimy streets, mills, warehouses, chapels, sluggish canals, factory chimneys vomiting smoke over hillsides scarred by terraces of squat grey houses like out-croppings of stone: behind them the road climbs steeply between unmortared walls to the edge of the hill and beyond it to barren sooty moors: they excited me strangely, an excitement that deepened to pain, fingers pinching my heart, when the train ran under the viaduct a mile from Whitby, and slowed down past the upper harbour with its empty shipyards, old mooring-posts, grey gleaming water, ruined Abbey. If I took this route now, I should feel the same pain, useless, inescapable.

While we were there Bill caught whooping-cough from my young sister. At night I shut the windows in our bedroom and burned vapo-cresolene over a night-light. So that no one should know I was writing, I wrote then, kneeling on the floor against the chair that held the infuser: the tiny flame spread a circle on the paper, and I worked with an ear pricked to catch the first movement in the cot.

On one of these long nights, a character broke into my mind without any warning, from nowhere, from the darkness outside the weak ring of light. A round-faced disreputable little man, limping and voluble, called Poskett. I knew all about him: I knew that he had had trouble with his wife, and why. I knew his weaknesses, his shocking habits, his one endearing virtue. I scribbled like a maniac, my face burning. The child woke coughing, and was sick: I made him comfortable and went back to Poskett, who for that matter had never been out of my thoughts as I spoke soothingly to the child and watched his eyelids flutter for a moment, then close. I wrote until pain in my knees, cramped fingers, and the winter cold of the room drove me into bed.

Less than a fraction of what I knew about Poskett went into the book. It never occurred to me that this fraction was the one splinter of reality in the whole preposterous business. No one told me so, and no reviewer noticed him.

If I had been told at this time that I could not write—least of all, a novel—I should have been startled and angry. But I should have found some way of learning. I was an uncouth blundering simpleton, but shrewd and obstinate, with my father's patience in finishing what I had started.

I did not finish the novel in Whitby, but I went on with it in the spring of 1916, thinking about it at intervals during the day, and writing, unless I were too sleepy, after supper. At last I finished, and had only to type it, rapidly, with two fingers, on my rickety machine. I gave it a title I thought in every way fitting, *The Pot Boils and the Scum Rises,* and dedicated it—a fleering joke worthy of Class 5b—to the man who ran the Shepherd's Bush coffee stall.

Choosing a publisher at random—Messrs Duckworth—I sent it off. In the greatest secrecy.

Chapter 22

Some time during the spring of 1916 my father's ship was sunk off the Irish coast by the German cruiser *Moewe*. The *Moewe* was on her way home at the time, and the *Saxon Prince* was the last of her victims. Her commander took the crew on board to join the crews of other ships, and landed the whole lot at Hamburg. From there they were sent first to a military camp, then to a concentration camp for civilians in Brandenburg. In the letter my mother wrote, telling me about it, there was an undercurrent of bitterness, as if she could not entirely forgive him for being safer than his son.

Harold was now a 2nd Lieutenant in the Flying Corps. He had done his pilot's training in France, in June 1915, after being given the D.C.M.—'For conspicuous coolness and gallantry on several occasions in connection with wireless work under fire.' (*London Gazette* 30.6.1915.)

A boy's hand moves slowly across the thin paper. It might be any one of the young unlined hands of that time, making their last signals to an indifferent world.

> 'In the Field
> August 16th 1915

'. . . Some days out here it is stifling all day, then when night comes, cold, strange, a heavy dew.

'Myself and another chap are living in a small tent we made of old fabric off the aeroplanes, it is quite up to date. He fetched a stove back with him when he went on leave, my bed is of canvas slung on two sections of a wireless mast and my comrade's bed is of sacking between two old aeroplane skids.

'Our larder is an old cupboard off an aeroplane, the framework of the hut split struts and skids.

'The floor is earth kept dry by a trench dug round it.

'The table is a sheet of ebonite.

'One thing about active service you find out very soon there is nothing you can not do without.

'I think when the war is over I will put all my worldly goods in a pack and go and bury myself in Brazil.

'Well I will finish now as time is going about as quick as my candle.'

The following March he did a short spell at home, but refused a job at Netheravon, as instructor. He was not at ease in a position which would have forced him to lecture and make social gestures; nothing in his short life had prepared him for it—and nothing in his nature, which was like mine, solitary and diffident, without the social confidence I can pretend to when I must.

Besides, he was afraid that if he stayed in England he would be overlooked.

'You see, if I stop in England I might miss promotion. You never know what's going on, why some get ahead quickly and others are kept back. If you don't do something they forget about you. I have to make them notice me.'

He had no schooling, no useful relations behind him; he had only his ambition and his share of a courage which grows like grass in our country when it is needed. (In other countries, too, but let them celebrate it for themselves.) In April he went back to France, to No. 19 Squadron, and after four months was promoted to Flying Officer.

It must have been the late summer when I saw him again, in Whitby. He seemed little changed, still a broad-shouldered gawky boy in the R.F.C. tunic (why on earth was it called a maternity jacket?) with its wings and ribbons, no lines round his eyes, and no hardening of his slow shamefaced smile.

We grew from one stock, but I could not talk easily to him: in every member of my family there is—was—the same profound sense of being bound to near kinsmen in a duty overwhelmingly stronger than any dislike or resentment, the same that stretched between our marauding northern ancestors, and the same reluctance in speech. Moreover, he lived now in a country as closed to me as the country into which the dead go alone. But he was moved to make an attempt, out of his awkward young kindness, out of his experience, to do something for me, his elder.

One afternoon—he never spoke of K. by his Christian name, but always formally as Mr C.——he asked me in a neutral voice,

'What is Mr C.—doing?'

'Nothing,' I said. 'Schoolmastering. He's in London, with his parents, until the end of his holidays.'

'Does this conscription affect him?'

'I don't know. No. Schoolmasters are starred, you know, and he's B2.'

'That won't mean much in a few months. They lost a lot of men on the Somme.' He stared past me. 'Why doesn't he try for the Flying Corps?'

'He's shortsighted.'

'Oh, I don't mean as a pilot,' he said with a short laugh. 'He could be an Equipment Officer, y'know.'

A familiar excitement seized me. I kept a face as blank and stolid as his own, and asked him what an Equipment Officer did. He told me, and added, 'If he thought of trying for it, I could write to a friend of mine at Adastral House, Major R——.'

Was he pleased to be able to give advice and help? I must have thanked him, but was it well enough done to give him any feeling of satisfaction with himself?

His name was in the *London Gazette* again in December.

'Military Cross. For conspicuous gallantry in action. He attacked a hostile kite balloon under very heavy fire. Later, his machine descended to within 150 feet of the ground, when he got the engine going again and recrossed our lines at 1,300 feet and returned safely. He has on many occasions done fine work.'

That month my mother was staying with me in Liverpool, she and my young sister sharing the comfortless second bedroom. She was still there in the first week of January when the telegram came, forwarded from Whitby by my aunt Jenny, to whom, when he knew my mother was not at home, the postmaster sent it—these telegrams were no new thing now, but they moved bureaucracy itself to take a little trouble, sometimes. If they could have been laid down, each as it came, one on top of another, a great barren pile of death, growing and thickening as more and more young bodies were pushed into the ground, the shame and horror would have sickened us. Or so I think.

I stood in front of my mother with the telegram in my hand.

'*Open it.*'

I opened it and gave it to her . . . Deeply regret to inform you that 2nd Lt Harold Jameson Royal Flying Corps was killed in action January fifth the Army Council express their sympathy Secretary War Office . . . She made the inhuman sound women make when they lose a son, a cry torn from the empty womb, and turned blindly, to go to her bedroom. I did not try to comfort her. What use?

At this moment I knew, knew beyond any question, that I would sooner K. had died. This had nothing to do with love. I loved K. more warmly than I loved my brother. But—I realized it then, and if I have forgotten the feeling I have not forgotten that it existed—in certain families, not otherwise eccentric, love is a paltry emotion compared with the ties of blood. From nowhere, from a darkness, the figure as I imagined her of Antigone came into my mind, and I thought: Now I understand you, I know why your brother had this hold on your will; it was not piety.

There is no explaining this impulse. Reason has nothing to do with it, and nothing to say about it worth hearing.

Later we heard what happened. He had been ranging our guns on a German battery when he was attacked from behind. His machine fell in No Man's Land, and some brave souls of the infantry ran out and carried him into the trench: he was breathing but soon died.

When I read this in the letter from the major commanding No. 6 Squadron, I felt a dreadful sickness in the centre of my body, an uprush of deathly fear—it was what he had felt in the first moment of falling. The moment when he knew he had lost.

We heard at the same time that he had been promoted to Flight Commander, a week earlier. Today (1961) I still feel glad he had that last small triumph.

All I could do for our mother was to listen without shutting myself off behind a wall of dullness, a trick I had learned young. I listened when she talked about his first leave after he became a pilot. She went with him to London. Once they were greeted in the street by an R.F.C. colonel who spoke with lively affection. 'Why, Jamie, my dear boy, it's you, is it? I'm delighted to see you. How are you, how are you getting on?' She had the same sense—a swelling pressure and lightness in her body—as when she read about him in the *London Gazette*.

'You could see how highly this older man thought of him. And when we were in Park Lane one morning he said: Mother, some day I'm going to have one of those houses. You shall live with me in it. You'll see. I shall be able to do something for you. If they'll let me I shall stay on in the Flying Corps. I might be a colonel then. You never know. This is only the beginning.'

I could scarcely bear her voice. It had the sound given back by a dry vase when you tap it. It was emptiness itself, the slow running out of meaning.

The frightful bitterness that came into it when she talked about my father was far more bearable.

'I asked him if he had written to his father to tell him about his second medal and his commission. Yes, he said, he had, and I asked: What did he say to you? And do you know what he wrote to the boy? He wrote: Don't think you've done anything, plenty of other men have done as well and fifty times better without getting a medal for it.' Her mouth worked in a way I could not look at. 'I shall never know what he did to the boy on that voyage. And then to tell him that he was nothing. I shall never forgive him for it, never. Never, never. I'm done with him.'

I listened. She was more capable of bitterness than I am, a simpler and more honest and straightforward human being. I gave a second's thought to my father in his German prison camp, but I don't remember that I had any pity to spare for him. Certainly she had none. The last flicker of kindness for him was dead. She would go on writing and sending parcels to Ruhleben. But give him, from now to her last day, a grain of warmth—no.

I understand that coldness.

Later, I saw that her son's death had been an end for her, a hard and bitter end of her deep life. From now on, for all she still had and was, it ran in colder shallower places, dwindling, in a drier country. At the time I did not see this. How could I, with my own life still quick and restless in me?

Chapter 23

My brother was not the only young man I knew for whom the war was a chance. In Archie's occasional letters from France my ear caught a ripple of excitement as far under the surface as the shadow thrown on the floor of a sea-pool by an unseen current, in every other way traceless.

'We are living in the cellars of an old brewery and across the road s the garden where D'Artagnan murdered somebody in an honourable quarrel. Did I tell you they had given me a decoration? I tried to find out why and had the correspondence returned. The party I sent to a saphead has just come back and the sergeant in charge reports the saphead full of Boches. I'm sure it can't be, because I was up there myself yesterday and found it full of water. Unless they are drowned Boches. I must go and look . . '

The decoration was the V.C., given him, I found out later, for an act of prolonged cool courage. The coolness is a sleight-of-hand and real.

Another letter had an effect he had not intended, making me grit my teeth over the memory of years when I had been rebellious and confident. 'When I crawled out of my cellar yesterday morning I found a whole bed of white violets. Signs of the times—in a Staff Mess of eight people, the *New Age, New Witness,* and *New Statesman,* are on the side-table every week. And the General looks graver and more puzzled all the time. There's a war on, of course, to distract our minds—and heaven knows they need distraction after reading the home newspapers. Did I ever give or lend you my *Spirit of Man*? My stock of quotations is getting low ... A funny thing happened the other day. You know there's a movement on foot to interest officers and men in social study with a view to simplifying adjustments after the war. The spirit of the thing is all right, but it's being run by generals and padres and people who still have to learn the rudiments. I say it's dilettante, and had better be run by omniscients from the School of Economics and sic-like people. I proposed a systematic education of padres and generals by the Central Labour College, and one red-faced High Priest got up and said, "You're little better than an Eikonoklast!" Truth will out, you see!'

The odds on K.'s being called up were shortening. I forgot that the mere idea of it used to dismay me. For one thing, I did not feel that he had any right to be safer than my young brother, and for another I was wryly certain that little harm would come to him on the ground. The excitement in my nerves was very like that I felt as a child, ankle deep in the sea, when far out the tide turns with a light all but imperceptible movement, which I could just feel. Also, I was shrewd enough to see what, for his own sake, K. ought to do now.

Early in February I persuaded him to write to Harold's friend in Adastral House: I drafted the letter for him, making it cool and urgent. It brought a reply at once—telling him to come to be looked over.

He came back delighted with himself. He had been accepted for training as an Equipment Officer, and was to go in the middle of March, to Reading.

I would follow at the end of March, after I had cleared up, and stored our furniture, and he had found rooms for us.

It never entered my head to wonder whether he would sooner have begun his new life without us. No more than it entered my head that I could stay on in Liverpool, in this detested house, waiting for the end of the war.

Duckworth returned my novel, but I took this lightly. A gaiety I tried to hide filled me, and, as soon as K. had left, an overwhelming energy. Confidence in my strength and cleverness swept away all the doubts I ought to have had about a reckless anarchic plunge forward, with a child less than two years old, into a future of which

I saw nothing beyond the first step. My craving to get away blinded me. I was madly happy.

One day I decided to sell the furniture. Not only because I needed the money—desperately: K. had left me half his last month's salary, but had very quickly written asking me to send him part of it to help pay for his 2nd Lieutenant's uniform and the rest—but I had never liked it. The thought of getting rid of it delighted me. When I remembered that I still owed my mother the hundred pounds she had lent me to buy it I felt a momentary check, but a number of excellent reasons (all fallacious) for selling it jumped into my mind, any one of which might convince her. (And almost did.) I sold the whole lot for thirty pounds to an elderly dealer, a daughter of the horse leech, and told her to take it away on the morning of my last day in the house.

My middle sister was staying with me for a few days: she was resting in bed one afternoon when the door opened, she looked up and saw me coming in with a ferret-faced crone who began silently to rap the bed with her knuckles and drag the blankets aside to thrust her horrible fingers into the mattress.

'I've sold your bed,' I told her calmly. With equal calm, she said, 'I hope not before I get out of it.'

Another thing I did, of which I was proud, was to withhold a month's rent, so that, when I left and gave the statutory fortnight's notice, I should owe ten weeks' rent. A woman who left the suburb had told me that the £25 she expected would be returned to her had been held back, 'until necessary repairs are completed.' Since the woodwork was gaping away from the windows, and you had only to rap the corner of a wall for plaster to drop off, the whole of her money vanished.

I paid all but two small bills, both to tradesmen: these I put in my purse to be paid as soon as possible. (I paid them in time, and my mother's loans, too: I have a puritan and Yorkshire horror of debt.)

It was during these last days that an extraordinary change took place in the movement of time. It accelerated, suddenly, and began to run past at a rate which has never slackened. I can put my finger on the moment when this happened: I had taken Bill to a large store, to buy new clothes for him now that he was going into the world: he sat on a high chair at the counter, bored, while I fingered woollen tunics. A sudden anxiety seized me—Am I going to be late getting him back for his sleep?—and in the same instant, exactly in this instant, time began to rush away from me as, one day years later, in Norway, the horizon rushed past when I glanced up and saw the coast galloping off out of sight on the back of a long gleaming wave.

I thought: You have no time. But it was not a question of time to do this or that. It was a passage into another country. The moment when I looked, smiling, at my child's bored scowl was the same moment when, a child myself, I touched the smooth veined petals of Grass of Parnassus growing from the red clay of a cliff at the other side of England. Both moments existed in another sort of time—now lost. Run as I may, turn as I may, shielding eyes and ears, I cannot reach it; I can only remind myself that it existed.

On our last morning I got up long before daylight. By the time I had packed the last things, and lashed the dress basket filled with blankets, linen, my silver forks and spoons (from my grandfather's hoard), and the china tea-service, which I was sending to my mother to keep for me, a grey light was welling over the top of the blind. It came from that other time, from an earlier setting-out, from a darkened kitchen with one lamp on the table, and the shadowy figure near me of my young mother.

If a doubt plucked my skin it must have been now, but I don't recall feeling doubtful. There was no time—we were leaving on a one o'clock train. At nine, the railway van arrived to collect the dress-basket and, pulling at the knots in the rope, the drayman told me I was a good lasher, which pleased me.

On his heels came the horse-leech's daughter, with a hand-cart and a thin boy, and began dragging out the sofa (it must still be somewhere, poor thing), hacking wardrobes in half to get them through the door, and knocking great lumps of plaster off the walls of the staircase. Much I cared how she destroyed her own or the estate's property. She carted off one load, leaving the rest scattered like driftwood, outside. I swept and dusted the rooms after her, gave Bill his last meal in the house, and packed the basket holding all he would need on the journey, milk, raisins. His clothes filled his own zinc bath, mine and the rejected manuscript went into a shabby trunk, and these with his folding cot and his carriage were all we had.

The cab I had ordered came. I told the man to stop at the estate office, and ran in and told a startled clerk gaily that I had left, and he could pay himself two and a half months' rent out of the deposit money.

'Oh, I don't think we can do that,' he exclaimed.

'I don't know what else you can do,' I said with the greatest composure and confidence, and hurried out.

I'm free at last, I thought.

At this moment I knew that I could do anything. Anything.

I have had precisely this feeling at a few other times in my life. It is a splendid, ecstatic feeling and an illusion.

I was, of course, mad. No young woman in her right mind chooses for her carefully-nurtured infant the hazards of lodgings and wartime journeys. I don't want to sit in judgement on the young woman, but to tell the truth. The only anxiety in her mind when she stood on the main line platform with cot, bath, trunk and the rest—and a porter to whom she would give sixpence (and be thanked for it)—was about getting a corner seat in the train. There was nothing outrageous in her decision to follow her husband about England. Perfectly conventional and sensible women were doing the same thing.

The difference between these sensible women and me was that they had decent settled homes to which, the war over, they would return: I had cut myself and my child adrift—deliberately. If you can call deliberate what is little better than an explosion of energy, of an old passion for voyages, tides, another harbour, another sun.

A departure. The wolf's teeth of life.

Chapter 24

I carried into our life as camp-followers all the anxiety about method and routine I had absorbed from my abominably enlightened book on the care of infants. Wherever we fetched up, I began by ingratiating myself with our landlady, so that I had the run of her kitchen to prepare my son's meals. It was this sacred routine, and my religious belief in it, and my ignorance, that almost killed him in Reading.

The book had so much to say about the supreme importance of fresh air that I was fairly convinced he would die, like a fish taken out of water, if I did not keep him in a current of air as often as he was not asleep. One day at the end of April the weather turned icy, showers of hail alternating with bursts of sunshine and a vividly blue sky. During one of these brilliant intervals I hurried him out into White Knights Park. On the way home a hailstorm caught us; he was warmly wrapped, but the treacherous cold must have reached him. At night when I was putting him to bed he was violently sick. He'll be all right after a night's sleep, I told myself. But in the morning he lay in his cot, waxen, with pinched nostrils and a faint blue shadow round his mouth. It was my first experience of the weak hold a very young child, even the strongest, has on his life; my heart turned over in me with fear—even though I did not yet know the danger.

He was saved by the accident that the doctor nearest us was an excellent children's doctor: when he came he ordered me, drily and quietly, to give him grape juice, or a tea made from raisins, but no milk, no animal food of any sort. I sent the landlady out to buy hot-house grapes and the best raisins, moved his cot into the warm living-room, and prepared stolidly to nurse him back to health. For all my agonized fear, strictly hidden, I did not think he was dying. The thought that he could die did not so much as brush my mind, not for one moment. Once an hour I gave him his spoonful of the warm raisin tea—he had rejected the grape juice by a weak pressure of his lips—but he still lay like a tiny marble statue.

The doctor came again in the evening: he said little to me, but— I knew this only later—he told K. not to leave me alone, the child would die any minute.

K. had been asked to dinner by another officer, and went, unable to face what was coming. I was immensely relieved to get him out of the way. As soon as he had gone, I made up the fire, pulled the curtains across the window, turned out every light except that of a feeble lamp, and settled myself to watch the child in the cot. I had the sense that a nerve in my body was joined to his. It was no effort to keep my entire attention on him; I should have had to make a conscious effort to turn it away. When, some time after midnight, K. came home and put his head round the door, I waited without patience for him to go and leave me alone with my child.

It would not be true to say that I concentrated on him the whole of my energy. It concentrated itself: the direction did not come from my conscious self, it came from a level far deeper than will. All through the night I had his life and spirit, as I had his small body, at the ends of my fingers.

At some moment in the first light I noticed that instead of simply letting me pour the drops of raisin tea between his lips, he was moving them to swallow. My heart turned in me again, this time with joy: I gave him a second spoonful, and another, and another. He opened his eyes and looked at me, a look as direct as a word—the first time for more than thirty hours.

When the light strengthened in the room I saw that there was no longer a bluish shadow round his mouth. He moved his hand in the light.

Today I see clearly that, although I kept him alive, the person who saved him was a doctor whose name and face I have completely forgotten. He must now be dead, or a very old man. If I were a Catholic I would have a Mass said for him. As it is—did I even thank him? I cannot remember.

If I did not, I deserve to be whipped. But I doubt whether I knew how narrowly I had escaped.

I had sent my rejected novel to Mr Fisher Unwin, and in the middle of June he wrote asking me to come and see him. Innocently, I supposed that he was going to take the book. By this time Bill was fat and well, and I could leave him with K. for an afternoon and go to London, less than an hour's journey. Before seeing Mr Fisher Unwin I saw his reader, who talked to me with great kindness, but did not tell me that the novel was no good: his kindness glanced off my specious self-confidence.

I have a clear image of Fisher Unwin himself, rosy cheeks, red palpitating scalp visible through his white hair, seated in his splendid room in an Adelphi which, thanks to the heroic work of our vandals, no longer exists. He, too, was amiable. He offered me—explaining that the novel I had sent him was unsuitable—a contract to show him my next six books. Innocent as I was, I saw that this committed him to nothing, and me to write an appalling number of novels on the off chance that he would approve one of them.

Politely—I am always polite unless I am angry—I replied that I would consider his offer. He walked with me to the door of his room, and at the last minute took a book from a shelf and gave it to me.

'Read this,' he said benignly, 'it will teach you how a novel should be written.'

I walked rapidly to the Strand, putting my rebuff in its place, the rejected manuscript under my arm, and there stopped to examine the book. The author was an E. M. Dell, and it was *The Way of an Eagle*. Somewhere between London and Reading, after trying to read it, I dropped it from the window of the train. I was tempted to throw the manuscript after it. Instead, I sent it out again, but I have forgotten where.

Shortly after this, K. was posted to Bradford. This time we travelled in comfort, since an officer in uniform could not be seen in the third class. Bradford was a disappointment. I had not the wit then to admire its hideous grandeur, streets plunging downhill into a cauldron of blackened mills and offices, a Wool Exchange in Venetian Gothic, and a Town Hall modelled on the Palazzo Vecchio in Florence (of which I had never heard). The moors were a few miles away, but I never got to them. And they were not *my* moors. I confounded the whole West Riding in my detestation of Bradford. Even today I find it impossible to think it as purely Yorkshire as the North Riding, or as handsome and arrogant.

Most of my time was spent in Manningham Park, pushing Bill's carriage up and down its asphalted paths; the weather was hot and airless, but if I tried to rest for a few minutes he flew into a rage until I set off again, down, round the lake, up, down. No doubt he was as bored as I was—I had not the least idea how to talk to a very young child. He was also lazy: when I took him out of his carriage and placed a ball in his hands he would throw it carelessly, then sit down and wait for me to fetch it back. Passers-by would stand still to admire him—he was a beautiful, a perfect human creature—and I was torn between pride and superstitious terror.

Without admitting it I must have known that I had advanced myself very little by bolting from Liverpool. True, I was free of a house, but I was not doing anything with my freedom. I read a great deal, and, when I was alone, dreamed absurdly of a brilliant future—I did not realize how pleasantly corrosive this habit of day-dreaming is until I lost the talent for it. In the meantime I made no efforts towards any future at all.

I had no impulse to begin a second novel. What was the use, since the attempt had been a failure? Without reasoning about it, I felt that there was neither merit nor sense in repeating an effort that did not bring in money or fame. That a book is written at least partly for its own sake did not then strike me.

Imagine what an instinctive writer would have done with my long evenings in that grimly fermenting town—a D. H. Lawrence, or (if he had not at the moment been in France) J. B. Priestley, born in the West Riding and as shrewd, greedy, possessive, as, with half my mind, I am myself, but born to write.

At the beginning of September K. heard that he was being posted to a Stores Park in Lincoln, and I decided to go there at once, to a farm outside the town, where his parents happened to be staying, until I had found rooms for us. I detested his father as heartily as he disliked and disapproved of me, but I would have invited myself to live with Beelzebub himself to get my child into country air.

After a week there—during this week I was ill, in acute pain, hid it from my father-in-law, a doctor, and imagined I had recovered completely—I took half a small furnished house in Lincoln, near the Cathedral: I hated the idea of housework, but the town was crowded and I could find nothing else fit for a child, *my* child.

I paid a month's rent, and for the rest of the month went hungry. K. had been kept waiting in Bradford, and though he wrote a couple of affectionate letters did not send the money I asked for. Worse, when he came he was in high feather because the bank had credited him in error with a second kit allowance, fifty pounds. He had spent most of it on taking the chorus of a musical comedy out for a moonlight picnic, in hired cars. I made a terrible scene. I was furious with his, as I saw it, incurable frivolity. Illogically, I was also hurt because he had not thought of spending any of the money on me.

Weeks later, Messrs Cox discovered their mistake and proposed to put it right by deducting two months' pay, and now that we were really in trouble I remained calm. I sent K. up to London to see them and beg them to repay themselves at the more merciful rate of ten pounds a month. They agreed. No doubt it was not the first time a young officer had snatched at what looked like manna from heaven.

He had been in Lincoln less than a week when he was posted away again—this time to a Training Station in Hampshire, near Stockbridge.

Chapter 25

Here begins a period in my life when I was almost continuously happy. We had rooms in a farm on the edge of a small village called Broughton, three miles from the airfield. Immediately behind the farm a field rose steeply to the edge of the downs: a chalky track led up, through oaks and beech-trees, to a stretch of turf as fine and springing as the cliff-top at Whitby, under a sky no less wide and pure than the sky over the North Sea.

This is the only part of England I love as I love the memory of my own before it was so nearly ruined: it is English in a different and kinder mode, the hills rounded and smoothly grey-green, the names of the villages—Tytherly, Mottisfont, West Wellow—gentler, the air without salt, but clear and fine. A famous trout stream, the Test, runs along the valley, not like our peaty moor streams but green and glassy clear. At night it was easy to see the valley and the downs as the Romans—who planted the first beeches—and the Norman-French saw them, ghosts no gentler than our Vikings, but carrying the seeds of another, subtler, civilization.

Three other officers with their families lived in the village, but in rented houses: I was the only one living in rooms, they teased me about my easier life and were gratified and amused when the wife of the farmer had her second baby without a midwife and I found myself looking after the house, and cooking not only for her and her husband but for a dozen harvesters. In fact, I did much of my own cooking, and learned to make cheese and butter—and in return was able to buy all the butter I needed, game, and illicit joints of veal and lamb: no child in wartime England fed better than mine.

The cheese was made in the cool stone-walled dairy: when the solidified milk had been cut into squares my job was to keep them moving until they reached the proper leathery consistency. I stood for two, three hours, gently drawing a hand through the whey, like a fish in luke-warm yellowish water, and with the other turned the pages of a translation of the Book of the Dead, repeating to myself with obscure excitement such superb phrases as *Apes that sing at dawn* (what apes? what remote dawns?), and *He becometh brother to the decay which cometh upon him*, and wishing passionately that I had had the luck to become an Egyptologist or almost any sort of ancient historian.

The whey softened my finger-nails, so that they broke off at the quick.

I took Bill for long, almost silent walks in the empty lanes—that is, I walked. He refused to walk for more than a few minutes. He was extremely stubborn, and had just discovered the pleasure of breaking things. I had to move everything breakable out of his reach before leaving him alone. One day, with great ingenuity, he succeeded in getting hold of a jar of face cream, the first I ever bought in my life, and flung it out of the bedroom window on to flagstones. I was heartbroken at the waste of five shillings. But I did not know how to deal with his child's instinctive malice, or with violent rages when he stamped his foot, shouting, 'No, no, no,' the only word he knew. He had only to look at me with wide brilliant eyes and hold his arms up, and I forgave him instantly. At these times I felt faint and dizzy with love, and the fear that I was unfit to have a child if I could not train him to be good and obedient. But I was unable to punish him. The mere thought turned my bones to water.

The happiness of these months after October 1917 is not something I imagine. It rings in my head with the sound given out by a flawless glass. I have been happy at other times since, in other places, but never with this insouciance, this certainty that I should never age.

And this in spite of K.

When I was thinking coolly, I reflected that our marriage had been eaten away until only the husk remained, and a few weak roots. He was enjoying his life. He looked well in uniform: the cross-over tunic, breeches, high boots polished to within an inch of their lives, suited his long-legged figure. Adjusting his belt in front of the glass he looked at himself with a pleased smile which— depending on my mood—irritated or touched me. So far as he was concerned the war could go on. It had given him his first taste of a good life, with a man-servant, dinners in mess, and the flattering sense of his reputation, pinned on him by his C.O., as 'the finest wangler in the area.'

I doubt whether he thought of me as an enemy, but he treated me as one. He knew that the moment the war ended I should begin trying to arrange his life again. My passion for managing exasperated him: usually, he gave way in the end, worn down by my greater energy and stubbornness—and then bitterly resented it. Expecting the worst from me, he often got it. Yet I had more kindness for him than he for me, far more. There was something comical in my feeling of responsibility for him. Again and again—either because I had caught sight of a crack in his jaunty self-assurance, or had behaved badly, and was seized by remorse—I made efforts to bridge the gap widening between us.

Sincere as long as it lasted, my good-will never lasted very long. It was quickly killed by K.'s suspicions. What is the use, I asked myself drily, of swearing kindness to a husband who takes so much pleasure in *seeing through me*?

Towards the end of the year I began writing again—for an excellent reason. And this time I was not trying to be clever or ironical. I tried instead, inventing a lame story, to record, before it sank without trace, the colour of our life, mine and the three boys', before 1914, the mad hopes, the idealism, the messianic dream. I wrote in the evening, on sheets of foolscap, with a fool's confidence.

My excellent reason was that the first book had been taken. When it came back from whatever publisher I sent it to after Fisher Unwin, I gave it one last chance, sending it to Constable. I sent it in K.'s name, from 92 Squadron, Chattis Hill, with the unscrupulous idea that they would reply quickly to an officer of the R.F.C., who might be leading a dangerous life.

They replied early in November, inviting him to come to London to talk about the book. Not to be caught twice, I wrote a polite careful letter, asking whether they had any serious intention of publishing it.

I destroy everything, but I have their letter, dated the 6th of November 1917, beginning: 'Dear Sir, we certainly did not write regarding your manuscript *The Pot Boils* without seriously intending to publish the book provided we could agree on one or two alterations . . .'

I found this letter only last week, in the back of a book, together with three pages of suggested cuts. When I re-read the last paragraph, I remembered sharply the scepticism with which I read it at the time. I never find it easy to believe praise of my work; I consider, and always have considered it, as a substitute for something I might have done better. And this time I was right and Constable and Company ludicrously wrong—'All of which being said, we can only endorse our reader's judgement that the book is a remarkable one and in places really beautiful.'

The letter had not been signed.

I was ashamed to call on another London publisher in my proper person of a gauche young woman. I made K. ask for business leave, and sent him with strict orders not to give me away. Naturally, he did. But it was an impossible deception, and the writer of the letter, Michael Sadleir, had no trouble in getting the truth out of him.

Some little time later, I went up to London for a night, leaving Bill with the wife of the farmer, to dine with my publisher. I had only one so-called evening dress, the short one made for me by a sewing-woman in Whitby in my first year at the university.

The room I was shown into appeared a mile long. I crossed it, dazed, towards two figures standing motionless at the far end. They came into focus suddenly, a smiling attractive young man and his very young wife. Betty Sadleir was small, slender, with the narrow face of a mediaeval angel, and a smile I found again later in Rheims, subtle and naïve, felicitous, very old: a thick plait of yellow hair crossed her head. Unless I am confusing this with a later evening she was wearing red-gold brocade. I cannot be certain of this: what is certain is that she was elegant in a simple way, and only mildly curious about a young woman in a shabby ridiculous dress, with reddened hands and nothing to say.

Like my mother when she went abroad, I took in avidly every detail of a dinner-table and rooms arranged with more elegance than I had known existed. They had a bad effect on me, rousing my latent greed to own beautiful things.

After dinner, Michael Sadleir brought out the now dog-eared manuscript of *The Pot Boils*—he had already deleted the rest of my title—and began tactfully going over passages he said were silly or injudicious. His tact was not needed. I seized the pencil he was holding, and ran it through every passage. This amused him. Turning to his wife, he said,

'She is the first author I ever knew to let herself be hacked to pieces without a murmur.'

What he took for submissiveness or timidity was nothing of the sort. It was a deep unrealized contempt for novel-writing as a serious use for energy and intellect.

This contempt still exists in me. It has nothing to do with reason. Rationally, I consider that the novel is one of the great arts, and I revere Tolstoy, Proust, Dostoevsky, Stendhal, as I revere, let us say,

Mozart and Rembrandt, whom I understand much less. And I have given the greater part of my life and all my wits to learning to write well. But—under all this reverence, which is genuine—a perfectly irrational contempt, indifference, call it what you like, persists in murmuring in my ear, 'Only an artist without the wit to become a poet (or a sculptor, musician, painter) turns to writing novels.'

Well, there I was—launched. Or so, with part of my mind, I thought.

Some weeks later, after the contract was signed, I needed money. There was nothing new about this, but I had a new idea of how to deal with it. I wrote to Constable and asked them for a small advance on the sum I supposed the book would earn.

I was far from imagining that it was no asset, but a liability undertaken in the hope of my becoming, some day, a novelist.

Only wretches unable to believe in the existence of publishers who are recklessly generous and kind-hearted will be surprised to learn that they sent me the sum I asked for, ten pounds. It meant that their loss on the book was precisely ten pounds heavier than it would have been.

Chapter 26

Unlike the Master, who, *pour tâcher de ne pas mentir*, wrote his memoirs twenty pages at a sitting like a letter, beginning each day where he had left off, without looking back, I start every morning by tearing up part, much or little, of the previous day's work and rewriting it in the interests of dryness and accuracy. I doubt if the Master knew any better than I do whether he was telling the truth of this or that episode which had disturbed him.

In August 1953, when I was in Grenoble for two nights, I reproached the head waiter of the Bec Fin for the carelessness of his fellow-citizens in not taking the trouble to make it easy for me to find Stendhal's birthplace. Here you are, I said, with the supreme good fortune to own the greatest of novelists, and . . . He interrupted me gently,

'Oh, Madame, n'exagérez pas.'

Which goes to show that Stendhal's *horreur peu raisonnable pour Grenoble*, and for *l'esprit dauphinois*, was more or less justified.

What follows has been torn up and rewritten five times; I must finish with it, lying as little as possible.

In 1918 my tranquil happiness was broken into and destroyed by the only episode in my life which deserves to be called an affair of passion.

June was a hot month, the roads and hedges white with chalky dust, the wells drying up, and the ground parched. Great chestnut trees sent up thick unmoving flames of creamy white and red, and the short grass of the downs was warm under the hand and scented with thyme and the yellow cinquefoil.

That month a squadron of the American Air Force reached Chattis Hill. K. made a song about his American parents (he had been born in Ireland, in Belfast, but he made it sound like Richmond, Virginia), and was soon friendly enough with the commanding officer, a captain, to bring him to the farm one evening, without warning me. From my bedroom I watched them climb out of the R.F.C. tender, and cross the garden to the front door. I did what I could, brushing my hair and powdering the end of my nose, to make myself presentable, and ran downstairs, only thankful that I had ready a cold chicken and cold gooseberry pie.

Frowning at me, K. said, 'I've brought a fellow-countryman of mine, an American——'

'A Texan, ma'am.'

'Oh, is there a difference?' I said.

After that, I said nothing. It has never embarrassed me to wear shabby clothes, but my lack of small talk was, is, a terrible embarrassment. The American talked easily, with an inoffensive irony, about his experiences since he landed his squadron in England. I listened, staring. He was strongly built, not tall, with a broad powerful head and noticeably small ears. He moved with a scarcely perceptible swing of the body, from his narrow hips, not, as most Englishmen walk, from the knees. He had a swarthy skin, eyes always narrowed, a direct guarded glance, and a short fine stubborn mouth. His expression was slightly arrogant, as though violence would be easier for him than argument, but he had a charming smile and a slow peremptory voice with more tones than an English voice.

Behind what I hoped was an air of intelligence, I was going through every sensation that the onset of an obsession—obsession-love—roused in me. It was so long since I had felt anything of the sort that I scarcely knew what was happening.

He must, I reflected, think me an imbecile.

When he got up to leave he said to K.,

'I certainly talk too much. Your wife is bored with me.'

'No,' I said, smiling warmly.

'Yes, ma'am. You were wondering if Texans are all as conceited. I've been talking about myself for three hours and a half.'

I had the sensation of jumping from a height, into total darkness: an astonishingly exhilarating feeling. 'It's an interesting subject,' I said, 'you could hardly have dealt with it in a shorter time. Not to do it justice.'

He took my mockery calmly, but K. scowled, and as soon as we were alone, said,

'If you had nothing sensible to say, why didn't you hold your tongue? You were damned rude.'

'Someone,' I said, 'should be rude to him. He thinks too well of himself.' My heart seemed to be beating in every corner of my body: I felt suffocated by it.

After this evening I thought about the Texan the whole time, whatever I was doing. When I sat down to write I was forced to drop my pen and give myself up to thinking about him, re-living, endlessly, tiny details, a tone of voice, a phrase. Now that I am incapable of behaving so fatuously, I regret the loss of a sensual trick so little harmful to anyone except myself, and so absurd and pleasant.

Ashamed to be wasting time, I made efforts not to think about him, not to stand looking out of the window in the hope of seeing him step out of K.'s tender. After a few minutes my mind rebelled violently and went back to its delirium.

The fear of mockery that froze me and drove me to silence in company vanished when he came into the room: I could say anything I felt. No need to pretend that I am a friendly harmless creature, no impulse to placate him. If I felt like jeering, I could jeer without fear of giving offence. The self I hide so carefully that few even of my intimate friends so much as suspect its existence, the fleering violent *northern* self, had met its brother. It was recognition—on a level below my absurd day-dreams. It did not brush my mind that so experienced and attractive a man would fall in love with me, but I had this other intimacy. It gave me the most acute pleasure.

My passion was a genuine one. It belonged to the same family as my delight in Marie Lloyd and all gross violent careless human beings. Is it possible that this derisive sceptical unpleasant self is my 'real' one, and that the moments when it gets free, the very few experiences it can take part in, are the only valid moments of my life?

It is quite possible. And that we begin dying, not when our body fails but much earlier, in the moment when we can no longer run the risk of a total folly.

One effect, good or bad, of my obsession was to ease my relations with K. The last of the quarrels in which he lost his temper savagely took place the week before he brought the American to the house. After that, nothing he said moved me, and when he left the house I forgot him.

Everything and everybody became unimportant to me except my son. He was and remained the changeless centre of my life.

Chapter 27

The Texan was exactly my age. Possibly he was inquisitive about a young woman who did not know that she was badly dressed, had never been trained to entertain a caller, and might at any moment insult him. He began coming to the farm three or four times a week. He talked to me about Texas, his father, the military school he was sent to when he was five, fence-riding, the Mexican expedition and, when I provoked him, about the English.

I had had no idea that the rest of the world did not humbly admire, and if not love at least fear us. I was astonished to hear him talk about our limited ideas, out-of-date traditions, laziness.

'But what can you possibly know about our traditions?' I exclaimed. 'Or our civilization.'

'Only that it's on its way out. Your traditions, whatever they are, won't be any use to you after the war, your people are tired, they don't want to work, we shall beat you to the trade of the world before you know what's happening.'

'How long have you been in England?' I asked.

'Four weeks, ma'am.'

'You have fine instincts.'

One day, when he had come up against the Wing Commander, he said with some sharpness that an Englishman's idea of co-operation is to decide what he intends to do, and leave the other fellow to think of a way to conform.

'But why,' I said, 'should you imagine you know what to do in a war that has been going on for three years while you Americans have been lending money at interest and writing pompous Notes?'

He looked at me for a moment. 'You have the tongue of a rattle-snake.'

Nothing in the world, not even to have him fall in love, could have given me a more sensuous pleasure than I got out of being able to say what I liked, no holds barred. It made up to me for my lack of all the qualities I knew he admired in women, elegance, social charm, the ability to ride and dance well.

I had few illusions about him. In any sense I could give to the word he was not educated. Behind his self-possessed politeness he was violent, with no desires or needs that could not be satisfied by intense physical excitements and money. If Stendhal could have made use of him in a novel he would have placed him in fifteenth-century Italy and made a soldier of fortune of him. (Later, he sold arms to both sides in the Sino-Japanese war, which shocked Michael Sadleir and struck me as typical of him.) He had curiosity and a hard brutal zest for living. This did not hinder him from being, in some ways, grossly sentimental: he had no moral sense, but a number of sentiments, unconsidered remnants of the idea of the Southern gentleman as it had come down to him, and as it concerned women, fighting, radicals. But—as Michael said of him—he made other people look like faint pencil-marks. He was violently alive, more alive than anyone I had ever known. And this was what infatuated me. I was half-dead, my energy, my mind, running to waste. He appealed to every impulse in me which sensible well-disciplined people either do not have or have had trained out of them. A part of me was gross, violent, sentimental, wanting change and excitement more than it wanted things in the end infinitely more important to me.

Good heavens, how is it possible to be so obsessed?

One evening K. came in with the look on his face, half-knowing, half-impudent, which meant that he had picked up a malicious story. It was about the Texan. The American squadron had given a dance to celebrate the building of their lavish recreation room. Ashamed of my poor dancing, I had left early, as soon as dinner ended.

'You remember the American nurses at the party last night? Remember the pretty red-head everyone called Oregon because she kept saying, "Y'know, I come from Oregon"? All our boys wanted to dance with her, but about one o'clock she disappeared with friend J., and spent the rest of the night until four o'clock in his hut. What a man, eh!'

A day or two later J. invited us to go into Winchester to one of the Saturday dances held in the Town Hall. I refused. 'I can't dance any of the new steps, and I have no proper dress.'

'There's no reason why we shouldn't go,' K. said. 'She's only showing off.'

His habit of taking me down in front of other people mortified me. To hide it, I said,

'Very well, we'll go.'

'Leave everything to me,' J. said.

At one o'clock on the day of the dance he sent a side-car and a gigantic sergeant-mechanic to drive me into Winchester, where he had taken a room for me at the Black Swan, so that I could dress in comfort. This I thought the height of luxury. When, late in the afternoon, he turned up in Winchester and asked my permission to bring two Americans from Pershing's H.Q. and a bottle of whiskey to the room for a drink, I felt doubtful—did he respect me?—and then exhilarated. This, surely, was the way people lived now.

Of the dance itself I remember nothing except one seductively silly waltz tune. The other day, a barrel-organ in a street off the Haymarket began croaking out the Missouri Waltz, and for a second or two I thought I should faint: it seemed that less than a breath separated me from a young woman in the claw of a ruinous passion, and that nothing, but nothing, equalled the loss of its agony and happiness.

None of this matters. What matters is to lose the power to regret.

We drove home after midnight, in an American tender, with K.

and three English officers. Shivering in a thin coat, I leaned my head against the side to be able to watch the hard outline of J.'s head: he had gone to the front, to keep an eye on the tipsy driver. The officers, not very sober, were dropped off at the airfield, and he came with us to the farm. He and K. were hungry, I offered to boil eggs, and for fear of waking the household I went outside into the yard, to the great stone barn, where there was a fireplace. J. had followed me. We got a fire going with sticks and I hung over it the black iron pan that would have held a score of eggs. I forget what we talked about in low voices—trivialities—but the few minutes of quiet untroubled intimacy in a darkness scarcely broken into by the crackling fire are still somewhere in my mind, if I could lay a finger on them.

I have completely forgotten what, about this time, I wrote to Archie, but I must, with this one of my few friends, have been indiscreet. He replied early in September, a letter which ended with a sharp rap over the knuckles.

'You're too expository about the Texan. If you want to run away, my dear, why don't you? You're not a soldier, and I'm sure Broughton is a miserably dull place. By the way, why doesn't the man join the army and come to France? There really are Americans out here fighting, I've seen them . . .'

I pushed his contempt to the back of my mind—where it went on working.

K. had a week's leave due to him. He wanted to take it in London and, reluctantly, I agreed to trust Bill to our landlady for so long.

Two days before we were due to go, he came home from the airfield, pleased with himself, and announced that J. had invited us to be his guests in London, 'in return for your endless hospitality.'

'I let him see that I thought it was about time he did something of the sort,' he said complacently.

The rooms J. had taken were in the Piccadilly Hotel, a suite on the top floor, two large bedrooms and a bathroom: the door from the corridor led into a long inner hall, and the three rooms opened off this.

We had not been in this, to my eyes, luxurious place, longer than twenty minutes when K. was rung up by the Adjutant. The Equipment Officer of one of the squadrons had come down with appendicitis, and he must come and take his share of the extra work. Almost with relief, I began repacking my suitcase—no long job.

'Don't be an idiot,' K. said sharply. 'You'll stay here, of course,

J. will look after you, and I'll be back the day after tomorrow. I know friend B., he loses his head if someone mis-counts a screw.'

J. took no part in the argument: his sexual vanity would make him careful not to say the wrong thing, or show surprise that an English husband thought it common form to leave his wife in an hotel with another man, and that man himself. I cannot be certain why K. was so eager for me to stay. The most likely answer is that he was showing off: one of his fantasies at the moment may have been to show how magnanimous, how nobly trusting, he was. He may even or also have been trusting.

My only clear feeling was that I should bore J. For the rest, I seemed to myself to be indifferent.

I went with K. to the station, then dawdled back to the hotel. To tell the truth, it alarmed me by its size, and the quantity of gay pretty women, smiling and well-dressed, sitting about everywhere. I caught sight of myself in a long glass, a thin shapeless figure in my five-year-old coat and skirt. Letting myself into the suite without a sound, I sat down in my room to wait until something happened. After a time, I had a vexed sense that this was no way to spend time in London. Not certain whether J. was even in the hotel, I ran across the hall and knocked on the door of his bedroom.

'Is that you, Margaret? Come in.'

I found him lying on his bed, a book he was not reading on the floor, and the obligatory jug of iced water within reach of his hand.

In five minutes we had quarrelled, I forget about what, but I had one of my rare paroxysms of rage when something like an explosion takes place behind my eyes, blinding me. In the same instant I was in his arms, abandoned to him, trembling, my throat hard, the veins of my body like straw in a fire. The next moment I was on my own side of a gulf, detached, cold. Why? Heaven knows.

I tried to move away.

'No,' he said, 'don't move.'

'Please let me go away.'

'I can't.'

A sentence jumped into my mind, and I said drily, 'You must think I'm Oregon and that this is your hut.'

He let me go at once, stepping back, and I walked out of the room to my own. I sat there wondering what cold devil had taken possession of my body and mind in the very moment when they were being offered all I had imagined and craved. I did not understand either why what I said had defeated him, but I had known it would:

the words were put into my mind as though someone had slipped a knife into my hand. All I had to do was use it.

After a time, an hour or less, I heard J. in the hall. He knocked, and said,

'Don't you want to eat dinner?'

'In the hotel?'

'Why not?'

I opened my door. He looked at my outdoor clothes, and said in a gentler voice,

'Put your hat on, child, we'll go eat in the grill.'

He had realized that I had no idea that in a grill room (in those days) a hat was obligatory. In the crowded restaurant I felt dull and awkward, without an idea in my head. J. was gay and talkative, ordering for me things I had never eaten, *huîtres Mornay*, and drinking a great deal. At that time I never drank, not even wine. Naïvely, I expected him to make some remark about—what ought I to call it? the fiasco?—but he said nothing until I told him I was leaving the next morning.

'You don't have to do that,' he said. 'If you're afraid of me you can lock your door.'

Confused, I said, 'I'm not afraid.'

'It would be a hell of a silly thing to be. Things don't happen twice.'

'You meant it to happen. But it was partly my fault.'

'Listen. Only a fool worries about what happened yesterday. Tell yourself: That was yesterday. And forget it.'

He was a little drunk, not drunk enough to frighten me, as people who have lost control of themselves do. But the only thing I wanted was to get away, out of sight of the person who had seen me lose my head and behave badly. We finished dinner: he saw me into the lift, and went away in search of a more amusing companion.

In my room, I packed my suitcase: I meant to catch the first train, at six o'clock. Then, switching the lights off, I opened the window, thinking that if I couldn't run about London I might as well look at it.

The windows on this top floor were casements, neither high nor wide: a low parapet cut off the view. I pushed a chair under the window and climbed out on to the sill. It was of stone, fairly broad, and I sat there dangling my legs, and staring. I saw roofs and the black gulfs of streets, an alphabet I could not spell out, and behind them a sky with a veining of darker clouds like twisted roots.

Lifted up at this height above London, I began to feel self-possessed, and then coolly excited. This excitement had nothing to do with J. It sprang somewhere in the nerves of my mind. I shall do something, I thought; there is a way out, and I shall find it.

This was not Rastignac's cry, looking down over Paris from the Père Lachaise: *Et maintenant, à nous deux*! Alas, I am not so single-minded. I want, even then I wanted, too many things which cancel each other, solitude, a bare life, and the pleasures of theatre, concert hall, travel; honesty and a reputation; wealth without crawling to get it; to live like a monk and a foot-loose unbeholden eater of life.

Naturally, I achieve none of them. Nevertheless, when I come to die, among the minutes I shall remember gratefully will be the thirty or so I spent on a top-floor window-sill of the Piccadilly Hotel, in 1918, confident, and madly happy.

I began to feel cold, and scrambled stiffly back into the room. I was afraid I should over-sleep, but I had not the courage to ask a servant to call me. I lay down on the outside of the bed, half-dressed, sure in that way of being too uncomfortable to sleep long. I woke at four, dressed myself properly, and at five started to go downstairs, carrying my suitcase. Not only was I too ignorant to know whether, at that hour in the morning, the lifts would be running, but I dreaded the glances of servants.

Not until I was sitting in the train out of Waterloo station did I begin to wonder what I was doing, and why, without in the least intending it, I had refused a man for whom I felt a violent lust—no other word for it. I had only to watch him cross the room to feel myself on the edge of fainting.

All this will be incomprehensible to young women today, and seem very silly.

It may have been both—but I had not been able to help myself. An impulse stronger and deeper than the one that threw me into his arms had driven me to draw back, escaping by a trick, a jeer that stung him so sharply he would as soon have slept with an adder—or a rattlesnake.

What, as the train hurried me back to Stockbridge, baffled me was: Why? Why, involuntarily, had I failed to behave like the loose woman I obviously must be?

I had no feeling of guilt. I did not believe it would have been immoral to take what I wanted with such violence. Ungenerous towards K., yes, disloyal, not immoral.

It was partly caution—a shrewd hard sceptical Yorkshire caution —hating to be overreached, hating to give myself away. I could lose my head—to a point. That reached, I drew back.

My upbringing, too, a puritanism not mine, given me. But more, far more, my instinctive certainty that the American was uncontrollable, I should not have been in control of my own life. *And that would never have done.*

It turned out that all the qualities I most disliked in my family were stronger than I was.

I had a moment of overwhelming relief that, in spite of my grasping mind and desperate fatuous day-dreams, I had been too much for the alien he was—a crude greedy over-confident alien.

No doubt, Archie's contemptuous letter had reached in me a self I could no more repudiate than the colour of my eyes or my hard bones.

I decided not to tell K. about it. For two reasons, one more presentable than the other. In the first place, I could not trust him to hold his tongue. He would enjoy a public scandal in which he played the part of injured husband and friend, betrayed by a scoundrel.

The second reason was an instinct. The thought of giving one man away to another in an affair of this kind shocked me deeply.

I told him I had been worried about Bill, and let him suspect that I had made some sort of dumb fool of myself.

I see as plainly today as then that to give way to my obsession would have been a disaster. I see, too—what I did not then—that for moral health a sensual passion should be given in to at once, or strangled. During the next few months I did neither. I thought about J. day and night, sometimes with an agony of regret. To endure it, I reminded myself of his bad qualities—he was violent, uncontrolled, uncivilized. And then I thought: But with him I was alive, not as I am, half-dead.

I was out of my mind. In everything else I had self-control and good sense: I looked as carefully as usual after Bill, and when some malicious friendly woman spoke to me about 'your Texan' I kept a smooth face. It was a relief when, not long after this, he took his squadron to France.

At the same time, K. heard he was being moved—to Canterbury. My heart sank. 'When?'

'In four weeks—at the end of October.'

The thought of moving to a town where, for all I knew, none of the things I gave Bill, cream, butter, fresh eggs, plump partridges and chickens, existed, horrified me.

I decided to take him and my all but finished novel to Whitby until K. had found us rooms at least half as comfortable as the farm.

Chapter 28

Some time this summer, the last of the war, my father benefited by the exchange of older civilian prisoners and was sent into Switzerland, where he was kept for a few weeks in hospital. I had not been at home many days when he returned. It was a strange homecoming. My mother met him in the hall, let him kiss her cheek, and asked coolly,

'Well, how are you?'

He gave his short laugh. 'Oh, I'm quite well.'

A few more words, and she went back into the sitting-room, closing the door. Tea had been laid for him in the breakfast-room, the first of many meals he would take there alone. Afterwards he drifted into the sitting-room and my mother talked to him, politely, as she might have talked to a not very welcome stranger. Perhaps trying to please her, he took notice of new things she had bought, a small old writing-table, a looking-glass, and she told him in an indifferent voice that she was going to Scarborough the next day to look at carpets for this room.

He lumbered away upstairs to his bedroom at the top of the house. When he came down again he went into the breakfast-room, and I followed him. Someone, I thought, should show interest in him.

The pity I felt was almost impersonal. None of William Storm Jameson's children had any liking for him; we scarcely knew him: as children we wrote brief empty duty letters to him, when told to, and fixed into albums the coloured postcards he sent us from the cities and harbours of a score of countries.

What became of these many hundreds of cards, fragments of a sunk world?

His youngest child could not stand him: her dislike of him had been born with her. I was the only one of his four children who felt a little sympathy for him, and that was a matter of nerves: his loneliness, his quick defensive lying when my mother accused or contradicted him, were the habits of a child lost at the age of thirteen. For a moment something infinitely baffled, tortuous, afraid, came close, and fell away again.

I tried to think of something to say to him. 'Were the Germans decent to you?'

'Oh, they were all right,' he said, indifferent. 'They knew what they had to deal with in us English. We didn't stand any nonsense.'

This was something he believed, as he believed in quinine. I saw him, gaunt, shabby, wolfish, shuffling about the camp, holding round himself the rags of his captain's authority, neither submissive nor defiant, preferring some of his German guards to some of his fellow-prisoners: he judged people solely by their attitude to him.

'I suppose there were all sorts in the camp.'

'Ha, yes. I didn't speak to many. Two or three was quite enough. The Brandenburg camp was worse than the other, they burned some of the prisoners.'

'What do you mean?'

'A hut caught fire and the men in it were burned to death,' he said carelessly. 'Queer people, them Germans.'

I did not know whether this were true, or something he had imagined. He said nothing more.

'Did you see the *Saxon Prince* sunk?' I asked.

For the first time he was roused.

'Yes. She went down very gracefully.' He laughed, a short nervous laugh. 'She didn't dive. She went down—down.'

He held his hand out, palm downwards, and moved it slowly down.

'What did they do? Did they torpedo her?'

'Yes. Two torpedoes.'

Between his son's death and the murder of his ship, there could be no doubt which went to his heart.

The breakfast-room had a french window opening on to a verandah and a small sunk garden. If a house keeps the impress of people who have lived in it, that is one of the two places where he still is, a tall shambling figure, head bent, fingers absently stuffing a pipe, eyes staring into the garden at a remote horizon. In later years, when he had left the sea for good, he lived in that room during the day. Once, for the sake of saying something to him, I complained of a large starling which drove the smaller birds from the crumbs I put out.

He frowned. 'I've been watching that bird,' he exclaimed. 'It's a very well-behaved bird. It's not a starling at all, it's an over-grown sparrow. I daresay it's the grandfather of the others. It's not greedy, it eats a lot because it needs more than they do, it's older.'

My bedroom was next my mother's now. On the night of his homecoming he was the last to come upstairs; I heard him cross the landing and hesitate outside her door for a moment before calling,

'Good-night.'

Silence. I held my breath. Isn't she going to answer him? He repeated it. 'Good-night.'

In a lifeless voice, dry, without warmth, barely audible, she said, 'Oh. Good-night.'

Listening with all my ears, I could not hear his footsteps going away up to his room on the floor above. He walked like a bear, moving his heavy body without a sound, in the way he crept up behind his officers on board ship.

The only person for whom my mother felt warmly anxious was her youngest. She had years ago given up trying to rule this child, as she had ruled the others, by fear and pity. No punishments were any use. An appeal to her emotions—which had brought me to grovelling remorse—only hardened Dorothy, and a threat of whipping sent her into such frenzies of rage that my mother withdrew in alarm. 'Go to your room and stay there until you are sorry,' she ordered. Hours later, it was she herself who gave in, touched by the sight of a small face closed against her like a fist.

She was too tired, spirit and body too worn, to master a young creature so stubborn, so capable of a harshness like her own earlier harshness.

It was as if, at a moment when she no longer expected anything of her life, she had turned a corner and come on her own younger self, pale with revolt and anger. The hand lifted to punish dropped. How could she punish herself in this last-born? How treat roughly a child for whom, now that she knew what bestial cruelty life is capable of, she feared as never for anyone.

At twelve, Dorothy was tall, with thin supple limbs and an exquisitely fair skin. Now that she always got her own way, her tempers were soon over: she was generous and straightforward, a miracle of energy. My mother's face changed when she spoke of her, softened by a half-foolish pride.

I saw that she had transferred her ambitions to this child. First it was I who was to compensate her, I thought, then Harold, now Dorothy.

One day, she told me, 'I dreamed about Harold last night. We were walking along a country road, and we came to a large house, with great trees round it, and he said, Look, Mother, this is where we're going to live now. The rooms were large and beautiful, like the trees—I've always wanted to live near trees. And then he began going away, I tried to keep him, but he was gone, and I woke up.'

My heart seemed to shrivel with pity. I did not know how to answer her. There were weeks when, my mind full of its own thoughts and wants, I did not give Harold a thought. I saw that there were no days when she did not think of him and the useless bitter waste of his life.

'One day you may have a house like that.'

'No.' She smiled unkindly. 'No. It's too late.'

The rawness of her grief scalded me. As did her reliance on her youngest child. I was afraid of another disappointment for her.

I did not resent it that she had written me off as no use. It certainly looked as if I were a failure.

During the first fortnight at home I expected every day to hear that K. had taken rooms for us in Canterbury. At last, when I had written to him twice, he replied that there were no rooms to be had, he might be moved again in a few weeks, I had better stay where I was. And be careful with money, since he had had to spend a good deal lately and wouldn't be able to send any of his October pay.

I felt something wrong with this letter, but could not put my finger on it.

That morning we were waiting for news of the armistice. If the Germans signed, a gun was to be fired from the cliff battery. We kept the windows open, and towards eleven I went outside into the road to listen.

I did not hear the gun, because suddenly all the ships' whistles and sirens sounded from the harbour, and then the bells, first from the church on the east cliff, then all the rest, peal on peal. A flag went up jerkily in the garden of a house farther down the hill, and another and another. I spoke to a man running past the gate.

'Is it the peace?'

He was beside himself with excitement, stuttering, waving his arms. 'Can't y'hear them? Can't y'hear t'whistles?'

Oh, pity, pity us and our weak useless hopes, the fraud, the treachery, the profit drawn from tears and death, the young dead, and the barren old carrying their bodies to the end. Or don't you hear them?

I went back into the house, trembling, scarcely able to speak quietly. 'It's the peace,' I said.

My mother's face was made ugly by her tears. 'What is the good of it to *me*?'

True—what good was it to her? I felt ashamed and helpless. In the same moment I was filled by an insensate excitement: I could not believe that this was not, for me, in some way a chance.

K. did not write again. He left unanswered the letter I wrote suggesting that he should approach his old headmaster in Liverpool and find out whether there were a place for him. Heaven knows I did not want to go back to the Suburb—but I would have gone. No question but I would have gone.

Nor did he answer another letter asking him to send me a little money, a pound, even ten shillings. I had nothing. There I was, twenty-seven, a married woman, and borrowing from my mother for our small daily needs, mine and Bill's.

Who wrote to me—Archie?—that he had heard there were openings in an advertising firm in London, the Carlton Agency. 'It might be something for K.?' I wrote to K. at once, begging him to apply.

This time he answered, a short letter. 'I'm quite capable, thank you, when the time comes, of arranging my own future. It's kind of you and all that, but I don't happen to need your help. Your letter made me smile. I fully appreciate what a disappointment I am to you, and you so clever and all. Don't get *too* clever. You'll go off in a cloud of hot air, and then what should I do? . . . I'm having an amusing time down here. Learning to dance . . .'

Had he not enclosed ten pounds from his November pay, I should have felt more mortified.

Chapter 29

I cannot remember when the idea came to me to write to the Carlton Agency myself.

It is difficult to write, without distorting it, about a decision which, now, seems to me coldly unforgivable.

Horror at the thought of leaving Bill—where? how?—wrenched the nerves of my chest in the very instant of writing to the Agency. It was a sharp pain, purely physical. I carried the letter to the post, refusing to think what I was about.

He was now three and a half, a strangely self-contained child. He had begun to talk, with the greatest reluctance, using long words but rarely making a sentence of them. I knew how to care for him so that he would grow strong and handsome, but not how to amuse him.

I thought: *I can't go.* Behind everything I was doing, the senseless dialogue went on . . . I can't go, I must go. What thanks will he give you for staying with him, when he is older and you have no money to spend on him? . . . Dialogue? The chatter of apes or the insane.

As soon as I had an answer from the managing director of the firm, asking me to come and see him, I spoke to my mother about it. She listened with genuine interest.

'But it would mean leaving Bill,' I said.

She did not offer to keep him. She had no heart now, no energy, for such an effort. She was far too tired. He was very wilful, and her youngest child more than a little jealous of him.

She was not sorry to see me trying, after so many years, to make something of my life, but she could not go the lengths of burdening herself with my child. I don't remember that it so much as crossed my mind to hope. I was too sharply aware that he was *my* duty.

She looked meditatively at me from her clear pale Gallilee eyes, a glance that seemed to come from an immense distance.

'We'll think of something,' she said slowly. In the same slow absent voice, she added, 'K. isn't much good to you, my girl.'

Repeating to myself, even believing, that nothing would come of it, I went up to London on the early morning train, and saw the director that afternoon. He turned out to be a polite middle-aged man, with a yellow skin and quick nervously intelligent glance. Because with half my mind I hoped to be turned down, I felt neither anxiety nor embarrassment. The interview was not a long one. He asked—looking down at the letter in which I had set out my degrees—what work I had done.

'None.'

'No experience. And no training?'

'No.'

He smiled slightly. 'What do you think you're worth—in the way of salary?'

In the train I had decided to ask for five pounds a week. I lost courage, and said,

'Four pounds. At first.'

'Very well.'

I said nothing—and felt nothing.

'When can you start?'

'In January.'

'We're badly under-staffed. I should like you to come before then.'

'I can't come before Christmas,' I said.

'At the end of December, then.'

'Yes. I can manage that.'

He may have felt that I ought to show a little gratitude to him for taking on an entirely inexperienced young woman. It did not occur to me. He rose politely and walked to the door with me. Possibly he was amused.

I remember nothing between leaving him and getting into the night train. I spent the evening with Archie, who at ten o'clock put me into the train, and hired a pillow for me. I was unused to such attentions, which no doubt is why I remember it. The journey itself, huddled in the corner of a third-class compartment, my head slipping off the pillow, has run together with all the other night journeys I made between London and Whitby to see Bill for a few hours, the sooty comfortless carriage, the long wait in York station, from two o'clock until five, the cold dirty platforms, the light coming greyly through the glass of the roof, the phantoms of other solitary travellers.

I tried to think clearly. From a single moment of exultance in having landed the job I dropped into the blackest pit. To give up my child in return for four pounds a week in an advertising office was plain madness, a folly for which there was no rag of excuse. Don't go, I told myself, don't go, don't go, don't go—tolling of an undersea bell.

I must, I answered.

I was not reasoning with myself, I was adrift, driving before a wind out of the past.

I could have said—it would be true—that I felt responsible, solely responsible for our future. Justly or unjustly, I was quite certain now that K. would never do anything, for himself or us. I read his few letters with an eye that saw only their levity and what my grandfather would have called bombast. He has the mind, I thought cruelly, of a precocious schoolboy.

Some years ago, in a bus rattling towards Amiens, I overheard the woman in front of me, a small pale creature smelling strongly of cloves, talking to her friend about her husband: he was a miser, he tormented her and their daughters, etc etc: at the end, with a gently ironic smile, she said, '*Eh bien, que veux-tu, il est mon homme.*'

I am incapable of such unthinking unasking goodness.

My poverty and insecurity were a torment, and my blind wish to do the best I could for my son. (That this did not necessarily involve having money did not brush a mind haunted by too many hard-headed ghosts.) By keeping mum about my ambition, boredom, restlessness, I could make out an excellent case for myself. Any sensible jury would applaud it, and it would be a lie . . .

My mother did not advise me, for or against, but she helped me to go. She had remembered a Miss Geeson, a woman in her forties who ran a small morning school for very young children and was said to be kind and good. Perhaps she would take Bill to live with her. She lived in Ruswarp, a small village a mile out of Whitby— less, if you could have walked along the estuary.

I went to see her, and liked her—she was clearly a kind woman. She had brown hands and soft embarrassed brown eyes. Telling her that he must have the best of everything, the best milk, the best soap, I asked about her fees. With a little diffidence she wondered if two pounds a week would be too much.

'No,' I said, 'I can manage that.'

'Of course, his clothes . . .'

'Buy him anything he needs, I'll repay you at once.' By the time he grows out of what he has, I reflected, I shall be earning a great deal more money. Rashness for rashness, what was there to choose between me and K? Today I cannot imagine on what I rested my confidence. On energy and ignorance, no doubt.

K. wrote genially: 'Well, well. To think that you could nip in and sneak my job for yourself. Congratulations . . .' He said nothing about Bill.

In the short time between my interview at the Carlton Agency and the end of December I was very active, and stupefied, like a man walking through a thick fog. I had moments of frightful unhappiness, from which I rushed into activity, any activity. Methodically, I planned, added to the pile of Bill's clothes, drew up a list of my few debts, all without reflection. The truth is—is it the truth?—I was in the claws of a raging want. There is no arguing with a raging want; it can be hit on the head, but not by an argument.

Feelings of guilt and regret are nowadays in disgrace. One cannot be seen with them in intellectual circles. But no one is forced to read a book in which I am trying to write without lying.

Perhaps one day, when I am very old, and frozen, I shall be able to think coldly about this time.

The evening before I was due to go, packing my own and his clothes in our room, I began for the first time to cry. I have always refused to believe that mental agony is as intolerable as physical pain, but during these moments and in the years that followed, I became a little less certain. Flowing through the whole of my life, an icy current, running at a great depth, avoided as often as possible and stumbled on suddenly, at home or in the street, at receptions for the great, on journeys, in sleep.

When, after putting him to bed, I went downstairs, my stolid face must somehow have given me away.

'You know,' my mother said, 'you could still change your mind about going if you don't feel altogether happy about it.'

'Yes, I could,' I said calmly.

I had arranged for him to reach Miss Geeson's house at bedtime, so that he would fall asleep at once, and wake in his new life. I could not explain anything to him. It seemed better for him to come in from a walk and find me gone. So, in the morning, I dressed him and sent him out with a servant. I watched from the window. As they reached the top of the hill, the cab I had ordered crossed them on its way to the house. My mother was standing beside me.

'I was just thinking,' she said, 'he's very little, after all. I hope he'll be happy with her.'

'Oh, I expect so.'

'I wonder what he'll think, when he wakes up in the morning in a strange room.'

Does she know she is torturing me? I thought. When I stepped into the cab he was still in sight. My mother pointed to him from the house. Turning my head away, I smiled at her. The cab jerked forward. I sat with a hand pressed to my throat. It was only a short distance to the station, I had no time left.

To write this makes me feel ill.

How ridiculous it will seem to . . .

Chapter 30

Why should I have expected the London of January 1919 to bear even a family likeness to the London of three poor scholars? It did not. Of all the Londons, lying one below the other in my skull, from the streets known to the captain's wife and her little girl to the London of eyeless façades and heaps of rubble, it is the shoddiest and least generous. Under a grey sky it awaited the harvest of millions of fresh young bodies pushed hurriedly into the ground, their eyes and supplicating hands, out of sight.

I have a poor head for dates; my memories of the next six years, in which my life fell into the folds it has kept, are hopelessly fragmentary and confused, a fresco of vivid details and great gaps where line and colour have vanished.

I spent my first night in a small dingy temperance hotel in a shabby quarter of Bloomsbury. Not reflecting that London would be full of visitors crowding on President Wilson's heels, I had done nothing about reserving a room, and for some hours thought I should have to sleep in the crypt of St Martin-in-the-Fields, opened to the homeless. In despair I went into the blue Y.W.C.A. hut set up in Trafalgar Square; the kind soul in charge telephoned a dozen modest hotels before finding one.

The bedroom was penitential, and I spent one of the worst nights of my life, weeping tears as bitter as vitriol.

Next morning I presented myself at the Carlton Agency in Covent Garden, and said coolly that I must be allowed a day or two to find lodgings. Since I had never been a subordinate, it did not occur to me to behave like one. This attitude, completely involuntary, did me no harm. The managing director—call him Shaw-Thomas—was an educated and passably intelligent man, with, I now suspect, fewer commercial instincts than he needed for survival. On the few occasions when he called me into his room, he talked to me as though I were socially his equal, a civility I was ignorant enough to take for granted.

Some time during my first week, he gave me a brief lecture on the art of advertising.

'Let us call it the art of persuasion. One of the applied arts, Miss Jameson.' He smiled, pressing his hand down on his desk, stressing a great many words, and showing small very sharp teeth. 'How many novelists and poets manage to get themselves read by rich, poor, superior, ignorant, successful, happy, miserable, snobbish, unimaginative, resigned? Remember always that people *choose* to read a novel, but you must *trick* them into reading an *advertisement*. You can do it *only* if you *believe* what you are writing, if you believe whole*heart*edly in the virtue of the soap, the face cream, the tobacco, you are trying to sell. Avoid *cynicism*. It is incompatible with emotion—and great advertising is the expression of great emotional sincerity.'

I listened with all my ears. The trick, I told myself, is obviously to describe, as vividly as possible, the flawless skin, and to overlay this image with an image of the soap, the face cream. Persuasion is a matter of evoking the right images in the right order.

My cleverness enchanted me. In the same moment I was very slightly revolted, as if I had been made to swallow the skin of rice pudding.

During the time I worked in the Agency—much less than a year —this mute sense of outrage became loathing. It was not the fault of my colleagues. An edged gaiety made the days tolerable, and I think with affection of certain nameless faceless men, hard-working, sceptical, who took some trouble to teach an awkward provincial her job.

Apart from typists, I was the only woman on the staff. My immediate superior, Mr Foxe—I have forgotten his real name—was patient and friendly, a man of forty odd, slight, brisk, frankly concerned about his looks. 'In business, one can't afford to age,' he told me one day when we were both tired. 'D'you know what I do? At night before I get into bed, I stretch a narrow piece of sticking-plaster across the lines on my forehead and at the ends of my eyes, to smooth them out.'

'How clever,' I said falsely.

He smiled. 'You have no lines yet, Miss Jim, but you will, you know.'

This minute I could write an essay on the beauty and holiness of the art of advertising—forgive me, persuasion—and avoid calling up a single image which might rouse in its readers a suspicion of the truth: that the use of words with intent to sell something is simply the art of telling convincing lies. The accident that what you sell is harmless, or even useful, does not cancel the lie in the soul.

Great emotional sincerity! There is no polite word for it. Balderdash! (George Gallilee.) Modern advertising is a disease, a skin cancer galloping through the cells of society. Modern advertisers—highly-talented men and women, paid to lie.

Within limits (drawn by my profound boredom), I became a skilful copy-writer. Admirably persuasive about face cream, admirably succinct and convincing about roofing tiles and arc-welding lamps, charmed by type-faces, I could no more invent a slogan than sing. None the less, a career in advertising lay open to me if I had had the will to look for it. A more adroit or clearsighted young woman would, without fuss, have split her mind, devoting one part to writing copy and preparing schemes, the other to honest work, and built a wall between them thick enough to keep one from contaminating the other.

This sort of inner duplicity—'controlled schizophrenia,' Klaus Fuchs called it—is too common a habit in our day to be noticed. Noticeable are only the rare exceptions, the one or two incorruptibles—like R. H. Tawney, that very great man and arbitrary saint. It is not to my credit that I resisted one form of the infection.

Ridiculous as it seems, I must have believed that I need only get myself back to London for all my unused energies and talents to flower at once. And here I was, doing work I knew to be worthless, making barely enough money to keep alive, and bored, bored, bored.

During those first weeks, I spent every evening, unless the weather were too abominable, walking about London from Oxford Street in the north to the Strand and the Embankment in the south. I was living in north-west London, I have forgotten where, in the house belonging to the widow of an officer killed in the war, a pleasant slightly *louche* young woman—I have a talent for finding landladies suitable to my condition. I had a small but not uncomfortable room, and would have done better to sit in it in the evening, since walking made me hungry.

I was singularly alone. None of my few friends were in London: Archie had (I think) already married his gay spirited Scotch girl, or was about to marry and go off to an Indian hill station, Sydney was in the West Indies, Oswald was marrying and beginning his career as schoolmaster in Yorkshire.

Why didn't I begin to write a novel? Because I lacked the sense to arrange my life sensibly. Because of the fever in my mind. And because I am a novelist *faute de mieux*.

I was dying of discontent with myself. And with London. This—these endless cold streets smelling of mud, sweat, petrol, these cafés and restaurants I could not afford to enter, these people with their flattened voices and faces, seeming to be nothing and nowhere, like shadows in water—was the London I had been praying to return to, and given up my son for it. Fool!

Wherever I went, at any moment, in the middle of a street, waiting to cross, crossing, in a cheap café before a scone and a cup of coffee, waking at two a.m., the same thought wounded me. Pressing its thumb into my brain, the image I had made for myself, of Bill looking for me in silence, became an illness. (I laugh like a dog when I think that these self-inflicted tortures belong to the same family as those I had felt thinking about the white rabbit.)

Walking along the Strand past Simpson's, I suddenly remembered that I had taken him there on our way to Hampshire. We had reached London at two o'clock, the two of us, and the train to Stockbridge did not leave until five. Carrying him down the long platform, I wondered anxiously where I could give him his lunch, and remembered that Simpson's, a place I had never been in, had a reputation for good English food. Nothing less would do for him. I took our luggage—cot, baby carriage, tin bath, dress-basket—to Waterloo station, and another taxi back to the Strand: I could never bring myself to risk him in the crowds and chance infections of bus or underground. (No wonder I never had two shillings to rub together!) When we reached Simpson's, it was three o'clock, and even in the doorway the place felt empty. We were directed up a flight of stairs. It took him a long time to climb them, and the large room was deserted. A man in a frock coat—I looked at him haughtily —led us to a table, and with his own hands placed a hassock on a chair to bring Bill's head above the edge. He gave me the menu— the prices were no worse than I had feared. I ordered lamb cutlets stewed in milk for Bill, and for myself mushrooms on toast—1/6. The cutlets were a long time coming, and meantime a round dozen of waiters gathered in the service doorway, smiling and pointing at the two-year-old customer who wanted stewed lamb at three in the afternoon. The chef brought it himself—no doubt he had heard the joke—and set it in front of Bill. A common waiter brought my mushrooms—two.

The memory of that afternoon only fifteen months ago caught me in the throat. Tears ran down my face in a stream I could not check, I stumbled along the street, praying that passers-by would take it I had been smitten by influenza. An elderly woman stopped and said hesitantly,

'Can I help?'

Scowling at her, I said, 'No!' in so foul and surly a voice that she stepped back. I hated her with such venom that it stopped my tears.

Hell, says Sartre, is the others. Nonsense. Nonsense prompted by a metaphysical vanity. Hell is five or six memories which are able occasionally to enter the intestines through the mind and tear them. That's all, that's all.

Chapter 31

I am writing this on the 17th of November, 1961. Yesterday I took the chair, with reluctance, at a dinner celebrating the 40th anniversary of the International P.E.N. About a hundred and fifty guests, including a charming old Dickensian professor from Moscow called Kirpotin. He had brought his interpreter, and throughout my speech—into which for his benefit I dropped the names of Pasternak and poor Ivinskaya—I was distracted by the muttered word-by-word translation going on in my left ear. Two other speakers, critics or dons, spoke amusingly: the second ended by calling for a toast 'to the distinguished women writers present, Dr Veronica Wedgwood, Dame Rebecca West, Miss Rosamund Lehmann.' This, I reflected with surprise, is the first time I have been publicly confronted by my own invisibility . . . I left the moment dinner ended, avoiding the kind of writers' talk which curdles my soul.

Dawdling along a cold brutally lighted Piccadilly towards my bed for the night, I made an effort to consider soberly the probable end of a freak.

It was no use—I could not keep my mind on my precarious future. Seizing the chance offered it at night, only at night, an older London tapped me on the shoulder. Friends, including one or two of whom I never now think, so undemanding are they, so withdrawn into their dark silence and peace, ranged themselves on either side of me, and we walked about unnoticed in streets no less immaterial than they were. I felt crazily exhilarated. My ghosts vanished, but, in spite of the cold, the gaiety stayed.

Why, I asked myself, do you write books? Not to be praised. There is not a single moment, during the many months or years of a book's conception and raising, when the thought: Will it be liked? Will it be damned? enters your mind. At this level, praise and dispraise are strictly irrelevant.

The person in my skin who flinches when damned or mocked is not the writer. The writer is deeply indifferent to opinion, fretted when she has not done her best, protected at other times by her ineradicable barely articulate conviction that novel-writing—or, more narrowly, her novels, for all the intense pains taken with them —are not serious, not worth a tear.

The one who flinches is the beaten child, afraid with an old fear. But there is no need to be sorry for her.

I walked about for an hour in my lost city, the happiest and no doubt the most foolish of its ghosts. No fine thoughts came to me, only lines I am certain of not forgetting.

> . . . I said to Lord Nelson at three
> Pore devil, look at 'yer
> They built y' a stat'yer
> They built Piccadilly for me!

Some time in the spring of 1919 my first novel was published. Trying to grope a way back to what must surely have been a time, however brief, of intoxication and expectancy, I remember nothing. Nothing at all of the feelings of an obscure young woman. I was seeing no one to whom I could have talked about it. Not that I had the least wish to talk; I would rather run a mile than be seen caring about the fate of one of my books.

I was too ignorant to be surprised that it had a great many reviews. I kept them, good and bad, for some years before tearing them up. Nowadays, I destroy as I go. I have no intention of leaving driftwood.

Today, such a novel as *The Pot Boils* would not get itself published. Or if a rash publisher took it for its promise—what the devil did it promise?—it would not meet any such body of criticism. The room into which a young writer steps now is so overcrowded that he is lucky if he is not suffocated in the first five minutes. And even if he is noticed he can hope for useful advice from, at most, two quarters. The rest will be no good to him. Unless he has laid his lines beforehand—unless, that is, he has *friends*—the so-called serious journals will not notice him at all. In this way, his lot is harder than mine in 1919. So far as money goes, it could scarcely be harder. Ten pounds, and that not earned! (Unless I have forgotten.)

Mr Shaw-Thomas caught sight of a review and read the book. He called me into his room, to talk about a campaign for a new firm, and said, smiling, 'I had no idea we had a novelist on the staff. Nor that you were so intelligent.'

I smiled. But—as my grandfather would have done—I thought his remark impudent.

K. was still in Canterbury. If I had not been so engrossed by my exasperating work, I might have been surprised by the fewness and brevity of his letters. He turned up one evening without warning, and took me to dinner in the brasserie of the Café Royal.

Intoxicated by so much food and by the delicious warmth and liveliness of a place which—thanks to the mania for change of fools who cannot see to the ends of their noses—no longer exists, and pleased not to be alone, I was immensely grateful. An old tenderness woke in me. I would give a fortune, I thought, to be living with him and Bill in some quiet place. Rashly, I said so.

He said he might be moved to Netheravon.

'But I thought you would be demobilized any day now. Haven't you heard anything?'

'Not a word,' he said gaily.

'Would they release you if you applied?'

'My dear girl, why should I? I'm quite snug where I am, thank you.'

I had enough sense not to say: But the longer you stay in the Air Force, well-fed, going to dances, working easy hours, irresponsible because nothing depends on your efforts, with a servant to polish your beautiful boots, the less fit you will be for any other life.

'But you will have to leave in the end—and the longer you hang on the worse your chances of a job. Why not try at once for a school in London? We should both be earning, we could have a house and a nurse for Bill——'

'You dislike houses. How often have you told me that one room and a suitcase is all you want?'

'That's true,' I said, 'but Bill——'

'But any stick will do to beat a bad dog,' K. said, in an amused patronizing voice. 'How you enjoy managing my life for me. You're pricelessly funny when you imagine you're being subtle, my dear. But you don't impress me, you know. You always wanted to get away, you've got away, and blow me if you're not still dissatisfied! How'd you have liked it if I had rushed out of the Air Force, back to Liverpool and the Suburb?'

'I would have gone with you.'

'And made my life hell by grumbling!'

True enough, I thought. My hatred of a settled life, my unhappiness when I thought of Bill, started up in me in the same instant, throwing me back into the confusion I lived in. How unreasonable, how feeble, to wish that K. had settled the problem for me.

'Don't you want us to live together?' I exclaimed. I meant: have you no feeling for us as a family? No single impulse to make us safe?

'I knew we should come to that! And mark you, *I* didn't ask you to leave the boy and betake yourself to London. You did it entirely to please yourself. Don't try to blame me.'

I was only too ready to think everything my fault. When he had gone, leaving me in Regent Street, I reflected that, though I disliked my life in London, I had no great wish to live with K. To tell the truth, I thought, angrily, you don't know what you want or what to do next . . . I felt demoralized and incompetent. I did not believe in my talents as an advertiser—still less, as a novelist. The only person wholly important to me was my son, and I had left him to a Miss Geeson.

The cold night air sent a ball of blood to press at the roots of my brain. I walked home in a state near insanity. There seemed no way out of the confusion. The idea of going back to Whitby, a penniless failure, was intolerable.

I have failed at everything, I thought.

In May I took a night train to Whitby. Travelling both ways at night, I could spend two days with him in my mother's house, and be at my desk, heavy-eyed, on Monday morning.

Walking out to Ruswarp to fetch him, I prepared myself for everything but the shock of hearing his voice. He had not been warned I was coming: he was in the garden, hidden from me by the hedge, when I rang the bell.

In a high clear thin voice he called out, 'Is that my mother?'

He has been learning to talk without me, I thought.

We spent the day on the sands. Light-headed with happiness, I forgot that he had not had the practice in climbing of three other children, and brought him back up the face of the cliff. For most of the way it was easy enough, only the last ten or fifteen yards suddenly became steep, hard slippery clay. Here his feet slid under him and he looked up at me quickly in fear. Hiding my panic, I said, 'You're all right, son—use your hands and knees.'

He reached the top without help, and stood smiling.

Love crossed with pride gives birth to the most surprising sensation, of a sail furling and unfurling in the pit of the stomach.

When I took him back to Miss Geeson on Sunday evening he did not ask any questions—Are you going? When will you come back? I put him to bed, and waited until he fell asleep, one arm flung out, long dark thick lashes feathering his cheeks.

'Do you ever feel sorry you went away?' my mother asked.

'Something had to be done,' I said.

To this day, if I am incautious enough to go near her, the young woman I buried alive claws me.

Some short time after this, I told Mr Shaw-Thomas that I could not go on working for four pounds a week.

'Why do you want more money?' he asked kindly.

Without reflecting, I knew that it would be a mistake to say: Because I am always a little hungry, and because my son is growing out of his sandals and cotton smocks. I smiled at him.

'How can I hope to buy a new coat on four pounds?'

'Very well,' he said, 'we'll make it six. But you must give your whole mind to the job. You're not writing another novel, by any chance?'

'No.'

How easy it is to exaggerate. The habitual state of my mind when I am not working is one of happiness, or at least detachment. That year there were days, of superb weather, when it amused me to dawdle about London. My best moments were those I wasted daydreaming. That I was famous, that I had written a masterpiece, or become a rich implacably clever business woman, or—equally consoling, and not a whit more absurd—that I had saved the life of a royal personage and been rewarded with a sinecure: better, the life of the director of the Ritz, who gave me two modest rooms looking across the Park, and the run of my teeth, for life.

Or I thought, less often now, of the Texan. The details of the scene in the Piccadilly Hotel, which had taken only a few minutes, lasted me through an entire evening spent under the trees of the Green Park, or walking slowly the length of Oxford Street, Regent Street, Piccadilly, St James's Street, the Mall, Constitution Hill, and Park Lane, dust everywhere, and the splintered voices and eyes of passers-by. I felt light and feverish, and deliciously free. Since I was not with him, I could give way safely to any delirium of my senses: the coolness, the vanity, needed to defeat him, were not needed.

It is when I recall the image of another person, or a place, that they give up to me the pleasure, even the ecstasy, missing at the time.

But there were moments that I really did see, did feel. I remember an evening in July when, walking across Trafalgar Square, I saw the pillars of St Martin-in-the-Fields as white as bones under a brilliantly blue sky; a sickle moon hung in it, and every object in sight, the edges of buildings, the fountains, Admiralty Arch, the pigeons, sprang out as clear as light. And there were innocent mornings when, even if the night before, in bed, alone, I had cried scalding tears, I woke certain that happiness was within reach of my outstretched hand.

The triumphs allowed the old are less insensate, less poignant, less ravishing.

Chapter 32

The image for my life in the years between 1919 and the end of 1923 is that of a vacant lot between crowded streets. I worked, idled, was poor, earned money, spent it recklessly, schemed, confided in no one, wasted time and strength, ignored opportunities—behaved, in short, with the utmost folly, while seeming to be responsible, reliable, intelligent. But give an account of it—impossible.

In contrast, my memory of the three days J. spent in London in the summer of 1919 is sharply clear.

He had not changed, voice, quick supple movements, energy. I felt all the happiness of coming, half-frozen, into a room alive with warmth and light. A gaiety I had forgotten—yet it was mine, natural to me—filled me: I had to use all my strength to speak in a cool voice. I forget where we dined; I forget at what point in a story he was telling me he broke off, and said, 'How long will it take you to get divorced in this country? A month? This is my last leave, I must go home and get myself demobilized. I don't want to have to wait when I come back for you. Your taste in husbands . . . couldn't you have found something else to keep you busy?'

Exasperated vanity must have had a great deal to do with his decision to marry a young woman with so few of the qualities he admired. He expected only legal delays. It did not cross his mind that I might find it no easier to be his wife than his mistress. As I always do when I am at a loss, I began an argument a little to the side.

He remained good-humoured. 'Don't you want to marry me and go live in a real country? This one's finished. Europe is finished. I'll say this for you that, without the war, you might have held out against us for another twenty years. But you've nothing left.'

His grotesque arrogance amused me. It was at least thirty years before I realized the crude truth in his boasts. (If this makes me seem to have been half-witted, reflect that only fifteen years before 1919 English imperialism had been at its glorious zenith. Merciful heavens, was there ever so rapid a descent!)

'I couldn't live in America.'

'Why not?'

'I would rather be poor and unsafe in this country than well off in yours.'

I said this thinking of my own poverty and uncertainty. But it was true. And had no relevance to what I felt. The thought of marrying him entered my head only to be ejected at once. I had no need even to hesitate. Put to it, I could have given reasons, excellent ones. The queerest thing about my destructive passion is that it was not blind. Or not more than half blind, half the dupe of my senses. I knew, I always knew, that there was no dignity in my obsession. In cold moments I saw him as any of my hard-minded upright forbears would have seen him.

The part of me neither blind nor duped judged him with shocking lucidity. The other part, the egotistical, ribald, unreliable, nihilistic part was wholly on his side. Had I been childless I might have gone off with him. It is possible. But I doubt it. I doubt whether any Gallilee woman could have brought herself to marry an ungovernable foreigner.

But what had reason to do with it? Devilish little. I discovered reasons for rejecting him after I had done it. At the bottom of every gentle or violent feeling I had for him, below lust, greed, liking, was quite simply fear. Not a physical fear—something older and harder. Fear is the wrong word. Why—unless our bodies are a great deal more intelligent than we give them credit for—should it have been my senses, obsessed with him, that warned me?

It occurs to me, but only now, that in rejecting him I rejected, once for all, my violent self. Not that this freed me of it. Good heavens, no.

At some moment in an argument that went on during three evenings, I said,

'The whole thing is impossible. You forget Bill.'

'I do not. We'd take him with us—of course.'

The bare notion of involving my child in so unpredictable a life put it beyond conjecture. This was so clear that I had the calmness to shrug my shoulders, and—in bad faith, since it was irrelevant— say that K. was vindictive enough to try to keep him.

'We won't talk about K. You'll have other children. D'you think I don't want sons?'

Heaven knows where my revulsion came from—some dry bodily pride, nothing to do with my reason.

'I'm sure you do,' I said drily. 'Americans have all the right sentiments.'

Thinking about it, I see, with a little astonishment, that during the whole of that brief time he behaved with great self-control, even kindness. Not until he was leaving did he put his arms round me. 'Why,' he said, 'must you give us both so much trouble? You're mine and you know it. When you decide to have me I'm yours, and I never told you lies—except about other people to amuse you. You don't want to be half dead for the rest of your life, do you?'

I thought that I was on the point of fainting. But I laughed.

How absurd this will seem to young women who fall into bed with a lover as simply as into a hot bath. And I am very willing to believe that the sensible (enlightened, free) young women of 1960 are wiser than I was. But not that they are the happier for behaving like commercial travellers with no time to waste between sales. With fewer unnecessary scruples, less naïveté, less tortuous minds, their lives may be simpler. But less boring? I doubt it. There is nothing like imagination for reducing the risks of boredom in a love-affair.

After he had gone back to France, my scepticism made me think it unlikely he wanted a wife. It must surely have been a mood. Then, a few weeks later, I had a letter from Texas, from his father, a kind polite simple letter, telling me that if I cared to come over at once I should be welcome in his house.

This surprised and pleased me, but did not change my mind. Given a second chance, I should have behaved with precisely the same stubbornness.

I knew it. I knew, too, that the fever would burn itself out. There are no incurable fevers. Oh, well, one.

During the next year he wrote a score of times, from China, South America, Texas, admirable letters, written in an idiom as sharp, lively and common as Elizabethan English, only now and then boastful. I answered some of them and destroyed all. In one he used a phrase—'the cleverest woman I ever owned'—that made me smile. Owned?

It was true in a sense.

Chapter 33

This year (1919) I made a woman friend, the first since I left Leeds.

Someone, possibly Sydney Harland, wrote to me that one of our group at Kings, an Eikonoklast, was living in London in St John's Wood, married to a sister of the writer Stephen Graham: he had sent him my address. I was a little vexed. John Gleeson had not been a close friend: he was a medical student, an extremely ugly young man, lean, sallow, myopic—his eyes behind the thickest of lenses were like sea anemones—and a mystifier, always inventing stories about himself which amused us mildly and were, perhaps, now and then true. I had no wish to see him again.

When his letter came I delayed an indecent time, then, reluctantly, went. His wife opened the door of the flat, and said smiling,

'It's Margaret, isn't it? Come in.'

I walked straight into an intimacy which fitted me like a comfortable old glove . . . With my few close friends, it is always the same, no slow prudent growths, friendship at first sight. It is the only likeness between them.

She opened the door of the living-room. 'But what an enormous place,' I said, too horrified by the disorder, the eccentric poverty, the dust thick everywhere, on table, shelves, sofa, chairs, to hold my tongue.

Knowing perfectly well what I was thinking, Elizabeth only smiled.

We drank tea, and I learned that John was not practising as a doctor. When they had no money at all, he would answer an appeal for a locum, and pick up enough money to keep them alive for a few months. For the rest, he was writing stories, so grotesquely bad that again I was silenced. If he is as inept a doctor as a writer, I thought, he had better stick to writing.

They had a baby, a few months old, unbelievably sweet-tempered, who submitted placidly to being fastened in her bed in an empty room when they wanted to go out without her.

Elizabeth herself—ah, Elizabeth. She was not beautiful, her face was too long, her features, except for the eyes, too masculine, a wide sensual mouth, pale, its skin slightly rough, a strong nose: her eyes were long, narrow, a greenish grey and extraordinarily bright, their glance the flick through water of a fin: her hair, the colour of a brown fox, fell naturally into waves too coarse and heavy to be held by any comb. She was not intelligent—a certain quickness of under-standing—the mind of a lively adolescent, but with reserves. The brilliant trivialities littering it distracted attention, even her own, from these reserves: she must have glanced into them as seldom as possible, for fear of finding there nothing reassuring—or nothing.

She was charming. Her charm was a sixth sense; she used it as a violinist his bow, without vanity, to give pleasure, and because it was what she could do better than anything else in the world. Without vanity . . . her certainty that she was charming might look like vanity, but was not—unless the sun rises or a nightingale sings out of vanity. Gaiety, a childishly natural gaiety and wit, rippled through her like light through a wave—in her smiling mouth a small jest became high comedy. And warmth—she was a fountain of warmth.

I thought their baby neglected—she crawled about the unswept floor, pushing fluff and fragments of coal into her mouth—but the warmth, in those days, covered her, too. One day when I came in with Elizabeth we heard her crying as we opened the door: in spite of the straps, she had managed to kick the blankets off her bed, she was cold and hungry. The instant her mother spoke to her, her cries ceased and she began laughing.

I am profoundly incurious about my friends' emotional habits and disorders. It ought to have struck me as strange that she had chosen to marry a penniless, eccentric, ugly man. I don't think it did for a moment.

She seemed radiantly happy. If she grumbled sometimes that John refused to do any steady work, it was lightly, with an amused smile, as she might have smiled at a child's clowning.

In the meantime she did not try to lead a good bourgeois life. She had not been used to cleaning or mending or cooking—therefore she did not clean, or mend, and cooked as rarely as possible.

The flat was large, much larger than they needed. After I had been visiting them for a week or two, they offered me one of the unused rooms—it held a bed, a chest of drawers, a cupboard and a glass dangling crookedly from a nail. It was ridiculous, they argued passionately, for me to pay a landlady when I could have a room for nothing. This last tempted me. On condition that I paid something into Elizabeth's famished purse, if no more than would cover the cost of my breakfast coffee, I agreed to come.

I hate disorder, and that flat really was squalid, but I lived in it for—how long? a year?—in exquisite ease of mind and heart.

I say nothing of body. John's indifferences to illness in his family —I now being part of it—was prodigious. One day, after I had been running about London in shoes that let the rain in, a pain started in my side, and after a few days I could not laugh or draw a quick breath without groaning. At the end of a week of this, I came back to the office from lunch to find that I could not climb the several flights of stairs, the pain was so frightful. A little alarmed, I got myself, on foot and by bus, to a woman doctor in the Harley Street quarter whose name I had picked up somewhere. Dr Aldrich-Blake was, though I did not know it, one of the great women doctors, and must have been mildly surprised to see me, ill and ill-dressed. She treated me with enormous kindness and gentleness, and diagnosed an inflammation of the gall bladder. I had a raging temperature. When I told her I was living in a doctor's household, she said drily,

'A male doctor, I suppose. Well—' writing quickly—'give him this when you get home. And take a cab.'

'What do I owe you?' I asked.

'Nothing.' She smiled. 'Since another doctor will, I hope, be looking after you.'

I spent a week in bed, looked after with loving inefficiency by Elizabeth—and recovered completely.

Chapter 34

The day when I cease expecting, slyly, to be saved from despair by some insignificant little miracle, I shall be really finished. By the summer of 1919, the miracle was overdue.

It astonishes me now that I kept my place in the Carlton Agency: more than half my energy and intellect was running to waste, dragging furiously against the other half—furiously and blindly. I was more discontented with myself than ever.

What would have become of me if it had not been for the *New Commonwealth*, that shortlived and hare-brained enterprise?

Some time in the early autumn, I had a letter from an F. Thoresby: the address was of a reputable city firm, and his name appeared among those of its directors. But for this I might, with the scepticism praise of my writing always starts in me, have thrown his letter away. He had read *The Pot Boils*, he said, it had impressed him, he would very much like to discuss it with me, if I would have the great kindness to lunch with him, at Romano's . . . I was ready to endure anything, even the boredom of talking about my novel, for the sake of a meal.

He turned out to be a not too elderly man, stout, friendly, evidently solid and respectable, and not a noodle. He talked less about my book than I had feared, and more, much more, about himself. This I could deal with: I had only to bring on my face an expression of alert attention and leave it there while I ate everything I was offered, like a starved boa-constrictor.

Besides, I enjoy listening to people talking about themselves as much as I detest being asked about myself.

After a time he surprised me into lively curiosity. He was, he said, about to retire, and had bought an old-established weekly paper, the *Christian Commonwealth*: he had plans for turning it, re-named the *New Commonwealth*, into a mouthpiece for his views. About these, although he went into them at great length, I remained uncertain. I imagine, now, that they were a form of *Poujadisme* before Poujade, but with more heart, an honest business man's vision of a society run on the lines of a good firm, reasonably generous to its workers. Neither then nor later did I take them seriously. In any event, he changed his views fairly often—and without noticing it.

He told me, too, that he was a theosophist. I had never heard of theosophy: I hid my ignorance, and afterwards looked it up in a public library. Like his politics, it seemed odd but harmless.

Throughout this long explanation I was waiting, without specu-lation, to hear what it had to do with me. Nothing very much, I thought. I was all the more startled—I took care not to show it—when he asked me to think over the idea of sub-editing his paper: he himself would edit it, and he needed, he said, a young sub-editor, whose mind was not cluttered up with rubbish.

Lucky you can't see my mind, I thought. I felt much less respect for him now that I knew I had impressed him with my—what? intelligence? competence? malleability?

He startled me again, by offering a salary of fifty pounds a month. At the same time he asked, smiling gently, for the year and hour of my birth, so that he could have his astrologer cast my horoscope. Later, he showed me five folio pages of incomprehensible jargon, of which I recall a single sentence: The nearer the goat the nearer the god. This struck me as unpleasant. Luckily, it did not seem to alarm him.

All this makes it seem incredible that he was a successful man of business, and not mad. In fact, he had been very successful, in a discreet way. Theosophy and astrology were an escape valve for a romanticism, a warmth of heart, an idealism, he could not use in business.

I hesitated over his offer. Not because I knew nothing about a sub-editor's duties—if he had raked London he could not have found a greater dunce. It struck my Gallilee shrewdness as unsafe. But fifty pounds a month!

In the end I told Mr Foxe about it, and asked his advice. He refused to advise me.

'You must decide for yourself. And I know what you will decide.'

'Well, then, tell me.'

'No. But I'll write it down, and when you tell me what you've done I'll show you what I've written.'

He scribbled a few words on a memorandum sheet, folded it into an envelope, sealed it, made me press my thumb on the wax, and put the envelope at the back of his desk. Two weeks later I told him I had accepted.

He looked at me with a sharp smile. 'I was wrong.'

Opening the envelope, I read: Out of female loyalty, you will stay with Shaw-Thomas.

I burst out laughing. 'Perhaps I am less of a female than you think.'

The office of the renamed *New Commonwealth* was the top floor of a lean decrepit house in a square behind Fleet Street. The square itself was old and shabby, not a house in it but was on its deathbed. A narrow street, infested with lorries, led from one corner to the printers', and beyond that to the river. The floors of our two rooms sank deeply in the centre, so that chairs slid inward, and desks had to be stoutly wedged.

The middle-aged gentlewoman who had been a prop of the paper in its Christian era stayed on. It must have been galling to her to have an unlicked young woman set over her. I did not then realize what self-control, what patience, what desperate civility, she exercised. Whether out of good manners or despair, she did not teach me anything. The paper's printers did that. I was always behind time, and Mr Thoresby's habit of rewriting his editorial at the last minute—having changed his policy since the day before—did not help. On press nights I was at the printers' until two or three in the morning, reading pages as they came off the machines. A savage lighting painted the men's faces fish-belly white, and the clattering steel fingers unpicked the seams of my brain.

One night, when he brought me the ritual cup of deathly strong tea, a compositor suggested gently that there are less dull ways of making up a weekly review than by running articles straight on, three columns to a page, without changing type or lay-out. It had not occurred to me.

I thanked him, and thereafter produced a paper which looked a little less like a parish magazine.

At the end of these night sessions I walked home, from Fleet Street to St Johns Wood, through blessedly empty streets—tubes and buses had stopped, and I could not afford a cab. Besides, I enjoyed the walk. It was the only hour of the twenty-four when London became human, when a clock striking in the city could be heard as clearly as if the sound travelled over fields and villages, when an air from the sea, or a ship's whistle, reminded me, inno-. cently, of another life than this in which I made only mistakes.

I wrote a great deal of the paper myself: dramatic criticism, political notes, reviews, brief essays—all, except the first, with a lighthearted indifference to principles. Until the day when, between one minute and the next, I ran head on into a social conscience, into a passion, sudden and lasting.

I forget which newspaper I had bought to read over lunch: all I recall about it is the language it used to dismiss, as snivelling and a lie, the story (in another paper) of German and Austrian children dying of hunger. I did not know the facts, but the smell of hypocrisy and bad faith given off by the phrases themselves stank to heaven.

In those days we were almost innocent. Even the war, even the millions of young deaths, had not accustomed us to cruelty. The enemies this rancorous editorial wanted me to punish by starving them were infants, and I disliked the idea of an hereditary enemy with tiny stick-like arms and a swollen stomach.

For the first time in my life I had the sense, horribly familiar later, of a dark wave of pain, cruelty, fear, gathering force at the other side of Europe and about to rush down.

After this, no issue of the *New Commonwealth* lacked its paragraph —at least a paragraph—about Europe's famished children. Discovering the commonest of tricks for calling attention to an item of news by printing it inside a rectangular frame, I used it every week . . .

About this time we heard—John heard—that one of our King's College friends, a fellow Eikonoklast, was in a London hospital being treated for the cancer that had started in him at the end of the war. We went to see him, I with reluctance.

Red Smith—nicknamed for his romantic anarchism—was the youngest of us: he was very fair, with a childishly snub nose and clear blue eyes. Lying in bed in a small room, he greeted us with an indifference so unlike him that, although I did not know he was dying, I had the sense that he had half turned his back. He and I had shared a passion for *La Révolte des Anges,* and I remembered—I had never thought of it since that year—Nectaire's long account of himself and the other fallen angels as tutelary gods of Greece and Italy and their decline through the centuries to this moment when he was making a living as a gardener in a wood near Paris. It was all false, all nonsense, and a delicious sense of freshness, of marble gleaming in the sun, of the Mediterranean miracle of light, rose from it, intoxicating us both.

I was afraid to ask him if he remembered it. What could it mean to him in this bare little room, with the bed, the two chairs, the window facing a blank dark wall? His eyelids kept closing, and when he lifted them there was only an emptiness under them, shallow, clouded. I did not realize that he was drugged.

Suddenly he stretched a hand out and took hold of one of mine. Like any ignorant old countrywoman I believed that cancer is infectious. It was an effort to let my hand lie quietly in his. It lay there for the rest of the time, twenty or thirty minutes, that we stayed with him. I had to free it from his grasp when we left.

He mumbled a few words I did not catch.

'Goodbye, my dear, we'll come to see you again on Saturday,' I said.

It was not necessary to go again.

Early in life a death closes one door in an endless corridor of doors, all open. For a few minutes I thought about him, then left him, behind his shut door.

La nuit tout entière entendit la flûte de Nectaire . . .

Chapter 35

That year, 1920, my second novel was published—by Heinemann. Michael Sadleir had not liked it when I sent him the manuscript, and with all the indifference in the world I took it away from him. Nothing I could have done to it would have satisfied him, and the idea of throwing it away vexed my Yorkshire soul.

This book had two readers I know of—one of them John Galsworthy. Charles Evans of Heinemann sent it to him, and showed me his letter. 'I've finished *The Happy Highways*, and congratulate you on your choice. This authoress has done what none of the other torrential novelists of the last ten years has achieved—given us a convincing (if not picture, at least) summary of the effervescence, discontent, revolt, and unrest of youth; the heartache and beating of wings. I should like to meet her. She must have seen and felt things . . . To an old-fashioned brute like me, of course, the lack of form and line and the plethora of talk and philosophy pass a little stubbornly down the throat and stick a little in the gizzard, but the stuff is undeniable, and does not give me the hollow windy feeling I get from a German novel—say: nor do I feel suffocated by the crude ego that stalks through most of their novels.'

'I don't think we can ask him to let us quote it, do you?' Charles Evans said.

'Good heavens, no,' I said, shocked.

'I thought you would feel that.'

How innocent we both were. Today if I write a personal letter to a young writer who has sent me his book, I know perfectly well that he, and his publisher, will be outraged if I do not allow them to make use of it.

The second reader was in prison. One day my eye caught a newspaper item: a young American poet, Ralph Chaplin, condemned to a long term of years in the Federal Prison of Fort Leavenworth,

Kansas, as a pacifist, had chosen an English novel, *The Happy Highways*, to take with him. Astonished—surely he should have something weightier?—and delighted, I wrote offering to send him books, and made a friend I never saw.

My conviction that novel-writing is no profession for a serious-minded pauper did not lessen.

I did not expect Michael to be angry with me for leaving his firm, nor was he. He was critical of me, an ugly duckling who never properly became a swan, and kind and sweet-tempered and loyal.

'Promise me on your honour that you will never put me in a novel,' he said once. I promised—and kept my promise.

Indeed, I knew too much and too little about him to draw his portrait. Like me, but without my violence and crudity, he was a flawed rebel. His mother came from a family of rich wool people, originally Quakers—not, I think, like my father-in-law, Evangelicals, but there was a certain Puritan rigidity, a strictness, which set its mark on him: he rebelled against it, but without conviction. Some—I have no idea what—feeling of disappointment, some failure or desertion of an original purpose (I am writing in the dark), remained in him, a grain of sand which grew smaller and smaller, but never disappeared. His good looks—he was extremely good-looking—had the softness enclosing a hard core which is noticeable in the portraits of certain priests. He was romantic and shrewd.

His young wife was an enchanting creature. Only the other day, when, after an interval of many years, she came to see me, I realized that her enduring quality is a simplicity in which there is nothing childish—although her smile still has the gaiety and irony, involuntary and guileless, of a very young child's. It is the simplicity of a heart without a single tortuous or calculating impulse.

A streak of worldly corruption in me, rising to the surface again and again, forced me, in those days, to covet an elegance to which, on another level, I am deeply indifferent. One year Betty Sadleir designed and made knitted dresses to sell to her friends. Because I should have liked to be a young woman who could afford it, I bought one. No sooner had I carried it away than I knew I had been a fool—I ought not to have spent the money. The dress did not even suit me.

I cried with grief, rage, shame. I could better have spared an ear than five guineas.

It seems to me that I have only to stretch a hand out to touch this young woman in her cold room, crying over a wasted five guineas tears which very quickly became tears for an infinitely heavier loss and error—also her own fault.

Nothing could be more ridiculous than this.

Chapter 36

Michael took me to what, only half joking, he called 'your baptism into the literary world.' It was not his fault that I am incapable of being sanctified by rose-water.

Naomi Royde-Smith was a power in what I now see to have been a soberly decent Establishment. She was editing, with tact and judgement, the *Saturday Westminster*, and had made it a forum for any talented writer—even, in Walter de la Mare, for genius—except the unpredictably new or eccentric. On Thursday evenings her drawing-room in Queen's Gate might hold as many as fifty or sixty people, friends and protégés, and protégés of friends, who came to talk to her and each other. Was there coffee? I cannot remember. Cocktails, which have murdered conversation, were not yet the rule. It was not a clique, not a restricted circle of close friends, not brilliantly intellectual. None of the currents setting towards the future troubled this urbane backwater. I could not have learned there that the world of 1913 was shrivelled and in ruins, like the forms of Georgian poetry. The great figures who sometimes glided through were none of them rebels—Arnold Bennett but not D. H. Lawrence, Eddie Marsh, not T. S. Eliot, not even a young Raymond Mortimer. No cold gusty breath ruffled this placid trough between two waves. It vanished, leaving no ripple.

Naomi I found a little formidable with her air of a younger more affable Queen Victoria. But Rose Macaulay, who shared the flat with her, had been kind on my first evening, and I had no fear of her, nor of her salty tongue. She was enchanting to watch, a narrow head covered with small curls, like a Greek head in a museum, with that way she had of speaking in arpeggios, and the lively hands, the small arched nose and pale deep-set eyes.

For the next twenty years I saw her in this way, unchanged. Then, in 1941, Arthur Koestler came up to me at a writers' conference and said with smiling energy, 'I've been talking to Rose Macaulay. But what a charming delightful old lady.' I felt a stupefying dismay, as if, walking behind her along a street, I had seen her swallowed up by a crack opening in the ground.

One Thursday evening, I watched her with Arnold Bennett. He hung over her, mouth slightly open, like a great fish mesmerized by the flickering tongue of a water-snake.

Another of these evenings remains in my mind almost intact, because it ended in my disgrace. The room, more crowded than usual, was frightfully hot. I cannot endure hot rooms. I stood about, with a false air of ease, wishing I had not come. Three or four young men and women—not many of Naomi's friends were young—discussed hotly the correct behaviour to be followed by a young wife whose husband, a poet, had brought his mistress into the family: they were very emphatic that she must not be jealous or give way to a narrow-minded respect for convention. They did not ask my opinion, and I doubt I should have been courageous enough to say that I thought their new orthodoxy no better or wiser than the old.

Suddenly, Naomi called me to sit, with two or three other people, beside a very well-known critic and patron of young writers. She meant it kindly, and I was thrown into an agony of diffidence. I could not have said a word to save my neck. I listened. When I listen blankly, like an idiot, what I hear is less the spoken words than the sense of the brain behind them, even its nature. Usually I am prudent enough to keep my impressions—which may be distorted by the medium—to myself.

I was leaving when Naomi asked me, 'Well, how did you get on with E.? If you have anything you would like him to read, let me have it.'

Startled by the idea, I lost my head completely, and said,

'Oh, I don't think he is interested in young women.'

Her friendly smile vanished. In a voice whose coldness terrified me, she said,

'Don't repeat foolish lying gossip.'

I fled—and lay awake half the night asking myself why the devil this innocent remark had brought such a rebuke on me. Unspeakably mortified, I wanted to hide, to run back to Whitby. I can endure, I told myself, the Yorkshire habit of rudeness and derision, but I can't endure *these* people, *la canaille littéraire*.

When, after several weeks, I dared show my face there again, she had forgotten my crime, and complained, smiling, of my neglect.

'Rose calls you a most likeable child. I doubt whether you're either likeable or a child, in spite of your voice.'

Those Thursday evenings should have cured me of going into company. When I got back to my room my mind was in a frightful disorder: fragments of it had been left lying on the floor of overheated drawingrooms and in the limp hands of strangers; I had talked to a dozen people and said nothing that was not dull or indiscreet or at best meaningless: I had agreed eagerly with comments that aroused only hostility or derision in me, and made promises it would destroy me to keep. I was trembling with self-disgust. And there was nothing I could do about it—except turn the light off and sleep. Five hours of not-thinking, not-planning, not-regretting.

14th of January, 1962

Yesterday I was in Cambridge. Sun and ice-cold air, bare branches drawn with Indian ink on a cloudless sky, a light like brittle glass, the Granta running full and fast, and every college along its banks as white, sharp, radiant, as if new: a day of celestial energy, given once every hundred years. The evening before I had listened to arguments tossed between four or five enormously intelligent people, and had realized, suddenly, that I was not afraid of them. Remoteness had taken the place of diffidence and my instinctive fear of punishment.

It is because I am old, I thought, and because, when I dream *deeply*, it is of the young dead . . .

In 1920 I was still weaving blindly the pattern of my future. The dichotomy in my mind—it goes deeper, but the larger word frets me —was there to be seen, if I had had eyes to see it: the instinct to withdraw completely, and the desire to live a flashing life in the world.

How far back in the darkness must I force my way, to meet the self whose need was poverty, simplicity, solitude, freedom from possessions, and who was betrayed—oh, another of those large words—by the self hungry for a way of living which rests on money and power?

Come to that, they betrayed each other. In the part of the world I come from, we have a cruel saying: Let want be your master. My wants were completely irreconcilable, enemies of each other and me. In those days I ran about my life like a dog chasing a yellow leaf down a path, turning to chase another, and another. My busily wasteful days ended, not seldom, in useless tears.

There are plenty of people who can go into the world and take part in conversations and the business of a career without losing touch with themselves. Too late, I see that I am not one of them, I was only fit to live alone, in society I am worthless.

Chapter 37

Out of a lifetime of receiving and writing a monstrous sum of letters, say, a hundred thousand, I have kept only a few—fifty, a hundred? (Apart from those tied together at the bottom of a deed-box, which, when a time comes, I shall destroy.) Kept for various reasons—not always for what they contained: the ones I tore up were often infinitely more important, that is, indiscreet, revealing, interesting—I re-read them with reluctance. The person I am afraid of meeting in them is not the writer of the letter, but myself—quite possibly, a self I no longer know anything about.

One evening at Naomi's I talked, for a long time, to Frank Swinnerton. The only thing I recall is his light smiling voice: 'You know, I don't regard myself as a writer at all!' But this letter from him, written, in 1937, to thank me for something, says: 'Well, I have always been fond of you from the evening when we first met at a funny party given by Rose Macaulay or N. Royde-Smith, and I was moved to the heart by your sympathy over our baby. I know that although we don't agree about some things it doesn't in the least matter; and you *are* my friend, and dear to me, though (as is the case with most of my true friends) we don't meet . . .'

Why not admit that the person I should like to catch sight of in this letter is not Frank Swinnerton but an unrecognizable young woman? Damn it all, this must have been a half-hour of reality in a desert of pretence, waste of time, inexistence. And I must, for once, have been talking with no impulse to protect myself. And the whole thing has gone—vanished—sunk.

Here are ten letters from Walter de la Mare, beginning in 1921, and in three of them, written twenty, thirty, years later, he describes the same incident of that year. 'Not so very long ago—to all seeming —I was sitting on the top of a tram with you, ascending, not Parnassus, but Sydenham Hill, en route for the Crystal Palace station one Sunday night—and you weren't wearing a hat.'

No doubt because my hat was agonizing on its deathbed.

I did not go often enough to 14 Thornsett Road, in South London, where he was living then, not so often as I might have gone—afraid of outwearing my welcome. A quiet street—its trees, lilac and laburnum, make signs to me from a yet more distant past—of houses with modest gardens at the back. The lunch, on summer Sundays, was always the same, cold beef, and an opulently fresh fruit salad in a wide deep bowl. There were four children; the eldest, Florence, was a thin graceful creature, who drew well. I have kept one image of their mother—she was nicknamed Friday—standing at the foot of the staircase with a smile of great sweetness on her colourless face: she seemed to me older than her husband—but was she? *Bonne ménagère*, as she needed to be, with two daughters and two schoolboy sons to feed, clothe, educate, and not a great deal of money. I should have liked to know better the younger girl, darker, silent, with—or did I imagine it?—a faint shadow of defiance across her face.

Walter de la Mare was only half a creature of the human world. What other he lived in, with that serenity, that air of looking steadily outward, into infinite space, I have no idea: it would be silly to speculate. Very young children have this same open remote glance, but there was nothing of the child in him. He was more adult, more unshakably himself, than any merely practical man.

He talked—I hear him—rapidly and lightly, with a detached curiosity about everything except people: if by chance he had to talk about a man or woman it was the lightest possible touch, without a flicker of malice. This was not because he was kind or a saint, but from a fathomless indifference to personalities. He saw everything, from the nearly imperceptible fold at the corner of an eye to the smallest wrinkle in a leaf or frost-tipped point of grass, and each of these tiny marks was one letter of a language he never stopped trying to read: his mind was too engaged in this effort to have time to be malicious, or bored or impolite. It had the quickness, the gaiety, of a young wild animal and the wisdom of—but I don't know of what. Certainly not of this world. He was in every sense—except in the sense of being rash, eccentric, extravagant—unworldly.

Some time in 1921 I wrote my essay on him for the English Review. It must have been printed a little later, in 1922: I have not the slightest recollection of it, and neither patience nor the courage to look it up anywhere, it is so improbable that it was better than superficial. But that it pleased and amused him I know from a long letter he wrote on the 27th of December, 1921.

'. . . it really is rather queer that in the first few pages of your paper you should have attacked the one problem that has been puzzling and fascinating me for months past. What *being* have imagined characters and places? I can distinguish no essential difference between them and the so-called real, except a partial uncorroboratibleness [that extraordinary word, like others he invented in talking, had too many flying meanings]. Only partial, too, for Heathcliffe and Tess etc etc are mine now too. How can we find out; and what line shall we take? The odd thing is that the very instant such beings insinuate themselves (or arise) in "the imagination" they are as whole, infinitely explorable, pervasive and enduring as, say, Mr Janner or Miss Mule who may actually come to tea tomorrow afternoon. Indeed I rather fancy the prototypes of this real lady and gentleman may appear soon, some day—in a story! How Master Harrison can find the mind to suggest cutting this beginning out— well, I have never been an editor . . . Didn't I once tell you that you daunted me when we met at the J.D. [Beresford]'s? I thought you were an intellectual. And you are, of course. But then I didn't know there were different kinds. This is dreadful if you would prefer to be kind A. Do come and see us again soon, and tell me whether you really understand this misunderstanding. Friday sends her love . . . and I'm sending you a belated copy of *The Veil*. It was meant to come at Christmas; and now it will come at New Year. How strangely frigid and uninviting these portals always are . . .'

If he were alive now, I would ask him what happens to the selves we abandon in houses. Some of these must be at least as vigorous and enduring as the characters we imagine. I cannot believe that the house in Thornsett Road, Anerley, and the small garden behind it, have lost all touch with him or with them.

Places he lived in later would draw him less stubbornly. (When I went to see him in the larger house near Taplow, he complained, smiling, that he and Friday had been left alone in it. Had he expected that his children were, as he was, immune to time?) And, just as, so long as I am alive, he stands smiling and talking on a rectangle of grass in sunlight, so while he lived I was a hatless young woman on the top of an open tram at night.

Night, tram, poet, blown hair—the emotion stored in them must exist somewhere. But where? Frivolous speculations, of the sort he liked juggling with, infinitely saner than the Faustian speculations of nuclear scientists.

I have known two or three indisputably great men. Diffidence, the fear of boring, of not being equal to their scrutiny, the pressures of life, a broad streak of indolence, kept me from seeing them oftener, knowing them much better. I regret it sharply—but at least I have touched greatness with a finger. Say what you like, it adds a savour to life.

Chapter 38

I cannot remember when K. was demobilized—I think late in 1920— nor where we lived: we had two rooms somewhere in north-west London, but where? Elizabeth and John had left London. Defeated by lack of money and Elizabeth's smiling refusal to lift a finger to make their poverty bearable, John had found a practice in a poor quarter of Portsmouth, where he kept hundreds of half-crowns in a large drawer in his consulting room. I missed Elizabeth, the one person with whom I felt completely safe and happy.

So much had happened to me since K. went to Canterbury, leaving me to shark for myself and Bill, that I imagined I was safe from being harmed by him.

What could he possibly say or do to me now—now that I had had two books published, and visited houses where no one knew anything about me before the moment when they saw me coming in behind my warm lying smile? I even felt ahead of him in worldly sense. If, without a word to me, he had left the country, I should have felt little except relief from a burden. But here he was, my husband, with the rights of a husband, and I still too much attached to him to wish him gone.

That is not true. I often wished him gone.

But I have an unlucky talent for clinging to what I once had, a frightful moral inertia, the other side of my restlessness. Or another self, a coward, unwilling to lose all she has invested in the past. And a little afraid to be alone.

There was also the part of gentleness, but how, at this distance, can I measure it?

He had his gratuity, and felt he could take his time about finding work. He did not want to leave London again. Nor—though I talked of living in a cottage and writing novels to supplement K.'s income as a schoolmaster—did I. I believed so little in my future as a novelist.

He had friends in what Michael Sadleir called 'the third-rate Fleet Street set,' and spent part of every day with them. It distracted him from his mortification, when he applied for posts in London schools, at being told politely that he had stayed in the Air Force too long; immediately after the war he could have had a dozen jobs, now there were younger men available, to be had cheaper.

As the months passed, his gratuity dwindling all the time, he became discouraged. From one of these interviews he came into my room with tears in his eyes.

'I'm the most miserable man in London, a useless failure. I shall never get a job, I'm not wanted. I ought to shoot myself.'

My mind is at its nimblest and most astigmatic, not to say insane, when it is making plans. The plan it produced, some time in March or April 1921, for saving K. and restoring his self-respect was no madder than others I have succumbed to. It was to give him my place as sub-editor (acting editor) of the *New Commonwealth*, and find some other job for myself.

At that time, I never had any fears that I might not be able, easily, to impress somebody or other with my talents.

To be strictly truthful, the only time I coveted a job was before I had got it, when I was leading an older experienced man to take my usefulness to him on trust. I enjoyed using my wits in this way. The appointment was no sooner in my hands than I began wondering whether I really wanted it after all. When it turned out to need the whole of my time and energy, so that I had none left for anything else—for the writing I still did not trust as a profession—I soon loathed it. Let a way of escape offer itself—if possible, without discredit—and I leaped at it.

What looked like the most quixotic generosity—stepping aside for K.—was very little either quixotic or generous.

Diplomacy was called for—first to persuade K. himself that I was *not* doing him a favour, then to convince Mr Thoresby that I was doing him a great one in resigning and offering him K. in my place. I have forgotten how I went about it. But when the time came for the final step, when K. was going to see Mr Thoresby for the third time, I made the mistake of trying to advise him.

'He enjoys the sound of his own voice,' I said. 'You must let him talk. If you listen attentively, you'll hear what he wants you to say. Don't argue with him. Let him tell you his ideas, but don't, don't remind him that last time he talked to you they were quite different.'

'Dear me'—he removed his pince-nez, polished them very deliberately, replaced them on his short nose and stared at me with something between hauteur and insolence—'it appals me to think that this is how I must have been handled, before I married you. I know you very well now, you'd like to arrange my life, you're as shockingly domineering as your mother. Perhaps you think I don't see it. I do—but usually I'm too amused by it to point it out. What a pity you have such a low opinion of me, it leads you into making a fool of yourself.'

I was atrociously hurt—and lucid enough to see that he was partly right.

'My mother has always been very kind to you,' I said.

He went off, and I sat trying to quell the storm raging in the pit of my stomach, hating the room I sat in, hating London for mocking my hopes of it.

I jumped up and went to the window. I can see now the nearly black leaves of a yew in the sooty garden, and the pale streak of yellow below it, a late crocus. In the distance a child—it must be a child—was striking slowly the notes of a piano.

'Parthenophil is lost and I would see him;
For he is like to something I remember,
A great while since, a long, long time ago . . .'

Why Ford's lines should have come into my head at that moment, I can't imagine. They gave me an intense physical pleasure, which cured me for the time of discouragement and the anguish of feeling that there was neither sense, purpose, nor dignity in my life now.

When K. returned, triumphant, having been accepted, I had a moment of panic—I must have been mad to give up a place where I was sure of earning money. My looks did not give it away.

It was precisely the same feeling as when, very young, I dropped a sixpence in the street and it rolled away and vanished through the bars of a drain. A lady who had seen the disaster bent down and said kindly, 'What did you lose, child?' She was opening her purse. When I said roughly, 'Nothing,' she shut it again.

I used my first weeks of freedom to go to Whitby to see Bill. The summer before this I had had him for several weeks near me, outside London, living with one of the officer's wives I had known in 1918. I saw him every weekend, but it was not altogether a satisfactory place for him, and at the end of the year I took him back to Miss Geeson. Since then he had had measles. Miss Geeson wrote to me every day, but I went through torments of fear—and shame. That another woman was nursing him through an illness humiliated me.

He had grown. He was now almost six, tall, with his wide forehead, fair skin and eyes of a deep pure blue, more beautiful than ever—so beautiful that I was afraid. When I was questioning her about him, Miss Geeson said,

'He is sometimes bad-tempered.'

I looked at her in mute astonishment.

'He has fits of rage. I never know why. He lies on the floor and screams and bites the legs of chairs. I wait until it is over, then I ask him about it, quietly. It doesn't happen often. He's really a good child—kind and intelligent.'

It is my fault, I thought. It is because I left him.

When I had put him to bed that evening at home, my mother talked to me about him, repeating things he had said to her, and stories about his illness. For a long time, days, he had been listless, as though he felt no interest in getting well; then, about three one morning, when Miss Geeson went to look at him, he was awake, and she asked him, 'Is there anything you would like?' He said languidly, 'I should like a good cup of tea.'

'Then you shall have it, that good kind woman said, and there and then went downstairs and made it for him; he drank it and after that began to recover.'

Not for a fortune—not even to give her the satisfaction of knowing that she had touched me to the quick—could I show interest. Still less, tell her what I was thinking.

I listened with a polite absent smile. Behind it, my mind ran from room to room, scrabbled at doors, beat itself against the walls. There was nothing I could do, there was no going back—nothing, nothing.

My mother looked older than her years, and tired. When I saw her, sitting for hours in the window of her room, idle, her eyes empty, or fixed on a point so remote that it could only be her own youth she saw there, my heart moved painfully and quickly, and I began to talk about trifles, a dress she needed, a new hat.

'Nay, I can't afford it,' she would say, and wait smiling to be contradicted.

'I'll give it to you for your birthday!'

'We'll see.'

'When my ship comes in, I'll buy you a fur coat.'

When she laughed, her face changed and softened. 'Your presents!' she said gaily and ironically. 'You'd give away your own silly skin.'

Chapter 39

When I went back to London, to K.—as always, hopefully, but with a cynical readiness to be disappointed—I decided that before looking round for another job I would finish the novel I had begun. Miraculously, I had a little money in the bank, and in July I was offered fifty pounds for what was to be a month's research, but turned out to be much more exacting. Mrs Margaret Sanger, an American crusader for birth control, had written a book filled with statistics—of population, incomes, venereal disease, births per age, per profession, per year, I forget what more. They were all to do with the United States, and she wanted them replaced by the corresponding English figures for an English publisher.

I set out lightheartedly on a wild goose chase. More than half the statistics did not exist in England, and had to be made out by inference—invention is the correct term—from such facts as were on record. I ran about London, from library to institution and institution to the Reading Room of the British Museum—and once ran for my life from a place where, I realized suddenly, they supposed I had come to be medically examined: I did not wait to explain.

In August that year the heat became terrible: the grass in the parks turned yellow, then black, the commons caught fire and smouldered. At nine o'clock, when I left the house, it was already stifling, and by midday a white oily light poured over the buildings and turned the streets into so many scorching gullies sending out a breath of acid dust. I walked about in a state of half-drunkenness—drunk with heat and the black coffee that was all I could face—eyelids half closed against the searing light, wrists and temples throbbing. At the end of the day I reached a curious state of—I can only call it a mute delirium—in which I seemed to be moving in one world, and seeing in another, brittle and transparent.

K. had two weeks' holiday, and went away alone, to Dorset: I had neither time nor money to go with him; Mrs Sanger wanted her figures, I had already spent three weeks on them and they were less than half complete. (A generous woman—when at last I finished, she paid me a double fee.)

The day after K. came home, a letter to him, sent on from the hotel in Dorset, was laid with mine in my room. In the evening I gave it to him. In the instant of handing it over I noticed—with less interest than the eye gives to a flicker of light on the wall—a change in his face, almost imperceptible. I forgot it immediately.

Exhausted by the heat and my annoying task, I went to bed and fell asleep.

It was still dark, some time between one and two o'clock, when I woke suddenly. What had wakened me was a few words spoken, with the greatest distinctness, inside my skull—*That letter is important for you.*

There is no more earthy, stolid, less extra-mundane creature living than I am: visions, premonitions, rarely visit me. I cannot explain this solitary instance of—what am I to call it—clairaudience? divination?

I lay still for some minutes, vividly aware of the darkened room, the bed, my body lying in it. Then without reflection I got up and went into K.'s room at the other side of the landing. Groping my way across it to the chair near his bed, I put my hand in the pocket of his coat, found the letter, took it to my room, and read it. It was short, a fribble of a love-letter, and it took me a moment to realize that the writer had spent the first week of his holiday with him, and had been his mistress for a long time.

There will be other letters, I thought coolly. I went back into the other room, and without troubling at all to be quiet opened drawer after drawer until I came on a collar-box crammed with letters. K. half woke. I spoke to him, and he turned over and fell asleep again.

(The impulse—to know, to make sure—which moved me to this detestable act has in honesty to be told, but I wish it had not.)

For precisely the reasons that make it impossible for me to go on reading a bad novel, I could not read the letters, but I sifted through them rapidly until I found one signed in full, with an address in Kent.

Now, for the first time, I was seized by an overmastering excitement. I'm free, I thought, I'm free, I'm free. I felt I should go mad with joy and excitement.

Without warning, I began to tremble violently.

I was deathly cold, and could not get warm even in bed. Lying awake, I went over again and again, endlessly, the steps I must take when I got up.

Out of—bewilderment? fatigue?—I did nothing that day except take the train to Maidstone in Kent, and come back immediately. In London I walked about for a long time, until, feeling hungry, I went into a small café and ordered tea and bread and butter. My throat closed against the bread. I could, with difficulty, swallow the tea, but not eat. My tongue had thickened and become dry, like a strip of worn leather.

Intensely interested by these symptoms of an unknown illness, I made a note of them on the back of an envelope.

For five days I said nothing to K.—warned, I think, by the instinctive certainty that once I began to talk I should lose control of the situation. I had kept the letters, but, careless fellow, he did not miss them. On the evening of the fifth day—Sunday—I asked him abruptly, 'Why didn't you tell me you were in love with this girl?' He looked at me without replying. 'If you'll tell me about it, I can divorce you and you can have her in peace.'

One thing is certain. Had he said he wanted to marry her, I should have behaved well. Pride, vanity—call it what you like—would have guided me, I should have closed my mind at once to everything but relief, and the excitement of making plans for a new start.

He did nothing of the sort. His face worked in a very unpleasant way, and he said,

'Don't send me off, don't leave me.'

I see today that I was hoping for another answer. Taken aback, I began to ask questions. The story could not have been simpler: the girl had been a V.A.D. in Canterbury, his partner at dances—and when he took over the *New Commonwealth* from me, he had brought her into the office as a typist. At this point I remembered that one day when I called for him at the office I had been struck by the inquisitive glances of a new typist, and with a feeling of sickness I supposed that they had discussed me afterwards. Reason told me that they had not laughed at me and at their cleverness in pulling wool over my eyes, but I felt naked and ridiculous, a laughing-stock. One grotesque image after another rushed into my mind, detailed, lucid—and insane. And in the same instant a younger self, in the grip of all the ludicrous, unmanageable and laughably sincere emotions of that graceless age, clawed her way to the surface and took complete possession. She gave every sign of having returned for good, my tears of rage and despair were hers, my savage humiliation. This awkward young creature had never wanted to be rid of K., never prayed he would leave her so that without taking it on herself she could be rid of him. An incredulous grief at having been tricked filled her. There was no reasoning with her. Not that she had lost the power to reason: one of the oddest effects of sexual jealousy is to poison the intellect at the roots, so that it goes on arguing with impeccable logic, from a mad premise.

I did not fail to notice, at moments, that the greater part of my anguish was hurt vanity. To think that I had been hoodwinked, and for so long! It made no difference, there is no getting used to jealousy. Moreover, it was a blow to my self-confidence from which I never wholly recovered—all the more because treachery, to be made a fool of and lied to, was only what in the farthest recess of my heart I had expected. I suffered, too, because what had happened was irreparable. There was nothing I could do, I could not make a clever plan to reverse it, could not adroitly prevent the innocent past from being smirched and distorted by the present.

That first evening I asked so many questions, called up so many lacerating and ridiculous images, that I exhausted myself. When I got into bed I fell asleep instantly, sinking through layer on layer of darkness, a drowned body plummeting to the floor of the Atlantic. For a minute I heard dimly a knocking on my locked door: I would have roused if I could, but it was physically impossible, I could not move a finger.

In the morning K. said, smiling,

'You needn't have refused to open your door, I only wanted the book I left in your room.'

My behaviour during the next few weeks lacked elegance. I harried K. with questions, and when he told me that he had stayed with the young woman at the —— Hotel in Oxford, or at another in London, I went there and walked up and down outside, up and down, impervious to inquisitive glances, imagining their arrival in the cab, entering together, signing the register, going up the stairs to their room: the images I called up made a lunatic of me . . .

I had a resource which morally fastidious persons will find shocking. From the very beginning, I made careful notes. After an evening of questioning K. with imprudent cruelty, I hurried to my room and wrote down an accurate description of my emotions and of all I had been moved to say. A thrifty astute side of my mind knew that unless I recorded it alive, with the claws still in me, I should forget the exact taste.

I have a vague memory of reading that some famous writer made notes as he watched his child die. That revolts me . . . Surely, too, the only griefs needing to be recorded at the time are those which, however sharp, *do not go to the quick* . . .

Outwardly I was unchanged: I toiled over Mrs Sanger's statistics, inventing new and ingenious methods of hiding the gaps, worked in the Reading Room until it closed—it closes far too early—then went back to my room to go on working for another two or three hours. If K. were dining with his parents, I walked home, stopping on the way to drink coffee in a Corner House.

At these moments a familiar gaiety woke in me; the warm dusty air of the street touched my face with a friendly hand, stretched to me from my future, my happy future.

Chapter 40

Some time during the five days before I made up my mind to speak to K., I made an appointment with a lawyer; I no longer recall his name, nor who gave it to me.

Carrying the package of letters, I went to see him. A kind dry man, he listened with an expressionless face when I told him, curtly, that I wanted to divorce my husband, showing neither interest nor boredom. But, good heavens, can anything in the world be more boring than listening, year after year, to the confidences of men and women with a grievance?

He began questioning me—Where did you live then? Just when did you begin to suspect that your husband . . .? A clerk sitting with his back to me wrote down all I said, now and then scratching an ear or his leg with his pen. I kept my voice cold, and watched my life slipping from me; the house in Liverpool with its neglected garden and the rosy-cheeked infant in his high chair; all the rented rooms since then, where I had left a ghost of myself, frowning over a sheet of manuscript-paper, rolling a naked child in warmed towels, day-dreaming.

Another minute of this and there will be nothing left, I thought.

'How did you gain possession of these letters?'

'I stole them.'

He smiled very slightly, and turned the pages with a finger-nail. 'Letters of this kind are all alike.' He handed them to the clerk, who tied round them a length of pink tape. 'They are not, I must tell you, evidence against your husband, although they are written to him. They are evidence only against the writer.'

This seemed to me no more idiotic than the legal procedure as he explained it to me. I must now write to my husband, asking him to return—my face did not, I think, give away the fact that he had never left—he would refuse and . . .

Here I interrupted to ask what I ought to say in my letter.

'Use your own best words, I don't want to put words into your head, that would destroy the spontaneity. Draft a letter, and let me see the draft.'

'And then?'

'Then we shall bring an action for restitution of conjugal rights; he will decline to comply with the order—giving you fresh evidence of adultery. Then we shall begin the action for divorce.'

I smiled. 'Conjugal is a ridiculous word.'

'You must not see or be seen with your husband.'

Outside, the heat tasted curiously of salt; I thought that the skin of my lips was cracked and tried moistening them with the tip of my tongue as I walked along Holborn and Oxford Street. I walked for a long time, feeling the heat of the pavement through my thin shoes. With an icy clarity, I blamed myself for everything; I had been selfish, disloyal, arrogant, without kindness. The gesture of the clerk's bony hand as he tied together in a small neat bundle all the days of my life with K., hopes, lies, unkindness, kindness, an empty calico bag labelled Coal, Light and Gas, a green sofa—what had become of it?—struck me as obscene.

The thought of turning K. out was singularly unpleasant. Where would he go? And how, in this heat, with the births per age of unmarried mothers still to be arranged (by me), could I find time and patience to separate my books from his? The trouble, no less than the callousness, of leaving him, bent my shoulders.

If anyone supposes that, in an emotional crisis, straws weigh less than iron, he is a fool.

When I told K. about the lawyer, he looked at me with an air of defeat.

'This is too much,' he said. 'I've had a miserable day. Your friend N. treated me abominably when I called there to ask her to let me review for her. From the way she spoke to me you'd think I was nobody. And I thought she was a friend of yours.'

I felt angry that he had been snubbed. When he spoke in this voice, with this look of young unhappiness, my bowels melted. It reminded me of a time when I had admired him above anyone. It was in those days that he had discovered how to start in me a fever of anxiety. This habit of my nerves—surely only my nerves?—was the strongest hold he had over me.

I knew already that I had no heart for this business of letter-writing and pretending. I did not give way at once. As always when I am faced with what is in effect a moral decision to be made—and a tiresome upheaval—I fell back on doing nothing. I waited for a wind.

Moreover—how absurd this is—I felt ashamed to tell the lawyer, that dry correct man, that I had changed my mind.

I imagined him and his faceless clerk having a good laugh at me and my feebleness. When, after a few days, he sent me a long document he called my proof, I could not force myself to read it, only glancing through the pages to see whether it were recorded that I stole the letters. It was not.

In a note pinned to the document he reminded me that I was to draft a letter. I drafted it, and sent it to him. A day later it came back with two of my phrases corrected in a fine hand. This mortified me. Did the fellow know whose style he was correcting?

After another four or five weeks, I went to see him again, and told him, brusquely, that I could not go on. 'It takes too long, there are too many steps.'

'That is so,' he said.

'I am sorry to disappoint you.'

He gave me an impersonal glance. 'I'll have a parcel made of the letters.'

I had forgotten them. 'Oh, would you destroy them for me? If I have them, I might not destroy them, I might do something mean with them.'

'I can't destroy them,' he said calmly. 'I'll keep them in my safe for you if you like.'

I thanked him and left. Are they still at the back of a safe? Or did a bomb later get rid of them?

To punish K. for my want of hardness, I made an abominable scene. He endured it with some dignity, and I apologized, asking him to forgive me my indecent sarcasms. I then wrote them all down.

One promise K. made me at this time—for which I had not asked—was that if, later, I wanted to divorce him, he would take the whole thing on himself, invent evidence I could use, anything.

'Why?' I asked.

Clearing his throat, he said stiffly, 'I think I know what is expected of a gentleman.'

I had enough self-restraint to go into my own room to laugh. My laughter was an echo of my mother's at her harshest and most jeering.

If I had had any respect for him, I could not have laughed in that hateful way. But respect and admiration had long been dead, their place taken by pity—pity, a creeping plant, like bindweed, all but impossible to root up.

I am not naturally vindictive, I forget the names of contemptuous reviewers. If, for any peculiar reason, the injury some dog has done me stays in my mind, I never forgive him, but if a chance turns up to punish him, I don't take it. I am unforgiving, but not malicious. And I am lazy.

Since I am too lazy or indifferent to be tempted to avenge myself, I ought to have been able to forgive K. If only out of civility.

The truth is, a knife-thrust in one's vanity takes longer to heal than any.

During the day tranquil or happy, and hard at work, no sooner was I in bed and alone than the memory of this or that incident—with what I could invent—started up in my mind and drove me out of it. I have never been able to cry easily or with pleasure, or in public; my tears during these months were corrosive, as bitter as the aloes smeared on children's nails. But I did not only cry; I imagined biting phrases and wrote them in pencil on a sheet of paper I took care to have by my bed, and in the morning added to the pile of notes in my cupboard.

What a curious animal a writer is.

I remember an early morning, grey, very quiet, when something —the chorus of birds, a wandering scent of damp earth—flung me back six years to the bedroom of the house in Liverpool. The longing I felt was inarticulate—even I had no words for it: it was the craving for water of a man dying of thirst.

This time it was myself I laughed at, wryly.

Chapter 41

In 1922—or was it early in 1923?—the *New Commonwealth*, terribly emaciated, died. Mr Thoresby had lost rather more money than he was willing to lose on a hobby that came second in his heart to his theosophical studies.

He treated K. generously.

Before this money came to an end, his father made him the same offer he had made once before: to send him to a university—this time to take a Ph.D. at Oxford. Now that I have written this, I wonder whether it was not a small legacy that fell to K. at this time, which he proposed to spend in this way.

When he told me about it, and asked, not my advice but my opinion, I refused to give it. Partly because what I thought was, that at thirty-two, nearly thirty-three, he should have something more serious to do than go back to school with boys of nineteen and twenty. And partly—and even less avowably—I did not care in the least if he left me to make the best of things alone. It would put him in a poor light—and leave me free. Alone but free.

'If I go,' he asked, 'what will you do?'

I did not tell him that, for some reason, I no longer felt absolutely confident that I could pick up a salaried job. I had a moment's sickening panic. I have done nothing yet, achieved nothing, I thought. I swallowed my fear, and thought: But I will.

'I don't know.'

'You could go home. Your mother——'

'My mother will always take me in. But it is a little humiliating—married, with a child—to go back.'

'What can you do?'

So he means to go, I thought. I had the sensation of standing in the entry of one of the narrow openings we call *ghauts* in Whitby, flagged passages between houses on the east side, pitch black until you come out under the slope of the cliff. My heart sank, then flew up in a great arc, like a gull, up and away.

'I shall find something, I always do.'

'Very well, my dear. Since you want me to go to Oxford . . .'

I had finished my novel, the third. When, later this year, it was published, it got bad notices, no worse than it deserved. It was atrociously bad, far worse, far more pretentious, than *The Pot Boils*. The one person who praised it was my dear Michael; it pleased his romantic palate and he did not see that it was unspeakably over-written and affected, the worst kind of fake. The letter he wrote to me ended: 'I can promise a frank welcome at Orange Street if and when you return to us. I hope it will be soon.'

I decided there and then to take him my next novel. I had already started it, and I intended to use my notes.

I took the quarter-written manuscript with me to Portsmouth, when we went to stay for a time with Elizabeth and John. They were renting a large house on the edge of the dirty clotted streets that supplied John with his hundreds of panel patients. It was dilapidated, furnished, like the London flat, with odds and ends picked up in sale-rooms, and smelled vilely of the brewery on to which it backed: they were living in the same eccentric disorder, but with two servants, and sherry in the place of beer.

I trusted no one with my unhappiness, not even Elizabeth. But K., who had sworn to me that he would hold his tongue, gave me away to her the first day. He could not resist telling me, with smiling condescension, that she felt I was making an hysterical fuss about a very usual incident.

'So you told her?'

'Of course. Why not? I'm not, let me tell you, afraid of the truth, I shall tell anyone I please.'

I did not reproach him for this slight case of treachery. What good would it be—since he would only confide in Elizabeth that I had made a scene? But my contempt for him deepened. I sat with a fixed smile, hating him.

Elizabeth I did not blame. I knew too well that, talking to a man, any man, she could not help trying to seduce him. Nor did I tell her that I knew she had joined K. in laughing at me.

My love for her remained, so far as I knew, intact.

It must, I think, have been April—May or April—in K.'s one year at Oxford that I stayed with him for a short time. He had made several friends among the young men—and one older friend, a man of his own age who had come to the university after years in his father's financial house. R. was a Jew, good-looking, intelligent, capable of clever and charming remarks: he courted me—no other word will do—with the same charm and thoughtfulness. I tried, vainly, to fall in love with him: it would, I thought, cure me quickly of my habit of wincing, a mere twitch of the nerves, every time I passed a hotel or a restaurant where K. had taken the girl. He made all the right gestures: for the first time I had a suitor who came with flowers and volumes of poems. It half embarrassed, half touched me. We spent long placid afternoons on the river, and he read the poems aloud, in his admirable voice. I could admire it, and his good looks, and the quickness of his mind, but I could not avoid moments when I was repelled by his romantic hedonism: he wallowed in delicate emotions.

One afternoon, in the very middle of a poem he was reading, his own this time, I yawned. It was not meant; I was simply caught out. Looking at me sorrowfully, he closed the book and took me home. On another occasion, he had drawn the punt into the bank of a meadow so thick with buttercups it was like glancing at the sun: under the opposite bank a canoe held four young men who climbed out and stood there, charming gawky figures, like the boys on a Greek vase. R. looked at them, and sighed.

'How I envy them. Their youth. It saddens me.'

'Why?' I asked, astonished.

'You must feel it as I do. Which of the four would you like to fall in love with?'

'None.'

I have never been able to understand how an intelligent woman can become infatuated with a much younger man. *Chéri?* Yes—but Léa is not presented to us as intelligent; a beautiful young animal would give her all she needed or craved. *Phèdre?* But do we know how old Phèdre is? Is she much older than her rather stupid stepson? In any event, what we are attending to is the poetry—

> *Ce n'est plus une ardeur dans mes veines cachée*
> *C'est Vénus tout entière à sa proie attachée*

—exactly as, listening to Lear's cries when he fumbles at his dead child's dress, we do not stop to reflect that she brought their unhappiness on him and herself by her priggish refusal to flatter an old man.

One of K.'s young friends, nineteen years old, caught an ill-humoured passion for me, as he might have caught a cold in the head or measles. I dislike hurting people—a scruple which has cost me dear—but his emotional crudity, the right emotions for his age, bored me.

The only one of K.'s undergraduate friends for whom I felt genuine liking reminded me of Boris Droubetzkoï as he appears in the first pages of *War and Peace*. B.J. was friendly, handsome in a cool way, poor, and scrupulously neat—he had, I think, only one suit, and when he was invited to a fancy-dress party he could go only because I lent him a blue crêpe-de-chine smock in which he looked charming. A hard worker, with no useful relations, and more conscience than Droubetzkoï, he became the secretary of a Colonial Governor.

I wrote R. three or four indiscreet letters, literary exercises, which I later took from his room. You can see that I have a talent for the theft of letters.

Chapter 42

Towards the end of that year I finished writing *The Pitiful Wife*—an admirable title for a novel spongy with emotion—and typed it laboriously from the manuscript, working until all hours, without benefit of green tea. Charles Evans of Heinemann was expecting it, but I had decided, out of love of Michael, to send it to him. I could act in this unscrupulous way because—in memory of Fisher Unwin, no doubt—I refused to sign contracts for more than one book at a time.

I wrote to tell Charles Evans what I was doing: it says everything for his patient kindness that he later took me back into Heinemann's bosom, without reproaches. He was a good man, and my friend. He would never, as did an elderly director of his firm, Mr Pawling, have taken me out to lunch and lectured me solemnly on the duty of a young writer. This was, if you believe me, to live for art, not money. It was too much for my—at the time—famished stomach.

Michael was delighted with the book, and paid me a hundred pounds in advance of royalties. I had not the slightest suspicion that it was a bad novel: at this time, thoughts and feelings started a fever in my mind, and I was under the delusion that this fever had some connection with literature.

Almost at the same time, K. sent me, unasked, a cheque for fifty pounds. I hesitated—but not for very long: it went against the grain to throw away money for a gesture, and I took it, with exaggerated thanks.

Now that I was so well-off, I decided to take rooms for myself and Bill—near enough to Miss Geeson's for him to go there daily. To my great surprise, my mother took it in bad part.

'The child is well enough where he is,' she said, in her coldest voice. 'You may very well want to go away again, and you would have unsettled him for nothing. And—you might find that Miss Geeson was not willing to take him back.'

The tone of her voice, harsh and cutting, travelled by a short cut to the child always expecting to be whipped for some misdeed. I flinched.

'But I'd rather have him with me.'

'You must do as you please.'

'I thought—I could write in the mornings and when he is asleep.'

'Miss Geeson has been getting him into good ways. You'll find he behaves much worse with you, I shouldn't be surprised if he begins his fits of bad-temper again.'

'He behaved well enough with me when he was a baby,' I said.

I have never been able to answer with dignity when I am castigated—unless I can feel angry. I hurried out of the room, up to my bedroom, trembling with resentment. She is perfectly right, I thought, but no one ought to speak to a grown woman in such a way, without a trace of respect.

It did not enter my head—it has done so only at this minute—that a jealous grief lay under my mother's words. Why should *I* be able to take my son back, when she . . .?

Downstairs, she struck a note or two on the piano in her room: her voice, for a moment clear and strong, rose in the first bars of *O Fair Dove,* weakened, missed the higher note, and broke off. A fury of love for her seized me. Why aren't you still young? I cried, Why was there so little for you?

Pressing my forehead against the window to cool it, I watched the wind rush down the field at the other side of the road, whitening the grass—then still a meadow, not yet groomed into the park where, when she was much older, I took her to sit staring at tulips and forget-me-nots with eyes as empty as an infant's. Grief caught me by the throat. Why must she die and lose sight of the wind in the grass? I saw her hands, fingers a little swollen, drop from the piano.

When I went downstairs, she was still in her room, talking now to a small lean bird-eyed woman in a thin coat, who listened with a guilty smile. The contrast between the two women struck me: my mother was older and frailer than her friend, yet had more life in her little finger than the other in her whole body.

'You shouldn't *do* it, Mary. *I* wouldn't. I wouldn't slave like that for any living soul. Visitors or *no* visitors, I wouldn't *do* it. Tell them you *won't.*'

For a moment I felt closer than their skin to all tired, anxious unattractive women, coming into rooms with propitiatory smiles, closing doors softly, opening and shutting windows, drawing blinds up, drawing them again at night or against the sun, turning down the sheets on beds, preparing trays, climbing with them up flights of stairs, hurrying to answer bells. The woman's thoughts rose in my mind in pale wisps and spirals . . .

I took rooms for us in a house on the edge of Miss Geeson's village: it stood alone in a field, and if I took the flagged path through this field, and through the next four, I came to the place where I was once nearly strangled by a lout, and so to Waterstead Lane and its mossy walls, and Park Terrace . . .

> *Et je voguais lorsqu'à travers mes liens frêles*
> *Des noyés descendaient dormir à reculons . . .*

The estuary, narrowing as it neared the first hills, lay beyond the house. In the afternoon we walked, I racking my brain for something to talk about to a child not yet eight: usually silent himself, he responded only when something I said amused him. He was quick, graceful and lazy, hating to exert himself. We had been living in these rooms for six months before I discovered that he was only pretending not to be able to read: he preferred to be read to.

In July that year there was an epidemic of diphtheria in Whitby, and one night he woke me to tell me that his throat hurt.

It was four o'clock: I got up, dressed, and spent the hours until I could summon the doctor, planning. I was determined not to let him go to the fever hospital. Nor did he. My calm certainty that she would allow us to stay in her house intimidated the poor woman. Like any other country wife, she was mortally afraid of infection, but I bore her down.

He had the illness lightly, but for the first two nights I did not dare to sleep. I floated a night-light in a chipped saucer, and placed it so that I could see the outline of his little body under the blanket. A dozen times in an hour I bent over him to make sure he was still alive. He slept through every night without moving.

Lying in bed, he drank milk and egg flip, and ate fish, white grapes, honey. He grew rosier daily. To hold the cup for him to drink suffocated me with joy. Told by the doctor that I must keep him lying flat, I read to him, hour after hour, until my penny whistle of a voice cracked and I had to lean close to make him hear me.

One day during the second week I remembered suddenly that my novel had been published a week earlier. I felt a pang of dismay. Clearly it was a failure. I drove it to the back of my mind. Nothing mattered but to go on pouring Valentine's meat juice, honey, milk, down my child's throat. Time enough when he recovered to look at the minor disaster.

The next morning I was reading aloud, as usual, when I heard my mother's voice in the field outside the house. 'Are you there, Daisy? I want you.'

I ran to the window and opened it. Because of her fears for my young sister, she would not come nearer than the flagged path. She stood there, a newspaper open in her hand, smiling.

'It says here that your book is fine and exquisite. A masterpiece. Wait, I'll read it to you.'

She was radiant, her eyes as blue and living as a girl's. I had never seen her so excited. A delicious feeling of warmth and confidence spread through me. Now at last I have done something, I thought; now she is pleased with me.

It was the feeling, half relief, half happiness, that I had when the news came of my scholarship, and when I could wire her that I had a First. Those other triumphs had led nowhere, disappointing her. Now something more splendid was beginning. A sense of power seized me, my energy starting up in my midriff like a famished wild beast. I laughed secretly.

Here, I thought, here begin the life and works of Daisy Jameson.

'Thank you for bringing it.'

'I always knew you would do well,' she said, smiling. 'Though I didn't expect anything so good as this.'

I could not endure to see her so pleased with this tiny success.

'It's only one review,' I said.

'There will be others.'

My courage came back, and I boasted,

'If it sells I'll buy you something you really want.'

There were other reviews, equally astonishing and fantastic. Nowadays when *The Times Literary Supplement*, as it has done for the last several years, treats me scurvily, I cannot help smiling when I think of the praise it gave a very bad novel.

One critic was not taken in: in a curt review Raymond Mortimer said that it was the silliest novel he had ever read. Since I am always willing to believe the worst of myself, this remark impressed me. Two or three years later I knew that he was right. The only real fragments in the book—the dialogue between husband and jealous wife—were not likely to appeal to a male intellectual. What could he know about the emotions of a violent and undisciplined young woman? He knew bad writing when he saw it, that was enough.

When Bill was convalescent I wrote to Michael and, hiding my diffidence, asked him whether any money had come in. I hoped for a hundred pounds. With a kindness I should have been obliged for— if I had not been too full of my own merits to notice his—he sent two hundred and fifty. 'There will be more to come,' he wrote, 'perhaps not a great deal more, but certainly something. You'll die rich!'

This prophecy delighted me.

A warning voice, my own or my grandfather's, said swiftly: *Not you!* You were born under an awkward star, and honesty will keep breaking in. Besides, you squander.

I am inclined, now, to think that it rested with me to become a rascally best-selling fake, a hypocritical success of some sort. If I had used my talents for Jesuitry consistently, I might have become rich.

I should still have squandered.

I had no trouble in persuading my mother that I was rich enough to give her a fur coat. Half her pleasure in it would come, I knew, from being able to say to friends: My daughter gave it to me; her books, you know, do very well . . . We went, of course, to Scarborough. The man in Rowntree's fur department had known her too long to feel impatient as she tried on coat after coat, always with an eye on the one she had coveted at sight. The ritual over, he said sweetly, 'You'll never be sorry if you take that one, Mrs Jameson: it will last you for years.'

'Do you like it?' she asked me, frowning. 'It's a lot of money.'

'No, no, it's not too much,' I lied. 'Is it what you want?'

Watching her run her hand over and over the sleeve, I felt the same piercing happiness as when I gave my son something he wanted very much and I could not afford.

It must have been the same day that she admired a hat so expensive that even I felt it was out of reach: separate strands of black osprey were sewn round the crown in four rows. 'You have an osprey at home,' I said, 'in the drawer with the ostrich feathers: I think I could copy it.'

I made my boast good. I am clumsier with a needle than any woman in the country, but when it was a question of getting her what she wanted I was without fear.

Dreams of supreme triumphs, of becoming rich, did not last: I was tormented by the sense that money earned by writing novels is less safe than the money my grandfather made out of ships. Except during a depression, the builders and owners of ships were sure of their tomorrow. Not so the writers of books. Between one novel and the next you could lose your wits and your audience.

Though I don't remember it, I must have written in this tone to Michael Sadleir. In September he wrote that an American publisher, Alfred Knopf, who was in London, wanted a young man or young woman to act as his representative in England, finding books and authors for him. 'I have told him that you are competent and unscrupulous, and—naturally—he wants to see you.'

Leaving Bill with my mother, I went up to London, and called on Mr Knopf. To my astonishment, he was not only young, he was a copy of the Spanish king, whose photograph in golfing clothes I had just seen in an illustrated weekly. This—and the smiling candour with which he remarked, 'I believe in giving people enough rope to hang themselves,'—amused me so much that I felt there were worse ways of being hanged.

'I want my wife to see you,' he added. 'I never decide without her.'

The image I have kept of Blanche Knopf at this time is of a small golden-skinned young woman, enchantingly smooth and round like a Chinese idol.

I was not surprised to be given the job. Total ignorance of what is expected of me has never done me the harm that boredom does me every day.

Chapter 43

With the greatest naïveté and coolness, I wrote to every publisher and literary agent in London and told them that I was in the market for authors, the best authors.

Then, over my suppers of coffee and bread and honey, I tried to consider my tortuous life. I had lightheartedly promised Alfred Knopf that I would return to London to live. This promise, and much else, ran head on into a moral—if it were no stronger—obligation to live in Cornwall with K. With his Ph.D. thesis unfinished (he never did finish it), he had left Oxford in July and taken a post in a school in Launceston—encouraged to it by me. At the time I had thought Cornwall as good a place as any to bring up a child.

Turning the saucer of my coffee cup, my hand came on a chipped place. Instantly I was in the darkened room where a badly chipped saucer, a feeble circle of light on the floor, and another on the ceiling immediately above it, had kept me company as I held my breath to hear the breathing of a sick child. An irrational fear seized me. The more radiant a living creature is, the less use life has for him, I thought. If there were another war, I couldn't save him. Panic drove me upstairs to make sure that he was asleep and safe.

In November, I gave up our rooms and went back to my mother's house, putting off a little longer the moment when I should have to decide something.

After three days, I had a magnificent excuse for doing nothing: I fell ill.

I woke on the 11th with an aching throat and a body which seemed made of equal parts of cottonwool and rusty iron. To get up and dress, I had to fight off a nightmare weakness. My mother was expecting me to go with her to the Armistice Day service in St Mary's —on the East cliff—and it did not enter my head that I could disappoint her. The cold air, when we set out, steadied me.

Luckily, my mother had to stop several times on our way up the one hundred and ninety-nine steps that climb from harbour level to the church. For more than half the way the old houses went with us, one crouching above the other, and I remembered the servant's story heard when I was four: one rainy night part of the cliff fell away and in the morning the yards of houses were found choked with bones and the crumbling wood of ancient coffins.

The top step, worn deepest because here many turn, ends in a narrow flagged path twisting between the graves, with their sea-wrinkled stones, to the church porch. We turned—and looked down at the harbour, and to the hills drawn round it, and the great line of the coast curving north, and to the pale sea. We walked towards the church, passing to one side, to climb an outside staircase. The door stood open on a narrow passage running towards the gallery. We trod softly between the wall and the high wooden walls of pews. A little light came through low windows. The boards creaked.

To come this way, we passed my brother's memorial tablet— 'To the memory of 2nd Lt. Harold Jameson, Médaille Militaire, D.C.M., M.C., Royal Flying Corps . . .' fastened to the wall of the gallery at eye-level—and came out between the walls to reach my grandfather's pew: a cushioned bench ran down its longer side, and the latch of the door was set high, above the reach of a child's hand.

I looked down, over the edge, into the well of the church, into pews like square roofless rooms. In the three-decker pulpit an old priest made the superb gesture I had watched him make when I was a child, flinging his white surplice over his head and bowing his face in it.

This church is part of my life: it speaks to my skeleton, which remembers clearly the worn places in stairs, the grain of old wood, the moment—each time as piercing as the first—when a man crossing the moors above Sleights sees the sea leaning against the sky, the edge of the cliff, and the church kneeling on it, waiting, beside the ruined Abbey. How could it forget, since those who live in me— and live nowhere else—have stared at it from the moors, from the harbour, from the sea, for eight hundred years? There is nothing here but what's mine.

I have read, in the logs of old ships, long since vanished, the handwriting on the page withered to the brown of a dry leaf: 'At eight in the morning Whitby church bore N.W.N. distant three miles . . .'

The winter sunlight crept round the wall to touch a corner of Harold's tablet. This wait for the Silence drew the cords of my stomach into a hard knot. How much longer? Leaning forward, I could see the soldiers drawn up facing the altar. I watched their officer: a narrow face, the cheekbones like knuckles, fair hair, hot quick eyes: he doesn't care who looks at him, I thought. The sergeant-major at his elbow did not expose himself in that way: his eyes, small and deep-set, gleamed, but it was the gleam of decaying matter, as though the mind at the back of them were dead. He had an air not so much cynical as over-used, and he was singularly quiet with it. He knows his officers like the back of his hand, I thought; their vanities, what each can do, their lusts. He would have known each time K. had his young woman . . .

The sailors filled three long rows. They were a different species

of animal, and looked curiously naked in their tight uniform. Behind
them the pews were filled with men and women to whom the war
had brought gifts: a dead son, a new, more exciting life, money.
Many Whitby people grew as fat as Eglon the king of Moab (look
him up in Judges) on their war—like the elderly shipowner who
allowed young officers to buy drinks for him on the first Armistice
Day, and bought none himself. Perhaps these had come to give
thanks.

Here it comes, I thought.

It came, the Silence, like the doom of God, like the sea rising
between rocks. The great chandelier hung suspended in it; the tall
pulpit, the galleries, the painted pillars, the bodies of men and
women, were held upright in it. The great ball of air outside the old
church contracted and pressed on it, and I thought that only the light,
crossing and re-crossing between the windows, kept the shell of the
roof from being crushed. I could hear my heart. I saw my young
brother at the other side of a London street, his face bent down,
scarlet; he thought he was not wanted. I ran across the road between
the wheels of cabs. I called him. I touched nothing.

I thought briefly of other young men I had known until they were
killed. I thought of Red Smith, not having thought of him since he
died. I could not now remember the tones of his voice, nor anything he had said that was of the least importance.

The silence changed very slightly. Far out in the North Sea a
wave gathered itself to fall, to send a green shock against the cliffs.
No heads were lifted, no eyes that had been closed opened, the head
of the old man'bowed in the upper deck of the pulpit was not uncovered—yet there had been a change.

Nothing happened—except that a gun was fired outside, and at the
back of the church a man lifted his arms and sounded the Last Post.

Dreadful, lacerating, unendurable sound.

The last note came to an end, slowly, passing over the rank grass
of the cliff, over the harbour: it would be heard everywhere, except
by my brother.

I gripped the edge of the pew. Standing beside my tearless mother,
I was ashamed to make a sign of grief: her body heavy in its black
coat did not move—when the trumpet flew up in the Reveille, it was
a moment before she realized that all were not sitting. It would be
indecent even to let myself imagine what she might be thinking,
what she saw with that fixed remote glance. The frowning face of
'a black bairn'? A boy in clumsy khaki and thick army boots?

The old Canon lifted his head and sent his strong unpriestly voice through the church. My mother sat stiffly, hands lying on her knees. *It is raised in power; it is sown a natural body; it is raised a spiritual body.* What a mockery of the mother who wants nothing but the living body of her son.

I could do nothing for her. I thought—at this moment I thought —if by jumping from the edge of the cliff I could bring him back, I would . . . But how can I tell? Suppose I took a moment to reflect before jumping, I should draw back. Of course I should draw back.

Oh, my poor dear, I thought, you have no one for you, no one who cares more for you than for herself. It was for nothing, it was for this dry moment, that you endured your life, the births of children, heat and discomfort in foreign ports, illness, pain, anger, ambitions transferred to a daughter, to a son, disappointment, the new heaviness of your body. For nothing.

On the way home I felt confused and ill, the pain in my throat became worse, and as soon as we were inside the house I fainted.

It turned out that I had diphtheria. The doctor was convinced that I had had the infection since the time when, to read aloud to Bill, I was bending over him for hours at a stretch.

Little as she liked the thought of a fever patient in the house, my mother did not dream of sending me away. My middle sister was at home again and could nurse me. So, with a sheet soaked in some powerful disinfectant hung across the door of my bedroom, I had my diphtheria in comfort.

Ordered to lie flat because diphtheria puts a strain on the heart, I persuaded my sister to bring me my typewriter, and sat up in bed typing letters to publishers and writers. I did not dare interrupt the correspondence I had started. A qualm of conscience made me add a postscript to the letters: I have diphtheria, burn this if you are afraid of infection. This drew, from John Buchan, a copy of his *Lodge in the Wilderness*, which brought a breath of cold clear air into the room, and a letter from Middleton Murry, whom I barely knew, of such kindness that I almost wept: he wrote that Katherine Mansfield had been delighted, at a moment when she was feeling wretched, by a review I wrote of one of her stories, and if I needed money he would like to send me twenty pounds from her.

I refused the offer, but I must have written more than once. I have a letter dated the 23rd of July, 1953, in which he says: 'For some inscrutable reason I am tidying up the accumulation of years. In doing so I came across and re-read letters of yours, written in 1923. And they touched me so that I felt it was sad, and somehow wrong, that I should have entirely lost contact with you . . . I remember you as I first saw you, at a sort of party at J. D. Beresford's . . .'

I remember him at that party, a young man with dark eyes which never rested on the face of the person he was speaking to, but flinched aside. I had not taken to him—because of this glance. I thought it sly and evasive. Perhaps it was—but it masked a delicacy and a kindness I was never, after 1923, tempted to mock.

No sooner had I recovered strength than I began to plan my future, mine and Bill's. I had less scruple now in leaving K. alone in Cornwall: during my illness, by a piece of carelessness that was like him, one of his letters had given away that he was still seeing his young woman: he had folded into it a scribbled list of the things he must do during a visit to London, and among them was: Meet D. 6:30 Marylebone Hotel . . . I threw it away. I was humiliated, but I had the honesty to remind myself: There was a time when you hoped he would leave you.

Yes, yes, leave me—not stay to make a fool of me, not force me—me—to put an end to our marriage. If he had taken himself off, I should have been cured of him in the time it took to close the door on him.

If you think with enough energy about a hoped-for event, it will in the end happen. Not because you willed it. Because it was all the time in your nature. But this trick has one fatal flaw. The moment an imagined event emerges into the real world, time leaps on it and gives it a twist that deforms everything. A spring you had supposed dry overflows, the looked-for ground gives way, and down you go.

Jealousy is a disease we should catch as seldom as possible. It is incurable. All the same, one recovers from it . . .

Michael recommended a school for Bill near Weybridge—forty minutes by train from London—and I decided to go there in January.

The day before we left Whitby, I walked to the moor above Aisalby. From here the road ran north to the coast with its hard-set fishing villages: inland, looking west, dark spongy peat, crossed by pale dry-stone walls and severed by deep valleys. The country of my heart's heart. Why am I going away? I wondered. I am a fool.

I thought a little about K. I felt absurdly sorry for him, because of his carelessness. In some inexplicable way, I was still bound to him. Am I a coward? I wondered. Am I afraid to be alone?

An extraordinary gaiety seized me. I shall do something with my life, I thought; who, what, could possibly defeat me?

Chapter 44

Competent and unscrupulous . . . I acted as the Knopfs' representative for more than two years—until they had the fatal idea of starting their own firm in London. Nowadays, American publishers take a short and easier cut to a stall on our market; they buy an English firm, plump it out by methods known to every breeder of geese, and under cover of its name sell textbooks by the hundred thousand to peoples who are still anxious to pick our brains after getting rid of us as overlords.

As an agent I was a success. As well as being lightheartedly unscrupulous—doubtless there are pirates and wreckers among the honest smugglers in my ancestry—I was as green as I was bold. Riding light—without rules or ethics—I expected to win against the field. In fact the field was almost empty. There must have been older, staider agents at work, but I did not hear of them. It was, too, the Silver Age of English publishing, almost the age of innocence, when a publisher such as Victor Gollancz, who not only *meant business*, but said so, gave offence.

I ran about London like a dog, scarcely taking time to eat, pricking my ears in publishers' and agents' offices, my tongue dripping honey. For winter I had an excellent dark green coat, bought under the slightly disapproving eye of Betty Sadleir, who knew I could not afford it, and a hat I trimmed myself with a sweeping feather. Summer—well, in summer, let us be honest, I had the airs of a moulting sparrow.

I wrote to every well-known author under the age of fifty. I had a few civil phrases on the end of my pen . . . my profound admiration for your work . . . should you, at any time, consider changing your publisher in America, I beg that you will give me the chance to . . . your reputation, your etc, etc . . .

The writer—more especially the novelist—who has not, at one moment or another, considered his publisher unworthy of him, has still to be conceived. And behold, waiting on the moment, a smiling young spider with the web stretched in sight of the fly.

Quite often, what I said was what I meant. When a writer caught my imagination, I was, in those days, only too respectful.

And I had my moments of long-sight, as well as moments when I fell in friendship with a writer and was prepared to risk my neck in the rope for him. (Let me say here that, for all his ferocious words, no hand was ever more reluctant to hang a sinner than Alfred Knopf's.) Any agent would have felt safe in buying Francis Brett Young, but I went farther on the road to being hanged. One day I read, before it was published, a novel called *My Name Is Legion*, by an unknown writer—unknown to me. As a novel it was impossible, with a streak of something wild and ambiguous—a smell of sulphur. Obviously it would sell two or three hundred copies and be ignored by any sensible agent of an American publisher.

I was instantly attracted. I wrote to the author, and went to see him—and at once felt for him and his young wife the sort of pleased love one can feel, at sight, for a fine landscape or a painting. Hilda Morgan was an enchanting creature, with red-gold hair and clear eyes, a flicker of malice pointing their gaiety. Charles himself was a portrait by either of the Cranachs: his face had that delicacy and energy, and, even then, a faint tracery of lines, like the surface, *craquelé*, of an old painting—more the shadow of it than the later reality.

After the failure of this novel there was a long gap before *Portrait in a Mirror*. Something, during this time, happened to the madman hiding in an obscure corner of *My Name Is Legion*: he was cured, exorcized, cast out, what you like. Possibly Charles had taken the measure of himself and his great talent: since he was the most reserved of men—and, which is more remarkable, of writers—who knows what he paid for the serenity and impeccable good manners of his writing from now on?

I forced him on the Knopfs, who did not keep him very long—

incompatibility of species rather than any failure of Alfred Knopf's foresight.

'Alfred doesn't believe in the book [*Portrait in a Mirror*],' Charles wrote to me in 1929, 'though Macmillan's acceptance shook his unbelief a little; and even if I sent him all the reviews, he still wouldn't believe; only thousands of copies will convince him, I am afraid, and I don't hope for much in that line . . .'

This did Alfred Knopf an injustice. It was Charles himself in whom he could not believe—as if he were a hippogriff, or as if he were seeing him in a glass which reflected only Charles's more arrogant traits, his aloofness, his Platonic idealism, his distaste for anything that offended his style as a human being. The two men never met, however often they may have sat at the same table.

I think Alfred had moments when he believed that Charles was a figment of my feverish invention.

Yet no one was more acute, more open to reason, than Charles. Three years later, when *The Fountain* was an enormous success, he still hesitated to give up his position as dramatic critic of *The Times*. 'I'm frightened,' he wrote to me, 'of depending on novels for fear of being compelled to write them not in my own time, and with care for the financial result. Journalism is a guarantee against that and enables me never to spend a penny that comes from novels or to rely on them in any way. The question is whether it's better to keep this absolute independence and to write novels, as I wrote *The Fountain*, in holes and corners and scraps of odd time (which means endless rewriting to preserve continuity) or to throw up *The Times* and venture. I don't know. And I'm becoming desperate because I can't get a clear twenty-four hours anywhere to write even the first paragraph of a book that has been boiling in my mind for ages . . .'

It was not then (1932) too late for me to notice the implied warning, and profit by it. But it brushed past me at a moment when I had just taken the notion that I could learn to write well. For years I thought of little else.

Today I see too sharply the folly (blindness, recklessness, ignorance—choose your term) of relying on writing for a living. The model for a young writer is Stendhal, who became a consul, or Tolstoy who was a landowner, or even X, Y, or Z, niched snugly in a warm corner of the cultural factory. I am dubious about the last: cultural officials lead narrow etiolated lives.

Is there any more futile and pitiable career than that of the writer compelled, year after year, to do his tricks on the same scrap of threadbare carpet, only in order to eat, poor acrobat? I suppose a minor actor runs him close. Or a fifth-rate politician. But these two probably have thicker hides, and feel their ignominy less.

This is a terrible digression, which has taken me too far from the young Charles Morgan, and his not yet bridled and bitted demon. Perhaps I am inventing the demon. The copy of *My Name Is Legion* was stolen from me, together with that other early book on his experiences in the Navy, so that I cannot track down the whiff of sulphur.

Chapter 45

As a publisher Alfred Knopf has no equal in his country. True, publishing in the States had not then become what it is now, a vast industrial enterprise, heavily capitalized, employing an immense corps of editors, experts in publicity, professors of (God help us all) Creative Writing and, by a strange necessity, writers: unlike the others, and like commercial travellers on a commission basis, the last are paid by results. But in 1924 the current was already setting that way and away from the kind of firm, small, choosy, he had imagined when he began. This elegant ghost never let him alone, egging him on to publish some books because he liked them, though he had no hope of making money by them. Whether saleable or not, every book had to meet his exigent standards of printing and binding. Not, mind you, that he would ever have been content to become an honourable failure; he was too ambitious, too shrewd, too intelligent. Curiosity and a fine palate drove him and his equally ambitious wife to pick up writers in every country in Europe, from Poland to Spain—at a time when translations were neither fashionable nor obligatory. He had—I should write: has—a knowledge of publishing comparable only to that of an English publisher he admired greatly, and sometimes quarrelled with: they were both as stubborn as the devil.

I had been working for him about a year when one day I answered the telephone to hear a voice I knew well, because it imitated so precisely the fluttering gesture of his hands when he was talking—Stanley Unwin's.

'Miss Jameson, Alfred has called me a *pig*!'

What was I to say? 'I'm dreadfully sorry.'

'Oh, it's not your fault. But I'll have nothing more to do with him.'

I did not believe the estrangement would last. Nor did it. The respect, not to say affection, between these wholly dissimilar human beings was too strong to be ended by a tiff.

To my spiritual and moral profit, Stanley Unwin became my friend. Wise, knowledgeable, shrewd to a fault, incorruptible, he was kinder to me than I merited. There may have been something honest in me, even at that simian time in my life, which caught his sympathy; or his sharp twinkling eye noticed that 'this devil is but a Simpleton, after all.' I made excuses to go and see him in his somewhat shabby office in a quarter of which he owned a sizeable part. His mere physical lightness enchanted me, so much that sometimes, in the pleasure of watching his hands fly up his with voice, I forgot to listen and had to improvise my reply . . .

One warm light evening during the last war, I was walking towards Pall Mall, and came on the half-destroyed front of the Carlton Hotel. I did not know it had been bombed, and was startled into standing to gape at it—long enough to let the ghost of a young woman in a hurry slip past me between the broken walls into the diningroom not there. I knew her: she was expecting six guests—and they were all on time: two of them had simply to forget that they had died several years before, and the others to leave less than twenty years in the lobby with their hats, to be able to go straight to the long light room, where tables, chandeliers, waiters, and *suprême de volaille Montpensier* ordered by the young woman beforehand, needed only their goodwill to be waiting for them . . .

When I had been working for them for five or six months, the Knopfs arranged for me to sign the bill at the Carlton, so that I could—not too often—give lunch to their own writers, and writers I was angling for. I might—they trusted me enough not to ask for names—have fed every needy writer I knew, but I was at least scrupulous enough to stick to writers worth seducing, and only once or twice to slip in a poor unsaleable honest little lark with the peacocks.

With a clear conscience, I invited a critic or two with the clerisy. Today, most reviewers of novels would have to be invited to nursery tea, but in the 'twenties they were serious thoughtful adults: fiction was not then considered a sort of writing only fit for an apprentice to cut his teeth on.

During these years I came to know so many people that I almost died of it. I have, thank God, forgotten nine-tenths of them: those I remember clearly have stayed in my mind either because, like Charles and Hilda Morgan, they became my friends, or because they were eccentric or impressive or gave me far too much trouble.

Romer Wilson died young, of tuberculosis. The first time I met her was with Blanche Knopf, who had come to rely on me to cast out devils in writers she found unmanageable. She got a half-malicious amusement out of watching me make myself affable to a Swedish or a Spanish novelist, neither of us having a syllable of the other's language. Asking me to help her with Romer Wilson, she said,

'You'll be able to handle her. I can't talk to her at all, I think she is insane.'

When she came into the room, Romer Wilson's dark eyes were rolling like those of a nervous horse, but she was not insane. She was simply a self-consuming genius, not a great genius, but of the cloth.

An infinite number of accidents—a love of going much into company or disliking it, having a sensual robust body or a sickly crippled one, being brought up Catholic or Calvinist—decides the answer that the sensitized nerves of the writer (painter, musician) make to his world. In Romer Wilson, genius took the form of a short cut between her senses and her half-conscious mind. Read *Dragon's Blood*, written before 1926, for her prevision of the bitterness and insanity which served Hitler's purpose. It is easier to describe water than to give an account of genius. One of its needs, or effects, seems to be a tension or peculiar instability of the nerves.

It occurs to me that this is why there are so few women of genius —tension and nervous instability do not go with childbearing.

The condition of genius may begin to be as common in women as in men only after several generations in which enough women renounce their biological functions. (I offer the idea to feminists.)

Possibly, too, the instability explains why a male writer of genius can cut down to the quick of a woman: any talented writer can produce semblances of human beings to fill out his tale, but when it comes to touching the naked rage of their lives he can only make guesses—it takes a Tolstoy to *know* what drives a woman to suicide or adultery or self-sacrifice.

You have only to compare the male characters invented by that highly-talented writer Charlotte Brontë with the male presences in *Wuthering Heights*.

It is not an accident that so much genius dies young, either stiffening into talent in Picasso, extinguishing itself in Wordsworth, dying in the flesh in Mozart, Keats, Emily Brontë, an endless line of brutally snuffed-out candles. If it can find a way to feed on others it can go on living; if not, if all it can do is to offer itself to its dear vulture, it dies—of T.B., or syphilis, or a stroke, or . . .

When I saw her alone, I got on extremely well with Romer Wilson. We are both from Yorkshire, and I understood her form of honesty, her form of timidity (more than half arrogance), her form of insanity—which was partly a total indifference to appearances and partly the dangerous lucidity with which, when she was writing, she heard and saw.

She told me once that she did not write with the conscious or deliberate intention of writing what, when she came to read it through, was there on the page. For weeks, months, she felt no impulse to write at all; then the wish seized her, she shut herself away from everyone, husband, infant son, friends, and wrote until she was physically and mentally exhausted.

If Mr X or Miss Y had told me that their admirable mechanically-articulated novels were in this way *given*, I should not have believed a word of it. I believed Romer Wilson—if only because no fragment she left, however trivial, is less than alive.

Chapter 46

Is it to my discredit that so much I remember is laughable—even when the memory that makes me laugh is attached to a person I genuinely like, or admire, or respect? Perhaps if I had had the courage, or the impudence, to laugh aloud at the time, I should have fewer memories, but they would be less unsuitable to a work of this sort.

Am I lacking in reverence? I think not. There are many people I revere with heart and soul, not only men like R. H. Tawney—there is no one like R. H. Tawney, and never will be—and women like Q. D. Leavis, but certain of the exiles I know, who are, quite simply and without knowing it, heroic.

But, in spite of my respect for her as a poet, as a high-spirited rebel against an aristocratic insolence she nevertheless fell into whenever she or her brothers were attacked by a plebeian critic, and as a hater of cruelty (except to critics), when I want to recall Edith Sitwell as I saw her in 1924, what springs into my mind first is not the really impressive figure she made, sitting, in a dark dress and immensely wide black hat, upright against yellow cushions at the end of the sofa in my room, her hands, her incredibly long fine hands, folded in her lap. No, I see her in her own sitting-room in west London, and myself choking over the hideously dry bun I was foolish enough to take from the tea-tray and too intimidated to leave uneaten.

Just as I had made up my mind that I could leave, a young man, fair-haired, tolerably good-looking, came in.

'You know Peter Quennell, of course.'

I did not. And when he knelt on a hassock and looked up into her face with what I daresay was genuine adoration, I merely thought him affected—*a fond ape,* as the ill-conditioned member of 5b, never far below the surface, would have said. Later, when his essays on the

French Symbolists came out, it was years before I brought myself
to open the book and discover how admirable a critical work I had
almost missed.

And here—saved from the fire by having been pushed inside his
book on Einstein—are three letters from J. W. N. Sullivan. Alfred
Knopf had written, urging me to get the manuscript from him, and
I went to a house in Pond Street to ask when it would be finished.
Misled by my awe of mathematics, I had supposed J.W.N.S. to be
a very old gentleman, who should be waited on. I found a dark
heavily-built man in his late thirties, who there and then invited me,
very pleasantly, to become his mistress. He took my refusal pleasantly, too, adding that he felt sure he would very soon convince me
that I was making a serious mistake. I was embarrassed and bored—
and anxious not to seem *provincial*. Even if I had found him attractive
—on the contrary, he very slightly repelled me—I was infinitely too
calculating and fastidious to enjoy a casual affair.

Not long after, he came up to London from Surrey, where he had
a cottage, and walked me about the Embankment a long time, two
or three hours, talking brilliantly about music, Einstein, Katherine
Mansfield ('You're very like her, you know.'), and the benefits a
young woman from the provinces could look for in being 'educated',
mentally and sexually, by himself.

The walk ended in Trafalgar Square, where we sat, in chilly sunshine, on the parapet of a fountain, and he said with energy,

'You are not a child. Why must you behave like one? Or like a
cold-hearted Puritan. Here am I offering you the companionship
for as many years as you like, and the devotion, of one of the great
intellects of our day—I won't speak of my other talents—and you
mock me.'

He was certainly vastly intelligent, not only able to argue in
German with Einstein himself, but a learned and passionate lover of
music. When, much later, I read the sentence in which Stendhal says
he cannot understand why Méthilde rejected him as a lover—she
was politically in disgrace, she had allowed him three years of intimate friendship, she loved him, and yet, yet, she refused to become
his mistress—I thought at once of J. W. N. Sullivan. I understood
Méthilde perfectly. With his brilliant mind, his youthful passion for
mathematics, his wit, his knowledge of music, his apparent self-
assurance, Stendhal must have been more than a little like him. My
passion for Stendhal, as writer and human being, is barely this side

idolatry—but I could not have fallen in love with him. There is a certain fatuity, physical not moral, not even spiritual . . .

The last letter from him (the last I kept) came—shade of Stendhal! —from Italy. '. . . why not run over here, straight into my outstretched arms? We have the *Spring* in Italy now. And living here is so cheap. Einstein will come along presently . . . And I have begun another NOVEL! I spend eight hours daily in writing. But that leaves time for other things. An Italian lady here tells me she never knew what happiness meant until I showed her . . . My dear little conscientious Northerner, come south for a while. *I mean it*, you know. You collect experiences, don't you? Well, I'm an experience (a delightful one, I'm told) and remember, *age* creeps on. And I know you. In your autobiography you will refer with veiled pride to your liaison (in Italy in the spring) with a certain well-known writer. And I will introduce you to Norman Douglas, a wise and charming blackguard . . .'

If I read this letter the first time with a detestably derisive smile for its fatuity, and if, re-read, it still strikes me as clumsy, ridiculous, insensitive—he was not insensitive—a little remorse seizes me: because he is dead and I have lived so long . . .

How carefully I cherish—between layers of blotting-paper—the youth of my friends! One young man's flaming hair, another's loud crowing laugh; Archie as a youthful lieutenant-colonel; the exquisite head, its line unmarred by its fleece of dark-red curls, of Amabel Williams-Ellis; Noel Streatfield, a lovely creature, tireless and witty, amused by her own preposterous life as a young actress *en tournée*; an absurdly thin Richard Hughes. He was living in a flat not far from the British Museum, with his mother, and I fell momentarily into disgrace with her when I went to see him in the hospital where he was recovering from appendicitis and told him a comical story about a poet we both knew which made him laugh, causing him exquisite pain.

Should I trouble the sleep of another ghost? One evening, at a large literary dinner-party—how I dislike these gatherings of enraged egoists—someone pointed out to me a small elderly woman sitting alone, neglected by chattering writers and camp-followers.

'May Sinclair. I wish you would talk to her.'

'But what shall I say?'

'Anything, anything.'

Her eyes were those of a very young child, incurious and a little unfocused. I stammered some phrase or other of admiration for the one of her novels I had read at the university. She made little or no answer. I went with her into the dining-room and helped her to find her place at the long table. From mine I could see her, with an empty chair on her left: the other, on her right, might as well have been empty, since its young male occupant ignored her throughout the meal. When coffee was served, Arnold Bennett, who was leaving, paused to speak a word to her as he passed behind her chair: after this, she sat silent, looking down at her cup. I turned over in my head the sentences I would run and say to her as soon as we rose, but before then she stood up alone and began to walk away. She had to walk the length of the room, and when she reached the door could not find her way through the curtains drawn across it. She glanced round, at a loss, then fumbled through them, distracted by her scarf. Too timid and self-conscious to get up and cross the room to help her, I watched her until she disappeared.

For weeks, I could not think of this episode without shame for my part in it.

I think it was this same evening, when I was standing near her, admiring her beautiful ruined face, that I overheard Violet Hunt say smilingly,

'My dear, Mary Borden sat all day at my husband's feet. He wrote her first novel for her. Many of the critics, I'm told, consider it her best.'

Chapter 47

In the autumn of 1924, I took a large room in Sloane Street, and provided it with a sofa, a walnut tallboy, a kitchen table, and some oddments of Victorian furniture. I was pleased with it: one very large room is all I need to live happily alone.

In 1924 it was still possible to invite people to tea—I am talking, obviously, of a very distant time. Once in a while I invited—separately, I think—two young men who were close friends: they had been at Cambridge together after the war, and were living side by side, each with wife and a child or two, in the country near London. Of all the too many people I knew, turning my life into a cheap circus, they alone seemed familiar.

An illusion, the accident that they reminded me of three smiling poor scholars, innocent scoffers with whom I had felt more at ease than with any of my new friends.

I liked the two, Gerald Bullett and J. B. Priestley, very well. They were as dissimilar a pair of friends as ever was: Gerald appeared the simpler, only in the sense that he was simple enough to believe he need only write his best, and all else, recognition, a secure living, would be added unto him. His friend—even then—knew better. Years later, with regret and sharp humour, he said to me,

'The mistake our Gerald made was to bury himself in the country. I told him: Get out, do as I'm doing, get to know people, make yourself felt, go about. He didn't listen.'

The advice was useless. If Gerald had been able to take it, he would not have needed it. He had two traits that ruined him for a life of getting about and getting to know people: a sub-conscious lethargy, which may have been physical, a deeply-rooted indifference or carelessness, as if he had thrown himself once for all into a stream and was letting it carry him where it pleased. He struggled, did well the work offered him, broadcasting, reviewing; he wrote, with immense effort, novels which give an effect of ease and grace, even lightness; he had more than one of your serious novelist's virtues, ingenuity, an almost innocent eye for the lies, ruses, self-deception, the blundering decency and compassion of ordinary men and women, a distaste for rhetoric. And all the time he was drowning in the very current that held him up: it was a slow process, and, when I first knew him, had scarcely begun.

Would he, if he had been born able to choose, or if he had not had his friend's example inciting him, have written novels? His rather clumsy head and body housed a poet of extreme elegance, of an almost Chinese elegance, able to make complex statements as if they were simplicities, so acutely attentive to the dissonance of life that in a chaos of sounds he could pick out the single note of existence itself. One says Chinese, thinking of the delicacy and purity of his poetic language, but the word is misleading: in his verse he was an English mystic, one of God's honest stubborn lazy eternally youthful

English: the landscape of his poems is a loving yet cool pattern of
sensuous detail, English in its smallest strokes.

I loved him for his gentleness. Not that he was soft-spoken, still
less bland. He was as capable of a tart or malicious speech as the rest
of us miserable sinners. But he had more gentleness, more charity,
more singleness of mind than was good for him if he had wanted
success as much as he wanted—ah, what did he want? To be happy,
to be a little better-known, to have time to write a few more poems,
time to look longer and closer at a leaf, a child, the surface of a
stream . . .

He was fond enough of me to forgive me—except when it exasperated him too much—what he called 'your abominable and inflexible
energy.'

I did not like the other young man any less. In one sense I liked
him, at that time, the better of the two—but my liking was not
straightforward. Imagine yourself walking along an empty street,
and suddenly met by yourself, coming the other way, in a mirror—
the shock of recognition, the instinctive fear and refusal. Hence my
instant sympathy, instant deep liking—that is, liking at a deep level
—and all but instant rejection. I think coolly that it is not my fault
we did not become friends. If I, without knowing it, rejected an
image of myself, he did the same, with instinctive mistrust.

Here is an odd thing. When I think of Gerald, it is only the last
glimpse of him which is clear in my mind. The others are blurred
copies. A door opens, he comes in, moving slowly and a little
heavily, his large head thrust forward, coming from nowhere, going
—where? But my memory of my first meeting with J. B. Priestley
in the summer of 1924 is curiously distinct.

He came to tea. I had taken it into my head that he might be even
worse off than I was. This was certainly not true; I had no reason to
think it, but I did—and offered him, in the Yorkshire phrase, an egg
to his tea. (I think he refused it.) We talked—or rather, he talked and
I listened.

The shadowy outline of a room in Herne Hill rose behind this
more presentable one. I felt affection, warmth, ease and a wary
scepticism. The thing most to be feared in a Yorkshireman is not his
shrewdness, his black sense of humour, his scoffing disrespect for
authority, his grudging temper—but his secret fear that he is not
accepted at the price he puts on himself. Touch that in him, and you
will not be forgiven.

I have always loathed and despised the grudging take-you-down-a-peg side of the Yorkshire character as heartily as I admire certain others of their virtues and vices: their brusque charity, tenacity, self-will, impatience of control, self-biting wit.

Nothing saves me from being the worst of Yorkshiremen except a profound indifference which comes from some other strain (Gallilee?). In my heart of hearts I do not care whether I am respected or disliked, or even injured, by *these people*.

'I had a look at your last book,' he said, smiling. 'I don't say it's bad, but all you women writers are the same, too careful or too violent. You s'd strike out something for yourself, not keep on hashing up all that old stuff. You haven't much invention, have you?'

Since my vanity does not lie in my writing, I took this for what it was, a nearly impersonal dressing-down. Moreover, I had begun to think he was right.

He talked to me about the book he was writing, and about himself. I listened. Later I discovered that he was carrying about with him a heavy weight of anxiety. True to his and my kind, he had no intention of showing it. His irony, his sardonic self-confidence, delighted me, and for a moment gave me the illusion that, with a cool blast of horse-sense, I could brush aside my mistakes, sins, follies. I was sorry when he got up to go.

Turning in the door, he smiled at me with the half derisive, half wary kindness familiar to me since my childhood.

'Well, you're not so bad,' he said. 'I thought you might be much worse.'

I tried hard to persuade the Knopfs that his novel was one they ought to snatch at once, without seeing it finished. Alfred Knopf did not agree—and lost *The Good Companions*. Just as well. The two of them would have been at outs in a year.

A few years later, when I was reviewing for A. R. Orage, I made him very angry by writing severely about his latest book. I have completely forgotten why I did it. The intellectual recklessness that seizes me when I am alone with a pen and a sheet of paper? A nearly impersonal Yorkshire malice?

I have never in my life altered my relations with a friend because he cursed or mocked my work—and I have had to take some pretty harsh comments. He is less indifferent, less sceptical about his writing, and—in a word—more honest. If I had imagined that my fault-finding would cut deeply I would have given my tongue to the cat . . .

This trivial incident tells nothing, or nothing of value, about a complex human being called Priestley. The person it reflects more or less accurately is a self-centred young woman, clever and imprudent.

Chapter 48

There are moments when it seems impossible that I am coming to the end of my life—and with so little of all I intended to do done, and without knowing myself better than when I set out.

A psychologist might find in the confusion, the persistent *lack* of plan in the welter of plans masking the deep-rooted improvidence and incoherence of my life, a secret wish to be punished for my errors.

On this reasoning, Stendhal brought all his frustrations and disappointments on himself, even his dull life in Civitavecchia, as a punishment for having been in love with his mother, who died when he was seven . . . *Quant à moi j'étais aussi criminel que possible, j'aimais ses charmes avec fureur* . . . But, good heavens, how boring an account of the author of *Lucien Leuwen*!

When we went to Weybridge in 1924, I and my eight-year-old son, I meant to live quietly, write a fifth novel, and begin to save money to send him to school and the university, even—but this I avoided looking at closely—to be able to have a house of our own. The novel was a necessity: we could not go on living on my salary as Knopf's representative.

Nothing turned out as I meant. I wrote nothing—the other work demanded too much time and drained me of energy: to have to do with so many people exasperated me; they pulled my mind to pieces with their monkeys' fingers and at the end of the day I was in a state of distraction, as little able to sit down to write as sing in tune, always beyond me.

I am lying. In time I should have learned how to live two lives without cheating either. What scattered my plans like dry leaves in a wind was a personal crisis, the sharpest of my life, into which I fell as soon as I started to work in London.

I am not going to tell the story at length. Like my happy difficult second marriage, it is part of the nervous system of my mind: to draw it out would kill me. What little could safely be turned into phrases has been told once already.

Outwardly, as it unfolded under the amused half-sceptical eyes of two of my friends, Elizabeth Gleeson and Michael Sadleir, it seemed no more than an obsession. Michael refused frankly to believe that it was either deeply serious or final.

'You'll fall in love a dozen times!' he said smiling.

Quite possibly, had there been no great difficulties, it might not have been a mortal illness or lasted my life. But the difficulties drove it into my soul, like a stain driven through a piece of cloth. They were not only concrete—we were both married, though not living alone. The most paralysing difficulty, the one I was weeks, months, learning to recognize, was impenetrable by sense or reason.

I realized quickly that nothing made Guy happier than to talk about the war. Certain names of places, Bapaume, Gommecourt, Hannescamp, Arras, had more than the charm or excitement of poetry for him. They involved feelings I could never touch. With a little despair, I guessed that his five years of war and Occupation had used up too much of his energy. During those years the relationship between him and a few men, a few places, between him and a battalion, had been complete and satisfying, as no relationship would ever be again. He was *occupied territory*.

'Thank heaven,' he said once, 'that my personal life is finished. The only pleasures I want are all impersonal. To work until I can't think any longer. Music. A decent bottle of wine. I'm perfectly content.'

Like other soldiers I knew, whose war had been long, he became tired, suddenly grey in the face, between one minute and the next. Fatigue made him cruel. 'Work is more important to me than anything. If you, or my wife, were to get in my way I should have to leave you out, do you understand, my dear? . . . I don't like being driven. The idea that I'm being held down to any set of circumstances, makes me want to move off, *foutre le camp*, before it's too late.'

Where he was concerned, I had no vanity, no pride. Spoken to by two voices at once, one of them his exhaustion and fear of failure, I heard only the other one. Nothing convinced me that, dryness and impatience apart, I was not loved, not needed. My mind had fastened on him with all its tenacity, with a total imprudence, obeying, this time, an impulse engaging body, spirit, imagination. All the energy of my tortuous and, as it was then, domineering nature was bent to one end—for the most part I was, am, too lazy, too at a deep level indifferent, to use it in this single-pointed way. It would be a great deal truer to say that I was possessed rather than possessive.

I saw him two or three times a week, and he wrote as often. A small pile of letters accumulated in a corner of my cupboard in Weybridge.

K. had become remote, a shadow on the edge of my mind. I suppose he wrote to me, since he had fewer distractions in Cornwall, and I answered, as is my habit, at once. Then tore up his letter and forgot him.

One incident of this time slightly alarmed me. I had a letter from an elderly lady he had met in a train, to whom he had said that I was the daughter of an Admiral and closely related to Dr Jameson of the Raid. I was used to his casual inventions—they were a sort of involuntary play-acting, little more sophisticated than a child's daydreams of being heroic and witty. This seemed a little worse. And if I were to be involved in his myths . . . (This mythopoeic trick of his did become serious, and later in his life began to fringe mania. Some of his inventions were less innocent than this one; there must be several people in the world who know about me disagreeable things in which there is not a vestige of truth.)

Since I could not answer the lady's friendly letter without giving him away, I destroyed it.

Chapter 49

Some time in March or April I came home from London early in the afternoon and found K. in my sitting-room. From his air of sullen dignity I saw that I was in disgrace. Drawn stiffly to his height of over six feet, he scowled down at me. The whole thing was arranged, even to his gestures. I felt contemptuous and uneasy.

It was soon out. He had found and taken the bundle of Guy's letters.

'Where are they?' I asked calmly.

'They're not in this house.'

My heart dropped. He was perfectly capable of reading them aloud to his friends. He would make a laughing-stock of us both, almost without knowing he was doing it. As for scandal, he enjoyed it.

'You've sent them away? Where?'

'Never mind what I've done with them. May I ask if you meant to tell me about this—this sordid affair?'

'No.'

I felt unreasonably bitter, and sick and tired of him. Yet, when I looked at him standing there, solemn, peevish, the dignified husband victimized by a dishonest wife—which I was—I had an extraordinary feeling of pity, almost gentleness. He has never grown up, I thought: he understands nothing, neither himself, nor what he did to us.

The fear that he might use the letters to harm Guy turned me to steel: I was determined to get them from him—by any means.

'If you imagine I'll make things easy for you, you're entirely mistaken,' he said sarcastically. 'I'm not going to hand my son over to you, to be brought up by you and your admirer—don't think it.'

I felt an access of contempt. 'Are you by any chance going to bring him up yourself?' I asked him in my mother's harshest voice.

There was a silence. Then he sat down and began to speak sorrowfully.

'I never thought you were tired of me. I've been looking forward to living with you in Launceston—I meant to work, and try to make something of my life. It's almost funny—you might as well have taken a knife and cut my throat. I would never have believed it of you.'

His face worked, and he covered it with his hands.

It would not be true to say that the grief which tore its way through my body, wrenching it horribly, was for him: it was for the past, for what he had been to me, for the failure I, I, had made of our marriage, for all the mistakes, disappointments, defeats, still in the closed hand of the future. A hand twisted the nerves above my heart. Am I going to die? I thought.

My will had not died.

'If you will give me the letters back,' I said, 'I'll give him up.'

'Do you promise?' he said sternly.

'Yes, yes, I promise.'

'Very well. I trust to your generosity.'

No, don't trust me at all, I thought. So afraid was I of wakening his anger again that I spoke under my breath.

'Where are they?'

He had made a parcel of them and taken it to the Left Luggage office at the railway station. At once, so that he would have no time to change his mind, I went with him to get them. When I had them in my hands, my strength left me and I felt deathly tired and weak, hardly able to put one foot before the other. I forced myself to talk to him in a gentle flattering way. He told me he was writing a novel, very outspoken. 'Bolder than anything you can do,' he said, smiling, 'or Bennett or Wells either. You'll see—your little K. will astonish you.'

Pray heaven he does, I thought: I shall feel less responsible for him.

Did I, even at this moment, intend to keep my promise? Almost certainly not. I made it without reflection, as I would have clutched the blade of a knife to save myself falling over a cliff. I felt neither shame nor guilt. Afterwards, in a confused way, I thought: After all, I may lose Guy, and then nothing I have promised will matter . . .

Some time this month—it may have been later or earlier: my uncertainty about dates is a scandal—I saw one of my first friends, Oswald Harland. With him or with one of the others, I was always happy. What other happiness in the world equals that of being remembered from childhood, and approved or disapproved of without irony?

He had had what he called an impudent letter from K. He told me nothing about it, and I did not ask.

'K. did you a great deal of harm,' he grumbled.

'I'm very hard. I've lived through it without damage—as you can see.'

'The damage isn't obvious—except to me. I knew you, don't forget, when you were a schoolgirl, afraid of nothing and nobody.'

'Not true,' I said.

'Well, let's say that in those days you had enough self-confidence to take you to hell and back. You've lost it, and you don't trust anyone. D'you know what Archie and I said to each other when you married K.? We said: And that's the end of our Daisy Jameson . . . It damn' near has been . . . Why didn't you leave him years ago?' He scowled. 'I haven't forgotten one episode in Shepherd's Bush—I thought very seriously of killing him then.'

I knew he was thinking of my fatuous impulse to kill myself, and my mind turned tail and bolted.

'You only saw his worst side, he had others . . . I couldn't have walked out of the house lugging young Bill, and his clothes and travelling bath and the cot, and all my books and the silver spoons my mother gave me, and my grandmother's tea service.'

'I never heard such nonsense,' he said, grinning. 'You're a queer dishonest chap, you know.'

'Then why bother about me?'

'I have m'reasons. You have an honest mind. No call to look pleased—you can't help it, and in every other way you're as dishonest as be damned. I don't suppose you've told yourself a lie since you began to think, but you don't mind how many you tell other people. You like them to think well of you, don't you?'

'It's my great fault,' I said, mocking him.

It was myself I mocked. When I was thinking coldly I thought that my ambition and impatience were more to blame and K. less than this friend, looking at me from our careless past, imagined. My own disloyalties seemed—seem—inexcusable where those of others can be explained.

K. began sending me terrible letters. I read them with a sick heart—and pushed them aside, almost unanswered. The half of me that cringed was strangled by another which scarcely believed in his unhappiness. I had come to an end of regret. And if not—not yet—to an end of concern and pity, these were drowned in an indifference that rose, a cold tide, from depths I preferred not to look at.

That was not all. 'An emotion can neither be hindered nor removed save by a contrary emotion . . .' (Spinoza).

Whatever might come of it, my new love—more despotic than any simply erotic passion—had freed me, at last, from everything except a guilt which had older roots than those still twisted round the man who had taught me to distrust myself, suspected me, hurt me in anger, and given me my first adult lessons in solitude and the unseemliness of relying on the kindness of another human being.

To avoid thinking too much, I worked myself to exhaustion. After long days, a few hours' sleep gave me back a body as light as when I was one of four poor scholars.

In just the same way as, after a defeat, there came to my side all the hidden exultance, the gaiety, of the child resolved *to get away*.

Chapter 50

It never struck me that hired rooms are no sort of life for a young child. Only very rarely, when he was more taciturn than usual, I asked myself whether Bill was happy living with me in Weybridge.

'What did you do today, my one?'

'Nothing.'

'No lessons?'

'Yes, I had lessons.'

'Do you like this school?'

'It's all right.'

'Do you like it better than living with Miss Geeson?'

'Yes,' he said, with indifference.

I saw that he could not tell me what he did during his days, because the repetition bored him, and because he had a profound dislike of answering questions. He answered them as shortly as he could, hoping there were no more to come.

With a little anxiety, I tried to hear myself as a child—and failed. It seemed that neither the streets and cafés of Antwerp, nor the ship's saloon, its air warm, stagnant, smelling of lamp oil and the steward's pantry, had been much troubled by my voice.

One day he left his composition book at home. The last two pages were filled, in his large straggling hand, by a piece entitled: How you write books. 'First you write what your book is going to be about, then you send it somewhere to be printed. Then if it is a good book it will be published and charged so much for, if it is a bad book it is Sent back. My mother Wrote a book each copy was so much money it took a very long time to Write. When it was finished it Was about one inch and ½ thick.'

Heaven be praised, he is not going to turn into a writer, I thought.

I spent too much time in London, taking the train as soon as he had gone to school and hurrying back in time to give him tea. Returning from one of these sorties I found Elizabeth in our sitting-room. She was playing with Bill, who for some reason had been sent home early, and she was on her hands and knees, her hair wildly in disorder, her eyes brilliant. I had never seen her look so beautiful. It startled me, and roused a little fear. With a wide sweet smile, she said,

'I have left John. Your landlady says she can let me have the bedroom next yours. Do you mind?'

I was overjoyed. The warmth, the gaiety, the ease she spread round her, without effort, in the movements of her large hands, in the tone, low and slightly rough—she smoked too much—of her voice, was what our life, mine and Bill's, lacked. I settled back into it as into my mother's house, with the same familiarity.

It did not surprise me that she had left John, but I was a little shocked that she had trusted her five-year-old Prue with the two servants. After Bill was in bed, she told me why she had left: she had fallen in love with the young doctor John had taken on as assistant, and John had found them together: the same day the young man left for London, and she, after a few terrible days of scenes and arguments, had decided to follow him.

'What is going to happen?'

She lifted her hands, smiling. 'Oh, I don't know. A divorce, I suppose. I'm not going to make any plans. What happens, happens.'

I asked no more questions. She lived in these rooms exactly as she lived anywhere, with the instinctive lightness of a seagull balancing on a rope, perfectly at ease and ready to take off any second. Our sitting-room became untidy and lived-in, she dropped cigarette ash everywhere, borrowed my books and handed them back with coffee stains on the pages. Once or twice a week, not oftener, she went to London to see her lover, who had taken a post of some sort there.

She seemed content to idle through the other five or six days of the week, sleeping late, reading, talking to me when I had time to listen. She talked a great deal of Prue, rarely of John. It was not she who told me, years later, that he had caught her when she was unhappily in love with a young man too preoccupied to pay attention to her: from the start, their marriage was made false and brittle by the pretence that she loved him. She, I suppose, did not want to look at a humiliating mistake; she would rather pretend, even to herself, that she had married for love. Yes, even, for a time, to herself. As for him, he loved her with a sort of ferocity—then.

I exaggerate, perhaps. After all, I lived with them for months without suspecting that they were not, in their different ways, devoted. What went on below the sparkling surface—made to sparkle by Elizabeth—was probably out of sight in those years.

She talked about her childhood with an intelligent charming father, who flattered her, and later abandoned his wife, leaving her to bring up—on a wretchedly small income—five children, including the daughter he had seemed to admire and love. 'When I was still in my cradle,' she said, smiling, 'he looked at me and said: Perhaps she won't be at all beautiful, but she has charm and an intelligent body.'

She refused to admit his rejection of her: alone of his family, she called on him in his editorial office in London.

Some of the tales she told about herself were doubtless touched up or untrue, but in a strange way they were all innocent, like a very young child's efforts to draw attention to itself by smiling and clowning.

Now that she was here I made use of her. Knowing that Bill would be happy with her—what her child had lost, that incomparable gaiety and warmth, mine gained—I could sometimes stay in London with Guy until eleven, the last train.

On one of these evenings, at the end of a day when the June sun and the dry wind had between them made a desert of London, I had a curious experience. Guy and I were going to dine at the Café Royal. As I followed him into the brasserie, I saw the Texan.

He was at a table against the right-hand wall, with a companion, a woman neither very young nor elegant. My heart moved heavily. I turned my head aside, vexed by the exquisite line of the Hampshire downs wavering across a cloudless sky: of all creatures in the world I did not want to see a young woman staring at it from her window, her ears strained to catch the sound of an American lorry in the lane from the village . . . I walked past his table to the farther end of the room, and sat with my back to him, uncertain whether he had seen me. In my one glance from the doorway I had the impression that things were not going altogether well with him.

When we left, there was no one at his table. I stood for a moment outside the entrance to the brasserie, waiting for Guy to fetch his hat from the cloakroom. A waiter, a thin smile of connivance on his sallow face, stepped up to me, and handed me a folded sheet of paper.

'The gentleman left this for you.'

I put it into my pocket until I was in the train going home. Two lines. 'I wrote you yesterday, to Whitby. Call me at the Piccadilly, tonight or tomorrow morning—your J.'

I neither telephoned, nor, when the letter arrived, opened it. And when he came into my mind, I turned him out. I wanted *not* to know what he was doing. An instinct he himself would have recognized ordered me: Don't look behind you.

For some days I said nothing to Elizabeth. When I told her, she looked at me with an equivocal smile.

'Didn't you want to see him?'

'No.'

'Why not?'

'All that's finished.'

'Perhaps. But I don't think I ever knew you do anything callous—before this.'

I was surprised. 'Callous?'

'Incredibly callous. I don't understand you.'

I should have great trouble in understanding myself. Perhaps I was simply a coward. But the state of mind I recall is not timidity or nervousness: it is indifference, a dry deliberate rejection—of a self which no longer interested me, and, naturally, of the man involved with it.

That was the end—except for a letter, some years later, from his father, asking where his son was. I answered that I had not the faintest idea.

Chapter 51

Things were not going well with Elizabeth. Though I did not notice it—I was too self-engrossed to see anything below the surface—she was adrift as she had never been in her life, and, perhaps without knowing it, afraid. I did not know that her love-affair was going wrong until an evening when I came back from London and found her in the sitting-room, not reading, seated against the wall, hands in her lap, head stretched back. She had an unusually long slender throat, with a barely noticeable swelling, and a long straight jaw. I noticed two things: she, who never used make-up of any sort, had covered her eyelids with oil, perhaps to disguise redness after tears, and she was deathly tired, the marked sensuality of her face softened by it.

She looked at me gaily. 'I never knew how many happy people there are in the world until I felt unhappy. This evening when I went out to the pillar-box, there were lovers in every gateway.'

I did not know what to say. I tried to hear her mind. 'Are you unhappy?'

'I'm usually very happy. When I'm dancing—and on warm fine mornings . . . Have you been dining with Guy?'

'Yes.' I did not say that he had been in a black negative mood.

'Well, you are luckier than I am,' she said lightly. 'D'you know, I have made the most humiliating mistake—he doesn't care for me any longer. I offered to live with him on any terms, and he refused.'

Pity would be another humiliation. 'Do you mind seriously?'

'Of course.'

She was smiling ironically. Her hands were perfectly steady. I thought: I shall never see her cry.

'I can't comfort you.'

'A stupider person would try,' she said quickly.

She lit another cigarette, and went on to tell me, in the greatest detail, how things had begun to go wrong from the moment she came to Weybridge, and repeated, calmly, even smiling a little, with the same fold of irony at the ends of her mouth, the insults vented on her by a young man who was clearly tired of her and afraid of scandal. I listened without speaking. I was slightly shocked that she could expose herself so nakedly.

I had no impulse to confide in her in my turn. There is no doubt, I thought, that I am showing as little self-respect in my own affairs, but I shan't speak about it or let anyone know what I am going through.

But, merely by listening with my entire mind, I drew so close to Elizabeth during this hour that there was no need for me to say anything. When she stood up to go to bed, I felt an impulse of pure love, a strange mixture of liking and identity with her. Neither of us was in the habit of caresses, but at this moment it seemed natural to lean forward and kiss her very gently on the lips. She smiled without speaking.

A week or two later, she went back to John. I never stayed with them again, and on the one or two occasions when she came to stay with me in London after I married Guy, there was a light sense of —not estrangement, but distance. We talked, laughed, were happy, across a small dried-up stream. In some way I made no effort to fathom, she had drawn back, her gaiety, her brilliance of life, very slightly blurred.

Guy was not charmed by her, and this itself set a curious no-man's-land between us, created by my anxiety that she should not notice it.

Possibly she only came once.

She died suddenly, in 1934, in her sleep. Of heart-failure? Perhaps.

After the shock of grief, I closed my mind against a smiling ghost. I preferred not to think about her life during the nine years after she went back to John. If I had thought about it, I should have been forced to see that she had been defeated—under my averted eyes. Forced to know that, for all her warmth, her charm, her hunger for safety and kindness, her deep reserve about the real things she felt, she was a swimmer in a strong stream clinging, with the strength of her fears, to a root in the bank.

With the strength of her fears . . . And I left her with them. Why?

I am old and she a ghost. Who are so unforgiving as the dead? It is useless to ask them to forgive.

Chapter 52

At the end of July I took Bill to Whitby for the summer. I was making plans to move to London, to the room in Sloane Street. I had a respectable reason—it had become very difficult to work for the Knopfs from Weybridge—but this was not the real reason.

Living in London, I could see Guy more easily, in a less hand-to-mouth and unsettling way. For this I was going to uproot Bill again and send him as a boarder to his school in Weybridge.

I knew—beyond any question I knew—that if K. were to stand on his legal rights and force me to decide between son and lover, I could only choose my son. That was as fixed and cold in me as iron. Did knowing this let me put him second in lesser choices? . . .

I have few memories more absurd and vivid than of the meeting, after I had asked K. to divorce me, between him and Guy. They met in my room. Guy turned up first: he was curt and distant, as though he were feeling ill. No doubt he was. I felt completely detached, a spectator of what, after all, concerned me gravely.

K. arrived on his heels, greeted me in a formal way, and Guy with what deserved nothing better than to be labelled stately courtesy. With a flicker of the jeering Yorkshire irony I detest, I thought that he had chosen the role of man of the world—a little spoiled by the shape of his nose.

They sat at opposite ends of my sofa. To give myself something to do, I took a number of papers and letters from my desk and began destroying some and sorting the rest into their kinds. After a moment's silence K. said haughtily,

'I understand that you wish to marry my wife, if it can be arranged.'

'Yes.'

A fit of laughter seized me. I did my best to stifle it, but it was too violent. Both men turned to look at me, K. gravely, Guy with surprise and displeasure. I was ashamed of my misplaced gaiety.

Which shrewd derisive forbear is it who takes possession of me at the very moments when I ought to be most moved or most dignified? For the rest of the interview, very short, I had no further temptation to laugh.

When Guy had gone, thankful to escape, K. dropped his sublimity.

'Don't send me off at once. Just think—I'm going to be alone for the rest of my life.'

Little likelihood of that, I thought. He was looking at me with a lamentable face. Not a line on it, not the faintest trace of a line; he was thirty-five or six, and except for a coarsening round the nostrils, his face was that of a man of twenty. For a disagreeable moment I saw the road we took out of Leeds on summer nights, stumbling over the roots of trees in the darkness, the spoiled runnel from the factory glittering in the moon. Disgusted by my folly, I thought: Forgive me, it was my fault—in the end I was the stronger and harder of us. I said stiffly,

'I haven't been honest with you these last months. I'm sorry.'

A look at once sly and bitter came into his face. 'Why should you assume that I'm going to let you keep Bill?'

This threat—the single indestructible hold he had over me—he repeated at intervals during the next few years. He never tried to carry it out, even when he could have done so. He was not unkind enough—and he did not for a moment want the responsibility and cost of a child. But the threat never failed to send a pang of fear and rage through me.

I steadied myself to answer coldly. 'For one reason, you have never, since the end of the war, kept him yourself. And for another, when I gave up my divorce, you promised that if at any time I wanted to leave you, you would take the whole thing on yourself. I am not asking you to do this. But you have no right to take Bill from me. Rather than lose him, I would call off the divorce—I tell you that frankly, so that you know where you stand. But it wouldn't do you any good—I don't dislike you, but I would never live with you again.'

'You're very hard.'

'Not until I'm forced to be.'

'I shan't take the boy from you,' he said. 'I'm finished, you've done for me . . . My girl, *must* you do this to me?'

I felt—not pity followed by indifference, but indifference, pity, contempt (for his asking to be pitied), sympathy, and an old habit of responsibility—all in the same breath.

I said nothing. He stood up, and looked round for his hat.

'Even now I can't believe you mean to get rid of me. I don't know what to do with my life. I feel like shooting myself . . . Sunday afternoon, too—it's awful, awful—not a thing to do and nowhere to go.'

The prospect of entertaining him for the rest of the day filled me with despair—as though I were agreeing to live with him again. 'Is there anywhere you would like to go?'

'Yes,' he said, 'yes. When I was coming up this morning I thought: How wonderful if a miracle happened, and instead of kicking me out she said: Hurry up, we're going to Richmond—just as we did, you remember . . .'

'Very well,' I said, 'let's go to Richmond.'

We spent four hours there, walking in the Park, gossiping, discussing his unfinished thesis, his novel, his social triumphs in Launceston, like old friends . . .

In November Guy's lawyer summoned us to his office, handed each of us a document, and made us stand against the window of his room, as close as possible to the glass. It looked out on a narrow yard, below the level of the street. Four figures in single file walked at the pace of a funeral across this yard, faces over their shoulders, like maladjusted puppets, staring at the window. K. first, in the overcoat I had given him on his last birthday; a large woman, with a grimly displeased face, the chambermaid from the hotel; a pustular bully in a navy suit, who was the inquiry agent; and a young wizened man, a solicitor's clerk.

This astonishing procession passed. I turned to Guy. He was no help to me: hurrying me out of the house, he said, 'I'll see you to-morrow,' and fairly ran from me.

I walked across the square, looked back, and saw K. striding towards me. I waited. The wind flattened his overcoat against his long thin legs; with his narrow head he looked more puppet-like than ever.

'Well,' he said jauntily, 'what are you doing this afternoon?'

No more able to disappoint him than if he had been a child, I said, 'Nothing. Would you like to have tea somewhere, and dance?'

'That suits me.'

The ball-room of the Piccadilly Hotel is a well-lighted over-heated room below the ground. We drank hotel tea, and danced—since that was why we had come here—and talked. He was in a boastful mood, and I felt the old impulse to encourage him, for my own comfort more than his. His mood changed suddenly. With a mocking glance at me, he said, 'You look older, my dear. He didn't wait to see you home, your new lover. Well, if you change your mind about him, you can always come back, I shall welcome you with cheers. No doubt when I'm sixty I shall give up feeling. At present I still think about you.'

I acknowledged his right to mock. It struck me that, unreliable and useless as he was, he had never wanted to convince me that I was less necessary to him than other things. I neither liked nor respected him, but I was not, not yet, free of him in my mind. Should I ever be?

When the dancing ended, at six, I shook him off, as gently as I could, and set off to walk home. I was in a fever of impatience. It's not even true, I thought, with despair, that I am doing what I choose . . . My brain seemed to be boiling in my skull; I thought I was becoming insane . . . I could be living with Bill, simply, I don't like London now, in another ten years it will be uninhabitable by anyone with a nose and ears. I don't want to know people, or be known—that at least is true. And this, this, is the moment I choose to lose my wits again, for a difficult self-centred lover. Well, I must do as I can—sit still in my bones . . .

I caught sight of my morose face in a strip of glass between two lighted windows, and laughed out.

For an instant I felt free and light, as though I were beginning again, with no hand on me to turn me this way or that, no son, no lover, no abandoned husband. I hurried on, breathing the cold damp earth-scented air of the Park, towards the illusion of safety in a room empty of ghosts, without thoughts, without anxiety, without plans.

Chapter 53

I decided—the wrong word, it was simply the next step along a road I was following like a sleepwalker—that it was time we lived to-gether: a life of meetings and letter-writing was a distracting com-promise.

As soon as it was decided, I felt qualms—and ignored them. I daresay that, used as he had become to the life of a bachelor with a good club, Guy had his own unspoken doubts. These, too, I ignored. I knew, how well I knew, that doubt, even hostility, can exist at the same time, towards the same creature, as an irrevocable love and dependence.

He left everything to me, and I found a small furnished flat, the attics of a house at the top of Primrose Hill. At night it was sus-pended over London like a lighthouse; lines drawn by the street-lamps crossed the hill in all directions, the circles of light becoming smaller and smaller until the last point merged into the half-dark-ness, thinly-sown with blades and tendrils of light, stretching to an invisible horizon.

I will not say that I lived here easily. Guy was at times unapproach-able, sunk in his work or his dry thoughts. And all I feared and dis-liked, disliked in my bones, a domestic life, was nailed to me again. I had brought it on myself. Alone, as I often was, in the flat, trying to write, I was mocked by a jeering northern voice asking me what I imagined I had gained by my headstrong folly.

My worst moments had to do with Bill. I cannot—that is, will not —try to decipher what kept me from carrying out any of the foolish plans I made to bring him to London.

No man is an island . . . what nonsense! The one certain thing we know about a human being is that he is an island, becoming smaller, colder, more sterile: the wildness of first love, the lovely ease of youth, the pleasures of hate, all slowly failing, until the day when only a habit of caring remains.

Guy's wife had put an end to their marriage in the most humiliating way imaginable. I understood her—no one can be so brutal, so blindly callous, as a woman in the grip of an infatuation. He had no conscious wish to redress the balance at my cost. In good faith he told himself, and me, that he was used-up, incapable of meeting the demands of an exacting love, unwilling to risk a second failure.

Possibly, I told myself, it is true. Possibly, as well as being naturally self-centred and self-absorbed, he really is incapable of self-surrender. Having once, without noticing it, given his whole confidence, with the recklessness, the happiness and torment, of first love, he is now half tired and half a coward.

I could not accept this. Hope is one of my vices. Beaten off at one edge, my fingers close round another—to this day.

Moreover, he was not consistent. There were moments or days when I was completely, madly, happy.

Like the Master, *je craignais de déflorer les moments heureux que j'ai rencontrés, en les décrivant, en les anatomisant* . . .

I shall not try. A decade of disorder and bitterness was behind me; I even felt an acute pleasure in the certainty that my life would be far from easy. I had done well to risk myself with Guy. I knew it— even at times when I lost confidence.

A year ago, at our first meeting, he had said, 'I couldn't read your novel. Do you mind? It's too emotional.'

A crack that was to become an avalanche opened in my mind. There and then I determined that, whatever else, henceforth I would write as drily as Euclid.

This was as far as my wits took me then—not far.

I should like to know whether I am eccentric in remembering places infinitely more vividly than I recall people. My skull is the walls of a vast museum of roads, streets, harbours, in foreign countries. And, if an incident I remember for other reasons took place in Whitby, I see it with every gesture, every tone of voice, every colour, as distinct and sharp as if it had happened this morning . . . As soon as his school term ended, I took Bill to Whitby, promising Guy not to stay longer than the end of the month.

On the first evening, my mother settled herself in her fireside chair, her dress turned back over her black satin petticoat, the palms of her hands resting on her knees, and prepared to astonish me with Whitby news. Her life, once rich in exotic memories, had narrowed to the streets and a few houses of a small port, and the doings of her youngest child.

I hated to deprive her of a familiar pleasure, but I had to tell her about Guy, of whom she knew nothing yet.

There was a long silence: she stared into the fire, her mouth working as it did when she was troubled or angry. The fear always at the back of my mind since I was a child, the fear of punishment, needled me. But she spoke gently.

'What is going to happen?'

'K. has agreed to divorce me. I shall keep Bill—of course. K. would not want to bother with him. He has taken a job now, but I don't suppose he'll do anything very much.'

'Not he,' my mother said contemptuously, 'he's lazy to his very bones, a good-for-nothing. A rare soft sit-down he's had of it all these years. I can't be anything but relieved that you have got rid of him.'

Ashamed to have thrown K. to the wolves only to make things easier for myself, I went on,

'The divorce won't be heard before May. And then there are six months before the decree is absolute. I thought—I can't see the sense of waiting a year—I thought we might begin living together at once. It would be more economical . . .'

'Everything is changing,' she said calmly, 'you must do as you think best.' Her face softened. 'You know that whatever you do you are still my little good child. You have always had courage for anything. You deserve to be happier.'

Relief, love, surprise, suffocated me. I could not put them into words. In my family there were few spontaneous gestures, few easy familiar words of tenderness.

'I couldn't have done anything but for you,' I said.

She seemed satisfied, her blue eyes less remote than usual. 'When you were a little girl, you were restless and patient—I used to think, how can she be both? And unbelievably stubborn. You don't take enough care of yourself, you live as if you were made of iron, and there is an end to that.'

'I haven't reached it,' I said.

Bill supposed I was going to spend the whole of his holidays in Whitby. I had told him, 'Ten days,' but, as children do, he put this aside.

Unless he wanted to do or be given something, he rarely began a conversation. I felt a blind ditch between our minds. Was it only because he had been so often away from me during the last six years? I had a heavy sense of guilt, of time rushing past. I want him with

The Norman Church, Whitby

its three-decker pulpit

The upper harbour, Whitby

Heavy seas breaking over the lighthouse

My grandfather
George Gallilee

A placid-faced schoolgirl
(seated, left)
Women's Representative
Council of the Union of
Leeds University 1911-12

An unlicked young woman—1920

A hat I trimmed myself—1923

My youngest sister in 1938

'The goose-girl of the German fairy-tales'

In Bratislava in June 1938, with Marina Pauliny (right)

me, I thought: he is the centre of my life, and Guy is an indulgence: I am a wicked woman.

When the day came to leave, I helped him to arrange his Christmas presents on a shelf in his room. 'As soon as I can I'm going to find us a house to live in. You shall have a fine large room in it.'

He did not answer. He had been talking, and now he had nothing to say, and, it seemed, no wish to listen.

'Shall you like that?' I asked.

'Yes.'

He doesn't notice whether I'm here or in London, I thought. I was going back on the night train. When I was giving him his bath, he said,

'Don't go.'

I no longer remember what, in my despair, I said. His face changed. He began to cry.

'You could stay here.'

'I must go, it's to get money for us, this isn't our house, you know, my little love, I'll come back for you in two weeks, I'll . . .'

Heaven knows what words I forced past the hard knot in my chest. He let himself be comforted and began laughing. When I was taking him upstairs, he said,

'I wish these stairs would never end.'

He had his wish. For ever and ever, as long as I live, I climb them behind him in the darkness, between the second and third floors of my mother's house.

The station at Whitby is alongside the harbour; I was early and had time to walk along the quay for a minute. It was full moon. The sky was a cold blue, as pale as the line of the water; above the skeleton of the abbey on the east cliff lay motionless feathers of cloud. The tide was out, and the harbour a stretch of bronzed mud divided by threads of beaten silver.

As always, my mind began throwing up plans, dykes against despair.

If, at the last instant, a soul is able to glance back over its life, what I shall see in the ambiguous moonlight will be a great bronze plain, crossed by threads of bright water and crumbling broken-off dykes which held back no destructive tides.

Chapter 54

I doubt whether I shall ever know what has forced me to live as if the one unbearable fate were to be settled anywhere. Imbecile.

Once, in the country between Bordeaux and St Emilion, I saw on the rough lawn in front of a small manor-house a young cockerel tied by a leg to an iron stake, and a boy watching its struggles to free itself; it rushed away, the length of the cord, returned, rushed off in another direction, returned, collapsed, rushed away again, now and then uttering cries more like a frog than a young bird. Its cord was seven or eight yards long; all the silly creature had to do was keep calm and peck where it could reach.

All I had to do was to keep quiet, bring up my child, cook, entertain my friends, learn to talk easily, cherish my husband, and cultivate my mental garden with patience and gaiety . . .

At Easter (1925), when I fetched Bill from Weybridge to take him to Whitby for the holidays, I thought he looked pale. Panic-stricken, I decided to persuade my mother into offering to let him live with her. A boys' school had just been started in Whitby by a woman I knew to be cultivated, warm-hearted, and a born teacher. My middle sister was at home now, and could take any trouble he might be off my mother's hands.

This sister, four years younger than I, began trying to escape from the family when she was three years old. Time after time, neighbours would meet her trudging up Waterstead Lane into the country and bring her back. Once she stationed herself with her doll's-carriage at the end of a line of horse-drawn cabs waiting to be hired. When she was seventeen, she began again. Each effort failed and she came home to be our mother's companion, housekeeper, nurse, depended on without mercy, scolded if she stayed out late. It would not occur to my mother—nor did it to me—to ask her whether she resented having a ten-year-old boy added to the household. Nor would it occur to her to protest: she had too much warmth, and the habit of obedience—and she had not given up all hope of escape. (She escaped after our mother's death—to New York.)

My younger sister was now nineteen, in her second year at a provincial university. Tall, immensely attractive with her cold clear blue eyes and marvellously fair skin, she was still the one creature my mother loved with passion. She was restlessly energetic, moving as quickly as a young lizard, and very impatient, except with her short-fingered hands. She said what she thought, without fear or mercy. Even a friend who had vexed her might be flayed and cast out for good. But she was as generous as implacable, and her malice was honest malice; the victim had not to fear an arrow in the back as he fled.

After all, I had no need to be jesuitical with my mother. She agreed almost at once that, yes, the boy could live at home now—why not? She may have regretted the moment when, weighed down by her body and her loss, and afraid—she who never in her life hesitated to scold and subdue even a married daughter—of the jealous temper of her youngest, she had let me send him to a stranger. Or was it a simpler impulse?

'He can have Harold's room,' she said, slowly.

Filled with heavy oak furniture—a wardrobe in which hung one of his flying jackets and his fleece-lined boots, two large chests of drawers, a bookcase, a desk—it was not a child's room, but Bill was pleased with it. To have a room of his own gave him a sense of safety and dignity.

The camera I gave him before I left was only one extravagance among others. He had seen it in the window of a chemist's, and asked me for it. So long as I had any money at all in my pocket, I had not the strength of mind to refuse him anything. Inside the shop, the man laid it in his hand. It was dearer than I expected. Seeing my hesitation, the man brought out a cheaper one, much cheaper, much larger, and, as he said, much more suitable. Glancing at Bill, I saw his face change: he said nothing, only stared at the engagingly small camera in his hand.

'No, I'll take the first one,' I said, sighing.

My son gave me one of his dazzling smiles, his eyes brilliant with excitement and satisfaction. I felt the happiness a woman is said to feel when she conceives, and that I felt only when I could give him something he coveted.

That evening, speaking about the camera, my mother said harshly,

'You spoil him. You're bringing him up to think he has only to ask and get. He asks, and you give. You'll ruin the boy.'

I had no answer. I lacked the courage, or the insolence, to tell her that she spoiled her youngest at least as crazily and without fore-thought as I my son, spending on her every penny she could get into her hands. And without my impulse to make up to a child for his loss of a settled life. The reserves of tenderness, indulgence, weakness, she lavished on her last-born child had accumulated during a lifetime. I did not feel sure of having a lifetime to indulge mine. There might be another war, then what good would strictness have been?

And—what had my mother's done for me except make me dis-trustful, of life itself?

I looked at her. As so often, she was staring in front of her—at what? My heart contracted with an old feeling of helplessness, an old rage, and I began to think: What can I give her before I go that she would really like?

Chapter 55

Guy, a great-nephew of Dickens's publisher, had as a boy two passions—history and publishing. His parents overrode both. Pru-dent elderly Victorians, middle-aged at his birth, they wanted to see their only child safely niched in the Civil Service, and from West-minster sent him to study law at Oxford. The War, and his father's death, cut him loose. In 1924, with a derisory sum of money, he started his publishing firm.

It was at least twenty or thirty years too late for the kind of firm he had wanted—a short list of scholarly works, translations (even of a few novelists, Paul Morand, Claude Anet), and minor classics of literature, superbly produced. Martin Secker in his young days as a publisher could indulge his polite tastes and live. (It is said, with malice, that when he was asked to send a book abroad, rather than fill in the many forms demanded, he dropped the order in the waste-paper-basket.) In 1924, a young man with scholarly notions and no money worth counting might, with luck, be taken on as an editor by some well-found firm. He had no other chance of survival.

From his two-roomed office in Adelphi, he published a few books of immense elegance (they included the *Historiettes de Tallemant des Réaux* translated by Hamish Miles, Charles Scott-Moncrieff's translation of the *Letters of Heloise and Abelard*, and the *Book of Wine* Morton Shand wrote at his suggestion).

He had as staff a secretary, Mrs B., a good-natured florid Cockney, so devoted that she was willing to work half the night, and so slow and conscientious—to all appearance—that she now and then did.

Some time in 1925 he took a pupil, Dennis Cohen, an uncommonly handsome young man, very like the fifteenth century portrait of the Emperor Maximilian I by (I think) Bernhard Strigel, but gayer.

In the autumn of that year it became clear that he could not carry on without running into debt.

He had two offers, one from Dennis Cohen, who wanted to start publishing and had a great deal of money, the other from Alfred Knopf. What Alfred wanted was his own English house. Impossible, after nearly forty years, to recall how we persuaded ourselves that he would be freer as a London manager for Alfred Knopf than as Dennis Cohen's partner. It was so obviously the wrong choice that I must have been responsible; it bears all the marks of one of my blind plunges. Or, I may only have wanted to please Alfred.

I have half erased the memory of my folly. As always, what I remember distinctly happened not in London but in Whitby.

In December, the negotiations with the Knopfs reached a stage when they asked us to come to New York for ten days, over Christmas. It was unthinkable that I should spend Christmas anywhere but with Bill. I sent Guy off to New York alone and went to Whitby.

My first glance—I had not seen him since the end of summer —gave me a child taller and stronger, his cheeks glowing, lips a clear crimson; even his eyes seemed bluer and more brilliant. An overwhelming relief consoled me: for once I had done a wise thing.

My father was at home between voyages, and vexing my mother by talking about two pound notes he insisted had been taken from his room. 'He makes these stories up,' my mother told me drily.

The second evening, when I was drying Bill after his bath, he began to cry, with shocking violence, shaking from head to foot; he told me that he had taken the money to buy, of all useless things, a gramophone pick-up he had seen in a shop, and coveted—heaven knows why, since he could never use it. My heart turned over. I recognized a trait of my own, the thing I wanted becoming an obsession, blinding me to every effect and every other impulse of my mind or body.

What was I to do with this child ravaged by remorse? By the code of my upbringing, he ought to confess his crime and hand over his pocket-money week after week until he had wiped out the debt . . . I could not inflict such humiliation on him—no more than I had ever been able to punish him except by the sort of angry remonstrance one child might use with another, younger . . . If I am doing the wrong thing, I thought, I can't help it—let it be on my head.

I forget what I said to him in the way of comfort and warning. I remember what I did. I tucked two pounds between my father's bed and the wall. When he found it, he told my mother triumphantly, 'You see? *She* took it. If I had said nothing she would never have brought it back.' *She* was the daily woman, whom for some reason he disliked.

'You never lost it,' my mother said ironically . . .

Without thinking about it, moved by an impulse which had nothing to do with my will or my reason, I tried blindly to guard my son from any of the feelings of responsibility, anxiety, guilt, with which I, a child, had been burdened. Even revolt against them is sterile . . .

I had been at home only four days when the Knopfs cabled that unless I came to New York nothing could be arranged. A fast boat, the *Homeric*, was leaving on the 23rd; I must catch it.

I had three days in which to get a berth and a visa, and get myself to Southampton. Somehow I managed it, and laid up for myself an agony still, if I am rash enough to lay a finger on it, searingly alive.

'I've been missing you so much,' Bill said, 'and now you're going.'

Neither time nor familiarity mitigate it. I should avoid touching it.

In the train I sat with my body clenched over the pain. Why am I going? I asked myself: no good will come of it.

I was not even sure that I had a berth on the *Homeric*. I had—a minute cabin on the lowest deck of the first class. I had never slept in what felt like the bottom of a hold, with the terrible weight of the Atlantic pressing against its sides. But neither had I sailed in any ship larger than three thousand tons. In spite of myself, in spite of an involuntary contempt for so much space and luxury in what passed for a ship, my spirits rose. When I walked into the vast comfortable drawing-room—an orchestra playing, waiters bringing elaborate teas to the small tables—I felt drunk with excitement.

For the space of a few minutes, it wiped out the burdened years separating me, as I stood there, from the child determined *to be someone*. Smiling, the two of us touched hands.

This exultance did not last very long. I am like my mother, for whom the sea was always only a boring hiatus between ports.

As for New York, I spent nine days there and did not see it.

Days in the Knopf office, that miracle of suave efficiency, were followed by evenings at parties where certainly I impressed no one by my wit or my one dinner-dress. It was the Prohibition era. Everybody—everybody we met—drank enormously and talked enormously about ways of getting hold of non-lethal alcohol. One evening, stupefied by the frightful heat and luxury of an apartment I had been taken to after a concert of Gershwin's music, stupefied, too, by the powerful voices of two coloured singers invited as guest-entertainers—it was also the era of Carl van Vechten and *Nigger Heaven*—I left silently, abandoning Guy, and walked a short distance, exasperated by the thought that I was being cheated of America.

I had no idea where I was. I seemed to be the single living creature in a wide tunnel driven between stone cliffs, open to the night sky, lit by two rows of street-lamps dwindling into the distance, and void —except of cars following each other endlessly and all but noise-lessly. The cold cut my breath off at the lungs. I was forced to get into a taxi and listen to an account of the driver's troubles with a faithless wife. The garrulity, or inventiveness, of New York cab-drivers has to be endured to be believed.

Another evening, at a party given by the writer Fanny Hurst, eighty or a hundred people stood about chattering and drinking in a room filled with ikons and church hangings: a long buffet held twice as many bottles as there were guests: there was also a samovar of ink-black tea—thicker than ink. Lady Colefax's black and white dress drew cries of admiration.

'Surely—Paris?' Carl van Vechten said.

'Yes. Worten. Designed for me.'

Five minutes later Alma Gluck, the singer, came in, wearing the same dress: before either could escape his malice, Carl van Vechten had seated them one on each side of him, to enjoy their absurd discomfiture.

Miss Hurst enchanted me. Under a long crimson silk shawl, heavily fringed, she was wearing what in my childhood I knew as 'dancing-class knickers'—row on row of white lace from waistband to knee: when she moved, the fringe parted to show them above black silk stockings.

I left New York thankfully, as ignorant as a carp, even of New York.

The English house of A. A. Knopf lasted three years. We left it six months before the end, without rancour: with characteristic reluctance to use the knife, Alfred allowed the rope to fray itself; I have never known anyone in whom generosity, kindness, acumen, a loyal warmth, and ferocity of purpose, were so inextricably mixed.

Both sides, we and the Knopfs, had been misled, or had misled ourselves: Guy supposed he was free to create a small wholly English firm; the Knopfs—more insistently after Alfred's father, a man to be respected and in his genial moods liked, his brain fitted with the tentacles of an octopus, began taking an interest in the firm —wanted something more rapidly profitable, and able to swallow at least a slice of their American list. Little of this admirable list was better than a dead weight on us. Two things might have saved the new firm: luck with an English author or authors, and a manager with less cultivated tastes and a great deal more commercial sense.

In New York it had been arranged that I should work half the week, with a salary half Guy's. In the event I worked five full days in the office. But—fatal circumstance, one the Knopfs could not have foreseen—I was bored. When the elder Knopf said to me, 'My idea of you is that you will want more and more to concentrate on business, and become less and less a writer,' I felt a violent revulsion.

It was less that I wanted to write novels than dislike of being tied down. Yet he was right to suspect me of an instinct for business. One side of me was pure Gallilee. By some freak—yes, freak—it had been yoked to an anarchist, a tramp, a *révolté*. The two cut each other's throats.

Chapter 56

I have few memories of this wasted time. One day—I was alone in the office—an old gentleman came in with a letter of introduction from I forget whom: he hoped we could give him a French book to translate. I eyed him stealthily while I read the letter; he was sitting expectantly, with all the air of a child waiting to be spoken to, too well-trained to speak first.

His name, Charles Roche, was not known to me. He was one of eighteen elderly journalists sacked from the *Morning Post* when it changed hands.

'Just think,' he said, smiling at me, 'eighteen of us were sacked at once, all those over sixty—without pension. I am seventy-two.'

'You look younger than that,' I said.

He was pleased. 'Do you think so? I ought not to take your time, but you are kindness itself. I'll tell you why I need money. My wife, my dear Annie, is dying. She doesn't know. I told her last week, "Annie, I've got the best job I ever had and as soon as you're strong again we'll go to France." Yesterday the doctor said, "I suggest giving a little stimulant." "I know what you'd like," I said to her, "you'd like some champagne." She only looked at me. Well, I went to my wine merchant, and I said, "Let me have one bottle of Moet '06; I'll pay you for it as soon as I can." And what do you think, he sent round half a dozen bottles that evening!'

'*How* long were you on the *Morning Post*?'

'Forty-two years, my dear Miss Jameson.'

I had to tell him we had no book he could translate, and promised him the first we had.

'You're too kind. Just think, eighteen of us in the same minute. An execution! One of us committed suicide.' He spoke with an innocent pride, like the survivor of an earthquake. 'I shouldn't like to blame him, but I shall not do that. Fortunately, it's forbidden. My religion is perfectly clear on the point.'

He rose to go. Trying to think of something I could say to please him, I said,

'I'll pray for your wife.'

'Oh, you're a Catholic!'

'No. But perhaps even a heretic's prayers may be a little use.'

'Oh, don't think I am such a bigot as that,' he cried, distressed. 'It's just that I never heard a Protestant speak of praying.'

I saw him two or three times again, then lost sight of him. He found some way of getting his Annie to France. A year after we left the firm, he sent me a photograph of her grave at Le Portel, near Boulogne. He cannot have survived her long enough to be chased out again, this time by the Germans . . .

I had a letter from Blanche Knopf asking me to see Wyndham Lewis (the painter and writer): we were not publishing him in London, but he had promised her his next book—whether a novel or literary polemics I forget—and now, in the way of very intelligent writers, in whom conscience is often in inverse ratio to intelligence, he had promised it elsewhere.

He came into the room and sat scowling at me across my desk, in a wet dirty mackintosh—the day was as vile as his temper—with a drop forming at the end of his nose: his eyes, furious, gored me. Politely and warily, I asked him why he had disappointed Mrs Knopf.

'Blast Mrs Knopf's soul,' he exclaimed, 'she hasn't said a word to me about the book for six months. How was I to know she still wanted it?'

Loud voices frighten me as much as bulls. 'But surely you realize how important any book of yours is?'

'Then why the devil didn't she write to me?'

'Why do you think? We were anxious not to annoy you by asking questions. But we expected the book, and the firm—the New York office—has been making every sort of preparation for it, talking to critics—' so far as I knew, this was pure invention, but it was what they ought to have been doing—'doing everything possible to make sure that when it came it was recognized as important.'

His terrible eyes shifted a point. Suddenly I felt his mind at the end of my own.

'I suppose you're talking sense,' he grumbled.

I smiled at him. 'I don't know. But I know how a book of yours ought to be treated, and how the Knopfs will in fact treat it . . . Can nothing be done? Have you the manuscript in your hands still?'

'I'll see what I can do.'

He stood up and began tying the greasy belt of his mackintosh, snatching a dubious handkerchief from the pocket to blow his nose dangerously. Spiritually arm in arm, we walked to the door together . . .

We, Guy and I, made one pure gain from our two and a half years' servitude—the friendship of Edward Thompson. We published his first two novels, *An Indian Day,* and *These Men Thy Friends*, two of the finest novels of a generation, and worked for them with the devotion they, and he, deserved. If at the Last Judgement, I were the 'prisoner's friend', allowed to put forward two, only two, of the Englishmen of my time as an example of the best we can do, they would be R. H. Tawney and Edward Thompson. The two of them were in ways alike: both had a consuming passion for justice, both were incapable of lying, both were loyal without flaw, generous without flaw. Both, without intending it, a little intimidated, or offended in their vanity, small mean men of power, who repaid them by neglect.

Dear Edward was like Tawney, too, in that the war (the first) gave him more than the bitterness and anger roused by its abominable side—I begin to believe that there is no state in which the minds and hearts of good men ripen so quickly as the state of war.

Tawney was the more arbitrary, with the involuntary arrogance of a man who is entirely indifferent to what other people may think of him and his merits. This in Edward became the fine muted rigidity of your bred-in-the-bone Nonconformist. His creed plagued him a little: to balance it he was a poet, with an innocent eye for all that can reach and touch the senses—only a poet could write the last twenty-five pages of *These Men Thy Friends*, or see the Indian scene as he saw and evoked it in *An Indian Day*. And *In Araby in Orion*, brief and elegiac, fine-boned, is one of the few nearly perfect *contes* of all time.

He loved his fellows, without sentimentality, with a singular clear-sight, indeed with irony.

He married the one woman he should have married, an American, the serenely beautiful child of American missionaries in Syria. They bred two sons as brave and honest as themselves. Frank, the elder, fought with the Bulgarian partisans, and was caught in May 1944 and executed. Left—of this splendid Puritan stock—a second Edward, as intransigent an idealist as the other . . .

As he grew older, Edward was a little humiliated by the retreat into which he had been forced. A letter he wrote in 1942—I had written to him about a volume of poetry, *The New Recessional*—gives out when I touch it a smiling bitterness.

'. . . I know the poem is good, but people whom I imagined friendly have not even acknowledged it, it seems to have shocked them; and in three months the sole reviewing has been three brief and all contemptuous notices . . . Brailsford and David Low privately have been enthusiastic. But when after hesitation I asked David, who has long been rather pleasantly friendly, if he would mind telling the publisher only that he found it readable, he has not answered. So that's that. Anyhow, I know that such passages as "By the Waters of Babylon" will last, if they ever get read at all . . . Frank after a year at the front is now in sub-caucasian Persia. He knows Russian, so may go further afield: I think, will. Palmer is training in the tanks . . . I do little and have been vetoed for India repeatedly . . . About your work: and mine: a lot you have had to put in former days into newspaper articles ought to have gone into criticism . . . But neither of us, my dear, have any right to blame ourselves, for what we have done has had to be done from necessity —my Indian scribbling was laid on me as a job for this incarnation, and my novels were an accident and then were a necessity to help pay one's way. We did what we had to do, and some of it was good . . .'

As always, he does himself a great deal less than justice—that 'Indian scribbling' covers historical works of high seriousness and importance as well as the enchantment of *An Indian Day*. And no war novel—of either war—is more worth remembering than *In Araby in Orion* and *These Men Thy Friends*. Oblivion, being blind, makes too many mistakes.

By a lucky accident, I re-read *In Araby in Orion* a week after a struggle, only partly successful, with one of the better artificers of *le nouveau roman*, Alain Robbe-Grillet. Suddenly as I read, a window was thrown up and I saw why, for all their virtues, intelligence, poetic double-sight, a visual imagination of peculiar intensity, Robbe-Grillet's novels are unsatisfactory, and, at a deep level, unauthentic. The writer who says mockingly, '*Ah, vous croyez encore à la nature humaine, vous!*' is condemned to work at a more superficial level than the one on which are conceived the great novels, French, Russian, English, and the miniature of *In Araby in Orion*, all of them resting in the affirmation that, by way of love and compassion—and, alas, of cruelty—men can, though imperfectly, communicate with each other. Without this single possibility of communication there *is* no human nature, no continuity of being. *Le nouveau roman* pushes to a limit the existentialist view of man as a project of action, immersed in becoming, disqualified from being. The characters in any of Robbe-Grillet's novels are a kaleidoscope of moods, no value judgements on their acts, thoughts, feelings, are possible or permitted. An axe is laid to the roots of any rational grasp of reality.

Clearly, all too clearly, this a-rational philosophy, this diminishing of the human person, this effacement of the classical-Christian-humanist idea of the individual, is as much a product of our mechanical civilization as Shell House and computers.

Two extraordinary paradoxes, two jacks-in-the-box, appear. Robbe-Grillet's scorn of 'bourgeois humanism' and of the pathetic human habit of 'appropriating' the non-human world by injecting emotions into it (the sad sky, the cruel sea) is mocked by his own intensely emotional link with natural objects. He seems not to know that his descriptions quiver and burn with sensual emotion. It is what saves his novels from dissolving in tedium.

And then his romanticism—like Sartre's—with its plumes from Kierkegaard, Rilke, even Byron! Lonely in the world into which he has been thrown, climbing with Rilke 'the mountains of primaeval sorrow', the solitary sport of moods, enduring *Angst* before the horror of the abyss, never in all literature was there a more relentlessly romantic figure than that imagined by the existentialist writers and their cousins.

Robbe-Grillet is a painter who has amputated his hands in order to prove how brilliantly he can lay on his colours without them.

Chapter 57

I was brought up to think that illness is shameful, and a doctor the last resort of a feeble mind. The body must do its best unaided until the moment when it surrenders unconditionally. For several years now I had been enduring an intermittent pain which grew more and more nearly unendurable until at last, in July 1927, I took myself to a doctor and discovered that I had waited too long.

On my first night in the nursing home—the operation was at eleven o'clock the next day—I had a vivid dream. I was walking slowly up North Bank, the steep straight road that leads from the harbour to 5 Park Terrace: it was night, I was naked, alone between the walls of the houses, feeling the cold and roughness of the stones under my feet. As I neared the top, the houses became unsubstantial and remote; I became aware of a shadow behind me, it took something of K.'s form, and his voice or another's said, 'Poor thrawn girl, come back again.'

In the dream, I wondered what on earth 'thrawn' meant. I half turned my head. The hill, the night, the voice, lapsed into vapour, into an overwhelming regret and longing.

I woke in the unfamiliar room and lay watching the leaves of a tree in the garden outside the window until the day nurse brought me breakfast I refused to eat. It was no use her telling me, and bringing the Sister to confirm it, that experience in the war had proved that soldiers who had been fed beforehand did better in an operation than men who had fasted. I knew better. It was my only victory over authority, which from now on did its worst.

I was furious with my body: it had been as soundly and strongly built as a ship or a tree, and ought not to have succumbed to my neglect. I could not forgive it.

Left alone for two hours, I began on one of the five books I had brought with me. It must be vanity that makes it easy for me not merely to ignore panic at these times, but not even feel it. I read placidly and carefully.

'And as the many tribes of feathered birds, wild geese or cranes or long-necked swans, on the Asian mead by Kaystrios' stream, fly hither and thither joying in their plumage, and with loud cries settle ever onwards, and the mead resounds; even so poured forth the many tribes of warriors from ships and huts into the Skamandrian plain.'

The list of captains and ships in this part of the Iliad had always bored me to yawning, and now gave me the most acute pleasure. Why? I suppose that terror is kept at bay by what is both serious and concrete in literature, where it would instantly break through a charming or flimsy or merely amusing book.

I had been told that people coming out of an anaesthetic talk wildly and give away their secret soul. Determined not to give mine away, I had written—on the piece of paper I was using as a book-mark—a sentence of which I had forgotten the origin; but that I had often used before when I was dejected. I hoped, by recalling it at the last minute, that it would come to my helpless tongue and save me from disgrace—'The last peaks of the world, beyond all seas, well-springs of night and gleams of opened heavens, the garden of the Sun.'

The nurse startled me when she came in at five minutes to eleven. 'Oh, is it time?' I asked.

'Yes.' She smiled. 'Nervous?'

'Not yet.'

She annoyed me by making me get into a wheeled chair, which a grinning boy held steady in the lift.

'I could have walked up the stairs in half the time,' I said.

'You'll be heavier when you come down again,' she retorted.

The operating room was large and light. To my first glance it seemed full of people, all women: surgeon, doctor, middle-aged anaesthetist, four or five nurses. When I lay down on the table, all I could see through the window was an elongated box, shaped like a coffin, of brilliantly blue sky. I thought: I must look carefully at everything. The surgeon's big white-clad body and brown face came between me and the light. *Last peaks of the world, beyond all seas . . .*

The anaesthetist looked down at me, smiling. 'Well, you look like a little girl,' she said.

Someone I could not see adjusted the mask over my face. This was the moment I feared—the choking. I made myself breathe gently. My doctor had come close to me: she took my right hand and held it in one of hers, and I gripped hers, so that they would know I was still conscious and not begin to cut me. My sight was failing. The outline of the window withdrew to a great distance, the waiting figures of the nurses dimmed. The silence became a presence. Shadows moved past my eyes. I lost the sensation of the doctor's fingers against mine.

Now an extraordinary thing happened. A thought—*I must signal to the last man*—pierced me. Why on earth should the scene in Giraudoux's *Bella* when Fontranges visits the disgraced Dubardeau brothers, read months before, float to the surface of my mind precisely at this moment? I had the impression that I was raising my arm and holding it straight out. I may have moved it, or my body on the table, because someone indistinct said in a quiet voice,

'Everything is all right, Miss Jameson.'

I was almost blind now, stubbornly widening my eyes to see the blurred form of a woman near me.

In darkness, for less than a second, I saw the figure of a woman bending over, something in her hands. Then, in terror, I hung in a black whirling flood, shot with red flecks, and supposed I was dying. Then I was fully conscious, of shadowy room, feeble night-light close to me, canvas straps holding me in a sitting posture, and at the other, the darkest end of the room, a nurse. I moved slightly, and the movement tore open my body.

I must have whimpered. The woman came and bent over the bed.

'Time?' I whispered. I was ashamed to ask her whether or not I was dying.

'After nine o'clock.'

I am a good sleeper, I can sleep through storms, in trains, sunlight, strange beds. The only sleepless nights of my life before this were during my child's illnesses. This one was sleepless with a difference. The pain in my body was shocking. I kept my eyes on the square of the door, outlined by a thread of light. My watch was lying in the weak glow of the lamp, and as my sight strengthened I could read the figures. It was five minutes to ten. Several hours passed, and I looked again. This time it wanted a minute of ten o'clock.

Once or twice the nurse spoke to me in a soft Welsh voice. When, without meaning to, I whimpered, she said, 'Poor rabbit,' and told me the surgeon had forbidden them to give me morphia.

'Why?'

'She said she didn't think you ought to have it. I'm sure I'm sorry. I would give you something, I would indeed, if I could.'

'Never mind.'

I walked through every room in 5 Park Terrace, noticing the wicker blind over the lower half of the kitchen window, of a sort no longer made, the horsehair sofa and chairs in the dining-room, the satin-striped wallpaper of my mother's sitting-room, the heavy furniture in her bedroom: next to my own room under the attics my brother slept, soundly and heavily, in his bed beside the small window, his doubled hands on the quilt.

I walked out of Whitby, through fields of buttercups to the Carrs, the river sleek in sunlight, the white dust, to Briggaswath and Sleights, climbed through the village past the old houses to Blue Bank, up which I toiled slowly, and turned away from the moors to follow the road leading down, down, to the lane with its foxgloves and honeysuckle, and the warm sound of bees. But not even here was sleep.

I never knew light so slow in coming, or bird to cry so clearly, piercing me to the bone with a moment's pure pleasure.

When the nurse was preparing me for the day, she patted my hand and chuckled.

'Do you know what you said when we were putting you into bed yesterday afternoon? You fought and struggled, we had to bring a third nurse in to help hold you. Sister was afraid you would open the wound. To think you could fight like that! And you kept on saying: "I must go home now, I must go home." We had as much as we could do to quiet you. My, you're strong.'

Weeks later, when I got home, I looked up *thrawn* in a large dictionary. It is a northern word, meaning: twisted, crooked, bent from the straight.

Chapter 58

During these years I finished a novel barely started in Weybridge, and wrote two more. I was trying, fumblingly, to write honestly.

I did not know what the word meant. I supposed it meant writing without affectation or uncontrolled emotion. I became hideously self-conscious, and touched an adjective as if it were venomous.

As a novelist I had for me only energy, curiosity, and my passion for looking. It is not enough. I read little modern fiction, and the chance I threw away in 1914 of making friends among people reaching out to new literary forms did not recur. I did not so much as suspect that the gulf between Tolstoy (or Stendhal, Balzac, Dostoevsky) and Joyce is one of intention, a choice between two ways of using language. Had I been told to define 'great novelist', I should have replied that a few novelists are great by virtue of an exceptionally profound understanding of human passions and a bold vision of man the social and political animal. In short: great novels are written by great men, acutely interested in the human comedy and able to animate it in depth.

That there is an entirely different species of novelist, interested first in what he can do with language, brushed my mind without penetrating it. The fragments of *Ulysses* I had read in *The Egoist* struck me as *de la blague sérieuse*. I read them with pleasure only because, in the absence of a living 'great novelist', *la blague sérieuse* was infinitely preferable to the swill of stock reflections and counterfeit emotions that go to make the bladder-novel, that great modern industry.

'*La seule excuse qu'un homme a d'écrire est de s'écrire lui-même . . . d'être originel; il doit dire des choses non encore dites, et les dire en une forme non encore formulée. Il doit se créer sa propre esthétique.*' (Rémy de Gourmont.) This was the only thing I read which put under my eyes the case for the experimental novel, for the growing impulse to break the traditional mould, achieve a new fluidity, new and personal symbols for human experience. I thought about it a little, and concluded that it was almost certainly impossible for a novelist to combine in himself the passions of a Tolstoy and a Joyce. The two impulses, I reflected, must diverge in the mind at an unseizably great depth, and the choice is inwardly dictated.

Today I am much nearer seeing Joyce as a purely disintegrating force, a sacred monster, uprooting established forms to create a waste land, a great anti-humanist, the destroyer by his devilish skill and persistence of the thin walls against barbarism. Writers who give themselves up to the disintegration of language are, so far as they know, innocent of the impulse to destroy civilization. But the roots of the impulse run underground a long way, to the point where the smoke from burning books becomes the smoke issuing from the ovens of death camps . . .

In 1926, when I was writing *The Lovely Ship*, I was even more ignorant, more out of date, than I knew. Fascinated by a past, still, in my fortunate childhood, within reach of my finger-tips, I wanted to record the Whitby that built ships and sailed them, a Whitby peopled by the great eccentrics of my mother's memory, men and women larger, more fiercely individual, harder, less lightminded than their successors who pull down decent houses to put up rubbish and vulgarize everything they touch. It took me three novels to write the life of Mary Hansyke, who became Mary Hervey, from her birth in 1841 to her death in 1923, and follow shipbuilding from sail to steam to turbines to her sell-out at the height of the war boom in shipping. This was something I knew all about. The three novels are like prehistoric animals reconstructed in a museum from clay and a few real bones.

When I sent the manuscript of the first to Michael, I told him I wanted an advance of three hundred pounds, a hundred more than he had ever paid.

At the end of a month I had not yet heard from him. I thought about it at odd moments every day, but said nothing.

Although, at this time, I was writing highly-paid articles for a newspaper—far too highly paid for their deserts—I needed money. I am one of those unfortunates for whom money has no *real* value. When I have it I spend it, seldom enough on my back—to my Yorkshire conscience, waste and extravagance only describe such inessentials as clothes and fashionable restaurants.

In those days, and, alas, still, the more I earned the faster I spent, and the end of every month found me ashore for money.

When at last it came, Michael's letter was a long one. ' . . . I think I had better say at once that I don't feel this novel is very satisfactory. My chief feeling is that you are trying to do something for which you are not fitted. I don't know why you have chosen to experiment in this method, which contrives to be dry and violent in the same moment. Your natural romanticism suited you better, and if you'll forgive me for writing bluntly—after all, the question of money does enter into it, since you are asking us to pay half as much again as we paid for your last novel—had a much better chance of succeeding . . .'

I put the letter away hurriedly, without re-reading, and without showing it to anyone. I had a sick feeling of disgrace.

The idea that I was almost penniless whetted my mind; it began its familiar trick of throwing out lines on all sides. I became a Yorkshireman with something to sell.

A short time before this, I had run into Charles Evans at a party, and he had said, smiling, that he hoped I would come back to Heinemann. Almost without reflection I telephoned to him, and asked,

'Do you still want to publish my next book?'

'Certainly I do,' he said at once.

'If I tell you that it is better, much better, than the last, would you be willing to pay me four hundred pounds advance?'

'Are you offering me the book?' he asked.

'I'm thinking of offering it to you.'

There was a brief silence, then Charles said calmly, 'Four hundred pounds sounds reasonable.'

My mind jumped a peg. 'I'll write to you or come to see you.'

Still without deciding, I felt stiffened to talk to Michael. But when I walked into his room, in the ramshackle house in Orange Street, and he greeted me with his familiar smiling affection, I felt a cold worm of fear in my belly. Fear and grief. I dreaded his possible anger, and shrank from the idea of hurting him, however lightly.

'Well, my dear?' he said.

'I can't alter the writing,' I said roughly. 'Or the book itself.'

'What do you want us to do? We'll publish it, of course. But I don't see how we can pay more than two hundred on this book, altered or not altered. What do you feel about it?'

At this moment, in one of those dangerous and deceitful flashes of lightning it was subject to, my mind cleared. I realized that when, reading the manuscript, Michael had caught sight of the real Storm

Jameson, he did not like her—his S.J. was the author of that neo-Gothic abortion, *The Pitiful Wife*. He had not the slightest idea what, blindly, I was trying to do, and if he had, would detest it.

This conviction drove every other feeling—gratitude, affection, diffidence—out of my sight. Every scruple, too. I had only one thought—to escape from his uncomprehending hands as quickly as possible and, if possible, without vexing him. Feeling my way, I said,

'I would rather you did not publish a book you don't like.'

What I meant was: I am going to take my manuscript away with me, now, and do what I can to throw the blame of the break on you . . . It had ceased to be a question of two or four hundred pounds, and become a question of freedom from a kindly critic who was in my way. We argued for thirty minutes. My stubbornness and lack of submissiveness surprised Michael: he was friendly and baffled, and I in the state of mind of a ship's captain with a crew of lascars.

I was too sunk in my purpose to have the faintest notion how I appeared to him. At last I said,

'Let me take the manuscript away to look through it again.'

'Very well—but don't decide now. Frankly, my dear, we'd rather publish the novel as it stands than let you go to another publisher.'

In my satisfaction at having got the book into my hands again, without a quarrel, I forgot to be politic.

'Thank you,' I said, smiling.

'For what?' he asked ironically.

'For being patient.'

Hurrying away along Orange Street, filled with remorse and a conscienceless gaiety, I turned over the phrases of the letter I would write, telling him—but in such a tone that I should not lose his affection—that I had gone back to Heinemann.

Friendship, affection—I have always placed a higher value on them than on love—*tout le corps, moins un sens* . . .

('*Alors, décrie-moi ton amitié. C'est une passion?*

Folle.

Quel est son sens?

Son sens? Tout le corps moins un sens . . . *Elle accouple les créatures les plus dissemblables et les rend égales.*' . . .)

I could not have acted otherwise than I did but, I see now, it was only one broken-off thread among dozens. There was less continuity in my life in those years than at any time since—though heaven knows how incoherent it still is. After its owner demanded back the flat on Primrose Hill we lived in four places before the end of 1928. We stayed for months in The Spread Eagle, in Thame, and made a friend of its eccentric proprietor, John Fothergill. Then we gathered my scattered pieces of furniture into a large flat in the fading late-Victorian gentility of Belsize Park in north-west London—the covetous side of my nature, momentarily unleashed, had laid hands on several antiques, chairs, tallboys, chests of drawers.

After a year, avid for country air, we moved to another flat, in a wing of a house near London. Designed by the architect of the House of Commons, it was grotesque, but it had caught the eye and heart of a gentle little City man—he fell madly in love with it, and it tyrannized over him like a rapacious kept woman, driving him to ruin himself to save it from the demolition it merited. The house itself had every discomfort, its only charm—to a cold eye—the large half-derelict park.

I brought Bill here, and sent him to the nearest preparatory school as a day-boy.

Why did I never think with misgiving of the confusion these many shifts must create in his mind? Small thanks to me that he grew up intelligent, brave, authoritative, to become an airline pilot of all-round excellence (*arete*), and cross the Atlantic both ways in a twenty-nine-ton yacht with, for crew, his wife and two very young children. That particular tenacity and indifference to danger he owes to a number of forgotten men and women—and first to one shabby taciturn old sea-captain . . .

Some nerve of my brain, an inner ear, was always, still is, on the alert to hear him breathe. I had an odd proof of this in the spring of 1929, when the three of us were staying in an hotel in Tunbridge Wells. He left my room on the fourth floor to go downstairs: the lift, an old-fashioned one, was at the far end of the corridor, and a minute after he had closed my door I heard the faintest of sighs. Nothing more—it might have been a leaf fluttering down. I knew in the instant what had happened. I ran from the room and along the corridor, running blindly. The door of the empty lift-shaft was open. I called—and his voice came back from the bottom of the shaft.

His only hurt, apart from shock, was a twisted ankle and the palms of his hands laid open. Without noticing that the lift was not there, he had stepped through the open doorway and fallen five floors on to the roof of the lift waiting in the basement: as he fell he clutched the rope running from top to bottom of the shaft; it tore his hands but saved him from breaking all his limbs or his neck.

'What in heaven's name were you thinking of?' I asked later—hours later.

He gave me the coldest of cold glances. 'I was thinking.'

'Did you call out?'

'No. I hadn't time.'

After one year in Harrow Weald Park, Guy and I went back to London, and Bill to Whitby again . . .

This unsettled life at a time when, if either one of us had had a grain of worldly sense, we should have been, as they say, *making ourselves a position*, was not entirely my fault. I had married a man as impatient as myself, and as unwilling to lift a finger to draw attention to himself. In love not with war, but with the conditions of war —sudden changes, no responsibility save to a few men—he took indifferently ill to the benefits of civilization. Except for a few of these—libraries, bookshops, a decent claret, the Savile Club. Turning the pages of those letters I must tear up before I die, I come, in every one of them, on phrases of exasperated discontent and boredom. —We must clear out soon—I wish we could travel together for a year—Do let us run away—I feel more and more impatient to get out and away from the Knopfs . . .

By the middle of 1928, the Knopfs were as eager to get rid of us as we to escape from an impossible situation. They could see Guy's total unfitness for the sort of publishing firm they wanted. What they did not suspect—or they mistook its cause—was my boredom, abysmal.

There was no quarrel. We parted so peaceably that my friendship with Alfred and Blanche survived, and with years became a solid faithful affection.

We had taken with us into the new firm the warm-hearted devoted Mrs B. Just when we left it was discovered that she had been robbing both the Knopfs and Guy for years, by an ingenious method known in the world of fraud as teeming and lading.

No one wanted the trouble of prosecuting her: she disappeared silently—like a cat slipping out of the larder.

Chapter 59

For all my, as I thought it, cynical understanding of human beings, I was still, when I married again, emotionally and intellectually a clever savage. My second marriage was a slow education, in many things. In trust first. Very slow, this—it was many years, a great many, before I even had the courage to say frankly that I wanted to do this or have that, I was so used to going by tortuous paths to avoid being seen, and perhaps mocked. Slow and not easy. I had more to learn and unlearn than Guy, whose life, the war apart, had been infinitely more secure, more polite, than mine.

In short, I was a savage, at best well-meaning, at worst pig-headed and lacking discipline.

If I have learned one thing about love, it is that no love endures very long, not even the most passionate, unless it is mortared by shared suffering. The birth of an enduring love is as hard and painful as any natural birth, and its growth attended by as many accidents. There is a passage at the end of one of Chekhov's tales which, when I read it as a girl, I did not understand: indeed I thought it nonsense. What the devil, I scoffed, have bitterness and pity to do with being, as Chekhov has it, 'properly, really in love?'

'. . . they forgave each other for what they were ashamed of in their past, they forgave everything in the present, and felt that this love of theirs had changed them both. In moments of depression in the past he had comforted himself with any arguments that came into his mind, but now he no longer cared for arguments; he felt profound compassion, he wanted to be sincere and tender . . . it seemed as though in a little while the solution would be found, and then a new and splendid life would begin; it was clear to both of them they had still a long long way to go, and that the most difficult and complicated part of it was only just beginning.'

Any marriage worth the name is no better than a series of beginnings—many of them abortive.

I was happy—that is, madly alive and interested—but my deepest coldest fears and hatreds coiled and uncoiled themselves, unchanged, below the happiness. My mania against domestic life was at its height. At one time in those first years we were the tenants of two places we never lived in, a large flat in Richmond and a house near Tunbridge Wells. I really meant to live in the house, lead a settled sensible life there, send Bill to Tunbridge as a day-boy, write, educate myself. And then, on my first visit to it after the contract had been signed, I was seized by the worst most unmanageable panic of my life and fled from it with the devil on my heels.

The flat was easily re-let, but the house remained on our hands for a long time.

Some time after the incident of the lift, in the summer of 1929, I made one of my sudden decisions. Less sudden than they look, no doubt—I imagine that my mind reaches a pitch of repressed fury when any decision is better than none. This one was almost sensible.

I went up to Whitby alone and arranged to buy a small house on what was then an edge of the town, on a road leading to Aisalby and the moors. As a house it was nothing, but, from the wide windows of the workroom I built on at the back, I looked across fields and the unseen valley of the Esk to the steep hill climbing to another moor. A road, up which I had often walked as a child, stretched across it, marked at night by the lighted window of a solitary farm.

The edge of the hill, where it met the sky, was a fine bounding line, as hard and pure as the line of the coast, as satisfying, giving me as sharp a thrust of pleasure.

For three years this was the view I had in my eyes when I lifted them from the paper under my hand. Since then I have lived in scores of places, without catching a glimpse, even in sleep, of the world bounded by a hillside, a dark belt of trees, a road climbing and turning, gleaming in rain and sunlight like a snake, in which, only in which, a freak, a savage, a child of one now marred edge of a province, is better than a stranger.

This was, too, the first and last time I had a room only to sit and write in.

As housekeeper I had a fifty-year-old villager from Ruswarp. She was completely illiterate, and at the beginning of winter drenched her short sturdy body in oil of evergreen and sewed it into a number of under-garments she did not take off again until May. As soon as she left the house at night, I opened the kitchen windows to clear the air which had become, as she would have said, *ram,* rank. But she was an admirable cook, and tireless, walking her two miles to and from the house in all weathers. She had innumerable skills, and a splendid natural eye for form and colour: the canvas-work seat covers she made, designing them herself, for my Chippendale chairs are still in use. Her life was one of continual excitement: any accidental touch, or a piece of string dropped in her path, might be a trick of Satan or an enemy. It was easy to see her accusing her neighbour of witchcraft and watching her burn with the liveliest most innocent curiosity.

A young niece lived with her in her cottage: she was always bragging to me about her as a *scolard*, who could read the newspaper, write, curl her hair, dance. This girl was a nincompoop, not worth her aunt's little finger.

For the time being, I was as tranquil here as in 1918 at Broughton. There are always these lulls, even during a typhoon.

One fine acid spring day, moved by heaven knows what premonition of change, I went out of my way to walk along Park Terrace. The life had ebbed from its faded narrow houses, and gardens filled with pampas grass and half-opened lilacs. I hurried past No 5 with a half-glance not quick enough to see the captain's young wife on her knees pushing a plant into the bed edged by exotic shells picked up on beaches at the other side of the world, and turned down North Bank. The tide was out, and in the harbour the gulls stepped delicately on mud goffered by their feet. On the other side a small shipyard was dying in its sleep, peaceably, after a brief flicker of life during the war.

Everything, I thought, has gone. But, resting for a moment on an old wall warmed by the sun, my hand let escape from me the child who stood there on just such a day, tasting the salt and honey of early light. For a moment, the gaiety, the simplicity, the modesty, of an older Whitby came close . . .

Chapter 60

At sixty-six, my mother's life was withdrawing from her as modestly as its life from the old shipyard. But I refused to believe it. Indeed, she herself did not believe it, or was surprised. Her heart was weakened, but she went up and down the steep streets every day. Why not? Her life was there, in the cobblestones and the dark older shops, smelling of cinnamon, yeast, coffee, malt vinegar, dry rot in the wood, calico, new bread. She would stand still to look fixedly into the window of some shop which, now, held nothing she would have as a gift.

'I bought my first pair of sheets here,' she told me. 'In those days every captain's wife knew decent linen when she fingered it. Now there's nothing.'

But she went on staring into the window as though it might be keeping from her in its depths a young woman who, if she looked long enough, would step forward to speak to her.

'Do you remember Crane's Christmas show?' she asked.

'Yes.'

Be sure I remembered it. For a week before Christmas Eve a blind shrouded the main window: the moment when it was drawn away to reveal a cottonwool snow scene, or dummies dressed as angels, or, one year, a Flight into Egypt with a Joseph so like the old Canon that he might have sat for it in his surplice with a drunken halo leaning over one ear, started in me a sensation that was purely voluptuous.

There was no essential difference between it and the pleasure to be got from looking at an El Greco: all was already there, even to the subtle distortions of art.

My mother spoke in the gay railing voice that broke from her when she forgot that she was an old woman. 'They don't take any trouble now, but why should they? Look at that—does that care about good linen?'

That was a young woman in Russian boots, hanging on the arm of a boy in the uniform of a third mate: a short skirt uncovered plump knees. After the age of thirteen, the human female knee is commonly an ugly joint, which doubtless is why in all classical statues and in paintings earlier than the nineteenth century, naked women are given the knees of a young Hermes.

'How long have I had this fur coat?' she asked suddenly.

'Seven or eight years. Full time I bought you a new one.'

'Oh, it will last me out,' she said. But she smiled, a quick, pleased smile.

Going up the steepest part of Flowergate, she had to stand still. She was breathing with difficulty, and her lips had a bluish tinge.

'What is the matter?'

'Nothing—except that my heart is a certain age.'

I felt furious with her for growing old, and for taking so little care of herself. 'You ought not to climb these hills.'

Her eyes flashed in the old way, the eyes of a girl in her lined heavy face. 'Nonsense,' she said sharply. 'If I can't come out, I might as well be in my grave.'

Her life revolved more and more narrowly round my younger sister, a lapwing circling its nest. It was the last and, I believe, the overwhelming passion of her life. She thought of this youngest child day and night, and talked about her—to me—endlessly, since I was the one person she could count on to listen with an attentive smile, and make the right answers. With me she had not to ignore an unspoken disapproval, or invent a good reason for spending money, recklessly. Anything Do asked for she got, and one year of her school in Lausanne cost more than the whole of my education. So far as I was concerned, this obsession was no different from lesser things she had set her heart on and I had encouraged her to buy, or tried to get for her. So I smiled approvingly when she broached another extravagance. It was, I thought, a harmless vice . . .

I see her stepping out of the London express in York station: she had been visiting Do, now married, and I had travelled from Whitby to meet her in York and see her through the rest of the journey, with its two changes of train. She looked at me with a young heartless flame of gaiety in her eyes, and before she had set foot on the platform cried the words that had been boiling in her throughout the journey.

'She is going to build a house, and I am going to help her as much as I can. What do you think of that?'

'I think it's wonderful . . .'

Did it for an instant enter her mind that she was treating unjustly the daughter, the other daughter, who lived with her and on whom, without even thinking about it, she depended? (My father, to mark his indifference to them, always spoke of Winifred as *that other one*, and of Do as *that one*: if he remembered my name it was because I was the eldest, the one in whom he had seen, perhaps, a thin reflection of himself.) If it did, she chased the unwanted thought out easily: there was no room in her mind for anything but this last passion . . .

When, at the end of her second year at the university, my young sister refused to stay up any longer and demanded to be sent to a secretarial college, my mother was disappointed. I set myself to put this right for her.

'Why not let her go?'

'I think she's much too young to be in London.'

'Not younger than I was when I went.'

'True, but she's not strong.'

At nineteen Do was as strong as a foal, but even to herself my mother would not admit that she was infinitely more careful of her than she had been of her other children.

'She can be secretary to a publisher or an editor. I'm certain I can find something for her.'

'Oh,' my mother exclaimed, 'she'll do well—of course. She's exceptionally clever, you know.'

'Yes, she is,' I said warmly.

As soon as she had trained I ran about London to find a suitable post for her. I should have been ashamed to fail, but in fact it was not difficult. She was attractive, tireless, and quick-witted, and had more sense in her little finger than I in my whole body.

This year, 1929, she married a young man she had known at the university, a scientist who had moved to the managerial side of a large factory in Reading. There she set up house, in a tiny flat, keeping her job in London.

When I saw her in her flat, self-confident, gay, delighted with her few possessions—'my good cups,' she would say, caressing one of them—her husband, her status as a wife, I thought: I am seeing Hannah Margaret Jameson in her first house, the one I don't remember.

Chapter 61

About this time my father sent in his resignation to the Prince Line. He did it without consulting my mother, who was bitterly vexed. She told me scornfully,

'I heard from your father this morning. He's retiring. After this voyage. He has written to the office already: they've promised him a yearly pension of three hundred—a grace pension, they call it. They're not bound to pay him a ha'penny. Grace!' Her mouth twitched with annoyance. 'The fool he is! And why retire now— at his age? He'll be bored to death hanging about the house for the rest of his life.'

'How old is he?'

'Seventy-four—seventy-five in October. Any number of older captains are still at sea. After all these years of being waited on hand and foot, he won't like it . . . But he has never taken my advice. Before the war, when shipping shares were going begging in the town, and he had a little money saved, I advised him to buy. If he had, he'd have been a rich man. As it is, the shares he did buy— because some man, a stranger, a Sir William Somebody, told him about them—are completely valueless. That's the kind of witless fool he is.'

'Thank goodness,' I said, to distract her, 'that you have a little money of your own now.'

I have in my ears, as I write, the terrible voice in which she cried, 'Too late! If I'd had it in time to help Harold when he was a boy!'

At this moment I would have cut my hand off to give her another life, which might turn out better.

The one my father led, when he came home for good, will be incredible to anyone born after 1900. During the early weeks my mother made a few careless efforts to accept him as a member of the family, but soon dropped them. Now that he was going to be in the house every day, for the rest of their lives, she lost the remnants of her patience. Quite simply, she could not endure him. The way he had treated his son was a living bitterness in her: after that time she had cut him off finally. To see him, to speak to him, cost her more effort than speaking to a stranger, and she hated strangers. His habits, his very voice, his presence in the same room, were insupportable.

If she were forced to talk to him, perhaps thank him for the Christmas and birthday presents he never failed to give her—anniversaries meant everything to her: she even expected her children to give her flowers on the anniversary of her wedding!—or to comment on the basketful of brambles or primroses he brought back from his solitary walks, she could not manage more than a dry, 'Thanks,' or a, 'Yes, very pretty.' Meeting him on the staircase, she would say, 'Good morning, Will,' in the detached polite voice she kept for a total stranger.

Mumbling, 'Good morning,' he hurried past, eyes averted.

Once I came out of her sitting-room where she and my aunt had been laughing like two schoolgirls over a memory of their terrible father, to find him close to the door, listening. What did her clear gay laugh remind him of? Furious at being caught, he rushed away, head down, walking softly and heavily, like a bear on two legs.

After those first weeks, he never entered either of her rooms except for chance minutes. He lived between his bedroom at the top of the house, the breakfast-room in which his meals were laid for him, and the kitchen where, at night, he smoked the strong American tobacco my mother detested, sitting for an hour or more staring at the stove—through it, rather, with his long-sighted eyes, drained of their blue by the sun. At what?

Sixty-one years at sea, from the age of thirteen, must provide anyone with as many horizons as he needs.

Or, in his clear slow back-hand writing, he filled another page in the latest of the large folio diaries he had been keeping for the past thirty or more years. He had no longer the incidents of a voyage to describe, but he recorded weather in a seaman's precise terms, and what his wife called cruelly 'his maundering notions': now and then he would leave spread open a page on which he had written a complaint meant for our eyes. He did not dare say openly what he thought about the way the house was run, or about Do's visits with her husband and their departure laden with gifts.

The sooner that one leaves, the better I shall like it, he would write. Or:

I don't care for living in a show house such as this. My idea if I should be left—he was nine years older than my mother, but he expected to outlive her—*would be a small place clear of the town, and then I think I should write a book on people I have never met but would like to meet.*

Unafraid of hurricanes or fighting-drunk lascars with knives—looking down from the bridge on to the lower deck, I once saw him separate two and shake them until the knives dropped from their hands—he was afraid of my mother, and full of impotent resentment when he thought of her extravagance and wilful half-conscious arrogance.

'She's always done as she likes,' he said to me in an unguarded moment—or did he trust me not to tell tales? 'There was all that furniture of m'mother's she sold—I daresay it wasn't worth much, but . . . and then buying more and telling me, That's mine. And Mr Gallilee's money—y'know, I never saw a penny of it. I didn't want it—not I—but she always said, If I'm left any money it will come in for our old age . . . Well, if it does, with *that one* about, I shall be surprised . . . Sixty-one years at sea—it was snowing when I saw my first ship—I was thirteen . . . Well, I've lived long enough not to expect anything.'

His short nervous laugh was an arm lifted to protect a thirteen-year-old boy's head.

When, as he sometimes did, he spoke to me in a genial voice, it did not seem incredible, that, a long time ago, there had been a handsome well-set-up captain who sang, not to his wife,

> Said the young Obadiah to the old Obadiah
> I am dry, Obadiah, I am dry.
> Said the old Obadiah to the young Obadiah,
> Are you dry, Obadiah? So am I . . .

Shall I be thought a monster if I admit that I had no affection for him? Since I had not to live with him, I could make myself seem friendly. And—perhaps only because I was born before my mother began turning away from him—I did not dislike him. What is more, I knew, very well, why he told absurd lies and bragged about the famous people who had made him the most astonishing confidences.

I don't think he was unhappy. After all, what difference is there between being solitary at sea, as the captain of a ship, shut in his authority, must be, and solitary at home—unless he had expected something better? His real life was lived outside the house, yarning with other old sea-captains, who may not have swallowed all his stories, but respected him as an experienced seaman, who did not find them grotesque—they, too, had heads crammed with foreign wharves, tropical scents, tempests—and in the long days he spent walking about the moors and lanes.

The blow that fell on him in the 'thirties still, to this day, fills me with anger.

How long had he captained Prince Line ships? Thirty, forty, years? The Line had become part of another larger firm, Furness Withy, and, finding no doubt that he was living too long, it reduced his pension abruptly to two hundred a year. And not very long after to a mere hundred.

True, shipping was in a bad way again, but I should not like to be the man who could bring himself to tell the oldest captain of the Line that he was worth less than two pounds a week to it at the end of his life.

When the first letter came, he brought it into the sitting-room and laid it in front of his wife with a nervous,

'Look at that, will you?'

She read it, and said drily, 'You were too eager to leave. If you hadn't been in such a foolish hurry, you might have got better than a promise they're not bound to keep . . . Economies! It's a rich firm, it pays a dividend. I'd dearly like to know what the man who signed that letter is sacrificing.'

She was as angry with my father as with the Line, and not surprised—it was a commonplace in Whitby to begin a sentence with: If there is a meaner creature on earth than a shipowner . . .

The second and savage cut woke in her something like pity for him. It vexed her to see him ashamed.

He was not going to starve, nor stand in a dole line. He had his house, and the few savings he had been able to make and would be forced to spend now. But he was pitiably ashamed. And behind that, behind the humiliation and bewilderment, was a real grief. To have endured at sea more than sixty years—forty-five of them as master— and to discover, with brutal suddenness, what the men who smiled and shook his hand when he walked into the office at the end of another voyage—'Well, Captain, had a good trip?'—really thought of him. Nothing.

Nothing at all. He had less to be proud of than the thirteen-year-old child blubbering secretly in his bunk.

My mother said warmly,

'It's a mean act. They've treated you abominably.'

But this stung him worse than her familiar coldness.

'No, no,' he muttered, 'they'll put it back later. It'll only be for a time. They'll make it right when they can. You'll see.'

When, some ten years later, the Line sent the usual letter of sympathy in the death of an old and valued etc etc, the acknowledgement I forced myself to write was barely civil.

Hypocrisy of this respectable sort is only the small change of our society: it was simple-minded of me to be nauseated by their letter.

Chapter 62

A few days ago, talking with an intelligent nineteen-year-old, I discovered, with surprise and some sadness, that the abyss between his and my generation was even wider than I imagined. I had been telling him about the confrontation between France and Germany which, during the twenties and thirties, took place not only before our eyes in events, but in our deeper consciousness, each country standing there not for a geographical area with a different climate, architecture, language, manners, customs, wines, but for a different state of soul. To him this antinomy, this once mortal contrast, was completely without meaning.

In the exterior world as in the dialectical one, nothing had interest or importance for him except the confrontation, material, intellectual, spiritual, between Europe and America or Russia, two giants of equal size.

'But surely you can feel the tension between two ways of thinking and feeling so different as France and Germany? And the need to choose between them?'

He was only puzzled. 'Why? Aren't they both part of Europe? And isn't Europe, which includes us, going to have to choose between uniting or being Americanized or communized?'

'Do your friends think that?'

'Of course.'

This sponge passed casually over the feverish obsessions and ferment of years when—so we felt—the whole future of the world was being played for disconcerts me. Who will now believe that there was a time, to be measured in heartbeats, when, with anguish, we watched the conqueror of 1918 stumble from one moral surrender to the next, and a crushed defeated Germany becoming every day stronger, more openly aggressive, more of a threat? And when nothing else seemed as important?

I have two countries, the Whitby of my birth, and France, the first secreted like a salt in my blood, bone marrow, and the cells of my brain, the other nursed by my foolish heart. The one lost, vanished, the other too large to be completely disfigured and spoiled.

My liking for France, for the country itself, is peculiarly English, a store of humble love, unasked-for by the recipient, unwanted, even mocked. Like all love—and all travel which is not simply globe-trotting—it traces the map of my heart rather than the contours of the country itself. At my first sight of it France became an idea I cherish, the idea of a habit of living which leaves room for more real pleasures than any we English have practised for at least a hundred years: the butter tastes of butter, the bread varies from one village to the next between toughness and an exquisite texture and savour, a village of a few poor streets grows its own wine, the stench of a cracked drain is followed at once by the smell of cooking herbs or the scent of lime-trees in bloom alive with bees. It is the country itself I love—I am neither naïve nor impudent enough to want to embrace its people —its fields, chestnut trees, olives, vines, its old houses, its country roads and village streets, even hideous. Part, no doubt, of my happiness in France comes from being where I am not known, but the greater part is the gift of the country itself.

(Nowadays, my happiness, no less acute, no less naïve than it always was, is edged by the bitterness of having been excluded from Europe by the will of one stiff-necked old man with the ideas of Charlemagne and the pride and vanity of the devil himself. To feel this about General de Gaulle is not to deny his physical and moral energy, suppleness, wit. He is a great man and it would have been better for Europe if he had been born in, let's say, Pennsylvania: a nature like his needs to be diluted by as many millions of men and acres as possible.)

If I were ordered to give reasons for my passion for France I could find plenty, and very respectable. France is the country where *le tact des choses possibles*, the instinctive knowledge of what is humanly possible and the refusal to strain beyond it, is least likely to be killed by an inventiveness which is taking not only the drudgery but the zest out of life. France may (pray heaven) have kept in reserve enough inefficiency to save its people from dying of boredom, enough modest households where the choice between buying a book or a bottle of wine and paying the first instalment on a washing-up machine is decided in favour of the wine or an edition of Stendhal's letters. Its provincial cities and towns have not yet been sterilized by the nearness of the capital; the life in its villages, on a working day so concentrated that they seem empty, suddenly breaks into a joyous childlike energy, perhaps a cycle race which brings out whole families for miles round and stops all other traffic, however serious. It is still, for God knows how short a time, the non-standardized country, the country where a mechanic enjoys repairing a foreign car with an inch or two of wire coaxed into shape by fingers that might be those of the anonymous builders of Chartres or the cave artists of the Vézère, where the *agent* bawls you out today for precisely the offence which, tomorrow, will move him to cover his face with one hand in mock grief and with the other wave you on, where museums are closed on Monday in one town and on Thursday in its nearest neighbour, where regulations are enforced or broken by an official's whim.

One day in 1931—it was the day after the abdication and flight of the king of Spain—I took my young son to see the flooded caves near Sare, right on the Spanish frontier: they stretch, in fact, between the two frontier posts. To his disappointment, they were closed, the season had not started. Ignoring rules, the gaunt middle-aged peasant in charge took us through them in his boat and provided from his own larder a meal of splendid bread, butter, cheese, and a bottle of strong unnamed wine. As we ate it with him, he talked with sharp gaiety about the fall of kings.

'For me,' he said, smiling, 'they cannot drop off too quickly.'

Lifting a hand the colour and texture of a ripe walnut, he wiped them off the end of his long Basque nose.

My France, yes—a lover's illusion of France, a country laid up in my memory. I do not offer it as a true image. It leaves out entirely an evil side of the very virtues which—for a lover—are the essence, the perpetually renewed miracle of France. Speaking in a secret session of the House of Commons in November 1942—and leaving little doubt in the minds of his hearers which of the two images he considered likely to please a God who at that moment seriously needed His good slow-witted English—Churchill said, 'The Almighty in His infinite wisdom did not see fit to create Frenchmen in the image of Englishmen.' The fact that, sitting at the side of a road in the Landes, eating French bread and cheese and drinking a bottle of Corbières, I say, 'And thank God He didn't,' does not prevent me from noticing that no more insular people exists, no people so innocently convinced that they belong to the greatest nation in the world, incomparably more intelligent, shrewder, more cultured, than any other, and speaking the only language worth the trouble of learning.

It is not possible that *my* France, still only half industrialized, out of step with less sane, less human neighbours, can keep the savour of a civilization founded on good bread, four hundred different cheeses, and heaven knows how many different wines (including the strong delicate *vin sable* a peasant in the Landes grows for himself and his family alone); can survive the monstrous deformation of our instincts forced on us by our own ingenuity and irrational conviction that we have an absolute right to indulge our intellectual curiosity about the universe to the point where, at any moment, we may annihilate it and ourselves; can keep its delight in *making*; can for many more years avoid being demoralized by the speed, the nervous tension, the efficiency, the growing incoherence of modern life; can keep a middle way between order and freedom, between the mechanized and the natural. Can look to a future which is largely a repetition of the past, so that a man is likely to die in the bed he was born in. Can enjoy a civilization predictable and subject to time. Modern technological civilization is almost wholly unpredictable (who knows where he will be this time next year?), unsettled, rootless, alarmingly subject to space. The former may bore the senses or the mind; the second plants a deeper boredom in the very spirit. No doubt it is an advance, but to what?

I suppose that soon the last traces of a backward France will have been effaced, the country will have been dragged up to date and saved for—heaven help us, for what? The long miracle of France will be over.

A Frenchman, highly intelligent, to whom I put my fears, said,

'What you are pleased to call our sanity, our civilization of the possible, brought us to the edge of the grave. Much good it did us in 1939 to be saner, more modestly creative, with, as you would say, more *nature* than the Germans. God forbid that we should ever again rely on our habits.'

'All the same, we need *that* France, we need, my God how we need the idea that bread, wine, and a margin of inefficiency are at least as necessary as speed and a sterilized efficiency. Water in a dry land—it might keep us just inside the humanly bearable.'

He laughed. 'Are you by any chance a poet? Come back in ten, five years' time, and exactly here, where a miserable couple of famiies has been scratching a living from lavender and a few olives, I'll show you a magnificent factory for electronic machines, employing hundreds of men and women and offering them, and the whole district, an ease, security, interests, they never had. Thank heaven that the future of this country is not in your hands.'

All right, thank heaven. Thank heaven I am old and shall die. Meantime I keep what are for me the living memories. The strange thing—is it so strange?—is that these are not, as you would expect, of Chartres, of Albi smouldering in hot sunlight, of Chenonceaux, of the naked brutality of Les Baux, but, returning only for me, of some unpaved square shaded by immense chestnuts in flower, some insignificant Café du Centre in a village with nothing to commend it but the age and strength of its houses (to an English eye stupefyingly shabby and neglected), of the dark shop, barely room to turn, in which, one torrid Sunday noon, I bought the finest bread in the world, of meadows where, as in a mediaeval tapestry, or as in fields I knew as a child, there are as many wild flowers as blades of grass, yellow ladies'-fingers, pink clover and ragged robin, red and purple vetch, pale mauve cuckoo-pint, blue speedwell, white bird's-eye, tall blazingly white marguerites, and innumerable creeping plants of all colours.

What have we done, in the past thirty years, to our English meadows?

And the rivers. Only the cold narrow Esk, flowing into the North Sea at Whitby, runs in me at a deeper level than Loire, Garonne, Dordogne, Lot.

My France, I say humbly, is these images and unnumbered others, and with them a few signs—again I daren't imply that they equal the reality—standing in my life for Stendhal, Péguy, and, yes, Jean Giraudoux.

In my green years I read Giraudoux with unfailing pleasure in a style which hovers between the baroque and the deceptively simple (a style full of paradox and half-relevant images, as fascinating as the movements of a skilled dancer), and a loyal refusal to notice his fiascos. I must be the only Englishman who has read all his published writing, parts of it half a dozen times. In Zurich, in 1947, I was impolite enough to correct a French writer on a detail in one of the lesser-known novels. He took it calmly since he knew, about Giraudoux, personal details he hoped would disconcert me. When I showed no interest, he went on,

'And, after all, as a writer he is an escapist. How like an Englishman to admire that!'

What nonsense. Escapist, the writer who returned again and again to the themes of treachery, madness, disappointment, death? He was escapist only in the sense in which Mallarmé escapes from the real world by substituting an image for a real event or emotion. And as Picasso deforms the reality in order to imply a truth about it. No writer ever came closer to dissolving in words the ambiguous and disturbing Greek smile, or the least reassuring Mozart.

I am very close to the moment when I shall be too dry of mind to re-read even those of his books in which the images had the freshness of a jet of water in sunlight, but I hope never to be so disloyal as to turn them off my shelves.

Older, much tougher, certain to last as long as I do, my passion for Stendhal is less easy to account for. (Can one account for a passion?) *Ce tendre et troublant Stendhal*, Paul Léautaud wrote in his diary on the 18th of March, 1901, and at another time: *Chez Stendhal, l'homme est si particulier, qu'il n'y a pas de milieu: on l'adore ou on le déteste.*

It is true.

His dry phrases, often careless, limpid to a fault, quivering with emotion below the surface, made a confused secretive adolescent free of a lively world, open on all sides, where any question could be asked, and no pretence was made of knowing every answer. A world exactly the opposite of the appalling closed world of Mauriac's novels with their final sense that everything has been exposed, and their suppressed pleasure in the defeat, pain, ugliness, of ugly defeated men and women.

But that is not the single reason for my abiding passion for Stendhal. There is no one adequate reason. It was instinctive. An instinct led me to the only writer who could explain to me, because he shared them, my hatred of authority, my inborn restlessness, my profound happiness in foreign places, fear of ridicule, distrust of human beings, my insanity. All these have their roots in my childhood, but they brought me, a masterless dog, to the feet of the one person I recognized.

Not that the instinct was a wholly fortunate one. Years ago Denis Saurat told me,

'You should read less French. French literature is poison to an English writer.'

I took this to be one of his sceptical quips until the day when I realized that I had caught an incurable disease, the taste for lucidity.

Chapter 63

What in the 'thirties I felt for Germans was not dislike, not fear, it was a cold passion of curiosity. I began to think it useless to look in my dear France for an answer to questions about the future. If anywhere, they were in Germany—about which I knew nothing except that my mother, as a young woman in Bremen with my father's ship, had seen a wife walking three paces behind her husband, carrying his heavy overcoat and what seemed to be a lightning conductor. No doubt he was expecting a thunderstorm.

In February 1932, we went to Berlin.

I lived there some weeks, fascinated, repelled, amused, above all disconcerted by a city unlike any I knew. Every other foreign city offers an image of itself in the first days, which may turn out to be incomplete or a downright lie, but is at least coherent. Berlin contradicted itself at every moment, and with the utmost violence. It did not even look like a capital city: there was scarcely a building anyone would cross the street to look at. Yes, one—the old guard-house on Unter den Linden which housed the tomb of the Unknown Soldier, a square of black lightless stone, with the date, topped by a great copper wreath; nothing else except the wreaths and two thin bronze pillars supporting thinner flames: the place was open to the sky, and the day I went snow was drifting down on to the tomb.

Other public buildings and most of the streets made an impression of middle-class sobriety and immovability, Victorian in its complacence. They evoked the most respectable feelings, but the writers and painters in vogue all belonged to an avant-garde devoid of any feeling livelier than disgust with life. Buttoned up to the neck in thick garments—it was bitterly cold everywhere—angry young men and women stripped themselves of conventional ideas and emotions, practising total evacuation as a moral hygiene.

A play that had been running for months, staged by a group of young out-of-work actors calling themselves Truppe 1931, was about the Marxian theory of value.

There was—this was not contradicted—a feeling of public tension such as exists in England only in the last few hours before the outbreak of a war.

As commonplace as a Baptist chapel to look at, with few trees, a wretched river, monuments of stupefying banality, Berlin at that time was conscientiously corrupt and gross, with misery, grey hunger, uncertainty, in the background—not so far in the background, either—but fascinating and heady, boiling like a crater.

An alienated city, living—it was impossible not to feel this—on borrowed time.

It fascinated because—where other capital cities are full of a past still living in their old houses or the wharves of their river or their bakers' shops—here what you saw was the future waiting in the wings for the curtain to rise. If I were to pretend that I guessed what the play was going to be about, it would be a lie. All I saw, tasted, felt, was the nervous gaiety, the eager abandonment and deriding of morals, the threat of social collapse, the paralysis of all ideals—including the ideal of freedom, squeezed to death between two extremes.

The first thing I saw when I came out of a dull declamatory meeting of the Stalhelm, a memorial service for the dead of the Great War, was a frieze of posters plastered on kiosks and bare trees: they gave the names (with dates) of people who had been killed by the Nazis during the month. On the other side of each tree, each kiosk, was a Nazi poster, with the list, much shorter, of their dead. Either the communists are worse shots than their opponents, I thought, or less savage. The young German with me said,

'It is a new war, yes?'

'As useless as the last.'

'No. This one is to defend our freedom.'

That same Sunday, in the evening, another German took us to the Bock-Bier-Fest in a working-class quarter. Cheaper and a great deal less comfortable than Haus Vaterland—where for a few shillings the clerk and his girl, the elderly official and his fat smiling wife, could choose between the scenery and eating habits of some dozen countries—it seethed with an animal gaiety: mountains of sausages and sauerkohl, tuns of new beer, singing to split the ear-drum, wall-paintings of innocent indecency and vulgarity, a Love Boat . . .

> *Einmal ist keinmal, drum trink' mit mir*
> *Und morgen ist alles vorbei . . .*

When we left, our German companion, shouting because I was temporarily deaf, nudging me in the ribs because I was wiping smoke-blinded eyes, said,

'See this street? Last week during a fight between our chaps and Hitler's swine, a child ran out of that doorway and got a bullet through its head from both sides. Absurd, eh?'

Nothing seemed absurd in a country where all contraries were equally possible, and where an inexhaustible vitality threw up in the same jet order and disorder, the most brutal theories of collective discipline and a reckless anarchy in personal life, energies as dangerous as Luther, Fichte, Marx, but also Meister Eckart, Beethoven, Goethe, themselves a little too much of a good thing . . .

Alfred Knopf was in Berlin for a week. He invited us to lunch at Horcher's. The small room with its faded olive-green panelling had seen and forgotten more princes and personages than other fashionable German restaurants remembered. I watched the waiter prepare a sauce, using double cream, an egg yolk, brandy, and a cupful of rich stock: he stirred them in a shallow dish over a flame, arranged in it the slices of venison, and let them simmer. As he passed, Herr Horcher gave the dish a glance from faded blue eyes. The vegetables were asparagus tips, kohlrabi cooked in cream, and potatoes dissolving in butter. I have forgotten whether I felt a little ashamed— perhaps not, since it was certain I should never sit in Horcher's again—but I ate everything. And I seized the chance to make a new contract for my novels which, as I expected it would, gave me the benefit of movements in the pound-dollar exchange.

'A much too shrewd businessman was lost when you took to writing novels,' Alfred said later. 'That's twice you've played the exchange against us.'

Outside in the street, the cold drove the breath back down my throat. It came straight from Siberia, and flayed the skin. Oddly enough, it did not destroy a petal of the snowdrops, narcissi, violets and feathery mimosa bunched together on stalls at the corner of a dull lumpish square.

If this nakedly pitiless wind made me flinch, what did it do to the unemployed who in the district north and south-east of Alexanderplatz outnumbered the employed? Face after face, the flesh sunk into ravines, had the waxen colour of hunger, but none of these skeletons was less than carefully shaved and very neat in his threadbare suit.

'When one of them loses hope completely, which may happen in his second year out of work—a man with wife and children is then allowed fifty shillings a month—he kills himself; his self-respect draws the line at dirt and rags,' my German friend said . . .

We were living in a boarding-house on the Kurfürstendamm. I could not call it an ugly street, since ugliness is itself a distinction, and these houses were as vacantly unattractive as a pile of rubble. At the lower end, the little cabarets and restaurants were simple and friendly, but one in every three shops was empty: here as in other streets the most noticeable object was the To Let signs.

On my fourth or fifth evening I was rash enough to ask whether anyone at the table took Herr Hitler seriously. The only person who did was a thin elderly spinster. She was put brutally in her place by our landlady.

Frau Broesike, a Saxon with the voice and moustache of a sergeant-major, was the widow of a professor of history; her boarders kept her alive, and she despised and bullied them. Striking her mouth with her hand, she cried,

'Fräulein Schön, if that fool should win in the election, you never eat in my house again!'

Did she later pay for this insult? Decent old virago that she was, I hope not.

'And Dr Goebbels?' I asked.

'Ah. He is not a fool, he is a devil. But he is not, as some say, a Jew. When he married, he offered to show his wife to any genuine enquirer, to prove that she was not Jewish.'

I burst out laughing. No one else thought the offer comic, and I reflected that what divides one tribe from another is less likely to be religion or politics, or a lack of oil or harbours, than different ideas of the ridiculous. To cover up my discomfiture, I asked,

'But who does support the Führer?'

'Apart from our sentimental Fräulein Schön?' Frau Broesike said spitefully. 'I will tell you. Small shopkeepers ruined by the crisis. And young men, trained doctors, who are glad to earn a few marks addressing envelopes. Do you know what we call our university in Berlin? *Wartehalle für Unbeschäftigte*—waiting-rooms for the work-less. The lecture-rooms are so crowded that students pin to the floor scraps of paper with their names, to reserve a few inches of standing-room. But, when we are on our feet again—and we shall be—you'll hear no more of Fräulein Schön's vulgar little friend.' She laughed like a mastiff. 'Do you know what she said about him the other day? That he was Frederick Barbarossa himself, come back to save us, ha, ha!'

I winced for the wretched Schön. It was unnecessary. After supper she drew me into a corner to ask if I had seen anything of 'our crusaders, our young archangels?'

I said I had. 'You have a song—I mean, they have—which begins something like: How fine to see the blood of Jews spurting under the knife.'

Her gentle face remained placid, smiling. 'Yes. Yes, it is a song. Like other songs.'

'Well, I don't know,' I said. 'It's not like any English song.'

'No?' A gleam of satisfaction came into her pale eyes. 'Much more lordly, no doubt.' . . .

I had a friend in Berlin. Some months before this, in the autumn of 1931, I was·in Scarborough at the Labour Party Conference. It was a dispiriting affair, both delegates and Executive wry-mouthed from swallowing MacDonald's 'betrayal'. Some at least of the dejected men and women on the platform must have seen it coming, but they were adrift and out of heart. I was standing outside the hall, watching their faces, when the secretary of the local party came up to me.

'I have a very young German here, a Miss Linke, I wish you'd speak to her.'

Turning, I saw what I took to be a schoolgirl in a shabby coat and a soft hat pulled down over her eyes. Reluctantly—I dislike getting involved with people—I went over to her and found myself looking at the goose-girl of the German fairy-tales, tall and slender, with a flawless skin, pale rose on white, red unpainted mouth, hair like fine yellow silk, eyes of a clear blue, the shape and colour of a kitten's. With some derisory sum in marks she had come to England 'to find out what my English comrades are thinking and doing.' Everywhere she had found friends, and shelter for a night or a week.

In poor people's houses she shared a bed with the children, as contented as when she could be given a room to herself. In the morning her hosts sent her on her way with advice and another address.

But of course, I thought. She is the Youngest Brother, whom everybody, peasant, old crone, swineherd, emperor, recognizes at sight and is compelled to help.

This was not her first journey. A year before, with two friends, boys as poor as she was, she had been to France. They visited the battlefields, and at Douaumont promised each other 'to be friends with all, to forget our losses, to build the future.'

Her English was eccentric, she was learning it as she had learned French, by ear.

'For months I, what do you say?, am scratching together pennies to come to England. I am happy here, *le bonheur fou.* But why is your Labour Party sitting glum and sad, repeating like old women: We must be calm, do not let us be excited, keep very quiet and all will be well? Why don't they wave their arms and shout: We are socialists, let us fight?'

'Perhaps because they are English.'

'Oh, no.' Her smile showed strong perfect teeth, very white. 'This four weeks I am talking with people of all classes, and they are not as if dead since years.'

In the few hours she spent with me in Whitby next day, I discovered her complete lack of self-consciousness. Words, gestures, actions, sprang directly from her nature, without vanity or calculation. I have never, before or since, known a man or woman of whom this is true. Born in East Berlin, the second child of a very minor civil servant, she learned during the War anything the Youngest Brother needs to know about hunger. After the War, a skinny fifteen-year-old with her first job, she learned to snatch her wages and run like a hare to buy the dress which in the meantime had centupled in price, so that it was as far out of her reach as ever. To say that she was a rebel against the stiff respectability of her lower middle-class family would be absurd; their ideas and teaching had no meaning for her, none at all. Her father's dull anger when she joined the young socialists, the tears and scolding of her mother, made her yawn.

She had been born without a sense of guilt. It did not occur to her to refuse to sleep with the young comrade she fell in love with at sixteen. To make any fuss about so simple a gesture!

The most common human vices—malice, envy, timidity, greed, jealousy, hypocrisy, fear—had been left out of her entirely. But her sense of responsibility was full-grown.

'What do you want most?' I asked her. The answer I expected was: To have the money to travel. Or: To be heard of.

In a serious voice she said, 'To live, to work, to build a world where is freedom and bread for all.'

Just as she was leaving, my mother came in, and without reflecting I said,

'This is Lilo Linke, she has come from Berlin.'

There was a silence. Then my mother said in a strange voice,

'I'm glad you are in England, we must forgive and forget the past.'

The words struck me as exaggerated. Surely, thirteen years after the war, a young German could be thought of as an ordinary visitor?

I had not the wit to feel the enormous effort with which my mother lifted her few words and laid them in front of the smiling young German. Who accepted them with polite simplicity. And why not? But I ought to have guessed that, only to be able to see distinctly, to reach the German girl, she had had to step over the body, its hands clenched, of her dead son.

In Berlin, Lilo was living in a two-roomed flat, not far from the Kurfürstendamm. She was immensely proud of it. It was so small that four pairs of legs filled the living-room, and so new that the plaster had barely set. Her few possessions stood to attention against the walls or on shelves: to balance her passion to be independent and free, she had a Prussian love of order.

'How,' I asked, 'can you afford this?'

The rent was very low, much lower than it would have been in London, but even at that little was left of her salary from the *Deutsche Volkswirt* (a journal she said was the Berlin equivalent of the *Economist*). The meal she had got ready for us was sparse, but I wondered anxiously whether we were eating next day's supper, too.

An efficient staff officer, she had drawn up a time-table for the next weeks, and I saw that I was going to have trouble to make room in it for what I enjoy in a foreign city, walking without aim, searching at the back of a café, between the half-closed shutters of a house, for the excitement, the sense of a mysterious other life, that when I was a child I got from the lights of houses rising suddenly out of blackness. The smiling fair-haired young man she introduced as one of her comrades in some Social Democratic youth front had been called up for duty to show us places she didn't want to see herself. His name was Werner. When Lilo was telling us how, as a child during the War, she had fainted in one of the endless queues and been charitably carried to the head of it, and after that, until she was found out, had pretended to faint in queues, happy to have stumbled accidentally on the right trick, he said,

'The only thing I remember about the War is my mother crying. She had hold of my arm and she was saying: Oh, your poor thin arm, where shall I get milk for you? Oh your arms, your arms! . . . But it was *after* the War, she had thought the blockade would stop, and when it was the same, still the blockade and no food, she cried. During the War—no tears. After the War, tears every day. That was very funny—yes?'

'It won't happen again,' Lilo said fiercely, '*we* shall see to that.'

Already I had my doubts about her leaders. Little turbulent as our Labour leaders were, I could not see them tolerating brutes like the Nazi storm troopers, encouraging judges to treat them with fatherly mildness, and allowing schoolmasters to sneer at the Republic and preach a violent nationalism to their young pupils.

Maliciously, I told Lilo that I had been listening to speeches by her Social Democratic leaders. 'Why do they go on repeating: We must be calm, do not let us be excited, keep quiet and all will be well? You blamed our people, but yours seem far timider, far more cautious and eager to show how correct and respectable they are. And we're not in danger, our streets aren't full of potential dictators. Why don't your leaders wave their arms and shout: We are socialists, let us fight? Anyone would think they are ashamed of having given birth to a Republic and want to keep it dark.'

'That's not true, you've been listening to old men. Who cares about them? *We* shall fight. Listen . . .'

She talked in a laughing authoritative voice about the new age, egged on by the smiling Werner. So long ago as it is, and Lilo dead, all I remember now is that suddenly I was madly happy. For the first time since 1914, I had the feeling of the years immediately before that war, the night-long talks about the future, the blazing excitement. It was like one of those dreams in which, ravished with joy, one is young and strong. These young Germans were talking with our confidence and gaiety, our mockery of the old, our rage against injustice. At one moment I could have sworn I heard a voice not heard since 1916—but that was too good to be true.

There were differences. Behind us in 1913 stretched years of solid peace, behind Lilo and her friends lay defeat, hunger, anarchy.

In a few months they discovered—as we had—how little the future was theirs, and how indifferently their leaders, not out of any ill-will, not for want of courage, had led them. Like ours, their new age died by default, surrendered by decent cautious men too much of whose energies ran away in oiling the machinery of a party: the machine functioned beautifully to reproduce itself, and broke down the moment it ran against passions it had no idea how to evoke on its own behalf and never came within worlds of controlling in its enemies.

The really surprising thing about the Weimar Republic is not that it lasted only fourteen years, but that it lasted so long. True, the rest of us did not do a great deal to help it elude its murderers.

Rather late, someone knocked at the door of the flat. 'That will be my boss,' Lilo said, smiling.

'Your——?'

'My editor. Dr Stolper. He said they would come—they want to meet you.'

But it was an elderly man—elderly or middle-aged, impossible to guess the age of these faces denatured by hunger. So ashamed to be begging that he was nearly inaudible, he asked for a pfennig. At most doors in the building he would have been lucky to get just that. The boy gave him ten, and Lilo—waving me fiercely back—another ten. She began to question him. Her candour reassured him, he poured out a torrent of words, cried a little, and stumbled away, his money in one hand, the other wiping his grey cheeks.

'What did he say?' I asked.

'Eight months ago he got a chance of work and lost it because he couldn't raise the fifteen shillings to buy a waiter's third-hand tail-coat. He cries because he doesn't understand how this could happen to him, he has always been a good waiter.'

Werner left. Soon afterwards, the Stolpers came: they had been to the theatre and were in evening dress, he a strongly-built middle-aged man, with a fine intelligent head and a smile at once friendly and arrogant, the unconscious arrogance, more an air of authority and success, of a man who knows he is better informed than anyone he is likely to meet. His wife had one of those narrow Jewish faces which suggest a Greek coin, an extreme delicacy and strength, dark hair, immense dark eyes with a flicker of gaiety in their depths, and the gentlest voice in the world.

Both treated Lilo with the indulgent interest they might have shown a young relative. At one moment, when she shook her head, refusing to do something Dr Stolper wanted her to do, his wife said quietly,

'But you must obey him, he is your boss—he is mine, too.'

Lilo gave her a brilliant smile. 'No. He is my boss in the office, but not outside. Outside I am my own boss.'

Her total lack of subservience was one of her most surprising virtues. Where had this East Berlin child, less than half educated, learned to defend herself and her opinions in any company, politely, but with unshakable self-will? No authority as such, no difference of age or class, made the faintest impression on her. She was never defiant. She was simply, in all times and places, her own boss.

Gustav Stolper and his wife lived in a society where intelligence, good manners, tolerance, uncommon sense, wit, worldly knowledge, join to quicken a cell which can only exist in a capital city, and there only at certain times on certain conditions. Their house in a suburb of Berlin, among pine-trees, was an instance of the new moneyed simplicity: the interior walls of four living-rooms could be rolled back to form a vast central square with immense windows and an invisible source of warmth: the nursery, which I saw when Mrs Stolper took me with her to say goodnight to her two young children, was divided at night by a sliding wall. The furniture in all the rooms was light and strong; there were admirable modern paintings, and, lying about, weeklies and monthlies in three languages. Had you wanted an example of the Berlin farthest from the one brawling in the streets, here it was, cultured, cosmopolitan—on the edge.

The talk at dinner was at first about politics—it could not begin anywhere else. A member of one of the centre parties, a liberal, Stolper refused, with a fierce controlled passion, to believe that Hitler would come to anything.

'No, no, everything is against it, every sane force, economic, financial, even social. Even philosophic—you can't found a society on a doctrine which is entirely irrational. But entirely.'

One of his guests—the American journalist Edgar Mowrer—said soberly,

'Don't be too sure that what looks irrational isn't viable. This country smells of trouble, as if somebody had buried a rat under the boards. If my experience of people—and countries—has taught me any one thing it is that if a man or a party can tap irrational energies they'll blow up Everest, let alone a single country.'

'Not this country,' Stolper said, with his fine smile.

Mowrer turned to his neighbour—banker or industrialist (I forget). 'What's your opinion?'

'Mine? Don't be too shocked if I tell you that, supposing he can take over the government—by any means—Herr Hitler will find more economists, bankers, diplomats, civil servants, field-marshals, even clerics falling over each other to work for him than he needs. The fact that he's insane—if he is—won't deter them for a moment when they're offered a chance to get their hands on the levers.'

Still smiling, Stolper shook his head. 'You're quite wrong. In the end unreason always destroys itself.'

Mowrer threw his hands up. 'Oh, in the end!'

The fourth man at the table—was he the banker?—had the face of an ecclesiastical official, perhaps a member of the Curia, smooth except for a few deep lines, all curved, widely-curved nostrils, downward-curving thin lips, a full womanly chin.

'My dear friend, my dear Gustl,' he said, laughing, 'you live in an unreasonable world. My cousin, who is a millionaire, has been placing money, gold, in half a dozen capitals. He can't get at any of it. How's that for lunacy! Europe is more than half off its head, and if all the statesmen, diplomats, economists like yourself, and financiers who are not mad, have neither will nor power to drag it back to sanity, why on earth do you put any trust in reason? Reason! My advice to you——'

He broke off abruptly, as if he thought his advice had better be given behind doors.

One of the others began to talk about a book he had been sent from Paris: from this, by way of Rilke and an argument about translating poetry, the talk was steered into thinner unpolitical air.

When I left, Mrs Stolper laid in mine a hand as light as a leaf and almost as narrow.

'I am glad that Lilo has made a good English friend,' she said. 'Perhaps she will need you.'

'Don't you agree with your husband about Hitler?' I asked.

'Of course I agree with him,' she said, smiling. 'He is always right.'

Later I discovered that this small dignified charming woman, often silent—who lived in and for her husband, believed what he believed, accepted as irrefutable all his opinions—had a mind little less cultivated and acute than his, and, as well, an instinctive wisdom which sometimes showed itself in a word or a gesture slipping from her unnoticed by her conscious mind . . .

What happened, later, to the Sportpalast, that monstrous building which served equally well for the six-day cycle race, memorial services, the stream of vitriol pouring from Dr Goebbels, and Communist rallies? The programme Lilo had laid down covered all these. The Communist evening was colder than any I remember, flurries of frozen snow and a wind like a flail. Over ten thousand people crowded into the place, solid patient faces of older workers, faces of nakedly angry youths, pinched faces of anxious women, children holding banners in their blue hands. A woman recited her husband's poems; the police had forbidden him to recite them himself. I tried to imagine which of our poets would be dangerous to public order. The words of songs were thrown on the screen. The one that fetched them all to their feet, bellowing, was about defending the USSR—it reminded me of the old maid in my boarding-house with her *leibliche Friedrich Barbarossa*. Why this passion for a Messiah, shared by both extremes? The last we had was Cromwell, an experiment never repeated.

Except when he halted the torrent long enough to ask, 'And who did this to you?' I could not follow the speaker. A roar answered him. '*Polizei!*'

Outside, arm-linked lines of the *Polizei* broke the crowd up into twos and threes as it came out into the brutal cold. The wind wrapped a piece of paper round my ankle—Vote for Hindenburg.

'Are you going to vote for him?' I asked Lilo.

'Of course. He is a decent old fellow, he will keep that devil Hitler in his place.'

The following evening—all part of my education—she and Werner took us to see a friend who was a Communist. He was also a scholar of sixteenth-century music and a composer. He and his wife had a flat even smaller than Lilo's, a room and half a room in one of the huge new blocks of workers' flats in north Berlin: luckily they were both very thin as well as young and very poor, and the room held only the essential minimum of furniture.

The conversation began politely, with a question Ernst Meyer asked about Dolmetsch, but in less than ten minutes a furious argument broke out between him and Lilo. Turning to me, he said,

'If she tells you that the Social Democrats are socialists, don't believe her. In 1916 they called out the army to shoot down the only honest socialists in the country, and they've been selling out to the Right ever since. In every crisis. All they think about is their jobs. Thanks to their treachery we——'

Eyes like a spitting cat's, Lilo cut him short. 'He has no right to talk about treachery. When I tell you that on the 9th of August last year his Party voted with the Nazis against Brüning! Think of it —*they voted with the Nazis!*'

'You know less about politics than this table leg,' Ernst retorted. 'The last time your people had an idea was 1848. Do you want a social revolution or don't you? If you did, you'd see that the only one way to it now is by backing Hitler against your shuffling old women who think about nothing but staving it off.'

'You're out of your mind,' Lilo said with contempt.

We were so jammed together that it was impossible to wave an arm; yelling was the only outlet. The gentle Werner, sitting beside me, turned out to have a drill-sergeant's voice behind his quiet one.

'No, he is not,' he bawled, 'but he has nothing in his mind except orders from Moscow. Fight the Democrats! Yes, sir. Vote Nazi! Yessir, yessir.'

In the foolish hope of pouring oil, I said,

'I admit I don't understand why the government allows the Nazis to preach murder, and plot, quite openly, against the Republic. It seems an odd way to defend yourself.'

Werner smiled. 'Ah, I'll tell you why. We must get the Treaty revised. So—if your English government sees that the Nazis threaten us, they will help us—yes?'

Taken aback, I said, 'Do your leaders really believe that?'

'Of course. I think it is sensible.'

'And do *you* believe it?'

Ernst said drily, 'No, he doesn't believe it, he's not an idiot. Nor do they. The fact is they don't know what to do, so they do nothing and pretend they're being very clever and cunning. And let me tell you——'

'Let me tell *you*, if you think that you can bolshevize us you're mistaken. We shall fight you.'

It struck me, even then, as ominous that they thought they could quarrel with each other, using the Nazis as a weapon. I must have shown my discomfort. Ernst smiled charmingly and said,

'We have not made you feel at home. Wait a minute.'

He fiddled with the wireless set. Through a screeching storm of noises, a few words were suddenly audible: This afternoon their Majesties left London for . . . Everyone burst out laughing. Ilse

Meyer, who had not opened her mouth during the quarrel, went out of the room and came back with a few sandwiches on a plate and handed them round, with a little air of anxiety . . .

For all her eagerness to embrace the world, Lilo was a loyal child of Berlin. She talked about it as though it were the centre of Europe, all roads led to it; it had the only swimming bath in which the artificial waves were as rough as at sea, the only museum with a complete reconstruction of an Assyrian palace, the only restaurant where each table was linked by telephone to all the others, the only production of the *Tales of Hoffmann* with a real horse and cab on the stage, standing outside a faithful model of the café where Hoffmann himself (or was it Offenbach?) spent his evenings, the only night club, open to all, whose habitués were inverts.

Werner was told off to take us there. He led us to a respectably ugly house, and into a room which would have been considered a little dull for a Methodist tea. I had supposed that these places were kept up for the benefit of foreigners who had been assured that Berlin was the most immoral capital in Europe. Not a bit of it: the small tables round the dance floor were all occupied by stolid Germans and their wives or secretaries, 'negroes', Werner said: provincials. The cabaret began at half-past eleven, with a plump woman in blue satin, opulent shoulders and arms bare and powdered, dancing politely with another, younger. But for their rouge and carefully plucked eyebrows they might have been a schoolgirl and her dancing-mistress—and but for the final gesture which revealed them, very delicately, as men. The next turn was a slender girlish creature, all but naked, her dress cut down at the back to the cleft of narrow white buttocks. She, he, danced alone, showing rounded thighs.

'He is alone,' the head waiter said, 'because his lover does not allow him a partner. See, he is here every night, watching.'

The elderly gentleman who might have been a civil servant rose at the end of the dance, bent to kiss the young man's hand, and escorted him to a table. My boredom was now intolerable, and I insisted on going home. Werner was distressed.

'Oh, but you haven't seen the other place, where the women wear men's clothes!'

Heaven forbid. Outside, his back against the wall, the man was still holding out the limp copy of a magazine he had been holding—how long? all day?—for several days. He made no effort to attract attention: perhaps the effort needed to stand upright in the icy wind absorbed all his energy, even the energy to move, to turn towards us eyes, I saw now, covered with a grey film, like frost . . .

'This evening,' Lilo said, 'I am going to show you the true Germany. Well, perhaps it is the true Germany. You will see.'

As I stepped inside it, the flat in Charlottenburg greeted me like an old friend. For some moments I could not imagine why it was so warmly reassuringly familiar. Suddenly, I realized how I knew it and where I had seen it before—not I, but my mother. It was one she had described to me, belonging to the German agent of the Prince Line in—was it Odessa?—where, a very young women, she spent several afternoons. It was her first voyage, and everything amused her, so that she forgot none of it, the German woman herself, so dowdy and submissive and good-humoured, the living-room where all that could be was over-stuffed, cushions, quilted curtains, sandwiches, and the room itself so crammed with chairs, tables, sideboards, a piano, whole services of china on the walls, every plate and jug carrying its warning—Gluttony is a vice of the eyes—Drink only with friends—Discretion gives long life—that once seated you could not rise without disturbing a table loaded to the edge with family photographs, or a brass bowl, or a lampstand in the form of a Nubian slave or a shepherdess embracing her shepherd.

Nothing was missing here except the warning signals and the Nubian.

My mother must, I reckoned, have been in Odessa for the first time in the eighteen-eighties, half a century ago.

It was a delicious evening. Dr Walter, an elderly professor of music, and his plump lively wife had chosen among their friends the three who could entertain us without needing a word of English: the young Jewish violinist from the Schauspielhaus orchestra who liked playing Bach, the old singer who could take the top notes in the Jewel Song almost without faltering, the not very young actress who was still—a little affair of jealousy—being given only minor parts but could, and did, recite long passages of Schiller with all the pleasure in the world.

A table had been covered with plates of sausages, salad, cream cakes. Between Schiller, Bach, a good-tempered debate about Webern with explanatory passages on piano or violin, noisy gossip about the theatre, and roars of homeric laughter, they ran to the table to swallow another mouthful, sang, shouted, and slapped each other on the bottom. The room was over-heated, shabbier than when my young mother knew it in Odessa (or Hamburg), but the gaiety, good-humour, gluttony, that vice of the eyes, the sentiments, the un-spiritual spiritual values, the pieties, were unchanged.

The true Germany? Well, perhaps—but fifty or a hundred years out of its time.

They had a past, these warm-hearted friendly people, but had they a future? Hadn't I, that very afternoon, seen the future in the form of a boy of twelve or thirteen, glaring at me, hands clenched, re-peating furiously,

'We young ones didn't sign that Treaty. No!'

'He's only been like this since he passed into High School,' his mother sighed. 'I try to teach him better.'

The true Germany? No other capital city I knew gave me this sense of improvisation and uncertainty: it was like a house the week before the family is due to move out because of an impending bank-ruptcy or divorce—dust, cracks in the ceiling, nothing quite in its proper place, an ugly feeling of exposure. As in a cubist portrait, all the fragments of a dismembered body were there. The disorder, the chaos, the distortion, had its significance, like a fever patient's chart.

It never entered my head that a people so in love with exaggera-tion, so quick to turn everything into an object of hatred or worship, so little in possession of itself, might begin to dream of possessing Europe.

Nor that the young ghosts haunting the fields on either side of the Marne would shortly be outnumbered by millions of ghosts—even of children, of women hushing a child as they carried it into the gas chamber. (But who could have imagined Auschwitz?)

Nor that the separate wills murdering each other in the Berlin streets were the shadow thrown by the passion for collective self-assertion, the romantic distaste for tolerance, compromise, individual freedom, which tolls through German history. Nor that that history has been made up of stupefyingly sudden changes, splendour to misery, empire to the most wretched anarchy. But I knew no history. Anyone knows more now who has seen the defeated despairing Germany of the twenties turn itself by an immense effort of cunning, tenacity, hypocrisy, moral and physical energy, shameless brutality, into the Reich which dictated to Europe, drove the Russian army to the suburbs of Moscow, only to collapse in ruins. And in fifteen years rise again, still mutilated, but rich and proud of itself. A country of diabolical energy where anything, any contrast, any self-con-tradiction, is to be expected.

On the 13th of March a mixed lot of Germans, Americans, English, waited in the offices of the *Chicago Daily News* in Berlin for the results of the Presidential election. The Germans, all members of the Centre or the moderate Left, were praying for Hindenburg. During the day I had noticed Communists and Nazis standing together outside the polling booths, almost arm in arm, shaking collecting boxes. This truce was not reassuring. The patient might die even if the operation were a success.

Sitting at an end of the long crowded room, as close as she could get to the loud-speaker, Lilo took down the figures as they came through, her cheeks flaming, red on white. She was by many years the youngest creature in the room.

'Ah—' a radiant smile—'*absolute Mehrheit*'—a frown and a heavy heaving sigh like a puppy—'*keine absolute Mehrheit.*'

One of the English journalists, Harrison Brown—humane, single-minded, pleasantly selfish and, except for Lilo, the happiest adult I have ever known—teased her.

'Your socialist comrade Hindenburg! Doesn't it ever occur to you that there is something very wrong with your party when it has to call out its followers in support of a reactionary old general, as stupid as a boot, and in the pockets of the East Prussian Junkers? Step by step you've retreated—into their arms! How do you like going to the poll hand in hand with Junkers? What good do you expect it to do you?'

Pushing her yellow hair back, Lilo said vehemently,

'He has sworn to uphold the constitution, he is a German general, not a devil.'

When we left, at two in the morning, Hindenburg's election was certain. A wind from the steppes was driving livid clouds overhead. The streets were empty, even of shadows, since the lights had been turned off. We groped our way in darkness.

'Are you sure,' I asked, 'that you can trust Hindenburg?'

'Of course. He has *sworn.*'

I was leaving Berlin next day. 'Well—you can always come to England.'

She laughed. 'What do you think can happen here? This good old man is a rock. Perhaps, as H.B. says, he is stupid, but what does that matter when there are a hundred men to be clever for him, and millions like me to prop him up. I'm not afraid.'

Chapter 64

From Berlin, the rootless alienated city, to my quiet house on the edge of Whitby, a long step backwards in time. If I had had the sense I should have seen it—correctly—as a rocky ledge out of reach of the tide racing to cut us all off.

I am absolutely convinced that I became a novelist owing to a serious misunderstanding with myself. But I doubt whether I can now find my way back to the source of the profound sense of failure, of spiritual dishonesty—in a word, treachery—that seizes me when I think about my novels. It lies a great way farther back than 1930, though that was the year it rose to the surface—a tormenting sense of dryness, *accidie*, futility. My mind, that clumsy dancing bear, went on inventing incidents and characters with fluent ease, but the labour of writing them down filled me with such mortal boredom that but for my insane obstinacy I should have given up.

Obstinacy and an equally insane belief that I had been born to be happy. Since I was no good now for anything but writing novels I decided, with a ridiculous excitement, that I must write better ones.

In civilizing a barbarian the danger is that something, some vital energy, irreplaceable, will be enervated at the same time as the barbarism. Possibly I educated myself above my intellectual level— *quelle blague* pas *sérieuse*!

A note in the margin of a book reminds me that it was on the 25th of October, 1930, that I began my first attempt to write well—that is, with unromantic plainness. *That was Yesterday* was meant to be an account of what happened to me between going to Kettering in the autumn of 1913 and setting off to London at the end of 1918, a little over five years. To avoid the odium of I, I, I, I wrote it in the third person, and omitted or changed the order of events to give it the form of a work of imagination. But I did not leave out events humiliating to me, and did not try to soften my own follies, failures, and the atrocious flaws in my character.

Timid and dishonest in company, the mere act of writing, alone in a room, forces me to be honest, and unconcerned to the point of recklessness.

The effort to discover what, during these five years, I had become, gave me back, for the time being, my pleasure in writing. It would disturb me to re-read this so-called novel, but it is a good book, one of the few in which I feel pride.

(Gingerly turning the pages, I have been hooked by this paragraph: 'At this moment, she felt sure that she would do something in the world. "Deliver us from temptation" should run: Make us to grow old, and our muscles to slacken, and our conceit to drop from us. Cause the young men to sharpen their wits on us. Bind burdens on us and make us afraid to run. Make one day like another and the nights the divisions between the days. Make us not to care.')

At last, I told myself gaily, I am on the right road.

It did not occur to me that I was on the point of disciplining myself out of one market without earning the attention and respect of my equals.

With smiling kindness, Charles Morgan told me,

'My dear Margaret, you know far too much about human nature, and too little about making what you know palatable. You don't give your imagination room to breathe, you dissect, and you write too many books too quickly.'

True, true. But I have no private income and I am a spendthrift. The worst of an income that rises and falls with the fury of a spring tide is that it is fatally easy to give away five hundred pounds, or spend it on going to France, since the next tide may—or may not— cover the rocks again.

None of this adds up to unhappiness. I have been madly happy for days at a time, and placidly engrossed for months or weeks. If only, I shall say to myself, when I am dying of not being able to stay alive any longer, you had had a little more coolness and foresight.

That Was Yesterday ran to nearly two hundred thousand words. (Who would have thought that my veins had so much blood in them?) In a recoil, I turned to the idea of writing a series of very short novels (*nouvelles* or *récits*, depending on the manner: we have no term for these forms), tenuously linked. Each was to be a portrait of a woman at the turning point, early or late, of her life, composed with the utmost scepticism about the feelings (love, friendship, loyalty, etc) we all profess, the self-deceptions on which we all depend: each was to convey through its form the essence of the character.

I wrote the first, *A Day Off*, with intense pleasure—pleasure in doing what I could do better than anything else, creep through the corridors of a brain and the veins of a heart. And unfailing pleasure in the view from my window. I had only to lift my eyes from the sheet of ruled paper under my hand to see the hill, the road climbing it, the edge of the moor, the wind-bitten trees on the horizon. No other scene in the world has, as that did, filled every crevice of my soul.

Ah, fool that I was to leave it and make an alienated city of my life.

It was not the first time that my craving for change, for a worldly life (something for which I have not a rag of talent) kicked my far deeper need of solitude into the cellar. Nor the last.

Was it about *A Day Off* or about a second *récit, Delicate Monster*, that R. H. Tawney said to me, 'You write like a devil!' The second, I think, but I am no longer sure, although I could not have been better pleased if I had been given the O.M.

A Day Off is perhaps the only genuinely imaginative book I have written. No, there is one other, published under a false name. Both were failures.

Telling myself that I had been rash to suppose I was capable of great things as a novelist, I began to write an account of my near ancestry and youth: I wanted, before it was covered by the sand, to record a world that had been destroyed in 1914. Begun in my room in Whitby, *No Time Like The Present* was finished in a London flat. But by the time I reached 1914 in it, I had had a change of mind or heart, and I filled the rest of a short book with my opinions. These were nothing if not violent, and it was an error in tactics to add them to an otherwise innocent book which had every chance of pleasing by its polite simplicity.

Chapter 65

Before we had been living in Whitby six months, Guy was writing from London: 'It is a fatal thing to settle down . . . I don't like London, but I think we must come back.' Yet in Whitby he worked no less hard than I. He was writing *A Passionate Prodigality*—one of the half-dozen finest books about the first war—planning his admirable life of Beckford, and editing a series of fine editions for Eyre and Spottiswoode. None of this satisfied him. I did not, then, realize that he would never be content, never be less than dissatisfied with himself and his work, a maniac for perfection as I for changes. Had I realized it, I might not have been infected so easily by his discontent with Whitby. It is just possible. Heaven knows I need very little to start up my restlessness. But Whitby is in my bones.

And, I had my view, that incomparable view of hill and moor road.

The surface began cracking in all directions. After many enquiries I had started Bill at a new public school, chosen because it was going to pay attention to biology, in which at this time he was interested, and because its founder had been the ruling genius of an older school. Genius he was and, I think, a bit of a humbug. None the worse for that—a touch of the charlatan is as necessary to a great schoolmaster as to an eloquent preacher or a politician.

In the summer of 1930 when he came home, I thought him wretchedly thin and listless; the panic always at the back of my mind started up, and although I listened calmly when the doctor advised keeping him at home for a term and talked about over-strain, over-growth, and a threatened lung, I lost what little common-sense I had about him, not much, and decided to send him to Switzerland. It was a bad move. The English school in Switzerland was expensive and not even good. It made him strong and tough, and taught him to ski, but little else. What side of his intellect went on growing grew of itself—acute powers of observation, a habit of accuracy.

For the rest, it became the mind of a healthy savage. I could have found some more sensible way of toughening him.

One of my misfortunes is that air of competence which persuades all but my most malicious friends that I know what I am about, when in fact I am totally without sense of direction, or much other sense. Very soon after I had taken my fifteen-year-old son to his Swiss school, I began planning, with suppressed impatience, another change. Guy was turning back to his first love, history, and my scheming brain threw up the idea that to work for a degree at the London School of Economics would give him the solid training he lacked. As an idea, it was suspiciously reasonable.

In the autumn of 1932 I rented a small flat in London, in St John's Wood, for three years. At the end of that time, I told myself airily, I can think again.

My mother, half resigned to the restlessness of her first-born, half saddened, pretended to believe that it was only a passing upheaval. When I took her her pre-publication copy of *That Was Yesterday*, she wished it luck, warmly—no more than I do could she feel that novel-writing is a safe way of living—and began to talk about Dorothy.

Without warning, she said,

'I wish you weren't going to London. I shall miss you, terribly.'

I hardened my heart against the pain that made a child of me. 'We must go, for Guy's work. I'm not selling the house, remember. We'll come back every vacation.'

'Yes, I know,' she said in an absent voice.

Her eyes stared through me. I had a sensation of emptiness, as when, at night, the darkness on one side of the road you are climbing begins to be the darkness of an unseen precipice. Her voice sent back an echo from it. What did she think about during the hours she sat in her window, hands folded? Not all the time about my young sister? About Harold? About voyages—the wild strawberries growing by the fjord in Norway, the beggar in Alicante, without arms or legs, rolling to her feet in a ball of rags, the agent's wife in Odessa, at whose submissiveness she had laughed unkindly, Vera Cruz and the scorching plague-carrying heat?

To distract her from the thought of my leaving her, I asked,

'Did you enjoy voyages?'

'I didn't care for the ship,' she said in a simple voice. 'And the long weeks at sea, often a bad time of the year, and no fresh milk, and quite often towards the middle of the trip there were maggots in the food, and your father hating fresh air, keeping the port closed and smoking his vile cigars. What I liked was going ashore.' Her voice changed, became younger, the smiling insolent voice of a girl. 'I liked Antwerp. I shall never see it again.'

'I'll take you there next May.'

'No. I'm too tired now.'

'We can travel comfortably, you know. Not like we used to.'

She smiled. 'We'll see,' she said, without belief.

She was right. We never did go to Antwerp again together. And when after thirty years I went there to look for her she was nowhere to be found. I counted on my body to recognize the corner of a street, a café, a shop window reflecting the silhouette of the captain's young wife, but for once it failed me.

The September day we left for London was cold and cloudily sunny. In the few minutes as the train drew out past the harbour, I felt myself isolated by a barrier of ice from every living human being, including the husband facing me. Like a knot of adders uncoiling themselves, one departure slid from another behind my eyes— journeys made feverish by unmanageable longings and ambitions, night journeys in war-time, the darkened corridors crammed with young men in clumsy khaki, smoking, falling asleep, journeys with a heavy baby in one arm. At last I came to the child sitting in a corner of a third-class carriage, waiting, silent, tense with anxiety, for the captain's wife to return from the ticket-office. A bearded gentleman in a frock-coat—the stationmaster—saunters up to the open door and says, smiling, something she makes no attempt to hear. Her mother walks lightly across the platform. 'Ah, there you are, Mrs Jameson. Your little girl was afraid you weren't coming,' he said amiably. Nothing less amiable than Mrs Jameson's coldly blue eyes turned on him, and cold voice.

'Nonsense. My child is never afraid.'

Not true . . .

Part II: The Glittering Fountains

O play the glittering fountains of the heart.
Here music ends . . .

H. B. MALLALIEU

Chapter 1

In London I rushed headlong into a life of seeing people, a great many people. I had taken a service flat, with a restaurant downstairs. Nothing simpler than to lift the telephone and tell the head waiter, 'I shall have four, six, eight, guests to dinner.' In the miniscule kitchen, barely room for me to stand inside and close the door, I prepared our breakfast and made coffee for our dinner guests. The food in the restaurant was frightful—like the bills at the end of the month.

Of the twenty-four hours in the day I may have slept for six; the rest were terribly occupied: writing a novel, reviewing (without pay) for A. R. Orage, running about London to political meetings, reading, to educate myself, economics and books on foreign affairs, and talking—no, not talking, listening.

It was at this time that I began the habit, kept up for many years, until it began to bore me, of writing down every night the conversations I had listened to during the day. Only certain conversations. Not any that were merely scandalous (these I buried in a corner of my mind, not deeply, but with no idea of resurrection). Only those attached to one of my obsessions.

Over twenty years or so I recorded many thousands of spoken words. I shall destroy the lot when I have finished this book. (Destroyed on the 26th of March, 1965.)

Lying awake—now that I am old—listening in the first light to a bird singing alone, I feel that only the thinnest least material of veils hangs between me and a meadow of my childhood; the wet grass bright with orchis and cuckoo-pint, the running stream, the clear pale northern sky and cool air, are within a single step.

To turn back into the thirties is infinitely less easy.

The survivors of my generation did not—then—realize that they had also survived an age and a world. Between us and that vanished world stretched four years of completely useless butchery, a wide furrow driven across Europe, crushing out bloodily the energy, genius, intentions and plain decent hopes of millions of young men. Those left were survivors in a strict sense, men living *beyond*—at the other side of a closed frontier. They lived, most of them, ordinary, sometimes highly successful lives, on this side of a country peopled only by ghosts, this side of a nearly incommunicable experience seared into their brains. The few who made the effort to force their experience into words would be the first to say that their account was incomplete.

Neither did we realize that what we were living through was an interregnum, not a new age.

The interregnum lasted some twenty years, traversed a series of conferences held all over Europe, where ageing men made the decisions which decided little except the death a few years later of their sons and the collapse into scorched rubble of their cities, saw the revival of torture as a method of government and the establishment of police states, broke down into another prolonged slaughter, and came to a sudden stop in 1945. Then, only then, the new age opened.

Looked at from this distance (1963), the interregnum itself splits in half. The twenties, for all their disorder, were lively with ideas, dreams, hopes, experiments. The illusion of freedom was intoxicating. When the change came it was like nothing so much as waking up in a grey light, with memories, half dream, half real, of a gay party, the only signs of it a deplorable muddle and a great many used wineglasses.

It was not so abrupt. But a moment did come—roughly at the end of the feverishly energetic twenties—when the moral and intellectual climate changed. Almost before they knew what was happening to them, writers found themselves being summoned on to platforms and into committee-rooms to defend society against its enemies. Writers in Defence of Freedom, Writers' Committee of the Anti-War Council, Congress of Writers for the Defence of Culture, Writers' Section of the World Council against Fascism . . . I forget the names.

The impulse that turned so many of us into pamphleteers and amateur politicians was neither mean nor trivial. The evil we were told off to fight was really evil, the threat to human decency a real threat. I doubt whether any of us believed that books would be burned in England, or eminent English scholars, scientists, writers, forced to beg hospitality in some other country. Or that, like Lorca, we might be murdered. Or tortured and then killed in concentration camps. But all these things were happening abroad, and intellectuals who refused to protest were in effect blacklegs. In this latest quarrel between Galileo and the Inquisition they were on the side of the Inquisition.

During the same decade, the cancerous poverty of the unemployed became, for many writers, what Quakers call a concern. (It still seems to me that there is little to choose between the ancient custom of exposing unwanted babies and ours of allowing an accident of birth to decide which child shall be carefully nurtured and which grow up in a slum.) Social historians of 2930 will ask why it should have stung the consciences of writers and other artists just when it did. Why, after all, should they fret about social justice? The savage injustices and cruelty of classical Greece, Elizabethan England, Renaissance Europe, did not distract them from their work.

Where energy and salt have not been choked out of a society, the writer can breathe freely. In the thirties, millions of half-fed hopeless men, eating their hearts out, gave off a moral stench which became suffocating.

There really was a stench. On one side Dachau, on the other the 'distressed areas' with their ashamed workless men and despairing women. Not many English writers had the hardness of heart, the frivolity, the religious certainty, the (why not?) noble egoism— noble or ignoble, the gesture is precisely the same—to hurry past, handkerchief to nose, intoning, 'My concern is with my art, what troubles are troubling the world are not my business; let those whose business it is attend to it, I must be about my own . . .'

By coming to London when I did, I moved from the margin into the centre at the very moment when the current dragging writers into active politics was gathering force. It was my road to Damascus. The heavens opened, and I saw that two principles were struggling for mastery of the future. On one side the idea of the Absolute State, with its insistence on total loyalty to the words and gestures of authority, its belief in the moral beauty of war, its appeal to the *canaille*: Germany awake, kill, hate, Sieg Heil, and the rest of it. On the other all that was still hidden in the hard green seed of a democracy which allowed me freedom to write and other women freedom to live starved lives on the dole.

In 1933 this explained for me everything in sight. I had no need to think further about the future, the destiny of man, or my own. I had my key.

The error—mine—was that I tried to open everything with it, beginning with my novels.

Moreover, I never succeeded in stifling in myself completely the promptings of a shrewd nonconformist.

For a long time, several years, I lived in a condition of violent self-contradiction. I was clear in my mind about the enemy. And absolutely clear that I was being urged to defend freedom by (among others) persons who knew much less about freedom than the policemen standing on the fringes of our meetings eyeing with the same stolid curiosity the political virgins and their seducers.

The fingers of the puppet-masters and the strings jerking us were perfectly visible. I knew I was being used. I knew I was wanted on committees because a pen in competent hands is a tool. When I stood on a platform and sang the Internationale—or would have sung it if I had not been as tuneless as a crow—I had no delusions about the doctrine of Communism as practised in Russia. In this I was more clear-sighted than some of my friends.

(Do not let us forget that the puppets could bleed: there were writers among the five hundred volunteers of the International Brigade killed in Spain—John Cornford, Julian Bell, Christopher Caudwell, Ralph Fox. True, these—since they had no prudence about risking their talents and their skins—might have died in the greater war they hoped to avert. But, at the age they were, a few more years is a long time.)

'Do you know,' an awed fellow-writer said to me, 'that Leonov and two other well-known Soviet writers were ordered to report to a factory in Siberia last month?'

'Why?'

'To write in praise of it, of course.'

'And you approve that? How is it better and less debauching than being ordered to write advertisements?'

(Or for that matter, I thought, than sitting in this damned room trying to draft a manifesto.)

'To have the privilege of working for the only free and rationally governed country in the world! You're being perverse, my dear.'

She was perfectly sincere. And certainly Leonov's was a more tolerable servitude than being ordered to hate liberals and Jews and acquiesce in their death by torture. (I knew less than I thought about Stalin's Russia.) And less sickening than the way politicians were refusing to *see* the barbarians on the move again at the other side of the Rhine. So—one of my counterfeit selves went on dumbly mouthing the Internationale on anti-Fascist platforms.

Put to it, I might have said that if my throat must be cut I had sooner it were done on behalf of Communism than by a Fascist. (This state of mind shows how little faith I had then in the triumph of that liberal humanism under whose banner I had enlisted.)

If I looked closely enough, I might see that what made me loathe Fascism was only my hatred of authority, only a mute rebellion against my violently feared and loved mother.

Perhaps the coldly precise reasons for rejecting a vile doctrine came after the instinctive revulsion? But does that invalidate them? Not at all. It is seldom that writers have so plain and comprehensible, if vile, bestial, and bloodyminded an enemy as Fascism.

The amount of time and energy I spent on reading and writing pamphlets, and attending committees and political meetings, was prodigious. And they bored me! I felt asphyxiated by the jargon that was beginning to take the place of criticism: it made the noise in my ears of water running over stones. Heaven knows how many hours I spent swallowing yawns in the company of writers talking about the materialist conception of history—familiarly, the M.C.H.—as if it were a formula for judging and even writing books.

A friend not to be suspected of liking Facism, Henry Harwood, tried by smiling mockery to convince me that I was wasting my time.

'What good do you think you're doing with your politics compared with the good you might do by getting on with your own job? Your conscience? You haven't a conscience, my dear, you simply like interfering.'

He was right—and unjust—and (since he was talking rationally to a monster of unreason) might have saved his breath. My own hard mistrustful Yorkshire nature, my upbringing in a society hostile to change, convinced me, secretly, that our protests were completely futile and certain to be defeated. An irrational instinct, a voice out of my childhood, deeper in me, tougher, older, than scepticism and *Angst*, retorted: Useless? Yes, if you say so. *But it can be tried.*

The loathing I felt for what was being done by barbarians who had taken over the Europe of Goethe, Dante, Vico, the very heart of Christian humanism and the classical Renaissance, was genuine. Concern may be only another name for the passion to interfere, but —such as I am—I could have done no other.

During those years I did not speak my whole mind either to friends or political allies. I recall—I have forgotten the date—a meeting between English writers and four Russians who had been brought to London by the organizers of friendship between our countries. Friendship has as many faces as uses. The face turned by the English wore a smile of eager good faith, curiosity and naïve willingness to make amiable signs to the country of Tolstoy, Chekhov, and the rest. The Russians did not converse, even through their interpreter. They made statements. Alexander Fadayev, author of a novel which had sold, he said, smiling, five million copies, made a speech. He told us that the qualities demanded of a Russian novel were realism and optimism; in Soviet Russia, since a society which is advancing has only hopes, this means that he need only report truthfully on the life round him. Subjective literature is bad, because distorted by personal ties, and in any case egotistical—that is, worthless.

One of our exiled writers, a German, was simple or malicious enough to say, 'Surely it is sometimes difficult? For me—to be forced to write in a particular attitude, however noble, or socially useful— would be boring. At the best. At the worst it would choke me.'

'On the contrary,' said Fadayev, 'I feel boundlessly free; I have a continent to write about, and the exciting advance in it of socialism, new cities are being built, a new happiness, new progressive men and women.' He spread his arms. 'With thousands of miles of progress to move round in, I am infinitely freer than any English writer.'

I had been nerving myself to ask him about a writer fewer people, at that time, knew. I stood up.

'What is Boris Pasternak writing now?'

Fadayev turned on me eyes so clear that they seemed holes, through which I saw a thousand miles—at least a thousand—of a dry cold country.

'Oh, Pasternak doesn't write now, he is busy on translations. He is very much happier.'

Even supposing I had had the contumacy to argue in face of the disapproval of the organizers of the meeting, it seemed, for Pasternak's sake, imprudent: I sat down, and closed my ears.

In twenty-five or thirty years' time, I thought, either I shall be translating (or telling hopeful lies in five million copies) for a living, or the whole of this debate will seem meaningless. No one in 1960 will believe that an English writer in his senses could ever ask himself whether literature ought to serve the projects of the State and its jesuitical priest, the M.C.H., or whether on the contrary he is bound, by a fierce inner command, to indulge his cruelly egotistical passion for uncovering the motives, stratagems, comic, foolish or agonizing thoughts of single human beings in the act of love, hate, treachery, murder, rejoicing, lust, death, ecstasy.

I had an impulse to get up and bolt . . . What the devil am I doing here? . . .

Apart from being secretly bored, I had other reasons for feeling uncomfortable in the company of politicizing poets and novelists. I shared their views about war and Fascism, but what they said often outraged me, or woke an uncouth jeering self I was too timid to let loose. I was shocked when a well-to-do novelist said at a dinner-party that one advantage of doing socialist propaganda was the chances it offered to get inside workers' houses—'to get the background right'. It's not her fault, I reflected, that she doesn't know and can't imagine what her kitchen looks and smells like to a poor woman when she lifts the blind at six in the morning on a dirty grate and the ring of rust on the stove, and can't *see* the woman's nail scraping the inside of a pan, or the gesture of her hand sifting ashes or setting on the table the little cake she has bought her ill-fed child for a treat. Not her fault, but, my God, the abysmal ignorance and silliness of supposing that she will discover anything by going to stare.

But I did not say this. I sat as dumb as a carp.

I did not even say that I saw no virtue in the much talked-of 'proletarian novel', that latest weakest version of the naturalist's 'slice of life'.

A comfortably placed poet, fifteen years younger than I was, explaining that when he thought of the poor he felt guilty, made me grin in my sleeve. The misery and injustice of poverty, the slums, the mean dole, made me blazingly angry. But guilt? I had brushed the edges of poverty myself, and his metaphysical distress bored me.

The one occasion when I spoke frankly did me no good. It was at a meeting, in a private house, of some committee summoned to draft a pamphlet in support of . . . to protest against . . . I forget. One of the young men I suspected of carrying a copy of *The Boy's Book of Civil War, or How to Build a Barricade* was talking about the benefits to a writer of joining the Communist Party. (He joined it himself—for a few days.)

'One will have the moral satisfaction of being able to look a comrade in the eye instead of skulking, head down, past chaps standing in the rain selling the *Daily Worker*, or picketing a factory.'

Exasperated beyond the diffidence which makes me incapable of sustained argument among people I know too little to be certain they are harmless—my brain moves only when I am alone, pen in hand, and three or four clear hours in front of me—I said,

'Is that what you think? Don't deceive yourself. Communism is no go in this middle class country, and even if it were they don't want your help. Nor mine. Don't imagine you'll turn into a revolutionary by going to meetings in shabby rooms and addressing the others as comrade. You're not their comrade.'

'I'm afraid you rather miss the point,' he said kindly.

I shut up.

Walking home, I passed through all the stages, very familiar, of discontent with myself. My heart beat so quickly that I felt suffocated. The truth, I told myself, is that you are not fit to go into company . . .

As I always do at these moments, I retreated into the last time in my life when I was wholly at ease—as a poor student in London. What do these solemn neo-romantics matter to me? Whom do I love? My son, my husband, my mother, at most three others. The rest of the world can hang itself.

I felt the crazy gaiety that always follows my black moments.

That night I had one of the dreams I remember. I was in a room, vaguely a café, with someone indistinct. I knew that he was dead. Class 1914, he said smiling. I had a terrible feeling of anxiety. We ought to keep together, I told him. He laughed and said: What is left of the company will advance in loose formation—or not advance. *I* shall advance, I said. But he laughed again, with heartbreaking kindness, and said gaily: Count on me in any personal way, but don't expect me to turn socialist with you. That's all moonshine. You're not their comrade, you're mine but not theirs . . . In the dream, I thought: But *I* said that . . . The light gay friendly voice went on: A new age is no good to me, my dearest. I shan't understand it and I shan't like it; Class 1914 was a damned fine class and it lived in a fine world. Hear me, I'm bragging, I know what England was like in 1913. You can keep the change. Comrades! I've s-seen comrades! I'll tell you something: the world you're part of, bone of, is finished. You believe in reason, you believe you can argue people into tolerance and goodwill. I tell you, my girl, that dream is as dead as I am. The new age is being prepared by unreason, to be brought in with violence. In that day reasonable people will be swept aside. This is something you don't know yet; you'll know it soon enough and you won't like it. This isn't the world I was born into, you'll say. Nor will it be. My love, your world's finished.

For less than a minute I saw his hands on the edge of the table. Then the dream vanished. I found I had been crying in my sleep . . .

The young Left-wing writers of the thirties were unlucky in so far as, thanks to the Second War, they became middle-aged and prudent without passing through a normal period of maturing powers: one to become a virtuoso in voluntary exile, another bedding down in academic exercises, a third in the barren world of international conferences and semi-literary politics. Today's respected *conférencier* is not as quixotic and engaging a human being as yesterday's histrionic young ass, but he is not more of a defaulter than the rest of us.

It would be neither perceptive nor decent to mock the comrades of the thirties. Their attraction to Communism was better than a literary fashion—although it was that, too. It was the outward and visible sign of a spiritual discomfort, distantly kin to that which drove Tolstoy into trying to live like a peasant, and, in every generation, drives a few generous-minded or thin-skinned members of the comfortable classes to give practical effect to their disgust with injustice and misery.

Why Communism? A complex of reasons: the *grande lueur de l'est*; the obvious weakness of social democracy; the greater logic and vigour of Marxism compared with the pliant doctrines of official English socialism; the attraction of a discipline (I offer you blood, sweat, tears, and the rest of it).

When the Spanish war broke in July 1936, and the democracies trimmed and lost the wind, Communism seemed *the* opponent of Fascism. In effect . . . in effect the fierce enthusiasm, the brave generous hopes, the courage, the young deaths, are not cancelled by the ugliness of the Party's tactics in Spain and elsewhere.

Chapter 2

The sudden—only apparently sudden—volte-face of leaving Whitby did not only plunge me into politics; it swung me round the compass as a writer.

After my Damascus vision, when I 'understood' everything, I understood that the two novels, *That Was Yesterday*, and *A Day Off*, which I had imagined were the start for me of a new truthful way of writing, were no good. Not that they were worthless, but they lacked, heaven help me, *social significance*.

This portentous phrase stupefied me. I had enough sense left not to translate it as the proletarian novel (that abortion), but it distracted me from my own narrow ravishingly subjective (egotistical) road.

Not that I should ever have drifted into the fashionable—is it still fashionable?—heresy of the 'pure' novel, in which form, composition, have the supreme importance they have in a painting. Brought up on the northern sagas and Dickens, I could not have swallowed anything so prudish and genteel as a theory of criticism which demonstrated that Tolstoy, author of 'large loose baggy monsters', full of 'queer elements of the accidental and the arbitrary' is a lesser artist than Henry James. Since the conclusion was absurd, there was a flaw in the argument. I felt certain that any novelist who starts from the impulse to create a style, to impose *himself, se créer sa propre esthétique*, has begun to separate himself from his age. And that, carried too far, this separation must end in sterility and the breakdown of communication. But between this respectable belief and my new passionate conviction that only society, only the crisis, was worth writing about lay an abyss I did not even see.

Like all reformers (including self-reformers), I set about hacking down the idols. No more atmosphere, I said, no evocations of rain and moonlight, even by a word, no 'inward landscapes', no peeling of the onion to reach the core of an emotion, no stream of consciousness, that famous stream we pretend to see flowing as we pretend that the water moves under Lohengrin's swan, no aesthetic, moral, or philosophical comment.

This neo-naturalism was as suited to me as his false nose to a clown.

The paradox of my life, which I am only now (1963) learning to see through, is that the genuine passions I indulged (hatred of war and injustice) did me as much damage as those I suppressed (violent hatred of a domestic life, love of change and gaiety). I was genuinely fascinated by the spectacle of a society in transition and convulsions. Even by its ugliness. From that I concluded passionately and blindly that the novelist ought to be a receiving station for voices rising from every level of society; he must be like the magi who heard of a birth and set off in the dead of winter, the way long and the roads hard, to find the place. The modern novelist's country, I said, *is* this new birth and the hard bitter death it involves: in one way or another its disorder must show through his words—or else he is a literary deserter and a coxcomb, a liar.

From this year, 1932, I began to *construct* myself as a writer.

I was no longer satisfied to try modestly, sceptically, to find the quick of a human being. I thought of *A Day Off* as a self-indulgence.

I was seized by the ambition to write a *roman fleuve*. I had its title: *The Mirror in Darkness*, and my brain spawned like a salmon scores of characters, politicians, ex-soldiers, financier, industrialist, newspaper proprietor, scientist, writers, labour leader, embryo Fascist, the rich, the very humble, the ambitious who knew where they were going, and the confused, the ruined, the lost. They pressed on me so thickly that I was sure I should die before I had given each of them his drop of blood.

I had not noticed that a *roman fleuve* is not the same thing as a human comedy, that Proust and Balzac start from two clearly opposed modes of the imagination. My conception was flawed from the beginning. At times the mirror itself—identified with that Hervey Russell who is and is not myself—supplied the images and ideas; at others, a character unfolded independently, alone or in a web of action. Because of this initial failure of awareness, no single novel of the series had a clear centre, and a far from despicable mass of knowledge, energy, insight, foundered—sunk without trace . . .

Possibly the cold bestiality of the immediate past would today defeat even a Dostoevsky. Nothing in the liberal humanism we were taught to revere prepared us for it. No earlier novelist, when he looked attentively at the life of his time, or when he strained his ears to catch the note of the future, was faced by chaos. There were fixed points, or which seemed fixed. Language itself did not break in his hands. Words had not been emptied of their meaning: if prisoners were tortured it was not called re-education; the term *final solution* did not imply the methodical killing by slow suffocation of six million human beings, old and young. Even in war certain acts were held to be too obscene. Certain principles still had enough force in them to restrain men able to read Goethe and enjoy Mozart from conceiving and administering Auschwitz.

It would need an inhuman detachment to forget that we have barely emerged from the smoke of burning flesh hanging over Auschwitz into the shadow of the nuclear age. But the intimate movements of the heart, the torments of sexual jealousy, the pain of betrayal, the secret stratagems of ambition, the private hell of lovers, dreamers, and neurotics, are the disguise the serious novelist must adopt before he begins to write about his time.

In 1932 I did not know this . . .

I am plagued by memories I have not had the courage—or the immodesty—to try to manifest. In November 1945 I was in Prague, and saw an exhibition of drawings made, in Terezín, by the artist Bedrich Fritta, who died there. And I listened for two hours to a young Czech doctor who went into Terezín with a few officials of the International Red Cross on the 4th of May, 1945, while the Nazi guards were still in charge. He risked going in because he had heard there was typhus in the place. Afraid of the typhus, the guards let them in and fled—after shooting some sixty people as a last gesture of authority.

I have twenty photographs taken by the young doctor. They are not more ghastly than others I was shown earlier that year in Warsaw, but they record, a needle turning in the brain, a cruelty, an indifference, so atrocious that the imagination cannot bear for more than a short time what men, women, children suffered—some of them for years. The images—a pile of bodies caught in the indecent attitudes naked and half-clothed limbs take when they are thrown down like butchered pieces of flesh, a hand covering the ruined sex, a mouth open on the blackness of corruption, the bones of a young woman's body standing out in the purulent skin, the tiny limbs of a child drawn into its body—remain.

Terezín—Theresienstadt—was not a concentration camp, it was

something differently unimaginable, a decent little garrison town which was turned into a transit camp for convoys of victims from all over Nazi Europe. It remained the simulacrum of a town—with hospital, mad-house, streets of barracks and houses, a baker's shop, a dress shop where second-hand clothes were bought and sold, lime trees, Town Hall, a restaurant, a coffee-house, a cinema, a theatre with numbered benches, a synagogue, a music-hall with singers, acrobats, a clown.

One day—for a day—it was given a new face, with flowers, white-washed house-fronts, a welfare centre, a shop selling perfume, a *Lebensmittel.* For the benefit of a visitor from the Swiss Red Cross.

The convoys were halted at a station a mile away. From here the passengers walked, carrying their baggage. In a large badly-lit hall names were taken down before some of the newcomers were sent on to Auschwitz to be gassed, or to Mauthausen to be used up quickly in exhaustion and filth. Others were allowed to stay in the town, for a short or longer time. Or, if they were singularly lucky or rich enough to buy their reprieve, to the end. There are degrees of degradation even in hell: the few rich were allowed, encouraged, to use their money: they lived, as a very intelligent and charming young Jewish woman—her name, which I have forgotten, began with K—said, 'as at Deauville', in their own rooms, with some penniless inmate as a servant, buying food from the thriving black market. When it was known that, to make room, another batch of men and women—once, four thousand at a blow—was to be sent off to be exterminated, they could buy themselves off the list. Always at least one of the Jewish officials making the selection was corruptible.

'For money,' K. said, smiling, 'you could buy many things in Terezín, even life.'

The wages she earned as a servant bought a touch of comfort for her mother and young brother. Then she was sent to Auschwitz and her brother to Mauthausen. There was something she recalled with great pride, some trifle, I cannot remember it, a stroke of in-tegrity in the man she fell in love with in Terezín and married three days before he, too, was sent to die in Mauthausen. Something he could not bring himself to do . . .

Like the *univers concentrationnaire* itself, Terezín would make sense to me if I could believe that it was devised by a wholly evil scientist anxious to fill out his knowledge of human nature by exposing millions of men and women to the extremity of pain and fear, to see what, to defend themselves, they would do. And what, finally, one of them chose to defend *in* himself by a refusal.

I looked long and closely at Fritta's forty-two drawings. The one that ran me through was of his infant daughter on her pot. It summed up what, in the bestiality of our age, is totally unforgivable—the violation of the innocent.

It is Dostoevsky's theme, I thought. How dare I touch it?

None the less, for a long time, years, I brooded over a book or a play laid in Terezín. It—Terezín—is, or was, an image of the human condition, a sealed world in which all the human virtues and vices, from the most abject treachery to the most genuinely modest self-sacrifice—doomed to be forgotten—had their chance to reach perfection. This book took possession of a whole level of my mind. For hours, days, I lived in a crowd, life-size, of its characters, not only the main personages of the drama, but the unnumbered others which no novel or play would have room for, but which existed. They became my familiars, I saw their eyes, their mouths, their gestures: the two women in the second-hand dress shop, the elder fingering hungrily a shabby fur, the other describing, for herself more than for her listener, the evening dress made for her eight years ago in Frankfurt by a half-French dressmaker, silver net, eighteen yards in the skirt alone, but a tight bodice, with no back, and a second dress in pinkish grey velvet she wore in winter that year; the girl and the skinny desperate boy looking for some place where they could join their bodies without being discovered; the mad mother of the little child on the pot; the bearded Jewish elder miserably or cunningly making his terms with the S.S. guard who lived, with his newly-married wife, in a villa near the ramparts and had two servants picked from a convoy for their air of vigour; the well-known clown making his jokes in the music-hall the evening before he was being sent to Auschwitz; the gesture of the man (moustache, yellowish face, long bony hands) piling the bodies on to the curiously shaped carts: they had sloping sides like the carts in French vineyards. And K. and her mother. The old woman survived Terezín. And because her young son had died in Mauthausen she could not forgive K. for coming back from Auschwitz.

'She has Terezín in her stomach,' K. said.

Why did I never write it?

Not because it was difficult and I was afraid of distorting an event almost past imagining. From a sort of shame. From pudor.

Had anyone who had not lived in that world the moral right to stare at it? Had I any right to press so much as a finger on the despair and nonchalance of the young, the panic-stricken baseness of the few rich, the courage of one woman, the creeping tide of insanity in another, the furtive sex, the innocence of the child on its little pot? I could not convince myself that I had.

Some future writer will be driven, as Dostoevsky was, to lay open in a novel unfathomed depths of the human possibility, led to them by what he is able to learn about Terezín and Auschwitz and the rest. I shall not now write it. Perhaps, surviving the death of my brain, a thought of mine will find its way into a cell of his.

Chapter 3

Early in 1933 I decided that at seventeen my son had wasted more than enough time in his Anglo-Swiss school, and I sent him, with some misgiving, to Göttingen, to live in the family of a retired professor. He stayed there until the end of May. Then—disturbed by a snapshot of him with a lock of hair across his forehead in imitation of the Führer's—I brought him home to be tutored for a year, although he insisted that nothing was happening at Göttingen, no one there had been persecuted. At that time, probably true.

There were only two bedrooms in the flat: I gave him mine, and slept in the living-room on an old Dutch day-bed, a very elegant piece of marquetry, too short to stretch out in comfort. For his six feet it would have been torment.

Even now, I cannot explain why I was never at ease with the idea that I had a child who was my own, not simply handed to me to cherish and bring up. By the time he was seven, he had learned that silence and a frown were enough to set me wondering anxiously what I could do to amuse him. He was an amiable child, but he would have been unnatural or a saint if he had not used his whip hand to get his own way. Almost always he got it. A vein of timidity ran through my love. In a moment of discouragement I tried to fathom why I felt this diffidence towards my own child. Because I want him to be pleased with me, I thought. Because of my unappeasable sense of an unfulfilled obligation.

He had rare bursts of talk when I caught sight of a speculative intellect hidden behind his one enduring passion. He wanted to fly.

He was going up to Cambridge in the autumn of 1934—to Trinity, which had accepted him after an interview, without an examination. In the meantime he wanted to take flying lessons.

'Now?'

'Why not? I'd like to have my A licence before I'm eighteen.'

I gave in. He was pleased. For less than an instant a child looked at me through his eyes, made a signal I could not read, and was gone.

For several hours I have been trying to compare our fear of war now (1963) with the fear that slowly submerged our minds during the thirties. (In 1934 an American reviewer, a woman, complained that 'like so many English writers, Storm Jameson seems unable to outgrow the war.' I retorted that the war we could not outgrow was not the one we had survived but the one we were expecting.) There is one overwhelming difference. The climate of fear is much the same, for at least three decades, but in the thirties we were facing an imaginable terror, one we could look at without falling, like Christian in Giant Despair's stinking dungeon, into a swoon. Today the imagination is stunned, paralysed. We look into a darkness without issue. What lies at the other side of nuclear war? A human remnant, mutilated in its seed?

As a writer with a mortal distaste for exaggeration I can find little that is fit to say.

In October I attended the first—was it the first?—meeting of The Writers' Committee of the Anti-War Council, in a shabby flat near Buckingham Palace. A very prosperous writer took the chair: he was willing, he said amiably, to do anything, he would even put aside his art, or adapt it to writing propaganda.

I looked from his smooth, healthy, wholly sincere and almost meaningless face to two others, the thin tired twisted face of the middle-aged Communist who was there to keep us straight, and W. H. Auden's heavy face, with its extraordinary patina of age. I have never seen so old a young face, it might have been overhanging

a mediaeval cathedral during centuries of frost and sun. He scarcely
spoke. Nor did our Communist, except when a writer said, in all
seriousness,

'We need a great deal of training. I shouldn't have an *idea* how
to set about pushing over a tram.'

'Don't let's talk nonsense,' the older man said icily.

As always in committees, my attention drifted. If no one else saw
the two young men in stained khaki come into the room, that is
not to say they were less alive than anyone there. The boy with the
blunt nose, thatch of flaxen hair, and pale clear blue eyes, looked
right through me to the worm under my breast-bone. The other
had kept his trick of waiting for the right moment to stutter a
derisive comment.

I was seized by an indefensible gaiety.

So you have come back, I said.

They burst out laughing. We never moved, it was you who left us.

That's true, I thought. What is left of Class 1914 has forgotten
almost everything it once knew and felt . . .

Every person in that shabby room was against war and against
Fascism. Only the middle-aged Communist with the nose like a
spiral of discoloured flesh separating his tired eyes knew that this
was a contradiction in terms. For him, there was no dilemma. He
was against Fascism and against any war *not fought by or in defence of
Soviet Russia*. What intellectual muddle we others were in did not
even amuse him.

I walked away from the meeting behind the strange shambling
figure, dusty bear on two legs, of Auden, wishing I had the courage
to say to him: Is this any use?

What a relief I should have felt if he had said: No use at all, but
that's not the point: like you, I am prepared to protest uselessly
against war, in dubious company.

(I suspect that Auden always had in reserve, even when young,
the inviolable egotism of the born writer, and an instinct for self-
preservation as dependable as Goethe's. One can divide writers into
self-preservers, like Goethe, and the self-squanderers, Stendhal,
etc, etc.)

Chapter 4

All through 1932 Lilo's letters from Berlin traced, without a sign of panic, the graph of a defeat. Writing about friends of her own age, she said,

'Our whole outlook was directed towards the future, only the future. We are like children forced to grow up in a week.'

In February 1933 these children began to be afraid, and her letters sounded like a child talking, to reassure itself, at the top of its voice. 'We are all here desperate, our hopes gone, only expecting dictatorship or civil war or even both. I feel confused and in some way deceived. Who deceived me, the others or myself? Since ten days I am trying to be calm. Marches, demonstrations, flags, my neighbours' wireless, voices shouting through the walls, a people mad, crying a thousand at a time "heil, heil", like wild animals. Every notice in the paper a provocation, every march hurts the heart. In the office we are working hard to record every event and every decree, for the future to read, and every word I write down is bitter to me. In the end one must either commit suicide or try to handle the situation, but I am too without experience to learn it quickly. There is not one of my friends who is not involved with it. That is the worst—this uncertainty which does not allow to see three hours ahead. Every ring of the telephone, every knock on the door, may begin that which would not be bearable. The faces of my friends are white, shadows under their eyes, even if we speak of something pleasant or indifferent, our minds are going on behind this conversation with fear. We are like strangers here, the people's festivals are not ours, the songs, the speeches, the words, the future. Suddenly we are cut off from everything round us, life has been taken out of our hands, we feel old and tired and do not have the comfort that those coming after us will carry on our work and ideas.'

This discouraged mood was not one she could live in. A month later, in March, she wrote, 'I was thinking very often of England . .

Now I am making a plan. When the fate of our paper is decided I shall rather soon come to England to look for a chance to live. Shall I not be able to write little articles in English? And so I hope to go on. Well, I shall fear nothing for the future, having here no present and the past wasted. I promise already not to show myself to you if I am once being afraid or dull.'

She stayed on in Berlin for two or three months after the *Deutsche Volkswirt* had been suppressed. When, in October, she came to London, Bill had gone away for a short time and I had a bed to give her in the flat. I was a little dreading her arrival; she would need more than a bed, I should have to do this, say that, to give her courage to pick up her life.

How little I knew her! She turned up at the flat when I was out; I came into the living-room and there, smiling her wide brilliant smile, stood the Youngest Brother. Delighted to have a story to tell, she neither expected nor wanted comfort.

I have known a great many people. I know no one more remarkable than this child of East Berlin. Not so much for her courage, gaiety, superb energy, refusal of boredom and despair, as for her indestructible self-possession. She was born free. As others may live in a state of grace, she lived in a state of freedom. In her way of looking at life and people, she was like a swift young animal, without the cruelty; there was not a cold fibre in her, nor (to come to purely human vices) a mercenary one. Her instinctive refusal to be shackled, emotionally, morally, intellectually, shocked some people—me, never. She herself said, smiling,

'I make no demands, I come and go, I am selfish, yes, but I don't ask anyone to give up for me one shred of himself.'

Some months ago, reading a new novel by a very intelligent woman (*The Golden Notebook*, by Doris Lessing), I was struck by its involuntary and complete misconception, parody, of the very thing it was supposed to be about—freedom, 'free women'. No human being was ever less free than these women struggling in the sticky web of their sexual needs like flies in a pool of treacle. They do not begin to know the taste, colour, shape of freedom. With no more trouble than a child takes reaching for a berry, Lilo took lovers, fought them sometimes, went through emotional storms if the weather set that way and came out smiling and heart-free. Perhaps the quality she possessed, and these other hopelessly un-free women had not, was innocence. Her intense sexuality had nothing complex or sombre in it. I almost wrote: nothing erotic. Her innocence leapt at any experience, but it was uncorrupted and incorruptible. Free of doubts, free of sin.

Possibly, the 'free woman' cannot be self-made. Like any other type of genius, she is born. With the necessary egoism and energy.

A race of free women would be the end of humanity, since freedom and childbearing are incompatible.

I am drawn irresistibly to all I am not and would like to have been, to the gross reckless vitality of a Marie Lloyd, violently herself, as quickly as to this German girl's energy, essential innocence, fearlessness, invincible gaiety.

From the beginning Lilo refused to fall into what she called, with smiling contempt, 'the refugee mentality'.

'They bore me with their talk about the past. Why waste energy on regrets when they have the whole world except Germany to look at? However long I live I shan't be bored.'

She had a little money with her, and she lived in my flat only a few weeks, long enough to find herself a room of her own, at a very low rent, with some woman friend, I forget the name. She made a new friend at every turn in the road.

Utterly unafraid, she would have argued with the devil. She wanted to meet R. H. Tawney, and I asked him to dinner. After dinner, when he made some statement she could not accept, she said so, with polite smiling vehemence, and refused to be shaken. If Tawney had told me the moon was made of green cheese, I would never have dared contradict him. He smiled at Lilo's want of subservience—but it took him a little aback.

She talked to me about the last few months, about her childhood, her friends in the excitable Berlin of the late twenties, and her first frugal journey abroad, to France. Among other things she did then, she persuaded the skipper and crew of a Marseilles fishing-boat to take her with them on a trip lasting several days. No one could tell a story better than she did, no detail, no touch of humour or poetry missed or blurred. I began to harry her to write down this French adventure, as a start.

After a few weeks she brought me the manuscript of *Tale Without End,* written in what she imagined was English. Everything was there, as vivid and racy as you please, but the language was no known language. I set to work on it. I had the idea that by making her follow every change I made, I could teach her correct English.

She would attend for a few sentences; then, seized by a fit of yawns, get up and go away, saying,

'Do it as you like, dear Margaret.'

I suppose I rewrote every sentence in the book. It remained un-alienably her work, her own voice.

The instinct that made her avoid my attempt to teach her was sound. In a few months, merely by listening, talking, reading (a little), she wrote clear lively English, as later in South America she learned to write Spanish.

I sent the revised manuscript to the firm of Constable, and Lilo after it. Enchanted by her—'How,' he said to me, 'could I refuse anyone with that smile and that face?'—Michael Sadleir took it.

After this, she wrote a longer book, *Restless Flags*, about a young Germany now stone dead. Then a novel, not a bad novel, but the trouble it gave her convinced her that she was no novelist. So, in search of something to work on, she went, with a few pounds in her pocket, to Turkey, and travelled in the hardest way, staying where she was invited, questioning any man, woman or child who could tell her anything. No one rebuffed her: the candour and smiling goodwill of the Youngest Brother served her here as again and again in strange countries, all her life.

The book she wrote when she came home, *Allah Dethroned*, drew an invitation to lecture on modern Turkey to the Institute of International Affairs. I trembled for her, but she spoke with the greatest simplicity and coolness to an audience which listened with respect.

When I say that no one ever rebuffed her, I don't mean that everyone liked her. Some of her fellow-exiles did not forgive either her energy or her frank contempt for their attitude.

'What the devil do you see in this half-educated conceited gutter-snipe with her intolerable airs of knowing better?' one of them said to me.

Would it have been any use telling him that a fresh spring is gayer than a stagnant marsh? Or that conceit is easily forgivable when it takes the form of courage and lighthearted egoism? He himself was intelligent and conceited, and unable to forgive a gaiety and success which seemed as undeserved as the Youngest Brother's good fortune always does—to the others.

Some time in 1938 she began planning to travel through the whole of South America, to write 'a splendid book, really truthful.'

'How long,' I asked, 'would you be away?'

'A year. Fifteen months.'

'If war breaks out next spring, you'll be trapped there.'

'There isn't going to be war.' She gave me a clear look, without a hint of derision. 'The English and French democracies won't fight, you know that.'

She had a German passport. When it ran out of date she had walked into the consulate and demanded a renewal. Glancing at her yellow hair, frank smile, and innocently blue eyes, the clerk gave it to her without asking a question. She was delighted by the success of her bluff, which convinced some of her fellow-exiles that she was not and never had been a refugee. Their suspicions amused her.

'I shan't be able to trick the devils again, but why shouldn't I do it this time? Without a proper passport I can't travel.'

With the one you have, I reflected, you'll be interned the day war starts. I took care to say nothing to dissuade her from leaving.

The outbreak of the war caught her in Ecuador, in Quito. She kept herself alive by teaching English in a boys' school. (I pity any young Latin male who imagined he could outface Lilo.) Soon she began writing—in Spanish—for a liberal newspaper. I have forgotten how soon after the war she decided to stay in South America, and became an Ecuadorian citizen. Nor am I sure when she began to be the personage in liberal circles she became. She wrote regularly on social and political affairs, visiting journalists and economists consulted her as an authority; she travelled enormously, she would go anywhere she could persuade her newspaper or an institution to send her. Many of these journeys, in the Andes, through the jungle, on the Amazon, were hair-raisingly hard and dangerous. They were her abiding passion—they and one other: her hunger to see justice done to the humble and oppressed. In her new country this became an assault, patient and vehement, on the frightful poverty and ignorance of the Indians. She loathed the oppressor and spent herself to drag and coax the oppressed out of their lethargy. As a passion it went back to her hard childhood and rebellious adolescence, a thread she never let go.

It was the most generous of passions. It was also the managing Prussian in her—the liking for order and authority that ruled her tempestuous life as it might have ruled any honest little workgirl. She detested and despised grime, untidiness, incompetence, weakness. In her shabby London room, the furniture and her books and clothes were always ranged *garde à vous*.

In 1937 when she and I were in Paris, it infuriated her that I paid no attention to the street-map. After we had walked for an hour in a strange quarter, she would halt and say,

'Now what is this square?'

'Heaven knows.'

'Margaret, you are absolutely intolerable, only last week I brought you to this very place and told you all the names. Don't you notice anything?'

'Only what interests me,' I said.

This struck her as a vice, as did my inability to keep money in my hands, and my willingness to tell lies to please people. Any lies she told were to please herself, and—she would have given her last shilling to a hungry man or woman—she never wasted a penny, and foresaw with horror and grief my end in a workhouse.

She came back to England from Ecuador, three, four, five times. Except that the yellow of her hair became tarnished, I saw little change in her: the gleam of white teeth, of cornflower blue eyes, remained that of the young girl. Her letters, long and marvellously vivid, charted a life which ran deeper and more calmly, but not any slower. I answered all of them, and did not keep one.

In May this year (1963) she was in a plane between Athens and London (coming to England as the guest of the Central Office of Information) when her heart—which I and all her friends imagined to be the soundest in the world—stopped.

Impossible, I said, impossible. I still say it.

Chapter 5

'English writers,' a French novelist stranded in London during the late war said to me, 'do not exchange ideas. I find this surprising—a little, what do you say?, debilitating.'

'Perhaps they have none to spare.'

'Perhaps,' he said reflectively, 'I ought to read some English novels. Thus I should discover for myself.'

I doubt he carried out a plan clearly distasteful to him.

He would have been just as disappointed if he had arrived in peace time. There is no literary society in London, in the meaning of the words: groups form and dissolve, like the tiny circular ripple an insect makes on the surface of a stagnant pond, nothing more serious. There is no room and I think no wish for the café society of a Place St Germain des Prés where new ideas and gibberish keep the air moving and dissipate the fog which had thickened round my poor Frenchman as he crossed the Channel.

During my years of seeing a great many people, I saw few writers. My close friends in the thirties were almost all politicians, usually of the Left, journalists, foreign correspondents, with a light sprinkling of historians and economists. It happened because my eyes and ears were fixed on the spectacle of Europe, and the only people I wanted to see were those who could tell me what was going on in a theatre where innumerable scenes were being played simultaneously, side by side and one above the other.

The past, even so vivid a past as the thirties, is a mural of which only fragments remain intact—a face, a gesture, a phrase. Philip Jordan's face had a very startling delicacy, like a Chinese painting: he had almost no eyebrows, clear pale eyes, a pale skin, and a trick of sending the point of his tongue rapidly across colourless and very fine lips, like the flickering movement of a lizard across a stone, when he made one of his sharp comments. He did it when he described an editor, Kingsley Martin, conscious of his exposed position on the Left, going into a theatrical wig-makers to order himself a crown of thorns.

He was the wittiest talker I have ever known, a fountain of intellectual malice, and incorruptible. He was also one of the kindest of men. He had, I think, fewer skins over his mind than other people, no protective layer of indifference, not enough moral egoism to keep him going for more than a short life.

A mind as thin-skinned as his could, perhaps, have been jarred into dying, suddenly, with no obvious physical cause.

After the aeroplane taking him to Jugoslavia during the war was brought down in flames he had bad nightmares, but can nightmares kill?

At dinner it amused me to place his deceptively transparent face next to the head—equally striking and equally not meant for long use—of the correspondent of two Scandinavian newspapers, Bjarne Braatoy. Bjarne's immense arched forehead seemed dragged backwards by very fair hair like a wig of tightly curled wire. The son of a Norwegian pastor, he was incorrigibly restless, ambitious, very intelligent, without stability or forethought—Peer Gynt in the flesh. Peel off his outer self, and another as lively, clever, and mercurially boastful, appeared: a hundred identical selves and no identity.

(Or was it reached at the last minute? Years of disappointment and failures in America, during and after the war, divorce, plan after plan falling to pieces in his hands, and then—at the very moment when the tide turned and he was given the position in the international Labour machine that he had craved and was well fitted for —he died, in a London hospital, alone. Perhaps he had no time to summon one of his English friends. Perhaps he had none left—or had wanted to establish himself before reappearing. He was vain, with the innocent vanity of Peer Gynt, one lie, one blunder, one misdeed effacing the last, leaving his mind swept clean for the next to be written on it. As his wife I could not have borne with him. Simply as a friend, I found it impossible to condemn him out of hand.)

He had married a young German woman from a cultivated, liberal, upper middle class family, the most charming creature in the world, polite, spirited, naturally elegant. She had the slenderly rounded body of a dancer, and hieratic good looks as indestructible as her air of race: arched nose, high cheekbones, wide straight sensuous mouth, hair like curled feathers springing strongly back from her forehead and small ears. One of her habitual movements, hands lifted in a gesture of tolerance and indifference, had a Mozartian wit and gaiety.

One evening in, I think, 1934, I invited together Philip, Lilo, and Aneurin Bevan. In a small room Aneurin's quicksilver energy was almost alarming, I felt that I was sharing his cage with a powerful wild animal. When Nye was telling a malicious story, which he could not do without miming it, gestures and voices, he was a great cat poised for a bound, claws unsheathed, eyes gleaming with savage amusement. He had a rich caressing voice, but there was no caress in his eloquence. Always double-edged, it could be corrosive. It secreted an unappeased bitterness—much as what some of his colleagues at this time thought his laziness secreted contempt and a turbulent ambition.

I had friends for whom he was the devil himself. They were off the mark. He was an earthy Welsh rebel, generous, likeable, pleasure-loving, highly intelligent, born a kicker against the pricks, a good hater who would have hesitated to guillotine a mouse. Since I had reached an age to distrust politicians of every breed, and since all breeds are forced, except in countries where power has congealed in a few hands, to promise their followers happiness, and no party has the courage to try to create a society in which the individual will see to his own happiness—the single chance of a civilized future for the human race, and probably humanly impossible—I could admire him without caring whether his eloquence were trustworthy or not. When his speculations about the future were based on reason and logic they were usually worthless, bound to be contradicted by the event. But so far as any politician is, he was honest—every politician is forced for his political health's sake to tell a number of lies. He might, seen eating and drinking in the Ivy, look like any well-off politician mixing sans-culotte sentiments with a good claret, but he remained furiously a rebel to the moment he died.

At the last minute Lilo rang up and said she would like to bring a friend she had just made, a writer, Ralph Bates.

All I knew about him was that he was the author of a volume of short stories, laid in Spain. Admirable stories, written, obviously, by a man who knew and loved an austere poverty-stricken Spain of workers and peasants tilling a handful of earth. They were, I think, the first notable re-appearance in our day of the Spanish myth—or metaphor—in which even before the civil war, before Guernica, Spain began to be identified with contempt for luxury and death, and the instinct to revolt.

'Of course bring him,' I said.

I expected a haggard Quixote. The well-fleshed young man—twenty-seven or eight?—who followed Lilo into the room looked like a responsible workman, a foreman come to weld a broken pipe.

He was self-assured and amiable. 'I've heard of you,' he told Nye.

He ate with extraordinary rapidity, and as he ate talked about himself. He was remarkable enough. Bored by his life as a railway-worker, he had cleared off to Spain, learned the language, and made friends among socialist workers.

'It's the only country,' he said, 'where the movement has kept its soul. Poverty and hard living—that's the secret. You won't see any labour leaders there stuffing themselves in the Ivy.'

'You enjoy your food, though,' Nye said, smiling.

'I can go anywhere I like,' he said calmly, 'food's the same to me wherever I eat it. What you have to remember about me is that I'm not only a writer, I'm a trained mechanic. I'm better off than any of your middle class novelists—I can always go back to that. And mark you, it's skilled work, it takes learning.'

Philip gave him a coldly ironic glance. 'Not like writing novels. Any fool can write.'

Not in the least disconcerted, the skilled man did not take the trouble to answer.

He was no fool, and not naïve. He had energy, the energy of imagination. About that, it is impossible to be deceived; either a writer, a painter, a musician, has it or he is merely clever: it may be a thin vein, soon exhausted, but there is no mistaking it.

When we went back to the flat, someone spoke of Oswald Mosley's 'amateur Fascism'.

'Let me tell you how that started,' Nye said.

Smiling cruelly, he described a meeting of the Parliamentary Labour Party, called early in 1931 to discuss a proposal, put forward by Mosley and backed by John Strachey, Nye himself, and one or two others, for a special conference to deal with the appalling unemployment. As he talked, his face lengthened and became Ramsay MacDonald's face, and his voice took on the softly unctuous tones of an old gentleman of failing mind and unshakable self-confidence. It may have been a caricature, but it was brilliant.

'Everyone of good faith knows that my government is doing its tireless best. Some of you are making speeches you should be ashamed of. It's an ill bird . . . You young ones don't understand how in the past some of us toiled and sacrificed, yes, sacrificed ourselves, for the cause. In those days we learned to put first principles first, we learned that everything must be done gradually, first one step, then another, and that each step has one behind it, that effects spring from causes, and causes produce effects, that if you drink too much in the evening you will have a headache the morning after, and if you have a headache the morning before. And that, friends, is the whole meaning of socialism . . . And he opened his arms—' Nye opened his—'and without blessing us he was parted from us and carried up into Park Lane to sit on the right hand of Lady Londonderry. The other so-called leaders went away, too, leaving four or five of us gaping at the empty platform. I knew then that Mosley would go. He was too impatient to realize that he was making headway in the country and had only to wait. X. gave him eighty thousand pounds, and he asked me to see the fellow. I refused, and left him.'

'The one of the three rats I don't understand,' Philip began, 'is Snowden——'

Nye grinned with amused contempt. 'He is eaten up by his own acid,' he said lightly.

A short time before this, my American agent, Carol Brandt, had asked me if I could take her to see Philip Snowden. I forget why—she may have been told that he was writing.

Out of politeness or habit, she dressed for the occasion as for an Embassy party, and Snowden was fascinated by the tassel of her small hat, dangling over one eye. We sat round a lace-edged table-cloth set with scones, sandwiches, a large fruit cake, plates of bread and butter, jam, a proper Yorkshire high tea. Snowden looked very old, frail and twisted, no flesh on his bones. I had been afraid he would sit silent, but he talked freely in his edged voice, and even laughed. Obviously he liked looking at Carol, who is a beautiful woman. Suddenly, when the ironic smile left his pale Yorkshire eyes, I saw the skinny white-faced child, shivering with cold, and hungry. I knew I could never dislike him, never condemn him, never not feel for him a sympathy of the nerves and the northern ice in my veins . . .

I was neither bold nor quick enough to try to defend him from Philip's forked tongue and Nye's contempt. How find defensible words for what is foolishly emotional and irrational?

When he left, Ralph Bates shook hands with me in the friendliest way, and said,

'You might ask me here again. I like you.'

Well, I liked him—but without sympathy or warmth . . .

The after-dinner gossip of foreign correspondents is the best in the world. Writers—and politicians—can be at one and the same moment intelligent and imposters, self-deceiving humbugs. A foreign correspondent is rarely a charlatan, his day-to-day work brings him into acid touch with too many events, physical and moral, of more than passing significance. No talker, and ignorant, I listened to them with passionate attention. I could live happily in a cell, I told myself, so long as the messages continued to come in from all sides.

Inevitably, during these years, from wherever a conversation started, in a short time it came back to our chances of escaping war.

Of one such evening, I remember only the angry Dutchman, a friend of Bjarne's, who had been travelling for his paper in Germany and had collected evidence—a quantity of evidence—that the Germans were preparing for war.

'With enthusiasm,' he said, stammering a little, 'with enormous enthusiasm. And I come here and find that decent intelligent men would rather walk naked down Whitehall than believe it. Are you all raving mad? Something worse than ignorance is driving you to suicide—sheep following each other over a cliff. God knows your shepherds are ignorant, they can't read German, they know nothing about history, nothing about Europe, but it isn't ignorance, it isn't for want of being told and told again, with proof and archi-proof. They *refuse* to know. Why? Why do they run up to Hitler with their silly throats stretched for the knife? Why do they believe he will say: I must spare these poor gentle hens? Why do they think that the sensible way to handle a thug is to give him everything he asks for? My dear fellow, we must redress your grievances, they say, take what you want . . . You know, I am baffled. I can't see any reason in what you are doing. It is somehow irrational. Your Halifax and Chamberlain are like those poor elderly gentlemen who ask girls to whip them.'

He laughed. I was surprised and embarrassed to see that there were tears in his eyes. I said diffidently,

'You say that the German government, that Hitler, is preparing to make war. Do you mean he wants to conquer England and France? Isn't that rather a mouthful—even for a dictator?'

His wide heavy face took on an extraordinary look of grief. 'You will see,' he said softly. 'When your decent pious respectable politicians—and *The Times*—have betrayed all the little countries to him, you will see how he will respect you.'

His voice dropped still lower. 'I am screaming with anxiety and despair,' he said in a whisper.

I must write this down, I thought (and did, as soon as he left). As usual, my ambiguous mind was thinking two things at once. I lived now in dread of another war, and by a sleight of mind believed it possible and impossible, in the same breath, with the same rage.

'I hope you are wrong,' I said.

This infuriated him again. 'You are not any better than your Cabinet Ministers and your dear deluded liberals. You shout: Down with armaments and God bless the League of Nations. Good,

good! You are against Fascism, of course you are against Fascism, you are an English radical, you detest tyrants, you are going to fight them. With what? With some old guns left over from 1918? Madness. You are mad. I must go, I shall insult you, and as soon as I have gone you will say: These Dutchmen have no sense of proportion and no manners, obviously he is out of his mind . . . Well, forgive me, I *am* mad.'

He turned with his hand on the door, to say, smiling,

'But, of course, if you believe that *nothing* is worth fighting for . . .'

He waited for me to answer. I said nothing. His smile broadened endlessly, and he went off.

I was too afraid of what I might see to look closely into the confusion in my mind . . .

I had the sensation, often, of listening to footsteps outside my room, drawing slowly nearer. If they stopped for a few minutes, it was only to make a bound and start up again closer. At moments the tension of listening became unbearable, as on the afternoon when for two or more hours I listened to Dorothy Thompson's account of the 30th of June, 1934, one of the coldest of Hitler's bouts of murder, when he saw personally to the killing of a friend and followers he had no further use for. It was stiflingly hot in the room. I sat without moving a muscle, as cold as a stone, sweat running down my spine, my stomach contracted in nervous anguish. When I stood up I found that my whole body had become as rigid as a clenched fist, and I could scarcely move it. Something in the incident—not, I think, the deaths—paralysed me with fear and curiosity. The curiosity of the writer. And perhaps fear of human nature itself.

I recall only one other time in my life when this strange physical rigidity seized me. That was an occasion in the brasserie of the Café Royal: I was listening to Harrison Brown who had come back from Berlin with evidence—at that time new and barely credible—of what Hitler planned to do to the Jews living in Germany.

I was still (in 1933) naïve enough to think that he had only to lay it before the editor of *The Times* to blow away for good every hopeful illusion about the Nazi regime. During the next two years that good man, Ebbutt, the paper's Berlin correspondent, broke himself against his editor's wilful delusions . . .

I should be lying if I pretended that I spent much time feeling anxious. Incidents like these were icy jets rising to the surface from an underlying terror. The surface itself was as lively as a June sea, splinters of light piercing the water, leaping, breaking, re-forming. What I remember about unnumbered evenings at this time is, first of all, an immense liveliness and gaiety.

I have never been so gay since, in any society.

Chapter 6

The Conference of the Labour Party at Hastings in 1933 was haunted by the ghost of German Social Democracy, in the shape usually of a young doctor or lawyer, with a pale intelligent face, and no money. What did these *revenants* hope from their assembled English 'comrades'?

I attended this conference as the delegate of the Whitby branch of the Labour Party, the first, and for all I know the last time that penniless branch sent one. I sat faithfully through every session, and shocked dear Philip Noel-Baker by raising my hand on his left in favour of workers' control in factories. He rebuked me very gravely. I assured him that I was only obeying the orders of my committee. In truth, like the group of born rebels it was, it had told me to vote as I pleased on every point. I had no principles and my instincts were those of an anarchist.

Every evening I wrote a racily detailed report for the famished and delighted eyes of a branch no one had ever heard of. None of the moments I remember most clearly found their way into the report.

One day at the end of the afternoon session, a gentle guttural voice—during the next few years this voice, in all its varieties, became very familiar—said in my ear,

'I think you are helping me. You are Storm Jameson, yes? I am—' I have forgotten his name —'from Berlin, a friend of Miss Linke. I am a lawyer, I have here very important messages and a letter from some Trades Union officials for Mr Arthur Henderson.

One of them is his friend for a long time. The letter tells him how he can help. I think you are taking me to him—perhaps now?'

With the desperation of the timid, I marched him across the lobby to the great man.

'Mr Henderson,' I said, 'this German has messages for you from a friend of yours in Berlin.'

I drew back a few steps and watched. For all I know, Mr Henderson was feeling an agony of grief. Nothing, no emotion of any sort, warmed a face the colour of a fishmonger's slab. I heard him say stiffly,

'What do you expect me to do?'

Pilate number thirty million, I thought, and hurried away.

I walked clumsily into old George Lansbury. He spoke kindly to me, and we sauntered together along the sea front in the last of the cool light. Outside one of the richer hotels, he halted me to watch three of his colleagues going in.

'Look at them,' he said, smiling. 'And all on the pennies of the workers. We ought to be ashamed.'

After this I avoided the German. On the last day he caught me as I stood watching the better sort, arms linked the length of the platform, singing *Auld Lang Syne*. Hugh Dalton, large gleaming head tilted back, only the whites of his eyes visible, smiling, at once cold and hearty, resembled nothing so much as a Chinese executioner. The guttural murmur began in my ear.

'This song, it has some significance, yes?'

'It has indeed. It signifies that no revolution will happen here, ever. Fortunately.'

Behind us a ragged handful led by Bill Mellor was trying to start *The Red Flag*.

'And this also you do not sing? Yourself?'

'I can't sing a note,' I said.

One can make literature of anything, even—or especially—of the cancer of violence, cruelty, despair, exile, eating into the thirties. As for exile, possibly only a writer who has suffered it has the right to try. The rest of us, with our guesses, are clumsy intruders. We do not know sharply enough what takes place in the brain and nerves of the man turning his back, not on possessions—within measure replaceable—but on the street he crosses to reach a certain café table, on his habit of pausing on his way home from work to watch a man fishing from a narrow quay, on a plane-tree always the last in his street to show green in spring, on the death he intended to die in his own place and time, on a worn-out school satchel kicking about in an attic with other rubbish.

Because of one incident in my life, I know a little about these losses. But not what it means to a writer to cut his writing hand off at the wrist, to lose by the same brutal stroke a country and his language, his own word for bread, house, sleep, child.

Departures are in my blood—voluntary departures. I belong to a country I left. Not quite the same thing as exile. Not the sensation of crossing a frontier into an alien language, an alien death. Still less the agony of being pushed on to the lower deck of a rotten ship, to be turned back from strange harbours, to drown in darkness, clutching the little terrified body of a child.

None the less, I never felt separated from an exile by more than a thin membrane. The refugees I began to be friendly with in 1933 were not destitute—or they would not have reached London. They still had something by which to hope, a cousin in Wisconsin who was going to send for them, a profession they might, in time, be able to use. (But I have never known what became of the old magistrate who had had the honesty to give a decision against two Nazi killers only a month before Hitler's triumph. Or what passed through the mind of the elderly Jewish woman who killed herself after arranging on the table in her room a strand of seaweed and a few shells in the shape of a bird.)

The evenings when I invited three or four of them to dinner had a taste my tongue recognized at once—the pleasure of being in a foreign town where I am limitlessly free. They were also exhausting: so many insoluble problems, so many hopes foundering, the icy sense—Henderson no doubt had felt it—of being responsible and helpless.

I had no idea how some of them were living, on what dole. And here is a curious thing I noticed. For all the weight of anxiety, discomfort, poverty, certain exiles I knew kept into late middle-age a sort of youth—as if beginning life again in another country had reduced the sum of their years. The eyes remained innocent.

Ilse Meyer's, for instance.

I have a sharp image of her, sitting, very silent, in a corner of the sofa while her husband argued with Lilo and the lawyer I had met at Hastings.

(The one object of value the young Meyers brought with them from Berlin was the manuscript of Ernst's scholarly work on English Chamber Music from the Middle Ages to Purcell: he ex-

pected to make his reputation by it. During the war, after I had
written innumerable letters, and with the help of some fund or
other, it was at last published, and praised at length and unequivo-
cally by the *Times Literary Supplement* for its 'great learning'. Was that
all he got out of it?)

Speaking to me—no doubt he thought I needed telling—the lawyer
said,

'Some cruelty shall accompany naturally the establishment of a
dictatorship. If minds and bodies are to fill a mould, some must be
broken to fit, yes? Is then the opportunity of scoundrels—such as in
my country flog political prisoners with steel rods, castrate, blind,
or arrest usually at night.' He lifted a short broken-nailed hand.
'Without extravagance, one may suppose national instincts. One
nation prefers to use castor oil and exile, another simple shooting,
another inclines to mutilation of the parts or other tortures. One
may even suppose that here, in England, brutality should be kept
low and the choice be of moral and economic pressure. What do you
say?'

I had nothing to say.

He went on, smiling, 'I am sure you will not, like your Labour
leaders, say: What do you expect me to do?' His chin worked in a
very unpleasant way. 'His friend writes: For God's sake help us.
And he answers, coldly: *What do you expect me to do?*'

'Well, what *did* you expect?' Ernst Meyer asked in his soft voice.
He had one of the most charming speaking voices I ever heard.
'First, he can't save everyone. Second, you ought to know that a
democrat is a man who bends before he is broken.'

Lilo turned on him a vindictive smile.

'And a Communist is a man who makes mistakes in order not to
learn from them——'

The quarrel raged for more than an hour. I effaced myself and
went to talk to the silent Ilse. It was hard work. The magnificent
dark eyes in her small face had a look of blindness or absence. She is
still, I thought, living in the tiny room in the Jäckelstrasse, she
hasn't yet let go of the life broken off short at a point she can still, by
looking obstinately back, see.

After a long time I felt her mind move at the end of mine. It was
not courage she needed from me; she had enough (and showed it
twelve years later, at the end of the war, when Ernst, still a faithful
Communist, left her and their five-year-old daughter in London and
went back to East Berlin with the English girl he had fallen in love

with). What she needed was some assurance that she existed. She smiled a little. Her hand moved from her lap to the arm of my chair.

Lilo beckoned me from the other end of the room. When I went to her, she said fiercely,

'Why do you trouble with her? She is mad.'

'Nonsense,' I said coldly, 'she is as sane as you are.'

'Well, there is no need to talk to her, she is not used to being noticed.'

Three more people arrived, a musician and his gently anxious wife, and a younger man, a poet. The musician I knew as one of those with a cousin in America; he was so certain of the future that he had recklessly given away part of the money they had brought with them. I made a great deal of fresh coffee, and hoped that the air of intelligence with which I listened to an argument about surrealist writing hid my exhaustion. I was so bored by it that when the poet said that surrealism is a new birth, I made my only comment.

'It looks to me much more like an abortion. The death by a thousand yawns of any literature worth the name.'

They fell on me in a body.

'I never dreamed you were reactionary,' Lilo said, with reproach.

'How is this? You hate what is new and damn it already out of fear?'

'Have it your own way,' I said.

Long before the last of them left, towards one o'clock, I was emptier of virtue than a husk. As I shut the front door, my furiously exasperated husband stamped out of his bedroom. He had stayed with the party—he was very fond of Lilo and liked the young Meyers—until the onset of surrealism. Then he could bear it no longer and shut himself in his room to work. He watched me stonily as I carried coffee cups into the ridiculous kitchen, emptied ash-trays, and straightened chairs. In reality I was collecting the scattered fragments of myself from all over the room.

'Why the hell didn't you turn them out sooner?'

I had a vision of the drab curtains and thin dusty carpet of an un-heated bed-sitting-room in West Hampstead.

'They were enjoying themselves talking.'

'No reason why you should kill yourself.'

I knew that my energy was inexhaustible. It might for the moment have vanished, but I could count on its return in a few hours, asking to be squandered.

Chapter 7

For some years after 1933 I lived in equivocal amity with pacifists and combative supporters of the League of Nations, adjusting my feelings, in good and bad faith, to the person I happened to be with. I swayed between the two like a tightrope walker, or a politician. My only immoveable conviction was my loathing of war.

In the autumn of 1933 this shocking indecision led me into more trouble than usual. Philip Noel-Baker asked me to help him to recruit well-known writers in defence of collective security and against war. His plan was to invite a number to dinner and talk to them. Then he decided that the dinner should be given by Viscount Cecil, and asked me to choose and invite the guests.

I was incapable of risking his disapproval by refusing. My respect for his courage and goodness, and admiration of his flawless profile, were both too great.

I brushed out of my way the uncomfortable reflection that a pacifist could support the idea of an armed League only if she assumed that the bombs of the International Air Force would never be dropped. My mind was far too divided to reject one more ambiguity.

What worried me much more was the all too likely behaviour of the well-known writers. I knew my fellows too well to share his confidence that they only needed a call to arms to come running. We shall eat Lord Cecil's salt, I thought, and nothing will come of it. Already I felt myself disgraced by a humiliating fiasco.

Racking my brains for a way to avoid it, I came on a half-formed idea that we might write a symposium on the danger of another war. Secretly I was convinced that we should be wasting our time, children throwing sand against the wind. I am rarely taken in by rhetoric, even my own, and I can never believe that anyone else is less sceptical.

Looking back, I see that in 1933 I was blinder than a bat to the real tragedy of our time.

What I saw then as an attempt of the reason, of reasonable men, to divert irrational forces driving us to war was not that, not that at all. It was a struggle of the human spirit *against* the intellect. Our intellect has betrayed us. Has set ajar the door of hell with a cruelty as frigid as that of German administrators and technicians opening the gas chambers. Today, Faust, in the person of the dedicated nuclear scientist, has prepared the extinction of human kind.

I chose a score of glittering names, and wrote my letters of invitation with tactful cunning, trying without frightening them to warn Lord Cecil's guests that they were going to be asked to do something.

The Wellington Club, where the dinner was held, was as imposing and reticent as any noble London club. Nothing could have been better suited to a gathering of distinguished minds and stomachs. The only faces I now see distinctly are those of Lord Cecil himself—great domed head and forehead, deeply-sunk eyes, superb beak of a nose, long prominent upper lip—and, flanking him on either side, Rebecca West and Rose Macaulay. (I have forgotten how I settled the problem which of them to place on his right: I think I tossed for it.) He looked like one of Jove's eagles overtopping two smaller vivid birds.

Towards the end of dinner, cold with the fear of ridicule, I suggested that we might write a book for him. I should have been certain that the task of editing it would be thrust on me. My heart sank. But food, wine, and the splendour of Lord Cecil had put our writers in a foolish state of goodwill, and rather than risk losing a fair wind I agreed.

It turned out a frightful labour—the writing with my own hand of a couple of hundred letters, cajoling, explaining, persuading, encouraging; not to speak of putting together the skeleton of the animal and struggling endlessly against the natural impulse of writers to promise one thing and write another—or not write at all.

Few of those I attacked had the hardness of heart—moral courage or sense—to refuse. One or two accepted out of vanity, the others from decency or sincere hatred of war. The greater the writer, the less trouble he gave. Edmund Blunden gave me none at all.

'It is very kind of you to invite me into the Disarmament Ring, and I hope I can produce something worthy of the occasion and th company. Some floating ideas might form a poem of say 100 or 150 verses, if you would take in so many. How long do you allow your Bards? I should like a little time. Can you invent a machine to reproduce the Menin Rd Battle for instance, so that some of our young may just look in at practical war? I could show them the way out of Hedge St, and eastward.'

The long poem he wrote, *War Cemetery*, is the single part of the book still living, still, as it was at the time, the only fragment of literature, a jet of truth from the heart and nerves of a poet.

My own opening essay on the revolt from reason was a fine piece of rhetoric and could have been written either by a devout supporter of the League or an out-and-out pacifist. Both of them were ad-mirably clear about the normal man's ambivalent attitude to war, and the nonsense of believing that fear or hatred of war has the slightest effect in preventing it. And about the banality of evil. (I was then far from imagining that sane men, with cultivated senses, can conceive and keep going an Auschwitz.) I wrote fluently about the Hegelian roots of Etatism, and the paradox of a rational theory breeding the irrationalism of the Absolute State. No one, I was sure, would notice the logical gap I skipped across to touch in lightly the idea of an armed League. No one did.

After trying in vain to persuade various better-found writers to provide the final essay, I wrote it myself. It contained—in 1933— an eloquent plea for a united Europe.

A splendid polemist was lost when I took to writing novels.

The book was published by Constable. It had the effect I expected —none.

This year, too, in November, I finished the first volume of the *roman fleuve* from which I expected so much, *Company Parade*. It was a good book. Yes, really a good book, crowded with men, women and a child or two, who are still breathing in a recess of my brain, though I have abandoned them. There is a great deal in it about Hervey Russell and her ambitions, blunders, joys, griefs; there are ex-soldiers, industrialists, a Jewish newspaper proprietor and his family, writers, a segment of the literary *panier à crabes* of the twenties, a Marie Lloyd figure, a young Labour politician and his wife—I forget the others, and have not the heart to look into a book into which so much energy, passion, intellect, and faith and hope disappeared.

The second volume, *Love in Winter*, took me another year, until November 1934. More characters forced their way into it, with ruthless energy, and truthful and sometimes bitter episodes from my own life in London in those years—Lord knows what more—the economic web, the social web.

I am coolly certain that, *fleuve* for *fleuve*, it ran faster and deeper than any flowering now, in the sixties.

But what a devil of an idea to set myself up as a Balzac. I must have been mad.

At the same time I was reviewing for A. R. Orage in the *New English Weekly*. Why add that to my other labours? For a reason, completely irresistible, which went back to 1913 and my joyous life then. Orage's *New Age* was the Bible of my generation. We would far sooner go hungry than miss buying it. We quoted it, argued with it, formed ourselves on it. I suppose he had a sharper influence on intelligent young Englishmen of that time—compare Alain's influence on a generation of Frenchmen killed in the War—than anyone else, and writers whom no one suspected of recklessness in money matters wrote for the *New Age* for nothing, simply because he asked them.

In March 1913, when he printed my first piece of writing, the gaily impudent essay on George Bernard Shaw, I would have gone to prison for him.

I did not meet him then. The idea of presenting myself to him never entered my head, I was infinitely too timid, I could not imagine that he would welcome a shabby student with nothing to say for herself.

All but twenty years later, in March 1932, standing in an icy Berlin street, I bought an English paper and read that he had come back to England and started a new weekly paper. I must have written to him, since he invited me to see him on my way through London.

He took me to drink tea in a small shabby café near his office in Cursitor Street. I had heard him spoken of as an intelligent charlatan, and came prepared to be disillusioned. He turned out to be direct, entirely without airs of importance, as easy as if I had known him a long time, and naturally charming, with a flicker of ironic gaiety that was rarely out of sight. It showed itself when he said calmly,

'Young writers are a great deal more commercially-minded than they were before the War.'

I supposed that our successors were not showing themselves very willing to write for nothing. In 1913 . . . I didn't need to dip Proust's madeleine in my strong tea to taste the gaiety, the causeless springing happiness, the feverish expectations and certainties of that year. Warm and alive, they were waiting in me to be discovered, as they will be waiting at the end of my life. Because of them, and to please more than one young ghost, I agreed to review for him. The idea of reading every month more novels than I care to read in twelve dismayed me, but I did not dream of refusing.

I kept it up for a time something short of two years, until too many other tasks made it impossible. When, with genuine shame, I told Orage I could not go on, he sent me the bound volumes of the *New Age*—would I had kept them!—and a comforting letter: 'My dear Storm, dear, you've served your time for a dozen volumes, so I still feel in your debt . . .'

Later I wrote a pamphlet for him on The Soul of Man Under Leisure. I have lost or thrown away my copy of this exercise. Did I believe what I wrote? Possibly. Certainly I wrote what, from so long a discipleship, I knew he believed. In those days I was an excellent mimic.

Three months later, on the 6th of November, I opened an evening paper in the street, and read of his death. It seemed that everything, the traffic, the thin bitter wind, ceased. This death, I thought uncertainly, is the end of more than a man, it ends a story, and the story of my youth. I had a sharp image of him, smiling. I felt in some way silenced and stopped.

None of these words is real. The shock and the silencing were real.

Chapter 8

One figure detaches itself from the dissolving phantasmagoria of my years in the St John's Wood flat. My younger sister steps forward smiling.

I saw her two or three times a week; either she came to the flat, or, oftener, I met her somewhere in the City, near the offices of the Amalgamated Press—she was on the staff of a magazine—and gave her lunch. Afterwards, if there was time, we walked about the City, looking at old squares and churches she wanted to see. In 1940 most of these disappeared; I could not now go back there to look for her.

At twenty-seven she seemed no more than sixteen, her very fair skin smoothly unblemished, like a young child's, the natural scarlet of her lips undimmed. She had my grandfather's and my mother's coldly blue eyes; one man or woman in every generation of my family has these eyes, a clear pale blue, without a shadow.

Intensely practical, quick-tempered and quick-witted, she had none of my fear of other people, none of my anxious need to be approved, no wish at all to please; sharp-tongued, frank, pitiless in her dislikes, wholly loyal where she loved. She loved only very few persons. She had some contempt for my extravagance, restlessness, and what she called my softness (with people), but she would have used her tongue on an outsider who criticized me, with very much the annoyance she showed if one of her possessions were belittled.

I should be put to it to explain the compulsive need I felt to give her anything I knew she wanted. It was not caused by the fifteen years between us, making her as much my child as my sister . . . Why are we afraid to talk about foreknowledge? . . .

Her name for me, Dear Dog, was half affection, of a rough un-emotional family sort, and half mockery.

The writing on a scrap of paper in the back of a notebook begins:

'Dear Dog, if you are coming to Reading on Saturday I'll make a fruit cake for you to take back, and some fresh eggs. The garden has suddenly exploded with roses, I have mowed and weeded, we are painting the kitchen, and it is all——'

There it breaks off, the light quick voice, full of pride in a small house in a street of small decent houses. There was not a single thread in her of my hatred of domestic life or any itch for change and foreign countries. She was never bored, never inactive, never tired.

At some time in the autumn of 1934 she told me she had learned that she could only have a child if she were operated on to correct a serious internal deformity. It was not an easy operation, nor entirely certain.

'Do you want to have children?' I asked.

She stared at me coldly from those far too direct eyes. 'Of course.'

'I'll take you to a London specialist.'

'The specialist in Reading is quite good enough,' she said impatiently. 'Don't let's have any fuss.'

The first time I saw her after the operation, she was still drowsy. Looking down at her, I had an extraordinary sense that she was separated from me by an immense distance in time, the half-closed eyes, flawless skin, short-fingered hands lying idle on the sheet, the slender body, were remote, something I remembered. She roused herself to ask a question, and my momentary discomfort vanished.

Outside her room, I asked the sister in charge, 'Is she all right?'

'Oh, yes.' She smiled slightly. 'When I saw her just before the operation I thought how calm and self-possessed she was for a little girl. I was astonished when I knew her age.'

Chapter 9

At the end of that year I sold the Whitby house. Clearly we should never want to live in it again, there was nothing for Guy in a remote little coast town, neither future nor, for him, past. It was my past I rejected when we left it, finally, on the 9th of January, 1935.

The light that morning had a familiar clarity, at once cold and gentle, almost voluptuous. Looking, for the last time, at the view from the window of my working-room I felt a mortal grief. 'I shall never see you again, old road, old hillside. You are scored on my heart, to be found again, perhaps, at the last minute—*on n'arrive jamais à la mort sans dot*—but so long as I live, nothing, no view, will remind me of you. I am a fool to go.'

I was speaking in the emptiness of the room already stripped of its few pieces, the old chair, the long well-scrubbed table, a desperate cry, heard only by my own inner ear. No one had forced me to go, I chose to uproot myself from the one place where I am not a stranger —happy or unhappy, but not a stranger. The few primordial images I

see my way by start here: the colour, in all weathers and seasons, of
the North Sea, the enchantment of distant lights, the hard curve of
the coast.

There was no room in the London flat for my table, nor for the
rest of the furniture. It would have to be stored. I have never had
the courage to get rid of certain objects some woman of my family
chose years ago. For all my dislike of possessions, I drag about with
me heavy tallboys, old chairs, old clocks, as if it were they who
would suffer if I abandoned them. Or as if such capacity for loyalty
and stability I have has taken refuge in them.

Explain why I threw away the piercing happiness my Whitby
view gave me every time I lifted my head from my desk—no, I
can't, though there must be a reason, other than insanity, why I
arrange to drift like an anchorless ship, moving myself and my pieties
from place to place.

Until this year the fear of another war had been balanced by a naïve
incredulity. ('It's not possible, after the hideous lesson of 1914-18,
for even a Hitler to risk war.') In 1935 it began to flicker continuously, just below the horizon, a lightning flash, a sudden thinning
of the clouds, another flash, another.

In March and April we lived for five weeks in a village on the
Spanish coast north of Barcelona. Since then, that coast has been, as
they say, developed—that is, its mediaeval poverty, dignity, bigotry,
and crust of old habits broken into. In 1935, the signs of civilization
were a handful of German refugees living on—mercy, what were they
living on?—and a school of young female artists, English, their
trousers, bangles, and high screaming laughter so out of time and
place that the Catalan women in their black dresses looked at them
without seeing them. There was a harbour, a lighthouse on a headland, a beach given up to fishermen and their nets—the few visitors
walked half a mile along the rocky coast to a narrow bay, the sea
rough and ice-cold—four or five thin dusty streets of secretive houses
and a few dark small shops where the owner began by offering the
cheapest thing he had, and dry hills covered sparsely with scented
herbs and shrubs. The single hotel was a large Catalan house owned
by (I think) a Swiss, and furnished in the barest way. Our rooms
were two cells, the stone floor and immensely thick walls meant to
defeat the sun. After five o'clock in the afternoon they were bitterly
cold, and the stove, burning green wood, filled them with a choking
acrid smoke, without giving off warmth. Meals were eaten in a small

courtyard round a wind-bent orange tree. A single Catalan waiter, with the face and bony elegance of Dürer's 'Death', did everything: without him, and without the pale smiling German-Jewish secretary, sitting in a cell at the back of the courtyard, gentle and exhausted, apparently unsleeping ('You want to leave at three tomorrow morning? I call you, I bring coffee. Of course I am awake, why not?') the place could not have existed.

A few hours, in the middle of the day, were hot, with a violent white light and a wind that exasperated the nerves and drove sharp grains of dust into the skin and under closed eyelids. After five it dropped, and we walked across the land side of a headland, following a path upwards between tall dry thorns and shrubs; these crackled like the snapping of innumerable tiny bones, on a note a degree sharper than the continuous creaking of the cicadas. There were no other sounds and even these ceased during minutes when the path crossed a naked slope, burned to the bone and eaten away deeply between distorted pillars of rock and dry earth. The path climbed interminably, rounding one headland only to twist across another; in the end we had to leave it and force our way down steeply between the crackling shrubs, two or three hundred feet, to the coast road; on the left the dark sea, the powerful acetylene lights of the fishing boats floating on it like comets, their tails lying across the ripples. Outside the village a man was still patiently turning over the few feet of dry stony soil on which he and his family —you could not say, lived—existed. A chorus of frogs made more noise than a dozen double-basses tuning up. The streets were empty, cold, silent.

My writing brain is at its easiest and most energetic abroad, or when I live in an hotel. If I could travel perpetually, only pausing for a few months in the impersonality of a hired room with a view, I should write with all the pleasure in the world. And write less, because I should not be bored.

My notion of perfect happiness as a writer is a foreign hotel of a decent simple bourgeois sort—I know a score of them, where I could be happy for a lifetime—a wooden table in a window looking out at the sea, a garden, hills, roof-tops, any expanse you like, coffee and croissants in bed, the morning and afternoon spent writing, the rest of the day sauntering, sitting in cafés, hearing music, seeing friends, reading, staring, making a few notes, while the next day's work ripens peacefully in the mind behind my eyes and ears.

During these weeks I thought constantly about a novel I had been meditating for several months, ever since listening to Dorothy Thompson's account of Hitler's 30th of June murders. What I wanted to do was to expose why a dictator is forced, almost always, to kill the very men who fought for him when he was only a brutal adventurer. I thought I knew why, and I could imagine an English Fascism, the brutality half-masked and devious, with streaks of a Methodist virtue. I saw scenes, landscapes, figures, but did not yet see clearly the figures of the dictator and his friend.

One night, between dusk and dark, I glanced from my window into the courtyard. It was empty except for two men, Spaniards, sitting at one of the small iron tables, drinking. The light from a single weak lamp fell across their hands lying on the table, and over the face of the older of the two. I had an extraordinary sense of the tension between them, a tension which was part of a deep wordless attachment. It struck me that there is a homosexual relationship infinitely subtler and more powerful than the physical one, subtler than any merely sexual intimacy, or than intimacy between men and women. The two men I was watching knew each other at a deep level: there was attachment and hostility, both a little dangerous.

I had my English dictator and his friend, the man he would have murdered.

Now I had only to write the novel. I began it in June, on a Norwegian island, Tjømø, in the Oslo fjord, so much more charming and likeable than the fjords on the west coast, which are a shade too handsome, and know it.

I was only retracing the voyage my remote ancestors had made—there are still Storms in Norway, and a vein of my mind is open to the older blood and the tart sceptical northern humour. It is certainly from them that I get my naïve belief in freedom as the supreme good . . . No Mediterranean warmth is as deliciously exciting as the brief summers of the true north; they don't soothe, they rouse. Tjømø is a small island, a wharf, a few houses and farms, fields broken by fantastic grey rocks. The water off-shore was like the air, as clear as the finest glass, and in the hot sun the pines gave off a heady scent of wild raspberries. There was a shabby friendly hotel, built of wood. Writing the whole morning, looking across a garden of long grass and fruit trees at a sky of astonishing purity, I was continually happy. Exquisitely happy.

In The Second Year has admirable passages. Since my interest, as always if I please myself, was in the extraordinary way human beings behave when they imagine they are being simple, heroic, truthful,

generous, it was a disappointment to my friends on the far Left, who
expected a direct attack on Fascism, with a Communist hero, and
the rest of it.

In August we moved to Oslo, to an hotel half way up the wooded
hill immediately behind the city, the most charming capital city in
the world; it was small enough to be held in the hand, and contained
all a capital city should, and once for all proved, if proof were needed,
that the real horror of modern life is size, the inflation of everything,
including cities. I hope it is still possible to leave the wide street
running from the simple dignified royal palace in Oslo to the
harbour, and, three-quarters of an hour later, follow a mountain
path between wild strawberries and pines. A recipe for happiness—
too simple to have any merit in the eyes of economists and politicians.

I am not suggesting that the Norwegians are simple people. On
the contrary. The farther south you go in Europe, the simpler life
becomes, and human beings. The endless winters of the north, the
corrosive cold, the long hours of darkness, encourage people to live
an intensely self-regarding life, and—of course—the more they live
inside themselves, the madder and more complex they become.

One evening in Oslo we dined with Bjarne Braatoy's brother, who
was a medical psychiatrist, and four of his friends, two Norwegians,
a shipowner and his young attractive wife, a Dane, and a Swedish
novelist. It was a superb dinner, afloat on aquavit and ending with
a vast bowl of cloudberries. The talk never stopped, immense good-
humour, violent arguments, outbreaks of crazy laughter, and not a
trace of vanity or the reserve noticeable in any gathering of intellectuals in London ('Am I giving myself away to a competitor? Am I
being impressive, witty, intelligent?')

Provoked by something Trygve Braatoy said, the Swede began a
half-serious half-mocking analysis of the Norwegian character.

'You think,' he said to me, 'that Norwegians are candid, simple,
spontaneous. Nothing of the sort. In the first place, they are all mad
or half-mad—the incidence of lunacy is the highest in Europe. How
many writers do you know in England who have been psycho-
analysed? One? Not more. Every one of my Norwegian friends has
been or is being analysed. It is an occupational disease. I tell you,
that old brute Ibsen knew what he was doing when he created
Brand and Peer Gynt, the monomaniac, all or nothing, and the self-
destroying braggart, the split man, imagination and no reality. At
this moment, yes, at this moment, what you are seeing is not a
meeting of simple souls, but a roomful of barbarians who have

never been happy or content since they were forced to give up raiding and stay at home.'

'Then that goes for you, too,' his host retorted. He had the same ear-splitting high-pitched laugh as his brother.

'No. We have civilized ourselves. We don't go mad, we drink to be happy, and commit suicide when we are sober.'

Inevitably, the talk turned on the threat of war. Frowning, the young Norwegian woman said,

'When I look at my two children I feel a little guilty because they are safe, and yours are in danger.'

'Are you sure you are safe?'

'Why, of course, who would gain anything by attacking us?'

'Now, the Germans are a simple people,' the Swedish writer said, 'if you like. They are still in the amoeboid phase of humanity, an active outer layer taking in food and ideas from all sides, an inner layer which is still fluid. The day when they split into two cells, ah, that will be the day.'

At midnight, I stood up and said we must go, we should miss the last funicular to our hotel.

'You can't go yet,' Trygve exclaimed. 'We are just going to eat— if this much-talking Swede will hold his tongue for five minutes.'

I forget how, after eating a great many thin rolled-up slices of almost raw beef, and swallowing more aquavit, we got home . . .

Back in England in the first week of September, with the finished manuscript of *In The Second Year*, I felt an irrational gaiety and hope. The Abyssinian crisis was in spate, and I ought to have felt anxious. In fact, I was convinced that there was no need to be anxious. Not because of what I learned from a friend who had been staying at Chequers, but from a purely irrational sense, born of the clear Norwegian air, the scent of pines and salt, the shiver of long sunbleached grass in a light wind, that war was an insanity impossible in Europe.

When I saw my young sister she told me that she was going to have a child next year, in February. There was still a risk for her in child-birth, but she brushed it aside as not worth a thought. To speak of her courage misses the point. She was brave, yes, and without being conscious of it for a single instant: what was at work in her was her will, she wanted this child, therefore it was not only possible but safe for her to have it.

She asked me about the crisis. 'When I told S——— that I was going to have a child she said she would be afraid to bring children into such a world.' She laughed contemptuously. 'Can you imagine anyone being so *soft*.'

'There isn't going to be trouble yet,' I said. I repeated what my friend had told me. 'We shall give Mussolini no cause to make war on us, rather than do that we are going to let down the Abyssinians and all the small nations.'

'Are you sure?'

'Absolutely.' I wanted to reassure her. 'The Italian government has spent seventy-five million—francs or lire, I can't remember—on seducing the French press, which asks nothing better, and the Banque de France has been financing the Italian war credit. They are all rascals.'

The eyes she turned on me had the same remote look as my mother's, as if she were raking a distant horizon from the bridge of a ship.

At this moment I decided that when the London lease fell in I would move to Reading to be near her, and in November we found a flat of fine large rooms, the upper floor of a house on the edge of Reading.

I took immense pains to arrange these rooms, setting out in them all my possessions, as if for a lifetime of peaceful mediocre existence. I found a housekeeper who had been kitchenmaid, then a year in the still-room, then under-cook, then cook in an aristocratic household, and now wanted an easier life. To all appearance I was as near being perfectly settled as possible.

On a sunny windless day, the North Sea is an image of calm enjoyment, not a cat's-paw of disquiet, above an unfathomed depth of restlessness and treachery.

When I visited my young sister during this time I was moved by her happiness and pride in the least of her possessions. She and her like are the salt of the earth, I thought: I am a wastrel. As her thin body became heavier, her face took on a serenity and an innocence it had not had when she was a child—as though she were no longer seeking anything other than she already had. Remembering the impatient rage my distorted body had roused in me when I was carrying a child, I thought that something essential had been left out of my nature, or some foreign body lodged in it, a grain of sand in a joint. No use to be sorry now.

Her son was born on the 17th of February, 1936. She called him Nicholas.

Chapter 10

After the 7th of March, the day Hitler sent his soldiers into the Rhineland, I seemed always to be listening to the sound of approaching footsteps and counting stairs.

One evening I had arranged to meet Guy and Philip Jordan in the brasserie of the Café Royal. The large room, when I came in blinking from the cold wind, was a chaos of fragments, a waiter sliced in half, carrying a bottle and two glasses in his one hand, a decapitated head with small malicious eyes and black whiskers, splinters of light, a woman's face, mouth open in a grimace of alarm, another mouth laughing brutally without a sound.

I saw a face I knew, Thomas Balogh, and paused to speak to him. The League Council was still discussing the Rhineland affair, he knew a great many people, financiers, politicians, journalists, and might have heard something.

He is the nearest thing to a heartless intellect I know. Not that he is without heart, but his brain functions with no interference by that refractory organ. This detachment is not unusual among genuine intellectuals, the Central European variety of the species particularly, but he must have begun as a child to bring it to a fine point of dry rationalism, logic, malice, acid wit. He told me once that one of his early memories was that of looking curiously at a dead body as he crossed a bridge in Budapest on his way from school, during the revolution. 'What revolution?' I asked. He shrugged his shoulders. 'Oh, my God, why ask? You wouldn't know anything about it.'

'Tell me in one word what has happened or is going to happen,' I said.

'There isn't going to be war. The Council is going to adjourn indefinitely, without waiting for that scoundrel Ribbentrop. The French get nothing, not even a military agreement with us, there may be an agreement with Germany, there will be no sanctions. The League is finished.'

'Are you sure?'

'Of course I am sure.' He smiled sharply. 'Yesterday I talked to a German in the Embassy, not a friend, but I know him very well. He was very cock-a-hoop. He said: We've let you kick our backsides from conference to conference for a number of years, now we're showing you other parts of our anatomy, you won't kick us again, that phase is over . . . He's right, but the truth is, all those victims of hardened arteries and renal disease in the Cabinet are too timid and prudent to kick a louse. It's amusing to watch them.'

'If one had no children,' I said.

'My dear girl, don't let your imagination run away with you. Keep it for a novel. I suggest you write one about a Czech or a Pole —one of those nice countries with nothing to brag about but their past—running from one international conference to the next, watching Europe collapse. Call it: Useful Spade Work Has Been Done . . . If you are hoping to judge affairs in Europe by any form of reason or sane thinking, you had better hang yourself. It is a bloody laughter, my dear, and you are wrong to take it seriously.'

'Thank you,' I said.

Philip had brought a friend with him, a Foreign Office official, one of those exaggeratedly lean, tall, well-bred Englishmen who look young well into their forties: the only mark of his age was a groove running from the sides of his blade of a nose to the corners of a thin mouth. Call him X. I repeated what Thomas Balogh had said, and asked if it were true.

X. knew him slightly.

'These Central Europeans are too clever by half,' he said lightly. 'There is no agreement with Germany, only pressure for it in some quarters; the political ground is too spongy for it to hold up. Otherwise he is right—to a point.'

'Why only to a point?'

'Because he knows, we all know, that there will be demands and crises and demands and crises, and a superb operatic performance, Hitler as Wotan—do I mean Wotan? the fellow who sings bass and is a bore—reciting his sad story, and prophesying the downfall of Europe if we don't all join him in crushing the Bolshies. A lot of chaps who ought to know better, important chaps, will applaud, and he'll begin to think he needn't manoeuvre us and can go straight ahead. What Tom Balogh and his kind don't know is the point when this will be too much for us to swallow.'

'Do you know?' I asked.

'Of course not.'

I had an inarticulate sense that this picture of us as short on logic, that dubious continental trick, and saved at the last moment by sound English instincts, was one of our vanities. But I held my clumsy tongue.

'By the time we reach that point,' Philip said drily, 'there may be nothing left to stand on, and nothing to do but invite Hitler to take over Covent Garden. And I detest Wagner.' His tongue flickered across his upper lip. 'They say Flandin blubbered like a calf in the Council.'

'My God, how would you expect him to cry? Like a film star?'

'The people I loathe,' Guy said, 'are the Liberals. When *The Times* says we mustn't offend the Germans it's only doing its duty as the last voice of Queen Victoria and some distinguished bird-watcher or other. But the Liberal newspapers make me vomit.'

At this moment, the finger I was running round the stem of my glass came on a slightly chipped edge, and before I could stop myself I was fingering the chipped saucer I had used to float a nightlight when my son had diphtheria. Something like a ball of blood exploded in my brain, I felt deaf and blind with fear and an insane anger. I stammered stupidly,

'Someone should assassinate Hitler now.'

I must really have looked insane. X. gave me a sweet condescending smile. I drew my shaking hand out of sight and tried to control my mind . . . The images in it were those any woman in any country might see, thinking of her child's brains spilled on the ground. In the 1914 war I had not felt this mortal anxiety for my friends who were being killed in France. Now, when I thought about my son, I became frenzied with fear. An irrational fear. But there was nothing irrational about my horror of killing, of the impulse, premeditated or blind, which sends men out to slaughter each other. Call it what you like—war, human butchery—nothing, not even the courage or docility of the soldiers, makes it less sickening.

I thought: And it will be no use. It will be like the battle of the Somme which went on for more than four months and killed the best in our country . . .

> The many men so beautiful
> And they all dead did lie . . .

If I believe that concentration camps, the torture of Jews and political opponents, is less vile than war, I must say so plainly, not pretend that the price is something less . . . With physical nausea, I thought: I can't say it.

I came back suddenly to the crowded over-warm room. Philip was talking, with a smile which curiously accentuated an air of transparence and bitterness.

'These Hoares and Simons would sell their own offspring to save their places and skins.'

'You're wrong,' X. said easily, 'they're all very decent public-spirited types, who wouldn't lie or cheat—except as a political duty. Or allow the Prayer Book to be messed about. In fact, that's one reason why they back the sober industrious tax-paying Boches against the corrupt immoral French. They may be limited and self-righteous, but they mean well——'

Philip interrupted, smiling. 'Yes, I know. If you talk to them about Dachau and all that, they think it's your dirty mind.'

I felt the instinct of an animal to bolt from my dilemma. Ashamed, I said,

'I couldn't go on living in England if we allied ourselves with these brutes.'

Philip raised nearly invisible eyebrows. 'Could you live in America?'

The pure line of the coast running north, seen from the East cliff, wavered behind my eyes. A stone leaning sideways in the rank grass had had its inscription eaten by the salt in the air, all but five words . . . *master mariner of this parish.* I felt an intense savage joy and pride in being one of the fraternity of master mariners.

'No.'

Guy said, 'The Germans have some virtues, but they're not house-trained—*sales Boches tout de même.* I'd join up again at once, to fight for France.'

But you were happy in the army, I thought without kindness: you were young then, and you enjoy not being responsible for yourself.

We drove back to Reading very late. Ahead of us on the Great West Road the shifting line of lights quickened an old excitement in me. A dark bubble formed of sea and sky closed round me; I had a sense, familiar and consoling, of time as a plain running out of sight on all sides, where in the same breath I was a child and dead, a phantom. I felt detached even from Guy. I thought: I've had several minutes of an absolute happiness in my life. In a final count, what matters more?

Chapter 11

I was writing far too much. I told myself so at intervals. You are writing far far too much. And went on doing it.

Was it at this time that I had a letter from Laura Riding ordering me to contribute to a volume of some sort? It would have involved hard work—I should have been ashamed to do less than I could—and I refused, explaining that I was already over my ears. I had a letter from Robert Graves, rebuking me sharply for not being delighted to put everything else aside when Laura had done me the honour of an order.

I could not feel about her, as he clearly did, and as she felt about herself, that she was quasi-divine, but, sceptic that I am, I had no impulse to jeer. She was as hard on herself as on others.

I finished (7th of March, 1963) *None Turn Back*, the third in the *Mirror of Darkness* series. In a long review in the *Listener*, Edwin Muir explained carefully why the book was an imaginative failure, 'because Miss Jameson's real theme is society, and all these people are seen as conditional responses to society; with the result that they must remain conditional, that they can never speak to us: society is their ventriloquist. The ventriloquist is brilliant and sometimes moving, but . . .' etc etc. At the end of his long analysis, with every word of which I agreed, passionately, as I read it, he said: 'The generous passion and the complete honesty of the story are beyond praise. The writing is sometimes exquisite, and always has the directness and candour of good prose. In spite of its faults, there-fore, this is a novel which no contemporary reader can afford to neglect.'

Most of them none the less neglected it. And I knew he was right about the imaginative defect. I knew, too, that the effort I had been making for the last three years, to uncover the social webb of the thirties and the men and women caught in it and struggling, was not contemptible. There are honest and moving things in all three books, and, what is worth more—part of an aesthetic creed too lightly decried now—they are, so to speak, built to be lived in. But, though certain of the characters refused stubbornly to die, and became central characters in later novels, I could not go on. Edwin Muir's criticism did no more than confirm in me my own frightful sense of dryness, *accidie*, when I thought about it. Dryness or spleen? I gave myself sensible reasons. That I was writing in a vacuum—not enough people were interested, and one cannot write without the complicity of at least a generation. That no one could write the sort of novels I had planned at the pace forced on me. What you need, I said, is a private income, time to spend several years brooding, re-writing, with no pressure to finish a book and be paid for it.

(When you come to think of it, the life of a professional writer is as horrible as would be the life of a politician condemned to offer himself to the public every year for re-election.)

All damnably true. But . . . to do what I wanted to do, give life and a form to the vision of England moving cloudily in my brain, I needed—what? The daemonic energy that drove a Balzac to empty himself to create a world, the egoism of a great writer, a Tolstoy, a Proust, forcing him to put everything, every human being, family, friends, himself, a bad second to his task.

The deep reason why I abandoned *The Mirror in Darkness*—but I see it only now—was a stifled instinct warning me that I was working against the grain of my talent. The restlessness and dryness were eddies, rising briefly to the surface from a subterranean river which was *my* truth, *my* reality.

I refuse to regret the energy spent writing polemics against war and Fascism. Still less the energy given to helping a few, too few, men and women to escape the hell of German concentration camps, and then to keep them alive. Nothing in me is fiercer, more obsessive, more nearly involuntary, than my loathing of the cruelty that issued in Auschwitz, except the sense that exile is only the human condition pushed to its farthest limit.

These images have burned me to the bone.

I could not have held aloof. No regrets. A concern with politics, a conviction that political activity was obligatory at that time, was right. Wrong as wrong was the fallacy that political passions I could not ignore had somehow to be pressed directly into my novels. I confused an inescapable personal commitment with a totally mistaken and crude literary one.

After *None Turn Back* I had an impulse to efface Storm Jameson altogether. Not that I had the wit to realize that my profound boredom with her was due to an obscure instinct that she was making a fool of herself.

Instead of turning the poor animal round to find her right road, I left her, and wrote two short books, and then a third long one, under two other names.

The first two, written this same year, were *récits*.

I began *Loving Memory*, by James Hill, on the 10th of March, an ironical story of a man's relationship with two women, one of them his dead wife. This—and James Hill's full length novel—were published by Collins, who loyally kept my secret.

The other short book, *The World Ends*, was a very different affair. I wrote it with intense care and the most acute pleasure—a story of the drowning of the world except for a fragment of Yorkshire moorland, an edge of the high moor springing abruptly from the plain west of Thirsk.

It was written slowly, through the summer and early autumn. I finished it on the 11th of October, and began an absurd intrigue to get it published. I decided to send it to the firm of J. M. Dent, only because I knew that one man there, Richard Church, would like it. The letter I sent with it was signed William Lamb. I don't now remember whether I intended to deceive Richard, but, when he wrote asking William Lamb to come and see him, I found that I could not, absolutely could not, bring myself to unmask.

I sent my young sister to see Richard Church.

The game amused her. I don't think he was taken in: he guessed, I think, that this slender blue-eyed woman was not the book's author, but he could not shake her self-possession.

He sent her a contract, which I have, signed by William Lamb in a fine sloping hand.

A few weeks later, I went to a dinner given by the P.E.N. Club, and found myself placed next to J. B. Priestley. Over dinner we became reconciled—so far, that is, as any Yorkshireman is ever reconciled to having been treated with less than the respect due to him. We left together, and on the way out, were stopped by Richard Church.

Going into company makes me reckless; I talk too much or I listen in silence, with approving smiles, to opinions that curdle my soul. Richard talked about publishing, and I asked him whether Dent's had any interesting books to come.

'Yes, one,' he said, 'an extraordinarily fine book by a new writer, William Lamb.'

'Ah,' I said, 'I'll read it.'

'I'll send you a copy,' he promised. 'We're going to make a handsome book of it, with engravings by John Farleigh.'

'I'll read it,' I repeated.

As he walked off, J. B. Priestley called over his shoulder, 'She'll cheat you, you know.'

What made him say it? A resentful memory of that harsh review? An atavistic instinct—one astute ironical Yorkshireman seeing right through to another's guile?

The World Ends finished, I turned back to Storm Jameson—I needed her—and wrote a long novel which was in reality a retreat. Into my mother's past and my own. *The Moon Is Making* was a Brueghel-like novel about the violently individual men and women, obscure eccentrics, dreamers, saints, their veins filled with the strangest fluids, whom my mother remembered from her childhood. Some of them were still alive in mine, in particular one, a Unitarian minister called Haydn Williams. His hatred of poverty and injustice devoured him. In an earlier century he would have been a Chartist, earlier still, a Leveller. When what had been a piece of commonland on the West cliff was enclosed to become part of the Spa gardens, he went there and tore down the iron railings. He was fined, jailed, and as soon as he was free, tore them down again, and again. The police lost patience and began to handle him roughly, and the common people he wanted to protect came out to laugh and jeer at him. A freak is a gift to men and women who have, after all, hard narrow lives and few amusements.

I was very young then, and I assumed that he was mad and said so to my mother. To my astonishment and mortification, she said contemptuously, 'You don't know what you're talking about, you little fool. What he does is useless and silly, but he's a brave good man.'

I daresay that few of her sharp speeches struck me harder. I don't say that it alone is responsible for my respect for rebels—which in turn is partly responsible for what I have made of my life.

Chapter 12

In May that year my mother stayed with me in Reading. It was a superb spring, the lilacs and chestnuts so full that each tree was a single massive flower, dazzling.

She could not walk far. I drove her about the countryside to look, with that blue fixed stare, at an inordinate beauty, almost too much, too cruel and insistent an energy.

'I shan't see them again,' she said suddenly.

To hear her say it angered me sharply, and I said, 'Of course you will, you'll be here next May and I'll bring you to see them.'

She looked at me without answering; she had wanted to be reassured and was not.

In August, my middle sister wrote from Whitby that she had had 'an attack', and was very ill. All the way in the train, an eight-hour journey, I was nagged by anxiety, and then impatient when I thought of the book I had had to abandon, and must finish soon: I needed the money.

'She thinks she has had a heart attack,' my sister said, 'so be careful.'

When I went into her room and saw her lying in bed on her side, my heart shrank; her face, her soft hair screwed into a plait, her eyes, all had in some way given up, as if this time she were really defeated. She spoke in a voice I had never heard from her, slow, slurred, coming from a great distance.

'I'm glad you're feeling better,' I said.

She was a long time answering. 'Am I?' she said at last, like a child who has been told by an adult something it can't take in.

I was both anguished and numbed, I refused to believe what I could see. Deliberately and yet as if blind and deaf, refused. She must not be dying—that was not thinkable. And, if she were, I could not leave her and go back to my life and my work.

Her recovery was very slow. Time confused her terribly. The

kind thing would have been to let her live in her own time, waking
and sleeping as she pleased. But she had to live by others' time, and
it was a torment to her. She slept, and woke bewildered; or she
forgot she had just eaten, and demanded her lunch, and then begged
us to give it to her, half weeping. Sometimes the railing voice of a
lively self-willed child broke from her; sometimes it was the strong
full voice of a young woman I could just recall.

I knew when she was living in the past, because her mouth shut in
a hard stubborn line; she was thinking of her dead son, and my
father's unkindness to him, or of some other bitter cause she had for
not forgiving her husband. She forgave him nothing. The dry indifference she had come to feel broke, and now she could not endure him. When he came into her room—as once a day he did, and
stood awkwardly, looking down at her, for a minute—she closed
her eyes.

'How are you feeling?' he asked, pretending ease.

'Better,' she said icily, and waited, clenched, until he had hurried
away.

I think that now she hated him simply because she had married
him, not for anything he had done. He stood for the disappointment
her life had been, for the absence of all an ardent quick-witted young
woman had expected from it and had not had.

We talked about my young sister, and her house and her baby,
endlessly, since I was the one person who would listen endlessly.
Even this was not completely safe, and once, as she had said about
the chestnuts, she said,

'I shan't see Do and Nicholas again. I shall never be well enough.'

'You'll be as well as ever,' I said lightly. 'You've had a bad heart
attack, but if you're careful you won't have any more.'

There was a long silence. Then she said slowly,

'I don't remember the heart attack.'

It shamed me that I, her child, was deceiving her. And that perhaps she was not really deceived.

One evening when she and I were alone in her room—she was
strong enough now to sit in the window, looking, looking, looking
—she said in a hesitant voice,

'Sometimes, in the night, Daisy, I feel afraid.'

I shut away, at once, the agony of grief. 'Why should you be
afraid?'

'I don't know. But I am afraid.'

'There is something you could say to yourself; you could say:

In quietness and in confidence shall be my strength. It's what I say when I'm afraid.'

I would not let her fear reach me. Would not. I kept it away from me, I would not know or feel what was taking place in her. She was not going to die, so why think about it, why suffer? I shut both mind and heart against what, if I let it in, would destroy too many of my defences and pretences. There were moments when I thought it would be better for us all if she died. And this, too, I did not look at.

Days and weeks went by. When she was strong enough to walk the short distance to the nearest shops, though not alone, I prepared to go back to Reading, to Guy and my unfinished novel. She did not want me to go.

It was like all the other times I had left her. I had to go, I had to get away—back into my life, into the world. As I had done at these other times, I hardened my heart.

To catch the only train that would get me to Reading that evening, I had to leave the house very early, at half-past six, and when I went into her room to say goodbye, she was half asleep: she was lying in the bed as though she were sinking in it, her eyes closed. I could scarcely hear her when she spoke.

'Don't go.'

For less than a moment I knew that I should hear that remote barely audible voice in the deepest recesses of my brain, and those two words, all the rest of my life. Then I closed my ears.

'I *must* go,' I said. 'But I'll come back—I'll come as soon as I can.'

She did not answer or lift her eyelids to look at me—as though she had lost interest. Or as though she had known all along that she could not count on me, had known I would fail her, and were turning away from me.

I did not go again until, in February, my sister wired me to come. Because, in winter, there were fewer trains to Whitby, the journey was endlessly roundabout, and I was tormented by the thought that I might not get there in time. Time for what? My mind drew back sharply from that edge.

The dark, the cold North Sea wind, the empty streets—it could have been any of the evenings when I jumped out of the school train from Scarborough and hurried home.

'Do didn't think of coming with you?' my sister said.

'How could she? She can't leave the baby.'

'Well, it doesn't matter,' my sister said wearily, 'she's forgotten her.'

'What do you mean?'

'Last week, when Do's box of snowdrops came and I took them in to her and told her Do had sent them, she asked: Who is Do?'

For all these years the abiding passion of every moment, and it had dropped out of her hand. Why, then you have had nothing, I thought, oh, my poor love, nothing.

She was reared up on pillows, her face empty, a skull, not a face, the cheeks sunk, the eyes a blue absence of sight: she was the image of her father, my hard grandfather: nothing of her was left except the life of her Gallilee tribe.

I bent down, thinking I should be able to reach her.

'Here I am, Mother.'

Slowly, almost imperceptibly, her eyes turned towards my voice. For less than a second.

'She's going fast on her journey,' the nurse said loudly. She saw my frown, and said, 'Oh, she's completely unconscious, y'know.'

I no longer remember whether she was two days or three finishing that journey. I slept through the nights. During the day, whenever I could be alone with her, I bent over her and said softly, 'Don't be afraid, I'm here.' But she made no sign that she heard me. Once I said, 'Don't worry, I'll look after Do for you.' I was forced to believe that, somewhere in the silence, she must remember her youngest. My breath was cut off in my throat by the knot of pain. Tears came against the hard effort I made; I could not bear it that she did not know I was there.

'You and I have been on so many journeys,' I said, 'and now you are going alone.'

I was ashamed to be crying, afraid that I was crying over myself, and ashamed to be seen crying. When the nurse came into the room, I hurried out.

On the second or was it the third evening my sister said that we had better begin to destroy or put out of reach things she would not want my father to touch.

She lay in her bed in the lighted room, seeming asleep, breathing lightly and rapidly, while her daughters turned out drawers and looked into cupboards. I came on the box full of my brother's letters from France. I began destroying them, then stopped. They can live with me, I thought: let someone else destroy them. I took the photographs of him, the young blurred image, a boy still, in the uniform of the Flying Corps, and the parchment *au nom du Président de la République,* awarding him his *Médaille Militaire.*

Laid under gloves in a drawer there was a letter from my father, written thirty-three years ago, in 1904. 'My darling wife, this wishes you Many Happy Returns on your Birthday. I am enclosing you £5 (five pounds) cheque to buy yourself something as a present. Well my Dear your welcome letter to hand well I am sorry you have such hard work and trouble with the children. You should let them run wild like animals that is what they are. It doesn't do any good making a fuss of them spending money on their clothes all they want is enough to cover them never mind looks. I don't give myself trouble about clothes and none the worse for it. Well we have had a lovely week. Sunshine all day and a smooth sea and this morning the sun is shining and a blue sky and 60° in the shade. I am happy and in good health and the air here is beautiful coming in the berth. Well my Dear I trust you are feeling alright and get all the sunshine you can for it will be best for you both for health and happiness. Now I will close with best love and best wishes and take care of yourself. Your loving husband Will.'

Very distinctly I saw the sea captain in his shabby uniform bent over the table in his cabin writing, in his backward-sloping hand . . . Why did she keep this single letter out of hundreds? Is it silly to think that, perhaps, under the bitterness, a single flicker, of warmth, regret, was still alive? . . . I put the letter in my pocket without showing it to my sister.

We found a large crudely coloured photograph of the three of us as very young children, my middle sister and Harold—he still in petticoats—smiling like idiots, I looking sullen and stolid. We laughed over it madly, and tore it up. I remembered suddenly that it used to stand in my father's cabin in the *Saxon Prince.* He must have brought it home, or it would have been sunk by the German cruiser in 1916, with his other possessions.

The night nurse came in as we were finishing. She looked closely at my mother and said quietly,

'She's going home.'

I would not take this in. Mechanically, without conscious effort, I refused. I went to bed and slept, in the next room, leaving her with the nurse.

Towards one o'clock the woman roused me. I went in. She died so quickly that even if I had cared to speak to her with other people in the room there would not have been time.

When I saw her again, it was daylight. Between them, the two nurses had made an image of her, lips upturned as never in life, an almost suave smile, not hers at all, her face ivory, small, ice-cold, fine soft hair drawn back from her arched forehead. Now I knew that she had really gone. It was a purely physical agony, a nerve being ripped out of me, slowly.

Downstairs in the hall I came on my father, standing at the foot of the staircase, crying. He was wearing the frightful suit, soiled and green with age, he insisted on wearing in the morning until he went out. I spoke to him awkwardly, with a false pity, and he turned his back on me, vexed. He cheered up later, and went out to be shaved in the town, first asking me if I had seen the chequebook of the joint account. I gave it to him and he took it away to his room. What a time he'll have going through the counterfoils, I thought.

When he came back, shaved, he handed me a paper bag. 'Here's something for you and the other one,' he said, smiling pleasantly. There were two grapefruit in it. He always bought these at Christmas, one for each person in the house. I suppose he had felt this was a day to be marked, and since the nurses had taken on all the business of a death, he had nothing to occupy him.

I kept going into her room to speak to her, when I could do it without anyone noticing. The cold of her cheeks shocked me, and the silence, but I could not let her lie there alone all day. (Why—since I had slept during her last night?) Each time, another piece of my life was ripped slowly out.

'I'm here,' I told her, 'I'm here, you're not alone.'

The agony came up again, tears poured down my face: I forced them back, and went away. No one must see me.

When she was alive, my father never entered her sitting-room. This evening, when the men brought the coffin, he came in. He was shivering with cold. He stood in the middle of the room, throwing quick glances round him, and said,

'I'll go out. I'll go out at the back.'

'Why?' I asked. 'Why go out? You're better here. Do sit down.'

He sat down in one of the armchairs, and began to talk about a pain in his chest. 'I shan't last long,' he said.

I despised him for trying to get attention and sympathy. Besides, he did not mean it; he had every intention now of living for ever. The men were walking about in the room overhead. I knelt and poked the fire noisily.

'Are you warmer?'

'Oh, I'm warm enough,' he said jauntily. 'I don't believe in warm rooms. Hers were always too warm for me. I've been forty-eight hours on the bridge in bad weather without so much as a hot drink. That's nothing, that's nothing.'

He laughed his short defensive laugh and went on talking about himself until the steps overhead ceased. Then he shambled away.

Later that night when I went into the kitchen, he had put aside his endless newspaper competitions—he never won anything—and was turning the pages of his scrap-book, and crying.

'Look,' he said, 'look what I've found.'

He pressed a long brown knotted finger on a yellowed cutting from some Australian paper. 'Y'see?'

I read the lines, shutting my mind against them.

'Then home, get her home, where the drunken rollers comb,
    And the shouting seas drive by,
And the engines stamp and ring, and the wet bows reel and swing,
    And the Southern Cross rides high!
Yes, the old lost stars wheel back, dear lass,
    That blaze in the velvet blue . . .'

'All them voyages,' he said.

What does he see? I wondered. A foreign quay that no longer exists as he knew it, blinding sunlight in a street in Vera Cruz, in Santos, in Montevideo, and a young woman who holds a sunshade over her as she walks with that light step towards the corner and the waiting cab, and is gone.

I left him sitting there. I had been sorry for him for a minute.

Shut in my room, I waited for him to come upstairs. When he had come and gone, padding quickly, almost silently, across the landing and up the further stairs, I went in to say goodnight to her.

'You're so cold,' I said to her.

I touched her hands, her cheek. The skin was soft.

'Goodnight, my love, goodnight, goodnight. Don't think about anything. The journey is over. Oh, my love, my love.'

Bitter grief hardened my throat and scalded my eyelids, and it was all no use.

The next day when I went in I saw that a faint colour had come into her cheeks. She seemed younger and vulnerable, and yet more nearly serene. This new image of her, this tranquil, inconceivably tranquil face, masked, at least for now, the tormented skull of the last days, and wiped out the image of the last few years, the blue fixed stare, the face which had become shapeless because her mind had given up bothering to mould it. Yet the last was what I ought not to forget.

I tried to recall other images of her. They must, each of them, have been familiar—the very young woman, tireless, the woman touched by time but still so eager to live. But nothing would come except an image drawn from a photograph, shallow and meaningless.

This smiling tranquil dead woman threatened to efface all the others. I turned away. Suddenly and piercingly, I saw her standing before the long glass in her other bedroom; she was trying on a new hat and looking at herself with such intentness that she seemed to be willing another self to step out from behind the one she saw.

My only chance of seeing her again is to catch her off guard in moments like this, I thought. And in sleep.

My father had been standing outside the room, waiting to say something. He was holding a painting on silk, made by a Japanese artist from the coloured photograph my sister and I had torn up. He gave it to me.

'It's no use keeping this,' he said hurriedly, 'since you're all going.'

I preferred not to glance at the abyss under the words—all but hidden from him, too. I am like him in the cowardice with which, when I can, I dodge an unpleasant reality.

It was her last day and night in her house. I went in and out of her room, and talked to her. The delicately flushed cheeks, the smooth rounded forehead, the smiling mouth, the rigid body, dreamed their own dream, indifferent to us, the living.

I stood there in the dark, alone as I had never been.

'This is your last night with us,' I said. 'Forgive me for all I have thought against you in vile moments, forgive me for all I did not do for you. Remember me only as the child I was, wholly in your hands.'

The searing grief ran over me. I felt drained of life, naked, and defenceless. Help me, I thought, help me.

That is a long time ago, many years. All but a few of the things she saw every day, and liked, have disappeared from my life. I keep a few. It is a long time, too, since I made the effort to see with her eyes the harbour, the old houses crouched against the side of the cliff, the abandoned shipyard, the old church, landmark for sailors, the fields and woods she knew. On the rare, very rare, occasions when I go back, no shadow comes to meet me. But—at any time since then I could have said this—the story is not at an end. Her life did not end then; it goes on echoing through mine, and will echo there until it and I are both silenced.

Chapter 13

For a long time I used to catch sight of her easily: she seated herself in a certain chair in her bedroom in my flat and looked with pleasure at the reflections of a vivid sunset in the tallboy (made in 1799 of mahogany for a Whitby shipowner and sent to China in one of his sailing-ships to be lacquered and brought back), or she came towards me from an old mildewed glass I had taken from her room. Objects have a long memory of their owners: her leather and silver travelling flask, when I touched it, had that instant been laid down by a hand swollen with age. These memories were wholly involuntary. I never sought them. A scene, a colour, a sound, split open as I brushed past it, and for an instant she was there.

In June, we went to France, and on our way to Royan stayed three nights in Bordeaux. The heat in that opulent city—which still, in some remote way, belongs to the English—was so heavy that it ran like a yellow oil down the old buildings on the quays, over the lighthouse columns, over the tracery of ships' cranes, and lay like a fog above the surface of the Garonne. I learned as a child the habits of a sea-captain's wife; it takes more than a violent sun to keep me from running about the streets of a foreign city, staring. I slept little —like Bordeaux itself that month. It seemed that only a few minutes separated the moment when I was looking at the Monument des Girondins, a white finger poked through the dusk, from the next when the rising chatter of scores of birds under my window in the Place des Quinconces woke me, and I got up to watch colour come rapidly into the sky over the harbour, obliterating first the street-lamps, then the single brilliant star.

On the second day we took a tram along the right bank of the river as far as a small village called Cambes. There was a very small hotel with a lawn of rough grass going down to the river and big coarse marigolds, and tables under the trees and on a wooden plat-form built out over the water. Barges passed very close, going down stream. At a table nearer the house, were three people who caught my eye, a boy and two middle-aged women, one in black silk with a great many old-fashioned gold chains and rings, dark-fleshed, her hair dressed in tightly-rolled curls over her whole head, the other also in black, shabby, leaning forward with an ingratiating smile, much too eager to please, or hoping for something. But it was the boy who attracted me. He was perhaps ten or eleven, very pale, with a head a little too big for him, the hair springing back stiffly, like fine wire. His hands, laid on his thin knees, were remarkable. He was frowning: obviously, I thought, he is both ashamed of his mother's anxiety and sorry for her, and a little anxious himself.

He and his mother were people I and James Hill had been looking for. The other woman, well-to-do and fleshy, I did not know yet, but I knew a little about her house in this village and its grotesquely ugly furniture and ornaments . . .

At that time—two years before the war in which it was flattened into piles of rubble—Royan was a little town of enchanting sim-plicity: a front, two beaches of clear sand, a street or two, a pleasant unassuming casino, a few hotels. The visitors were all French, no Germans, no English—bearded papa, plump vigilant mamma, chil-dren making no more and no less noise than birds, girls and sun-burned youths playing ball. My bedroom in a modest friendly hotel faced the sea, and after my coffee and croissants—served by the lean smiling overworked and completely indefatigable Joseph, who waited at table, ran up and downstairs with trays, swept, dusted—I sat up in bed and made notes for the full-length novel James Hill was writing, and read (since the central character was a musician) a life of Busoni, a volume of his letters, Berlioz's memoirs, and an account of van Dieren.

I have never known, and cannot imagine, a life of greater, more exquisite happiness.

On our way home in July we drove from Rouen to Arras through country which has been fought over so often that the dust must be more than half human, and certain names of rivers and villages are fixed in the brains of a great many living, and of a great many of the half-living—and who knows anything about the dead?—like nails. The country itself did not mean very much to me, but what I saw as a mere empty grass-filled depression between two fields, Guy saw alive with young bodies, restless with life. Many of them had now no other life. But there was one village—I have forgotten its name— where a few graceless new houses had been set down hurriedly in the middle of fields which still looked shabby and vacant: there were a great many coarse nettles and no trees. A long and unnecessary action had been fought here; it lasted for two days and a night, a short night, and some thousands of young men, English, were uselessly killed. Did the present inhabitants of this uncouth village ever feel that they were hopelessly outnumbered?

As soon as we were at home, I had to arrange for my son to start his training as a civilian air pilot, at Hamble. (Nowadays, that *air* before the word pilot seems superfluous. Not to me. When someone speaks to me of a pilot, I have first to rid my mind of a weatherbeaten face and robust body coming up the side of the ship, hand over hand, to take her into dock or to the mouth of the river.) He was twenty-two, tall, remarkably good-looking with his fair skin and speedwell-blue eyes: except that he had finer eyes and a long narrow head, he looked much as my father would have looked had he been carefully nurtured instead of starting at sea at the age of thirteen. Both had a northern look.

His single ambition was to fly. His career—what a word for so careless a passage—at Cambridge had been irretrievably altered by it. He went there to read for the Mechanical Sciences Tripos: in his first year, since he has a good brain, he did very well. Then, in October 1935, he was allowed to join the Air Squadron and thereafter did little except fly, and fall in love with a young woman a few years older than he was, a lively handsome creature, with whom he spent the time when he was not flying or making casual efforts to work a little. He listened amiably to his tutor's reproaches and complaints, agreed that he must do better, and continued to do as he pleased.

Very soon he was forced, with no regret, to give up hope of the Tripos. He did a little work, enough to earn a pass degree and lend him, for an hour or two, the disguise of a student. The rest of his time he spent, very happily, amusing himself and flying. He left Cambridge this year, when we were in Bordeaux, with his degree, a number of debts, and the young woman—she would have made a splendid wife to a less absorbed or more ambitious young man.

In my eyes he had changed little: looking at him I saw easily the engagingly beautiful child, amiable and quietly self-willed. The degree to which I was responsible for his indifference to success— no, his active rejection of anything except the one thing he wanted to do—is too clear. My restlessness, my profound loathing of a settled life, were being played through in another key . . .

The training at Hamble would take two years. He agreed readily —why not?—that it was impracticable to think of marrying before he had finished it. Now that he had got his way about flying, he was happy; he would wait, the young woman would wait; there were mitigations. I had no hope that a marriage I knew in my bones must end badly would not take place.

Chapter 14

Early in September, when Guy went to Spain to stay with his old friend Peter Chalmers Mitchell, I went with Lilo to Paris, taking with me—of course—a half-finished manuscript. I had agreed to live at the rate of her purse—she refused to help herself from mine —and she went ahead to find an hotel. She found it—a place meant for students—in the rue de l'Abbé de l'Epée, and engaged two attics. The rent in English money worked out at less than one and four-pence a night. You can easily imagine what, at that price, our rooms were like: low, narrow, a thin bed, a chair, a decrepit small table, a sort of wardrobe, all of the roughest sort and depraved by years of ill-usage, a strip of worn-out carpet, a cracked bowl and jug of cold water for washing. On my first evening I looked round it with unspoken dismay. No, this is too squalid, I told myself, I'm not young enough to live like this again. Lying down gingerly between the coarse sheets, I pushed from me a blanket which might be clean but did not look it—just as the stairs, polished by a servant who spent the whole day on her knees, had acquired a second membrane of hard ingrained dirt.

In the morning I saw that from my window I could look across the roofs of even shabbier houses to the dome of the Panthéon. In a strict light, the absence of all softness, all blurred lines, was suddenly exciting. Less than a quarter of a century ago I had been living, in London, in no better or more reassuring a room, without caring. I turned back quickly to rejoin a penniless young scholar hurrying to offer me her tireless body and joyously inquisitive mind.

I can live here easily for two months, I thought, oh, easily.

To say of Paris that it is cruel is a generalization for the simple. No city I know is so determined to endure, so clenched on an old root which reaches down, unbroken and still sappy—not only in carefully-preserved great buildings—in narrow foetid streets with overflowing gutters, squeezed between houses which have not had a sou spent on them in five hundred years, to the twelfth century. To stay alive for so long requires, no, involves, a certain detachment, not to say contempt for things and persons which are *not of the family*. Yet this city, this face stony with age, at moments wears a smile purely enchanting and as young as the infant born five minutes ago in a room of one of these ill-smelling dilapidated houses. Neither its hideous poverty nor its beauty contain it. At its coldest and most sordid it keeps a certain air of breeding, a suavity, little shaken by the barbarism of our age.

We breakfasted—a single cup of coffee (abominable) and a roll—in a small dark low-ceilinged bistro at a corner of the rue St Jacques—Abelard's rue St Jacques to the life and slippery gutter. A few workmen at the counter, taking their first drink of the day, had an air of unhurried enjoyment. Sometimes we lunched there, on another roll and a glass of yellow Anjou wine, cheap and instantly intoxicating—but the effect wore off before we reached the end of the street. This quarter was full of cafés, Chinese, White Russian, so cheap that Lilo was reluctant to dine anywhere else. Certain that I was being poisoned, I ate these appalling meals with a calm which went unadmired—except by myself.

To her overwhelming energy and curiosity, Lilo joined a ruthless discipline. We did not saunter through Paris, we walked, briskly, miles, visiting, quarter by quarter, museums, old squares, churches, palaces, the Louvre, modern painting in the Petit Palais, markets,

the outer boulevards, Montmartre, parks. To save myself from
dying of suffocation I took care, wherever we went, to look—that is,
look—at only one or two objects. This is why to this day I remember
every line and delicate feature of a thirteenth-century oak figure of an
angel, in (I think) the Musée de Cluny—long slender nose, curled
hair, strong childishly thin neck, closed lips turned up at the ends
in a smile of pure malice, which spread to the eyes with their suggestion of a pupil, and fine springing eyebrows. I remember it, too,
for another reason.

One morning, when we were in a café near the Halles, a young
porter came in, a magnificent animal, filthy and sweating. Lilo
looked at him with naïve admiration and greed.

'Look at that strong sunburned fellow,' she said gravely, 'I
should like to have him as my lover.'

'He'd probably beat you.'

'No, no, I should make him wash and teach him to respect me.'

'Never,' I said. 'Prussian though you are, he would defeat you.'

She laughed without resentment, a flash of her strong very white
teeth. 'Well, you are always right.'

It was the year of the Exhibition. We went several times, and
walked, in the torrid sun, from pavilion to pavilion, bored by the
loud-mouthed effrontery, smugness, or swaggering efficiency of the
great nations: only the smaller peoples know, or had remembered,
that a polite host effaces himself before his guests, does not bawl at
them, or insist on their admiring his wealth; again and again we went
back to the fountain of rose-water in the Bulgarian pavilion: the man
in charge of this unpretentious building, almost always empty, recognized us and came forward with a pleased smile. He had so little
French that he could only beckon us with gestures from one to
another of his few treasures, but he flattered each with his small
muscular hands, watching our faces to make sure we shared his
delight. Except for the enchanting fountain there was really very
little to see, but it had been arranged with intelligence, perhaps with
tenderness, and the effect, in the middle of so much that was alarming
or intolerably noisy, was very reassuring. After all, how young
Europe is.

Lilo had friends in Paris, an odd assortment. Where had she met
and impressed the Turkish writer, Halide Edib? We sat in the Deux
Magots with her for a long time, eating croissant after croissant,
for which she was going to pay, while she talked about her life in
Kemal Attatürk's army.

'I was a soldier, you understand me, I wore uniform, I fought as infantry-men fight. I was Kemal's friend, but when he made himself dictator afterwards, I turned against him, and left him and Turkey. Since then I am only a writer.'

Another afternoon it was a Jugoslav, a Professor Jovanovié, who invited us to the café at the corner of the rue Soufflot. To explain his politics to us, he raced through a history of Europe from the tenth century, smiling joyously as he presented first one and then another triumph of civilization—'*Donc, les autobus! Donc, les avions!*'—until he reached the crowning evidence, the Parti Paysan of Jugoslavia.

These were incidents: her closest friends, who became mine, were a lycée professor and his wife, Henriette and André Buffard. Any Englishman who has the luck to be invited by a cultivated Frenchman to his house or flat finds himself with delight in an atmosphere he has met only in the memoirs and letters of two or three finely cultured families of the late Victorian age. The affluence is missing, but the assured intelligence, the ease with which ideas are passed from hand to hand, the inborn goodwill and politeness of heart are there, as if these were still the only criteria of civilization. And with them a play of light, a gaiety, a cutting edge, which is not English at all, of any age.

Not only does André Buffard look as though one of his ancestors may have been a quick-tempered cat, he has a wholly feline independence of spirit, a little savage. Add that he is—there is no English phrase for it—*un coeur sensible,* an almost reckless sensibility, passionate to a fault—and you have, crudely drawn, the portrait of a natural anarchist, incapable of taking on trust an idea or a creed, instinctively mistrustful of received opinions, not because they vex him, but because they are hypocritical.

He was a close friend of another relentless individualist, Alain. His contempt for the politicians of the Third Republic was vitriolic. He mocked me smilingly when I said that another war was unthinkable except as a paroxysm of irrational fears.

'Why delude yourself that rational ideas have any place in politics? Certainly there may be war—there are enough idiots in all countries —and this time, this time, it will not unite France. You'll see.'

What I had seen or felt already was the curious difference between the war fear here and in England. I explained it to myself by the mere existence of frontiers: the Spanish war, now over a year old, roused violent feelings in England, but we did not feel the ground move under our feet. Open on three sides to Europe, the

French were less able to work off their fears in speeches from platforms.

Even the refugees from Germany—we knew several of these—living, many of them, in rooms shabbier and poorer than our attics, were tenser and more anxious. And this was not only because often they were really more insecure than their fellow-countrymen in London. One of them explained to me,

'It's infinitely more difficult to get into England than to get here, but once in England you are not continually harried, you have your papers. Here—' he spread his hands—'you can sneak in here without them, and then you spend your whole life trying to scratch together as many francs as will make all the difference between living, however uncomfortably, as a human being or as a louse, always in danger of being trodden on by the police, by a neighbour who dislikes Germans, by anyone.'

He was a gentle good elderly man, a painter of landscapes so innocently orthodox that he could, if he had chosen to close his eyes and ears, have gone on living comfortably in Munich: he was not a Jew. Here he lived in the city cellar of a house sinking under the weight of its age and filth, eating little but potatoes.

'They are cheap, and even more important, clean,' he said, smiling.

His closest friend was a young Berlin Jew called Emil, living, at the other side of Paris, in much the same conditions, except that his room was large and almost completely bare. One evening when we went there, the painter had carried across Paris the large water-colour he had just—a true miracle—sold. It was to be delivered, packed, to the buyer—a former patron, on a visit to Paris from Munich, who had accidentally discovered him here—at the Ritz next morning, and he was sure he could not make a decent parcel of it. Swathing it delicately in the clean remnants of a shirt, and paper he had begged from a shop, Emil said to me,

'Do you know what the fellow paid for it? I'll tell you.'

It was a very small sum.

He was whispering, but his friend overheard him and said reproachfully,

'Emil, you are still grumbling. And on a day when I am divinely happy.'

'He could have given you the proper price.'

'But,' the painter said gaily, 'he came to see me in my room, and he saw how little I spend. Why should he give me more?'

Both these men had the precious papers they needed not to be chased from their pitiful foothold; but they did not, for that, feel secure. Emil was working feverishly, like a spider, or like an old woman piecing together fragments of string, to get himself to America. It tormented him that he could not persuade the painter to move.

'You know, you can't trust the French,' he said urgently, 'at any moment they may round on us, they'd care as little what became of us as if we were stray cats.'

'I know, I know,' the other said, with his old man's innocent smile. 'But I can't run away any further, you must go, you have young legs. I'll take my chance here.'

No one in this room had better reason than I to be convinced that they were perhaps right to fear for their safety. The house I had just come from, to meet Lilo here, between Emil's bare cracked walls, had shaken more than one of my illusions. Listening to André Buffard's sarcasms about 'the other France', I had put down part of his savagery to an intellect which was all sharp edges. This afternoon I had with my own eyes seen 'the other France'—in a house in the seventh arrondissement. Impossible not to admire, coldly, the nearly inconceivable elegance of the women, an elegance no other country, even much wealthier, is able to bring off—I daresay unable to hit on the exact proportions of genius and hard-hearted insolence—and impossible to imagine anything more magnificent, more opulent, more imposing, brilliant, flawless, than the drawing-room itself, its rococo scrolls, curves, mirrors, chandeliers, and the rest.

I should have breathed easier in this room if it had been what it seemed, an incredibly lavish stage set.

The only person, apart from my half-American hostess, to whom I talked, a little, was a Madame de C., indecently rich, related by marriage to a Guermantes family. She introduced me to a middle-aged politician, slender, sinuous, bull-voiced, a human organ-pipe. I listened, at first idly, then with an astonished attention, to what they were saying to each other. Until this moment—although I had been told, not only by Buffard, that rich Frenchmen had only one emotion, the fear of losing their money, and would go to any extreme to muzzle persons and classes they suspected of being Reds —I had not believed that this feeling, if it existed, was strong enough to make two people, intelligent, without a drop of any but French blood in their veins, talk of Hitler as a Messiah and of an alliance with Nazi Germany as the quickest way—the politician's phrase— 'to castrate socialism and the Red swine once and for all.'

Madame de C.'s fine eyes softened as though she were going into
an ecstasy over a painting or a symphony.

'Castrate,' she echoed. 'Figuratively, of course. Why not?'

I had not the courage to say a word. I left them and wormed my
way towards the anteroom.

They are not, I said to myself, France.

I reached the arched doorway into the anteroom in time to see a
guest arriving alone. It was a long room. Two rows of footmen, tall
splendidly healthy young men, in silver and sky-blue, formed a lane
stretching its whole length. Along this lane the guest, a man, walked
rather slowly, the footmen bending before him like Lombardy
poplars in a wind. The two nearest the door, speaking together,
announced him, but I did not catch the name.

I watched him being politely mobbed. The celebrated writer who,
in the hour I had been there, had not altered by an eyelid his pose of
bored distinction, dropped it instantly, and began a deferential
sentence of which I understood only the first words.

'If your Excellency will allow me to . . .'

I had the curiosity to go back to Madame de C. and ask, 'Who is
it?'

She raised her eyebrows. 'Surely, you have met the German
ambassador?'

I thought: It is a rehearsal.

I did not entirely believe what I supposed I had seen. Certainly, I
told myself, if they could, these people would carelessly hand over
Emil and his friend and all the other refugees to be 'castrated'
(figuratively). But had they any power—except to live as the very
rich live?

After considering it uneasily for some time, I thought not . . .

The next day, we dined with Edgar Mowrer. I had not seen him
since the evening of the Hindenburg election in Berlin in 1932. He
and his wife had a fine apartment near the Chamber of Deputies, and
as we walked up the wide staircase I thought that these intelligent
Americans moving about Europe from one threatened country to
the other must have a vision of it which it would be interesting to
compare with that of a fifth-century monk meditating on the sack
of Rome.

With this in my mind, I was enchanted by his third guest, another journalist. Helen Kirkpatrick had the head, on a slender
American body, of the thirteenth-century angel in the Musée

de Cluny, the same firm delicacy of line, the same finely ironical smile.

During dinner I described yesterday's reception, no doubt exaggerating its flamboyance. 'But of course,' I said lightly, 'these people have no real influence or power.'

'Don't be too sure,' Edgar Mowrer said. 'Your Proustian epigones are a bad joke, but there are at least as many better-placed men and women, bankers, rich industrialists, politicians, who ardently admire and respect Hitler, here as in London. Monsieur X. may be more corrupt than most of them—no one believes that he cleans up less than a hundred thousand francs out of the Budget in the week before the new taxes are announced—but he isn't the only politician I have heard saying that he would rather give Chartres to Germany than see a socialist France. These people would feel *safer* as vassals of Hitler. Naturally they'd rather not go so far, but if they had to . . .'

'What has happened to this country?' Helen Kirkpatrick said, smiling. 'The French used to be fighters.'

I felt a prick of anger. 'Have you any idea how many Frenchmen were killed in the last war?'

'I'm only now beginning to realize *how* deeply that war weakened France,' Mowrer said. 'The standard of the reservists is very poor, and as for their generals! Weygand is so out of date it's not believable.'

I was experiencing a familiar difficulty in saying clearly what I thought; somewhere between my brain and my tongue the words fell into a helpless disorder. I said stuttering,

'I don't believe we, or the French, can be defeated by a people quite so intellectually repellent as the Germans . . . that frightful cold mysticism of theirs that makes them turn everything into abstractions—trees, the Rhine, human beings . . . They don't *see*, I mean, either things or people, they see abstractions they call the Volk, or the Jewish infection, or *Brutalität*, or . . . Our minds may be slow and untidy, but at least they're still in touch with the real world.'

'But there *is* something wrong with the democracies,' Mowrer said gravely. 'They didn't defend themselves in Spain—that war is lost, you know. Stalin doesn't give a damn about his Spanish friends —why should he, when neither your government nor the French can make up its mind which stinks worse, Hitler or Republican Spain?'

'England isn't France,' I said. 'We are still sound.'

'You may be right. But you threw away your last chance to trip up Master Hitler two years ago. If he had three divisions in the Rhineland that was the most. The French had four times as many behind the Maginot Line. My belief is they never had the faintest intention of trying to hold him off—they knew they couldn't. Now, the Germans are so strong that if you want to contain them you'll really risk a war. *Which you may very well lose.*'

If I had dared I would have said: Nonsense, the English don't lose wars.

It was what I thought.

I had a sudden uprush of fury—no doubt humiliated annoyance with myself and my tongue.

'If there is another war,' I said, 'we ought to scatter the Germans over the face of the earth afterwards.' I controlled myself. Looking across the table at Lilo, I said, 'I'm sorry.'

She gave me a warm brilliant glance. 'Perhaps five just men will be saved,' she said, smiling.

She left Paris a week before I did. The weather changed: overnight the bland honeyed warmth of September withdrew itself, and in the last days of October a cold west wind drove heavy clouds like Atlantic rollers across the whole sky.

I am never happier than when I am alone in a foreign city; it is as if I had become invisible.

The evening before I left I sat outside a café in the Place Théâtre-Français, watching the blown jets of the fountains and shivering a little: a fine rain, more mist than rain, more a cold breath than mist, clung round the street-lamps. If I were to stay another month, I thought, or if tomorrow morning I were to go south to Bordeaux, I could finish James Hill's novel . . . The daily business of living, about to close round me, would delay it.

If, I said to myself, you thought this or any novel more important than other things, you would not live as you do . . .

Before I could save myself, the finger of mist on my cheek had swept me as far north as Whitby: glancing over my shoulder I saw the flagged path across the fields behind her house, the line of bare trees, and on the left, across a valley, the hill rising steeply to the moors. How long before I cease to see this path and the two figures moving along it? Never. Unseen, unheard, unending, her life, like

mine, turns at the same point, on the same path, between the same
hill and thin pale line of sea.

Yet somewhere I had lost my way . . .

It was too cold to go on sitting here. I paid, and walked back to
my attic in the rue de l'Abbé de l'Epée. Refusing to think that it
was my last evening of freedom, I was very happy.

Chapter 15

The tension of the weeks after Hitler's triumphant march—a parody
of Wagner—into Vienna. Imagine a steel coil round the brain which
is slowly contracting. Or smoke thickening in the air from an
approaching fire. Any trivial incident reported in the papers, a
frontier shooting, a dictator's access of vanity, a speech by some
maniac, could mean that it had started and would go on from here.

On the afternoon of the 22nd of May I was with my young sister.
She was to go into a nursing home that evening, to have her second
child. The news was bad: Hitler had moved troops to the Czech
frontier and the Czechs were calling up their reserves, and the rest of
it and the rest of it. She said, casually,

'I suppose we shall be at war very soon.'

I supposed it too, but I said,

'It's not all that certain.'

She hesitated and with the same air of indifference—she would
cut her hand off rather than show fear—said,

'If it happens at once, where could we take the children—Nick
and the baby?'

'Perhaps to Canada? I know some people there.'

'Oh, no.' She shook her head. 'I didn't mean take them out of the
country . . . You don't know anyone who could tell you how serious
it is?'

'Yes, I do.'

With her watching me, I rang up Philip Jordan in London and asked him what the journalists and foreign correspondents he knew thought about the crisis. He was reassuring.

'If you'd asked me last night I'd have answered differently, but now the feeling is, strongly, that this isn't it, it's going to simmer down.'

I told Do. She smiled vaguely and calmly, without making any comment. Looking at her closely, I thought that she was too deeply absorbed in what was going on in her body, the child's movements there, to be much disturbed by anything outside. At thirty-one, she still seemed a girl of twenty—at most twenty. Her air of delicacy, the pure outline of her face, its brilliantly clear skin, hid a toughness, a northern toughness, that I had yet to see shaken.

Her daughter was born the next morning. In the afternoon when I went in to see her in the home, she said,

'I counted twenty-seven heavy planes flying over us about an hour ago.'

'Yes, it's an Air Day.'

Her expression changed very slightly. 'D'you know what I thought? I thought war had been declared and the Government was trying to reassure us.'

'Didn't you ask the nurses?'

'Of course not. They would have told me some silly lie. I waited for you.'

In June, as English delegate to the P.E.N. Congress to be held in Prague at the end of the month, I had to attend the dinner-party given by the London Centre before one of these affairs. I went with a light heart. The guest of honour was the Czech ambassador, Jan Masaryk, and, if nothing else, I thought, I can watch him.

Jan was an entertainment in himself, Elizabethan in its daemonic vigour and cheerful bawdiness, a miracle of wit and energy. He had more energy in his little finger than most of us in our whole bodies. Perhaps he enjoyed good food, wine, talk, and women, a little too much, but they did not destroy him. He enjoyed his life as might a fine animal who had been endowed with a human mind of the liveliest most acute sort. Even when he was unhappy, his dejection was shot through with an ironical gaiety as likely as not to issue in jokes that would have been in place in a barrack-room and did not endear him to the more formal of his diplomatic fellows.

'An outrageous buffoon,' one of these exclaimed.

'What,' I asked, 'outrages you more? That he sometimes plays the buffoon, or that he is not one?'

All I remember about the dinner itself is the speech made by old Henry Nevinson. In his nearly inaudible voice he talked about international decency and good faith, about Czechoslovakia, and the duty laid on us to help a small democratic country to defend itself against the lies, abuse, and threats heaped on it by a bully. I think he knew already that, for decent and indecent reasons, our statesmen had decided to try to buy peace by encouraging the bully to sate himself on this small country, and he was using up the last jet of his life's passion for justice, as, without thinking about it, he would have used the last drop of blood in his old veins. As I listened, I felt the deepest reverence for him.

After dinner, H. G. Wells, who was taking Masaryk and Baroness Budberg, a woman I admired very much, to his house in Hanover Gate, asked me to come with them. Afraid as I am of not being equal to the talk of very intelligent people, I was pleased. Not simply flattered. I would have gone anywhere to listen to Moura Budberg's voice. It is the most enchanting female voice I know, rather deep, but not too deep, with a double note in it which is indescribably moving. Goodness knows how many times, in a novel, I have tried and failed to describe it.

I suppose she was then in her middle forties, but she might have been any age; she was heavily-built and cared nothing about her looks—she had been beautiful—and dressed with lazy indifference. Why not? She has spiritual elegance. She belongs to a very rare class of human beings—if one can call a class that which is strictly a handful of unlike men and women who may lead lives of the greatest saintliness or the greatest amorality, without in either case ceasing to be given love and respect, since at no moment will they act against their nature, which is essentially good, sensitive, generous, and supremely tactful—that is, devoid, within human limits, of egoism.

H.G. loved and depended on her. His dependence took the form that evening of not wanting to let her out of his sight. When she left the room for a minute he followed her to the door, calling,

'Don't run away from us, my dear Moura. Where are you going? Don't be long. I want you here.'

She put up with his insistence as unselfconsciously as a child. Not that she was or is in any degree childish. It would be truer to say of her: She is a gentleman. There are honest gentlemen without a rag of charm: she charms as she breathes, naturally.

No doubt there are flaws in her—I certainly hope so—but what can they matter by the side of so much courage, warmth, nature, openness to life?

H.G. wanted to provoke Jan into indiscretions, the easiest thing in the world.

'D'y'know,' he said in his high weak voice, 'what a Conservative Member of Parliament, a woman, said to me the other day? "*After Czechoslovakia*, we may have to put our foot down." My dear fellow, there are men, powerful men, in this country who detest you and Beneš.'

Jan was in a ribald mood. Walking up and down the long room, twitching his lips like a clown, and drinking, he amused himself by imitating the Foreign Secretary.

'Oh, I know, I know. When I got the news about the German troop movements on the 20th of May, I went to Halifax with it and told him he must have enquiries made in Berlin. Halifax said, "You're always making us ask questions and we don't like it." I trembled, of course, but I insisted. I must know what the Germans are up to, I told him, because everything depends on me, and it's me they're attacking, not you. So Halifax told Henderson to ask Ribbentrop in Berlin.' He stood still, staring at us with eyes as impudent and lively as a schoolboy's. 'Your ambassador in Berlin is a scoundrel and a Fascist,' he said, smiling. 'Ribbentrop told him: Oh, just manoeuvres. And Henderson telephoned the Foreign Office that it was only the bloody Czechs trying to stir up trouble. Then more news came in, and back I went to Halifax and got him to tell Henderson to ask again. In the meantime we moved some troops, and this threw Hitler in a rage he worked off on Ribbentrop. So, when Henderson came in, Ribbentrop banged the table and spoke to him in language which has never been used in diplomacy. Not even by me. "What the hell do you mean by coming to me with this crazy stuff? Go and look after your ramshackle empire, which we're going to crack like a nut." So Henderson was annoyed and said, "What the hell do *you* mean by speaking to me like this. I'm His Majesty's representative, etc," and left. That helped us. Ribbentrop sent for our Minister in Berlin and told him, "Take your troops away, take them away, I say".'

He made a gesture I liked, scattering a pinch of dust with his fingers. 'Ah, if only he had said it to me!'

'You don't understand,' H.G. said maliciously. 'You think you're an outpost of western democracy, wonderfully civilized and all that. You don't torture your political prisoners. You have no concentration camps. You don't give anyone any trouble. If you did, we should begin to respect you, and write to *The Times* warning people to try to understand your proud, frank, loyal nature.'

Jan brought his hand down on the table with a single obscene word.

'I'm devoted to you, all of you, you're the nicest people in Europe. But why in God's name are you so afraid of—whatever you are afraid of? Why do you let Hitler go on making a balls of Europe? Are you hoping he'll leave you alone and attack Russia? Would you? Would you go after a bear, with a fat sow of a British Empire within reach of your foot? You're mad. No, no, I don't mean you or old Nevinson, God rest his soul. But what the devil is your pious candlestick of a Halifax telling the Nazis behind our backs? What does he think would happen if Hitler were able to swallow us? Peace and —— everlasting?'

The malice in H.G.'s voice sharpened to the squeal of a hack-saw. 'Not Halifax—another member of the Cabinet—said a week or two ago in my hearing: The Czechs are a nuisance in Europe, that fellow Beneš is a nuisance, a common adventurer. If Hitler goes in we shan't stop him.'

Jan shook with laughter, fingers splayed out on either side of his stomach. He had a stomach. 'I'm delighted to hear that your Cabinet finds Hitler well-bred and dependable, it must console them when he kicks their backsides. We poor Czechs—so ill-bred we even keep our promises—of course we stink.'

Without giving myself time to lose my nerve, I said,

'No, it's nonsense. We can't afford to drop you overboard. For our own sake.'

He rolled his eyes at me. 'Why not? You let the fellow march into the Rhineland, re-arm, grab Austria, threaten. Why not my poor ill-bred little country? You'll ask him to promise not to do it again, of course. And Halifax . . . oh, my God, Halifax. You know, my dear girl, you English really are too awful, too supercilious. I happen to think Heine the greatest poet in the world, also I was brought up on the Bible, and I told Halifax, "Listen. If the Germans tried to take away my Heine and my Bible, well, I'm afraid I should fight." And he said mildly and casually, "Yes, old boy, yes, old boy, that would be awful." I started to be riled, and said, "Well, if the Germans came here and took away your Shakespeare and your Bible, you wouldn't like that, would you?" He got excited at once and said, "By God, that would be terrible, terrible." I said, "You see? It doesn't matter a damn about my little Heine and my little Czech Bible, but your Shakespeare and your Bible, that's terrible! You don't care what happens to my soul, only about your own".'

He began to laugh at himself, and said sweetly,

'Halifax is a good sort of a man. He rides and he prays . . . He is even a sportsman. Y'know, he shoots birds. So, when one of our policemen killed those two Sudeten chaps in Eger with one bullet, and I went to tell Halifax, and he sat there trembling and wringing one hand—the other is paralysed—and repeating, "The fat is in the fire, the fat is in the fire," in a shaking voice, I said, "Well, after all, Halifax, he got a double".'

He roared with laughter. His excitement was beginning to run away with him pleasantly.

'Our mobilization in May went off without a hitch,' he said, shouting, 'two hours quicker than we expected. And you know what? There isn't a Prussian second lieutenant who isn't ashamed to his guts of the march into Austria. The bloody fools drove tanks from Munich, three hundred miles, they were ditched all along the road. Why didn't they take the train or come by steamer like sensible people?'

For some time H.G. had been fidgeting in his chair as though he were tired of listening. He said in the strongest voice he could manage,

'I take it that, in Prague, I shall have a chance to talk to Beneš alone?'

Jan stared at him. 'Certainly. I'll arrange it.'

'I shall tell him the exact truth. Whether he likes it or not. I shall say, "Don't delude yourself, the men who have all the power in London and Paris don't love you. Or democracy. Their bank credits matter to them, nothing else. If you're relying on us to lift a finger to help you you're off your head. We haven't the slightest intention of risking trouble. If you'll take my advice you'll make terms with Russia. Now. Before the worst. It's your only chance—a risk, of course, but safer than trusting us. Or France." If he won't listen to me . . . well . . .'

He opened his hands and let Beneš fall to the floor.

'Ah, to hell,' Jan said, grinning. 'Of course the Germans are going to march in. We know it, and we shall fight. And lick them.

Every Czech man, woman and child, is ready to fight. In Prague last week I was talking to the archbishop. He said, "Though I am an archbishop"— y'know, he had all his robes on and you could see he wasn't Pavlova—"if Hitler came into this room now I would strangle him with these hands".'

He rocked from side to side, ready to burst with pride in his country, and so confident that I was tempted to tell him to knock on wood. Why didn't I?

When we left, at midnight, it was still warm in the streets. London was wide awake, people sauntering, standing under lamp-posts, and in doorways in each other's arms. The searchlights were closing in on an aeroplane, so high up there was no sound from the engines: caught in them in the dark sky, it looked like a very small weak moth.

Masaryk drove the large open car as though he enjoyed it, with terrific energy, talking all the time.

'Y'know, he's not a joke, Hitler, but when he says that as a passionate architect he can't bear the thought of Prague abandoned to the Czechs, you laugh, my God, you laugh.'

He put an arm round my shoulders. 'Who cares if you rat on us?' He laughed pleasantly. 'We have our army.'

Chapter 16

When we reached Prague it was already dark. My bedroom in the hotel in the Václavské Náměstí—the names were a reminder that we had crossed a frontier into another Europe—looked down on to a restaurant in the courtyard of an old building, not more than five or six small tables, a lamp on each, no other light: it had the look of a stage set, the opening scene of a ballet; at any moment the next to principal dancer would come on and begin his delicate lively steps between the tables with their motionless couples. It was deeply exciting, an old memory, its start far off at the very beginning of my life.

In the morning, after sitting for two hours, oppressed and silent, through a meeting of the Executive Committee, delegates from all over Europe under the chairmanship of an imposing Punch figure, Jules Romains, I walked about Prague, alone. The hot dry light-fingered sun made me feel that I could walk here forever. That and the exquisite pleasure of being in a city where the past is still confidently alive. A double past, mediaeval and Baroque. Other capital cities, as splendid, as careful to preserve their old buildings, are in comparison stiff and wrinkled. In Prague the seventeenth century has kept the ease, the supple limbs, the smile, the amiable boldness, of a young man. This week, too, the streets were full of the Sokol striplings, carelessly lively and free-stepping, the girls hardly less broad-shouldered than the boys, and older men in red shirts, with the Sokol coat flung across a shoulder, like soldiers off duty. Trained in groups, in villages and small towns, to the same music, when they came together for the first time in the Stadium they moved as a single body, a vast ballet.

To look at these confident children, brought up to the free use of their bodies and minds, and remember whose hand was reached out to strangle their country—oh, intolerable.

Later that day I watched a score of them, fresh from their village, marching through the streets as lightly as if they were at home in this superb city. As they were. Jiřina Tůmová, the secretary of the Czech centre, was with me, a small slender young woman; her face, colourless from exhaustion, was so small and narrow you could have cupped it in a hand, and she had a quick ravishing smile.

'See how gay they are,' she murmured, 'and proud, like dancers. When we train them for the Sokols we take care they are not stiff like Germans. It is a *free* discipline. They must be as if springing from their soles on the ground. You see?'

In the garden of the Ministry for Foreign Affairs that evening, she slipped from one group of chattering writers to another, listened for a minute, and moved on. With their instinct for what is perfect in itself, the Czechs had not brought out lights. In the half-luminous June night, the seventeenth century, smiling, vigorous, suavely self-possessed, had the Černín palace and its garden to itself.

'They are happy?' she asked me anxiously.

'You can see they are.'

'Yes—' she laid on my arm a light cold hand—'but do they know how madly hard we are working, so that no one shall be ignorant or too poor? When they go home will they tell the truth about us? Don't mistake me, my darling—' listening to the English, she had taken the word to mean 'my friend'—'I know that none of you will tell lies. You will write that Prague is beautiful, that we are kind and stubborn and eat a great deal of goose and dumplings. But . . . tell me, please, why does your Government not say to Hitler, "These dull sober obstinate Czechs are our friends, do not threaten them"? Why?'

'We can't let Germany overrun you,' I said uncomfortably. 'For our own sake. We're as selfish as any other nation, but we're not out of our minds.'

I could just see her face, paler than usual. She was not smiling.

'I hope you are truthful, my darling, as well as kind and clever. And I must tell you—if our friends refuse to help us, we shall fight without them. But I am sure you will not refuse. And France—' her voice rose to a bird note —'the French will never fail us. They have promised.'

'Do great nations always keep their promises to small ones?'

She was more than a little shocked. 'You are talking about France!'

She and Jan Masaryk, I thought, are two unlike faces of the same coin, the same country. I suspected that there was another Czech, shrewd, hard, with the hidden malice of a peasant, subtler than he seemed, and capable of a simple brutality as unlike the planned bestiality of his enemy as possible.

She and her husband, a doctor, took me back to the hotel in an open car. In the darkness I could only see that he was young, with a calm friendly face. He stopped the car at the other side of the river and told me to look back. The castle had been flood-lit, with the utmost delicacy and subtlety. Lifted up by its hill as by a dark wave, Hradčany rode at anchor above six hundred fathoms. I looked at it with joy, my God, what joy—and grief because in six minutes an airman could wipe out an angelic beauty that had stood for six hundred years.

'You have a superb country,' I said.

'And we shall keep it,' Jiřina said very calmly.

The next afternoon I was with her in the Street of the Alchemists, a narrow lane close to Hradčany. Its absurdly small mediaeval houses leaned against each other in the sunlight. H. G. Wells and Jules

Romains had asked for an interview with Beneš, and were with him in the castle now.

'What are they going to say to him?'

The warmth and the light made me reckless. 'I can tell you. They are saying that the only people in France and England who admire you for your reasonableness and honesty are middle class liberals and intellectuals, of no importance and without any influence. If you murdered Jews and socialists, and had a great many aristocratic families and powerful financiers, you would have many more useful friends.'

She shrugged her thin shoulders. 'You are joking, my dearest.'

'Not entirely.'

'Well, we are not afraid,' she said lightly. 'If we are forced to fight we shall. All the children you have seen will fight. And all the old. And we shall win.'

Later, Moura Budberg told me that H. G. Wells had said what he intended to say. Had warned Beneš not to trust too much in his English ally. And Beneš had smiled. It was impossible, he said, smiling, that self-interest, if nothing else, would not compel a rich civilized country to protest against international robbery with violence.

What Jules Romains had said she did not know, or did not tell me. No doubt he had been diplomatic and eloquent.

The P.E.N.'s International President had eloquence to spare. Behind a table or a rostrum, the shortness of his body was less noticeable; his large head, its features at once heavy, wooden, and delicate, impressed, even while it made an English listener think of Punch (without his friendly hunchback).

From where I sat to hear his speech when he addressed the Congress, I could see Jiřina: she was listening gravely, but with so clear and delighted a satisfaction that I began to listen to him more attentively. It is what the reporters scribbling at their table will call just and moving eloquence, I thought. Very just about the dangers facing the world, very eloquent about the deaths of civilizations, and with a curious echo—the sound a finger-nail would make tapping an empty vase.

'*Soyez sages, modérés, appuyés sur une tout à fait bonne conscience, équitables jusqu'à la générosité. Gardez-vous des maladresses, cela va de soi; mais gardez-vous au moins autant d'excès d'habilité; de cet excès d'habilité qui a fait quelques années tant de mal ici et là . . .*'

Did he, I wondered, think that a good conscience would serve in place of allies? Had he advised Beneš to be generous? To whom?

Such an abundance of crypto-clichés seemed excessive even for a French rhetorician . . .

I had looked at the baroque sculptures in the superb Valdštejn palace and noticed, for the first time, that there is a trace of cruelty in the smiles and bossed eyelids of these voluptuous angels, and in the delight certain monks and priests were taking in their own sufferings. This evening, the Minister of Education had arranged for *Romeo and Juliet* to be played, in Czech, in the garden room of the palace. There can be no more beautiful room in the world. Giovanni Marini built it, a few years after Shakespeare's death, at a moment when the energy of the century was approaching the height of its exquisite curve. We sat in darkness in the garden and watched the dancers move quickly and lightly up the shallow steps, and through the triple archway of white columns into the great room. The young men ran, fought, argued, with ravishing energy and boldness. Words I could not understand rang like gold coins, so new and un-handled that they might have been only just written down in time for the first performance. It was shockingly new. There was a moment when Mercutio, who must at that moment have cried out 'I was hurt under your arm,' turned his head towards a foreign audience he could not see with an extraordinary air of contempt. It reminded me of Jiřina saying, 'We shall keep it,' and my spine felt cold.

I was sitting beside Henry Nevinson. In one of the brief intervals, tired and a little sunk, he glanced round him—black trees, a sky the colour of blackish plums, swallows and flittering bats. Suddenly he took hold of my arm in a painful grip, long dry fingers.

'To think, Storm, that all this will go on and on, and in a few years I shan't be alive to see it.'

I don't remember what I answered. What answer could I have made to staunch *that* wound?

Are there left such men as Henry Nevinson was? Passionate quixotes who feel injustice anywhere in the world as a nail driven into their own flesh?

After we got home, he wrote three or four times a month in a hand which over the years became more and more broken and thread-like. I answered every letter and kept a few, out of piety. His house was damaged in an air-raid, he had to leave London, and his letters became the bitter complaints of 'a useless old man'.

'Can it be possible that we must spend another winter in exile? I had hoped to patch up our house, but it would be too expensive for the risk of another blast. I fear now that I shall die far from the centre, my inward life, and you. I look at the churchyard here and I don't like it, I should so much prefer a chariot of fire. I don't think even you can imagine what joy two days in battered London gave me. Here in Campden all is beautiful, but on every side an angel with a burning sword stops me and asks, "What dost thou here, Elijah?" I am saying goodbye to all my friends, but I will not say it to you yet . . .'

To whom were these scores of letters written? Not to me, not to any flesh and blood woman. To an echo, to the answers his own youth sent him.

It saddened me to watch this incomparable fire burning out, shielded by Evelyn Sharp's thin gentle hand. When he died in 1941 it was a ghost who withdrew from all the places he loved. Sitting immediately in front of me in the chapel, Evelyn looked too small and slight for so many heaped-up flowers, such a weight of death. When, to watch the coffin disappear, she stood up, she made the movement with her arms that a tired woman makes at the end of a hard day.

The Czechs had arranged a journey for us across the country to a summer hotel in the High Tatras, the mountains and mountain lakes on the Polish frontier. That was for the English. With a fine tact, they arranged for the French delegation something less spectacular and slightly more sophisticated and, above all, in another place. We travelled together as far as a Slovakian village.

A memorial service was being held there, in the single street. In 1918 four hundred Slovakian soldiers had refused to fire on a company of Serbs; their colonel, an Austrian, ordered the company to be decimated, and one of the forty young men on whom the lot fell came from this village.

There was a tablet, a file of soldiers, and a handful of peasants, men and women. An officer and the Lutheran pastor shared the clumsy platform.

Standing in the hot sun, we listened to the preacher's trumpet of a voice. Suddenly he spoke in bad English.

'Do not be afraid, Englishmen. We do not fear.' He smiled at us sternly. 'N'ayez pas peur. Nous, nous sommes heureux.'

The officer, too, was clearly a peasant, with a great beaked nose

and large hands. He spoke in a curt voice, each word a blow. The
Czech writer who was standing behind me muttered,

'He says: This soldier who was murdered by Austria is your
lesson. All of you, men and women, get it by heart.'

The officer stepped back, and a big lean man in a shabby French
uniform sprang forward and began to speak with a strong American
accent.

'English friends, I love America, I lived there honourably when I
was young. I say to you that we, peasants, have no time for things
of the spirit. You must enjoy them for us, you must keep them alive
same as we for three hundred years kept our freedom alive in our
hearts. Thank you. Glad you came.'

Climbing into our motor-coaches, we rushed away to a town
smaller than many English villages. The town band met us and
played us in, and we sat down in a great barn to a feast—soup, roast
goose and pork, cabbage with carraway seeds, dumplings, roast
chicken, salad, strawberries and thick cream, rich cakes, eight sorts
of bread—the whole grown, reared, given and prepared by the
women of the little town. It was a divine feast; I have never eaten
a meal like it, not in Paris. A torrent of fine white Mělník wine and
powerful home-made slivovitz poured down our throats. My tongue
loosened by it, I made an emotional speech, followed by one of the
French writers. Would we help them to defend Czechoslovakia? No
question, we were their allies, we would fight with them. Roars of
Na Zdar and, 'Come again!'

'Come again—you are our friends!'

'Next time,' shouted a young Slovak, 'bring your rifles with you.'

He laughed, his French and English friends laughed, the musicians
fiddling for dear life laughed. A troop of peasant cavalry had been
waiting, and galloped beside the motor-coaches for a mile, then
turned back, laughing and waving. I had the strongest possible impression that there was nothing to laugh about.

In Bratislava the Slovak P.E.N. was waiting to entertain us. I
have forgotten how they did it—no doubt the Danube was called in
to help. I remember two things. The face, charmingly serene, a
little the Flemish madonna, of the chairman of the Slovak P.E.N.,
Marina Pauliny—I sat next to her at dinner, we talked about the
Czechs, and for the first time I realized that they were not one but
two nations.

'They are a fine people,' she said carefully, 'but they look on us as their young brothers, who must be taught. We are less cautious, less—what shall I say?—*serviable*, but we are a nation.'

(Rather more than a year after this evening, she reached London through France, and in 1942, when I was living there, came several times to see me. She was so confident of returning to Bratislava that there were hours, days, when she forgot that, turning a corner, she would not see the Danube. Immediately after the war, she contrived to get herself a seat in one of the first aeroplanes going back; it crashed as it left the ground and caught fire.

It happens sometimes that I drive past Blackbushe airfield. I don't forget to pray shortly for the soul of Marina Pauliny, as she would expect of a friend. Not that her spirit would hang about that desolate place, it would go back directly to a country untouched by cruelty or violence, the only one it remembered.)

The other thing I recall was the walk I took, after dinner, with a professor of the Komensky university, Otakar Vočadlo. We sauntered along an embankment, the Danube moving with us silently in the darkness. Almost silently. Now and then an under-water sigh or whisper interrupted for a moment what my companion was saying. He was in love with England and English literature, and he spoke very simply about the time he saw coming when his fluency in the language would be useful to English soldiers.

I—even I—was exhausted by the travelling, the long days, and the effort of enjoying banquets where I was forced to make a speech. The kind of lucid penetration fatigue gives the brain before numbing it made me notice that there was nothing forced about his confidence in us: he believed—as a man believes in the friend he has known all his life—that, when Hitler attacked his country, we should come to its help. He did not rest his certainty on the sensible idea that, in our own interest, we could not let one of our friends be murdered. He *knew* that Chaucer, Shakespeare, Keats, Byron and the others would not let him down.

Shortly after Munich, in October, I had two letters from him, written without emphasis, his anger and disillusion well in control. In the first there was even a flicker of humour: he wrote on the paper of the Anglo-American Club of Slovakia, of which he had been president, and noted, 'This club is dead now, but I have to use up the stationery!'

'. . . across the Danube, where I walked with you after the P.E.N. banquet, I could see tonight a huge swastika made of electric bulbs. The Nazis have occupied the right bank and they don't let us forget it. But that is nothing compared with the invasion of purely Czech towns and villages. However I shall spare your feelings. It's according to the old *vae victis* formula. The difference is that we were *not* defeated but betrayed and, what is worse, prevented from defending ourselves, by our allies and friends . . .'

He went on calmly, giving me news of writers I had met, and of his plans. He had convinced himself that, whoever had betrayed him, it was neither Chaucer nor Byron.

On that June evening several of his sentences began with the words, 'I foresee . . .' Neither of us foresaw the moment, not many weeks in the future, when an English journalist, stopped on the Hungarian frontier by a single Czech guard, almost a boy, asked, 'Can we cross into Hungary?' and was answered, with a contempt that cut to the bone,

'You're English? Then you won't have heard—we Czechs haven't any frontiers now. Go where you like.'

Chapter 17

After Bratislava the English were alone for three days in an hotel in the mountains—almost completely alone; it was not the season.

I was born and bred by the sea. To be surrounded by jagged peaks of mountains cutting off the horizon keeps me awake. I feel that I should keep an eye on them. It was all I did—from the edge of the truly splendid lake. I could see them twice—when I lifted my eyes and again when I looked at the water; every rock and snow-veined crest was engraved in it as by an acid. The more energetic climbed to a pass where they could stand and look down into Poland; one of them, on the way down, took her shoes off on a smooth path; a solitary German tourist stopped her, pointing at her feet, and asked with grave eagerness, 'On what system do you walk bare?'

When the others left Czechoslovakia to go home, I took the train to Vienna. I was to stay a few days with Toni Stolper's sister, Anna. I went reluctantly—surely, I thought, they could not have wanted the trouble of a visitor now, when they are preparing to leave the country.

My first sight of Anna Jerusalem, in the doorway of the pleasant shabby house in the nineteenth district—Paradisgasse 20—reassured me. A human being of such goodness, such simplicity—not naïve— would not resent me, even now.

In her late middle-age Anna had kept the thin angular body of a schoolgirl, quick, a little awkward, direct. The clearest sign of age in her sallow face was in her eyes, large and dark, a little sunk; they were far older than she was, with the age and half-tragic half-humourous wisdom of her people. There are times when I feel that only Jews and Chinese are really civilized: no doubt each of them has, as a people, grave faults, but they are incontestably more philosophic than the rest of us.

When I asked her, Anna said that yes, they were arranging to leave, the children first, then perhaps, no probably, she and her husband, a professor of history, retired. The eldest daughter, the most brilliant, had already settled in Palestine, and the tall young son was on his way there. Time was running out, a Nazi official had been twice to look over the house, and . . .

'And we have been lucky,' she said, smiling. 'One morning not long since a storm-trooper came here and took away Leni and her sister to clean the Nazi barracks. I begged and implored him to take me instead. And do you know what he said to me, that boy? He said, "But would *you* let your mother go in your place?" He was shocked!'

'What happened?'

'Oh, in less than an hour they were back. I had a servant for years —until the order forbidding Aryans to work for Jews. She heard about it, and rushed off to the barracks, and rated the Nazis until they were thankful to send the girls away.' She smiled, her sad clown's smile. 'I don't think that would happen anywhere but in Vienna. But I must get them away as soon as I can. Next time we might not be lucky.'

I followed the glance she sent round the room. It caressed lightly, one after another, without showing any unjust preference, all the things, the old chairs, tables, a pile of linen sheets, worn thin, the set of small gilt and white coffee cups, she had loved and served all her married life with the gentleness, pride, and essential innocence of her love for her family. It seemed at the moment only absurd that the paranoia of an Austrian-born ex-corporal should deprive them of her.

Not she, a secretary of our Embassy, warned me not to be taken in by the dull surface, dulled by a foul breath, of Nazi Vienna. Under the surface, unpleasant things were happening, an unknown number of suicides, many arrests, a few known incidents of torture—a great many brutal confiscations. 'There is always the Danube,' an official told the young Jewish surgeon whose hands they had deformed beyond repair after taking away all his other possessions. He had asked, 'What shall I do?'

I told him I had to go to our Consulate.

He frowned. 'You won't enjoy it.'

When I went into the courtyard I understood him. It was filled to suffocation by men and women, Jews, hoping for visas: they stood, pressed closely together, some patiently, others angry and scolding; there were even children, gripping the skirts of mothers they hardly knew any longer, so changed were they by waiting and fear. Some of them had been coming day after day without getting near the stone steps leading up. A harrassed consular staff was forced to keep the door locked on the inner courtyard, letting in two or three at a time. The instant the door opened, an eddy set towards it, like the dead eddying and whirling about the blood poured out by Odysseus. I was ashamed to have thought this. What right had literature, even the greatest, here? And even more ashamed, after hesitating for a long time, of holding up my English passport when the door opened again, so that I was let in at once. I had promised one of the German refugee writers in London to ask if a young Viennese actress about whom he was anxious had passed through their hands.

The clerk who searched rapidly through the lists for her name did not find it. 'That doesn't mean she is still in the country. There are other ways of getting out.'

'How many of these people get a visa?'

He shrugged his shoulders. 'Not a great many.'

'What will happen to the rest?'

'Oh, if I knew! Probably nothing. Perhaps they will go back to the days of the ghetto. After all, they can't be killed off, can they?'

I spent hours every day walking about Vienna. After only four months of German occupation it had become a dull provincial city, the cafés half empty, the shops disfigured by paintings and blown-up photographs of Hitler and placards announcing that they were—or were not—in Aryan hands. The Germans could not be blamed for the unseasonable rainy cold, but like the notices forbidding Jews to enter parks and museums it seemed part of the spreading tide of pus.

And yet, and yet . . . With every step I took in the streets between Kärntnerstrasse and the Graben, another Vienna came briefly to life. June in Vienna in 1930 was cloudless and very hot. Walking about these same streets, then rippling with light, I stared into every shop in search of the right present to take my mother. It was always the same when I was abroad; until I had found her present I was anxious and fretted. What in 1930 I found, after days of looking, precisely in this small shop, in this narrow lane still blessedly free of obscene notices, was a bed-jacket of soft white wool, cunningly knitted, and almost weightless. She liked it—so much that she kept it between layers of soft paper and rarely wore it. I found it after she died and gave it to the two women who were dressing her, telling them to put it on her.

I stood there, in the fine chill rain, letting the threefold images dissolve into one behind my eyes—then, now, always—always the same moment, in which I was drawn backwards by so many threads that I knew as little where I was going as a sleepwalker.

I meant to lunch in the Hofkeller. Eight years ago we had taken most of our meals there. The food was admirable: a door at the back of the inner room led into the old Imperial cellars, and on our last day we bought six bottles of strong Tokay and two of yellow Chartreuse. The manager had become our friend, he told us where to go in the city and out of it, and one blistering Sunday took us by train and cable-car up the Raxalpe and made us walk down it into the valley. Long before we reached the bottom, my knees were on the point of collapse. To encourage me, Rudi pranced ahead on the steep path, jerking his broad middle-aged body from side to side, crying, 'Look at me, I am a horse, a little horse!'

He sat with us evening after evening, talking about himself with endless vivacity. In 1914 he was a waiter in a London restaurant: interned, he escaped in the last year of the war, stowed away in a Dutch boat, and walked across Holland and Germany to Austria, where he was put in jail. I asked why. He spread his hands. 'Why not? I might have been a scoundrel. I was lucky. "You are unfit for the army," they told me, "find yourself a job." So I apply to the Imperial Hotel. "Yes, you can have a job, but you must first get a dress suit." "Where?" By now, in 1918, there is nothing to buy in Vienna. "Perhaps you get some clothes from someone who has died." I look round and I hear of a woman whose husband is killed, and I buy collars and two shirts from her. Then I hear of another woman whose husband was a waiter and he has just been killed, and from her I buy, cheap, his suit. So in June 1918 I start in the chauffeurs' room, then outside, then in the dining-room. In November I give notice, not enough money—no tips. The manager sends for me and says if I stay now he will give me a good place later. So I stay. In 1919 I am afraid to leave. The other hotels have closed their restaurants, only in the Imperial is there food, plenty of food, white bread, meat, at terrible prices. Because of it, because if people knew, don't you see, they had to be very careful who they took as waiters. There was one very old waiter—Fürst. He knew all the Archdukes from children, he used to force them to order the most expensive dishes, lobster at fifty shillings a tiny slice and so on, nagging at them until they gave in, cursing. He was an idiot. One day at my table the customer said to him, "Fürst, I don't feel very well in my stomach, I want something very light." "Well, Excellency, we have some fine boiled beef and cabbage." "Get out, you fool!" So Fürst brings him the beef. The man doesn't touch it. "Did he pay?" Fürst asks me. "Yes, and he is very angry." "So long as he paid!" Then, in 1924, an industrialist I served every evening asks me to manage a hotel he has bought. The manager of the Imperial is so furious he almost strangles himself, but after two years he sends for me again and offers me the job of managing the dining-room. The industrialist has died, and I play a trick on his widow to release me from my contract. Then, last year, it is the Hofrat who sends for me. I know what he wants, but I go into his room and ask, "Well, Hofrat, what do you want with me?" "There is something wrong with the Hofkeller," he says, "it loses money. Do you know what is wrong?" "Yes, I know, and when I am employed I tell you. But first, what terms do you offer me?" Well, we argue a little, and in the end I make my own terms, perfectly fair good terms, I am an honest man: he must employ my wife, and he must give us a room in the Hofburg. So—here I am—as you see me, safe, well-off, as safe as the Hofrat himself. I crack my fingers—' he cracked them with a noise of tearing calico—'at the manager of the Imperial, at the politicians, at generals. No more changes. I know exactly what will

happen in the world—that is, in Vienna, that is, to Rudi Göldner—
for the next thirty years. Nothing. Nothing!'

He laughed, throwing his arms out. 'Look at me. An absolutely
free happy man.'

I went, more than a little reluctant, ready to turn back, down the
steps from the narrow Schauflergasse into the outer room. Rudi was
there. He knew me, but spoke without a trace of friendliness, and
sent a boy to serve me. I ate a dull uninspired meal, drawing it out
until I was alone in the place, so that as I passed him on my way out
I could say quietly,

'Vienna has changed.'

He gave me a sullen cold glance. 'Yes. For the better. Everything
is better.'

The rain had stopped, but it was still cold. I walked through the
outer courtyards into the Josefs-Platz and stood, my back to the
Pallavicini palace, looking towards the corner between the Re-
douten-Säle and the great Library, where, in 1930, an improvised
platform with a single lamp held the singers. It had been dark, a soft
warm night. Three or four rows of chairs faced the narrow platform:
waiting behind them for the opening notes of the Nachtmusik, a
silent crowd of Viennese, too poor to pay to sit down: some had
bare feet. Windows had been opened in the palace and in a few of
them an oil lamp, turned to its lowest, did no more than thicken the
shadows round a listening figure. In those years Vienna, still shabby
and straightened, brought to its sharpest pitch one of the oldest
pleasures in the world: music heard in the open air, at night. At no
other time, in no other place, have I listened to anything more
moving. And contrived by the simplest means. Showing that, thrown
back on themselves for the essentials, most people do not need to be
told how to live. (In 1945 I saw this again in the rubble of Warsaw.)

I was alone in the Josefs-Platz with, coming towards me from a
low doorway, the ghost of an exquisite happiness. What was happening in Vienna did not disturb it.

Egoist!

Chapter 18

At the end of the week I went to Budapest. On the Hungarian side of the frontier, the uniforms became sadder and dirtier, and the young man who checked my passport had the face of a diseased rat. Suddenly, pressing a yellow finger on the first page, he glanced up at me with a smile of astonishing sweetness.

'Ah,' he said, '*orter*!'

Was he an author himself?

In the hotel I was given a room on the fourth floor with a narrow stone balcony. It looked across a noisy square and across the Danube to Pest. In the evening light without sun, the river ran grey and oily. There were barges. Looking down into one of them as I crossed the bridge, I saw two, no, three naked children lying asleep, knotted together like little snakes. Farther along the embankment there were large buildings and cafés, but I was afraid to go into one of them. Besides, I was running short of money. I chose an unpretentious café near the bridge and ordered coffee and rolls: since I had eaten nothing since breakfast in Vienna I was hungry, but the happiness of being alone in a strange city was all I needed to satisfy me, and the coffee was very good: so were the rolls. Pretending to be absorbed in a German newspaper, I made these last out.

When I had finished it was fully dark, but I could not bring myself to go back to the hotel without at least glancing at Pest. The street-lamps along the embankment, and the lighted cafés and hotels, made it seem any capital city, but in the streets like walled drains open to the sky, running away from the river at this end, there were few lights. The black gaping mouths of courtyards gave out a sour breath—earth, sweat, excreta, and another pungent spicy smell I could not identify. I turned back. This place stank of violence in a way Vienna, for all its Nazi jails and barracks, did not.

The next day was very warm, light pressing down on the streets from a white-hot sky. I decided that coffee and bread every two or

three hours was an excellent diet in such heat. Both were very good
here, even in the smallest cafés; the bread was the best I have ever
eaten, better than French bread. I spent the day sitting in the gardens
and bastion of the Royal Palace near the top of the ugly dolomitic
hill behind the hotel, making notes for a novel. Two, three, novels.
Between a slight hunger and the delicious ease I feel when I can live
a completely irresponsible life, my brain raced ahead of me like a
colt. I walked a little in the dusty quiet square outside the gardens,
drank more coffee, and went back to my notes. When I closed my
eyelids, the sun drew on them a black sinuous line which was the
Danube.

I had brought two letters of introduction, one to a journalist, the
correspondent in Budapest of the *News Chronicle*, another to a
Madame F—— K——, from a friend in London who had asked me
to take her a tin of Earl Grey tea. Reluctantly, I had posted them in
Vienna, and when I went back to the hotel about seven o'clock, the
hall porter handed me a letter from Madame F—— K——, and a
visiting card. *Baneth Alexander, Correspondent of the London News
Chronicle. Hungarian Chamber of Commerce.* The last words had been
crossed out in pencil.

'The gentleman is waiting for you.'

Turning, I saw a short middle-aged man buttoned into a thick
overcoat. He had black hair, black very bright eyes, a creased white
face the texture of soft india-rubber, perfectly round. He was wearing
grey kid gloves and a monocle on a broad moiré ribbon.

He smiled and bowed. 'I got your letter from Vienna this morning only and I telephoned at once, but you had gone out, you are
very active, the English are all active. I am charmed to find you at
last.'

'It is kind of you to come, Mr Alexander.'

'Baneth. In this country we place the surname before the other
names. It is absurd, of course. I tell you because you will wish to
know everything about me. How long have you been in Budapest?
Today only? Good, good. What have you done already? Have you
seen some people?'

He had a clear soft voice, and his eyes never moved from my face.
'What are you going to do this evening?'

'Nothing.'

'Then you will have dinner with me? No, it is a pleasure for me to
meet a friend of the editor of the *News Chronicle*. I shall take you to
my club, it is fortunate I have no engagement for this evening. You

have just come in and wish to go to your room. I shall wait as long as you wish, I am not in a hurry. Though I am a Jew I do not run everywhere.'

With my indifference to people's looks, I had not noticed that he was a Jew. Now that he had told me, I saw it in the blunted softness of his features and long fine womanish mouth. He had very small soft hands.

We took a tram in the square outside the hotel, and crossed the bridge. He went on questioning me, with a gentle insistence.

'What is your position on the *News Chronicle*?'

I realized that if I told the truth he would be bitterly disappointed. 'I am a writer, I have written many articles for the paper.'

'Oh, you have written articles. I am sorry, I have missed them. But you are a friend of the editor? You know everyone in London? Why have you come to Budapest? You must not go back and say I am in despair. You can see I am not in despair. I am objective. After the war, Count Bethlen—you have heard of him—told me, "I can ask your opinion because I am sure you will give it without fear or politics." He asked me to do certain things for him.'

He broke off, to speak to the conductor with the same smiling energy.

'I know everyone. Not only Count Bethlen. I know the tram conductors and the dirty little newspaper boys. They are all my friends.'

Sitting opposite us in the tram was a remarkably handsome little boy, shabbily dressed, nursing on his bare knees a school satchel and a bunch of lavender. Leaning across, Baneth talked to him for a moment, then chose a stem of lavender.

'Please take this,' he said to me.

I gave the child an apologetic smile. Smiling back, he handed me several pieces of his lavender, whispering to Baneth.

'He says he would give you all of it, but it is for his mother.'

'In Hungary even the schoolboys are charming,' I said ridiculously.

'Well, he is a nicely brought-up little Jewish boy.'

Impulsively—it seemed the right thing to do—I gave Baneth a piece of my lavender. He took it, looking at me gravely, and throughout the evening kept on taking it from his pocketbook to smell.

We were now well into Pest. 'Here we arrive,' he said merrily. 'We are almost at my club. But first we shall walk a few steps, I want to show you something.'

We were in a wide square, scarcely lit by a lamp or two. Trees, possibly a park, stood about at the far side: in front of them a massive stone column rose into the blackness—the Great War memorial.

None of these memorials move me except those with no aesthetic merits, on the edge of a village or in the busy street of some small town, where it is possible to imagine that the dead young men crossed here between the narrow pavements or stood there, idly breaking a branch from the hedge. Great marble monuments mock the obscure dead. Who, looking at them, remembers a boy with unformed features and large clumsy hands?

Baneth was talking in a lively voice. 'Andrássy Street, behind you, is the finest street in Europe. It will be to let when they have got rid of the dirty Jews. Please look only at the base of the column—at the statue of Arpád. He was a savage who founded Hungary. I must tell you only the truth—he was not a Jew. But he chose the Jewish religion. He had all the others explained to him and decided on the Jewish. Repeat this, please, to a Hungarian who is not a dirty old Jew. Very likely he will not be a Hungarian either, he'll be a Slav or a Swabian, or a mongrel. I, I am pure Hungarian, my family has been living in Buda for hundreds of years.'

He smiled finely. 'Now, this way, please.'

We dined in the lighted garden of his club. I was the only woman there and the only Gentile. The other diners glanced at me inquisitively as they passed the table. Baneth fixed each of them with his single eyeglass, and answered their greetings with the greatest affability and the reserve of an important diplomat.

As delicately as I could, I asked him whether the Jews in Hungary feared trouble. He shrugged his shoulders.

'After Béla Kun a great many poor lower-class Jews were killed a little brutally. An old friend of mine, a Christian and a Conservative Nationalist, what you call a Tory, of very good family, made speeches saying that every Jew, rich and poor, must be stripped and driven out. I went to this man, and I asked him, "Why do you say these things? You know me. Do I deserve to be murdered?" He said, "Well, you Jews live at a swifter pace than we Hungarians. You are going to say that since the treaty the country is ruined and can't afford not to work quickly. Please don't be silly. To live as you do is against our Hungarian character—it offends us." Very well. I understand. I agree that the five percent of Jews in Hungary ought to give way to the ninety-five percent of Hungarians. But it ought to be arranged in a decent way, not in the cruel way they do it in Germany and soon will here.' In a meditative voice he added,

'I try to be objective.'

He held the stem of lavender under his nose. 'Do you see that man with grey hair?' His eyes sparkled with a youthful malice. 'He is one of the Jews I dislike. During the war he made clothes, rotten clothes, and became rottenly rich. He decided to be baptized. I asked him, "Why have you been baptized?" He replied, "We Jews ought to be assimilated. We must assimilate ourselves." I answered him, "If you mean by it turning a bad Jew into a bad Christian, then you are assimilated already".' He laughed gently. 'Some of these spoiled Jews do not like me. I make jokes about them. Before the war a schoolfellow of mine became a nobleman—I don't imagine what it cost him. You know—I explained you—we put the Christian name after the surname; his first name is Andreas, it sounds a little like Andrássy, and foreigners take him for one of that family. Do you believe he corrects them? One day he came into the restaurant of the Szent Margitsziget; there was no room for him, he made a row about it, and the head waiter suggested, "Perhaps you can sit for a few minutes at a table where there is only one gentleman." Very well, my assimilated friend looked round the room and saw a young man lunching alone; he went up to him, bowed like an officer, and said in German, "Baron etc etc etc von Nimburg. May I give myself the honour etc etc of sitting here?" The young man looked at him once politely and said, "Esterházy. Please sit down." You know what that means here, to be an Esterházy? Perhaps the story isn't true. I hope it is. When I am feeling sad about all these threats and assimilations, I remember it and laugh . . . What do you think?'

I thought that I had never seen malice allied to so much gentleness and serene smiling philosophy. I thought that, as a human being, he was probably worth a dozen Esterházys. Before I could say anything—I had no idea what to say—he went on with energy,

'Don't think that we Jews are wise. Our rich clever leaders are making frightful mistakes, for which we others shall pay with our teeth.' He smiled sweetly. 'But I am not consulted.'

Outside the hotel, he asked me,

'What will you do tomorrow?'

I had an appointment, I told him.

'Then you know some people in Budapest?'

'One or two.'

'They are journalists?'

'No—private persons.'

He swallowed his curiosity. Holding my hand between both his small paws, he said warmly,

'If you will be here another two or three days at least I shall ask my friend Count K—— H—— to dinner. He is of old family. You will like him.'

Sighing—I infinitely prefer to be alone in a foreign place—I asked him to come to the hotel tomorrow about five and drink coffee with me, on the terrace of the *Wellenbad*. Then I went upstairs to my room and patiently transcribed all he had said—no, all I thought worth remembering.

The St Gellért had two fine baths, one in the hotel where powerful sulphur springs lifted all but the heaviest bodies out of the water, and another outside, with artificial waves and a wide double terrace. It was again a day of stifling heat, but Baneth was muffled in his overcoat. In the strong light I saw that it was turning green, and worn down to the thread on the carefully-brushed cuffs and shoulders.

Stirring his coffee absently, he said,

'Yesterday you asked me how things are here. I shall tell you. The country is being driven to an abyss—' he pronounced it *ábbiss*— 'I don't even know whether it can escape. I will tell you another story—this Baneth, you will say, is always telling stories. When I was a boy an old journalist—he was a Jew, of course—told me, "If our mother has bad servants, she is still our mother. It is wrong to write what Hungary does against her Jews." Well, I want only that other nations should leave us alone and not write about us.' He paused and went on in a still gentler voice. 'How could the *News Chronicle* understand what is necessary for us, for Hungary? They do not understand—I must send *only* news which helps Hungary. They have been complaining of me in London?'

I did not immediately realize that he hoped I could put him right with the newspaper. Nor did I realize his position. Under a new law Jews were being thrown out of work in Budapest. His job as correspondent of an English paper was safe—exactly as long as he was able to send the sort of news they wanted.

'Things are difficult?'

'A short time ago something happened which I shall explain. A man came here. I did not speak to him, I avoided him on purpose.

He talked to a great many people, and he got a fair idea of what is going on. His article in the *News Chronicle* did not tell lies. But he told things I would never have told. Certain people here were angry, they thought I had given him his facts. A question was asked in Parliament, there were even letters in the press. No one gave my name. No one said, "Baneth the dirty Jew is sending out anti-Hungarian propaganda." But wait, please.'

He drew from his pocket a shabby note-book. Moving aside the stem of lavender carefully he took out a frayed newspaper cutting.

'Listen. It is written in a bad style—rotten—I shan't read much of it. "How long are we going to allow a dirty animal from the ghetto jungle to send lies about Hungary to an English newspaper? Somebody should slit the pig's throat. He would squeal on another note." I went to a friend of mine in the Government and told him, "I had nothing to do with the article in the *News Chronicle*. I would not write such things about Hungary." He was polite, but I ask myself did he believe me? In any case he could do nothing. Nothing.'

His black eyes sparkled. 'I told you I am objective. It is my religion. Religion of a dirty little ghetto animal.'

He stood up, and bowed to an almost naked young woman sitting at the next table. She waved carelessly.

'She is the wife of my friend Count K— H—. I think he is bathing. When he comes, I shall bring him to speak with you. He is of very old family—excuse me, I told you already. He is also well-known.'

The air, absolutely still and as if wadded, muted the cries and laughter from the bath. There was a smell of geraniums and heavily oiled bodies. Fully-clothed dancers crowded the narrow space between the tables and white wicker chairs. In spite of the heat, old gentlemen in high-heeled shoes leaped like goats, hands on the shoulders of young women who must have been more enduring than they looked. Averting his glance from them, Baneth said,

'Like every country which is on its way down, we are governed by a sick man. It has been so for years. In 1936 Gömboes was with a shrunken kidney already, and last year Dáranyi is a thyroid-deficient. It is very sad.'

'You have a new Prime Minister,' I said.

A smile ran through the creases of his face. 'Dr Imredy—I know his doctor—has an ulcerated stomach. My theory is proved. I hope he will recover. But he will not save Hungary from—what will they call it this time? A spiritual regeneration . . . Excuse me, I shall bring my friends.'

Followed by a yawning reluctant wife, the count was smiling vaguely. He sat down between her and Baneth, and became absorbed in pinching his body in its cotton wrap.

'You are cold?' Baneth said anxiously. 'The water is too cold for you? Why do you bathe? Your wife is wiser, she never bathes.'

'The water is unpleasantly warm, but my blood is slow,' his friend said, smiling.

'The K—— H—— family,' Baneth said to me, 'is one of the oldest Hungarian families. You need only to visit the crypt of their palace at Esztergom to see in stone nine centuries of our history. The count will give you his permission.'

'Certainly. Do you wish to go there?'

'I should be delighted,' I said. I had no intention of going. The count knew it without glancing at me.

'My wife adores England,' he murmured.

She looked at me for the first time. 'We go to London as often as we can afford it.'

Her body was a dark gleaming brown. A strip of thin blue cotton drawn tightly across her breasts drew the eye to them. Another strip shaped into narrow drawers vanished when she crossed her legs. Behind dark lashes her eyes were bored and greedy, the eyes of a clever slut. Her toe nails had been painted a black-red and trimmed into points. She yawned, showing narrow white teeth like a little animal's.

'You are tired?' her husband said gently.

'Yes. We must go. But give me a cigarette first.'

I don't smoke, but I was carrying English cigarettes to give away. I offered her the case.

'Oh,' she cried, 'wonderful. They are too expensive to buy here. I make my English friends bring them.'

'I have a friend coming in September,' I said. 'If you'll give me your address, I'll send some by him.'

The only reason I made the offer was to show Baneth that I admired his friends. Smiling innocently, he watched the young woman scrawl her name in my notebook, 'Margit K—— H——,' and said,

'She will not tell you herself because she is polite, but I can say it for her. On the envelope you must put: The Countess K—— H——.'

She grimaced. She stood up, and ran a finger under the edge of her drawers: a thin paring of white showed, exactly below the cheek. Baneth bowed deeply.

When they had gone he asked,

'Do you like the countess?'

'She is very pretty.'

'I don't like her nails,' he said in a gentle voice. 'And I am sorry I must tell you they are the only genuine thing about her. I don't like to say what would hurt the Count, who is my friend, but I don't know anything good about her. He—I love him—he is intelligent. It is a great pity . . . But I must make you amused. You are invited to dinner?'

Only for a drink, but if I said so he would certainly ask me to dine with him, and quite apart from preferring my own company I did not care to take so much from him: he was certainly not well-off.

'I was invited for seven o'clock,' I said.

'It is twenty past. You will be in good time for Budapest.' He stood up. 'But you must go. I shall take you. What is the address, please?'

'Malna Utca. It is on this side. I shall take a cab.'

'It is not necessary. There is a tram along the embankment. You will be there quickly. It gives me pleasure to come with you.'

We crossed the square to the tram. Baneth smiled at me. 'You see? I have arranged everything for you. This is the right tram. Not even a moment to wait. Please sit here. And now tell me. You do not know these friends? Perhaps I know them?'

I did not answer. For no reason whatever, I felt sure that, if he knew the F— K—'s, they were people he would rather I did not meet.

In the poorly-lit tram, he looked yellow and downcast. Rousing himself, he said,

'If I tell you what is in my mind you will laugh at me. All these troubles in the world are caused by sun spots. Thunder disturbs horses, and we are a very little, only a little, more intelligent. The sun erupts and destroys seeds in the earth, the brain, the womb. It is written in the Talmud, *When spots appear on the sun the Jew should be afraid.* You know in the Talmud one sentence often needs many pages of commentary. The commentary on this sentence asks: Why are the Jews to be afraid? And the answer: Because when the rod is brought out it is those children who have been beaten before who must fear.' He looked into my face. 'It is true,' he said softly, almost gaily.

We left the tram and I followed him through dark streets. It was still very warm, and a light breath from the Danube did no more than thicken the darkness.

'This is Malna Street. Do you know the number?'

I peered at the nearest door. 'This is it.'

'You see,' he said, with smiling triumph, 'you were right to trust me.'

'It was good of you to bring me.'

'It is my greatest happiness. I shall telephone to you in the morning.'

Madame F—— K—— was young and amiable. We sat in the courtyard, at a wooden table on which were glasses and an oil lamp. She thanked me for bringing the tea, and went on quickly,

'What a pity you came after dark. This house would amuse you if you could see it, it is small and very old. My parents bought it in 1918 when they came here from what is now Slovakia. My father said, "We must only buy a small place; we shall be going back in six months, this nonsense can't last, and we shall need our money." I was four years old. In six months we had lost both money and estate. I and my husband and my brother all live here. We didn't do anything to the house and at last it was so uncomfortable I said, "We must do something, we can't squat here any longer like Czechs." So now it is not so bad.'

Her brother came in from the street carrying a suitcase. He had been to look at a summer hotel in the mountains, and his sister asked him about it. Turning to me, she explained,

'Since the Tatras were stolen from us, we have to find other places for holidays.'

'The place was lovely,' her brother said, 'lovely, lovely. But the hotel was full of old post-office girls who went to bed every night at eight o'clock. Ferenc and I bought four bottles of wine and sang songs. In the morning they said, "You mustn't disturb the other guests." I said, "Excuse me, what is this? A hospital?" '

I had fallen, as one falls asleep, into a state of mind a great deal too familiar. The small courtyard, the weak ring of light in the centre of the table, the three young Hungarians—her husband had arrived and kissed my hand carelessly—the glass of wine in my hand, lost reality: it ran out of them as air seeps through a puncture. It became difficult to feel that they existed, in the vital sense of the word. They were there, dwindled, and drained of substance, I could make them out, but not add myself to them. Then the feeling of estrangement spread to my hands, my body. I began to lose touch with myself. (I imagine that dying, if one dies rather slowly, must be much the same sensation of withdrawal from the living and from oneself. A withdrawal of reality, and from it.) I have learned that to struggle against this annoying condition is worse than useless. It is, though, easy enough to keep up an air of being present—and wait for it to take itself off.

'Where have you come from?' F—— K—— asked me.

'Prague.'

'How do you like the Czechs?'

'They are very decent people.'

Both young men shouted at once. The brother's voice rang like brass.

'Oh, so you think that! Well, Mrs—I can't remember your name —I will tell you. In September there will be no Czechs. Hitler will march in, and we shall march into Slovakia at the same time. It will be after the harvest. These damned swine of Czechs have lived too long already. Look here, every Saturday I go into Slovakia to see my wife. They know me at the frontier, they know my wife is with her parents, ill. And every Saturday for a year they make me strip to my skin and search me like a thief. They do it to everybody. Every Hungarian. It's nice to have your shoes ripped off their soles. Once they smashed my watch and handed me a paper to sign that I did it myself, I was so gay I jumped on it. I said, "No, I don't sign, I don't sign nothing written in Czech." Very well, they put me in a room with nothing, no chair, no fire, it is winter, and say, "See how you like that." So in the morning I sign—or I would be there now. You think they are decent? Yes, you have an English passport. The swine smile at you.' He shouted with laughter. 'If I had *just once* an English passport!'

'He is telling the truth,' F—— K—— said. He told a long story about the meanly savage treatment of two Hungarian schoolboys, and exclaimed, 'It *must* finish. There *must* be war.'

'Perhaps you are shocked,' his wife said to me. 'But, after all, we must get our country back.'

Her brother laughed again. 'Now *I* will shock her. Mrs, there is a Hungarian officer going into Czechoslovakia, he is a spy, and they play a trick on him with an old lady. She asks him, "Please look after my luggage for a minute." Well, there is something, I don't know what, in the luggage. They arrest him. They beat him. They inject caffeine in him to bring him alive. They beat him again. Then caffeine.

Then beating. He is unconscious. They throw cold water over him. They take a piece of wood and scrape the flesh of his leg, to the shin bone. He is unconscious again. Again injections. At the end they empty him into a coffin full of nails, and roll and roll it until he is all, all, all, wounds, and throw him away, he is finished, dead, in a railway siding. Another Hungarian, a spy, gets to him, he is still breathing, and this fellow puts him in a truck, you know, covered up with coal. He is safely over the frontier and is in hospital for eighteen months. I know him.'

He waited for me to show my horror. I did not disbelieve him, but he might have been talking about puppets for all I felt or cared.

'But, Mrs, look here,' he said sharply. 'We don't act no different ourselves. Our soldiers captured a Czech captain two weeks ago. He was spying. My friend who was there told me, "Although his feet were broken, twice, and his arms and legs all broken, we didn't get anything out of him." Look here, that was a pity!'

'Never mind,' F—— K—— said, smiling. 'In September we march. In less than two weeks it is over. The French, pooh! The English——' he stretched his neck from side to side—'cluck, cluck, in Parliament.'

'The Czechs will fight,' I said.

His brother-in-law kicked his legs up like a schoolboy. 'Fight? They'll run when they see us. Look here, you're mad. They're all peasants and cowards.'

'And you've forgotten Russia,' I said.

'Russia has no officers! Stalin has shot them. There is only Jugoslavia. Look here, we don't want to fight the Serbs, they are tough!'

'Miss Storm Jameson will think you are both savages,' Madame F—— K—— said, smiling at me. She filled my glass.

'Tell me one thing,' her husband, said, almost quietly. 'Why doesn't your country make friends with the Germans? You won't be able to do anything against them, they're marvellous. Lions! That man Hitler is like God, he makes men. The German air force is magnificent: in Vienna they dropped thousands of men by parachute, with full equipment, on the Aspern aerodrome. The other day I went to see a news film, and there was your king, King George six, reviewing his troops. I was shocked. They held their bayonets up anyhow, as sloppy as girls. Then directly after, German troops—simply majestic—every bayonet in line. I was in Vienna when they marched in—with the goose-step—whack, whack, *bang*. Tears ran over my face, and I thought: Oh, my poor country, what could we do against these fellows?'

You talking ape, I thought remotely. I was not offended by his contempt for England. It did not occur to me for a moment to take him seriously. A dog lifting his leg against a lamp-post.

'You know,' Madame F—— K—— said, 'it's true. I dislike Germans, they are mannerless bullies. But our only chance is to march *with* them. If we don't, they'll squeeze us to death.'

They'll do that anyway, I thought. I made some polite meaningless answer, and looked at my watch.

'Don't go yet,' she said warmly. 'We're not really savages. How long will you stay in Budapest? You ought to see the country. Lake Balaton is very beautiful. We could drive you to see my husband's parents on Sunday.'

'My parents are mad,' her husband said calmly. 'They keep twenty-five indoor servants and my mother never buys a new dress. The whole of that generation is the same. Every soul in Hungary could be dying of hunger and they wouldn't know what to do. When we begin running the country we're going to break up the big estates and give the peasants some of the land.'

'But, look here, half Hungary really is starving,' the brother shouted. 'Go into the country and offer a child sweets—he'll think they're marbles. There are hundreds of young men, doctors, students, lawyers, thankful to address envelopes. If you speak about it to one of these damned old idiots, he'll whistle a song. Bah! We shall kick them out of the way.'

I stood up. The sense of unreality and absence was beginning to wear off, and the only thing I wanted was to escape. I thought: I don't understand these people. If there is such a thing as civilization, they haven't yet been *assimilated*.

'We should show her at least something,' F—— K—— said. 'Have you been to the Kakuk? No? No gipsies? Oh, but you must. To-morrow night—we'll take you tomorrow night.'

I hesitated over an excuse. His wife said quickly,

'Please do come. You have no engagement. I am sure you have none.'

Vexed by my clumsiness—I should have lied quickly—I said,

'Thank you, I should like it.'

In the morning, the telephone rang before I had finished drinking my coffee and reading through the notes I had made the night before. My heart sank a little. Although I was not responsible for the uncertainty of Baneth's life, and the dangers—these were certain—hanging over him, he made me feel guilty.

'Baneth Alexander. It is you? Good morning. How are you? I hope you will dine with me this evening at my club—if you do not dislike my club. I shall ask a friend——'

'Your club is delightful,' I said. 'But I am very sorry, I am going out to dinner.'

There was a brief silence. Since I had withheld the name of my Malna Utca acquaintances, he must be feeling certain they were the wrong sort of Hungarian, the sort which describes Jews as animals from a ghetto jungle.

'When are you leaving? I am afraid you will go soon. I am glad for you that you have friends here, but I wish you had none.'

'Tomorrow,' I said, 'I'm leaving tomorrow.'

The silence this time was longer. 'Your letter said four days. Perhaps I have miscounted.'

'Today is the fourth day,' I made my voice as affectionate as possible. 'Perhaps you could come here for coffee—if you can spare the time.'

'After six I have all the time,' he said quietly. 'I shall come.'

He came punctually. 'We will go out,' he said. 'I hope you did not come to Budapest to sit indoors. Besides, I have an appointment.'

'Surely——'

He interrupted me, smiling. 'Shall I tell you what Count Bethan said to me? He said that when he wants to know what everyone in Budapest—not a few people, but everyone—is thinking, he asks me to come and see him.' We were crossing the street, and he took my arm. 'This tram will move now. Please be careful.'

'Where is your appointment?' I asked.

'Here.'

We stopped at a dilapidated newspaper kiosk. The middle-aged woman inside, worn to a rag of grey flesh, looked at us without interest. Baneth glanced at his watch.

'It's later than I thought,' he said, grieved. He poked his head into the kiosk. His politeness forced him to repeat in English anything he said in Hungarian, even to waiters.

'I am asking her: Do you know that dirty little boy who comes here?'

The woman said something in a scrannel voice.

'No, no, I know it is not your son. Your son is smaller and dirtier. The boy I mean fetches your copies of the *Magyarsag*. He asked me for a paper fan, like the one I gave your son. I promised to bring it. Please give it to him when he comes tomorrow.'

He handed her the fan and turned to me with his sweet smile. 'Now we shall go to a place I know which is comfortable, and drink coffee.'

The café, a large one, was filled with Jews, and after a moment I realized that they were speaking German to each other. Baneth looked at them with a gentle malice.

'It is sad, but I can't help remembering what a French Rabbi said about the German refugees in Paris. *Ils sont nos frères, mais ils sont Boches.* These are all rich men, and I only like rich Jews when I remember they are in danger.'

'Are they really in danger?'

'The Jews in Hungary are done for,' he said softly. 'Perhaps Hungary is done for. For the Jews there is no perhaps. It is only a question of how many months.'

His face took on the look of a mischievous child it had when he was going to make one of his quips.

'There is a Press Control Board now, which is going to have a small percentage of Jews. One of my friends, a Christian, said to me, "Of course you will be on it." I told him, "No, I shall refuse." He asked, "Why?" "Because," I said, "if I take this place I am depriving some other Jew, with a wife and family, of a chance of safety. I will sell bootlaces. And I hope you have many many pairs of boots, because I am sure you will buy your bootlaces from me. But I am afraid you will not have any boots, and I shall not be able to live".' He lifted his hands. 'To be a poor Jew in a rich city is not a bad thing. To be a poor Jew in a poor city! They are going to ruin Budapest. All these restrictions on the Jews means ruin—for a simple reason. Only the Jews understand banking and business. Other Hungarians despised these professions. There was no law to forbid Gentiles to be bankers, journalists, business men. They chose not to be! Now they have lost their estates and they see the rich dirty old Jews, and want to step into their place. Why not? you say. I shall tell you. They are not fitted for this work. After they have killed the Jews they will kill Hungary. Even if I am dead or half-dead, I shall be in pain for the country . . . But now I sadden you. Forgive it, please.' He began smiling again. 'I am luckier than most of my friends. I have no wife or family. It is my only fortune now.'

His eyes sparkled. 'I couldn't speak of my salary from the *News Chronicle* as a fortune. They allow me so little that one of my friends said to me, "Other men keep an actress, you keep the *News Chronicle*." I laughed. I shall try to laugh—I am objective—when the

News Chronicle writes to me they must find a correspondent who is not a Jew, because a Jew cannot send the news.'

'Why not come to England at once?' I said. 'You have friends in London. If you wait until there are hundreds of refugees from Hungary, it won't be easy.'

My conscience was speaking. My heart sank at the thought of being obliged to think about him in London.

'You are too kind.'

'Good. You'll come.'

'No.'

'Why not? You would be safe in England.'

'I am so much a Hungarian—since I am a Jew—that I would rather starve in Budapest. It proves how tactless we Jews are!'

He told me several more stories, some amusing. When we left the café, and were sauntering along the embankment, I thought that the Danube is one of the cruellest rivers. Running out of the darkness of the past, it has heard so many cries, closed over so many victims like the man talking beside me, that it should be called Acheron. With a sudden real grief, I said,

'Do think again about coming to London.'

He laughed gently. 'How kind you are to think of me.'

When we reached the hotel, he asked,

'You are dining with the same friends?'

'Yes.'

'Where are you going tomorrow, when you leave?'

'To France.'

'Ah.' He sighed and smiled. 'I don't care for the French but I admire them. They refuse to believe that they have no longer any power over what happens to them . . . You are leaving by the morning train?'

'Yes—alas.'

I stood a minute and watched him walk away, with his short quick step, holding round him the folds of his absurd overcoat . . .

I do not know what it is that gives to almost any continental night club a gaiety lacking in the determined efforts of the English to enjoy themselves by paying through the nose for inferior wine, carelessly served, in a stuffy overcrowded room. I once put this question to an old Frenchwoman who had been, in the greatest respectability, the mistress of two well-known writers and was the widow of a third. Narrowing wrinkled eyelids in a smile, she said, 'My dear child, the emanations.'

'What can you mean?'

'Put one of us—' she meant her countrymen —'down in a *boîte*, even a stupidly fashionable one, and at once his mind begins to give off little wisps of amusement and interest and curiosity and malice, so that the air in the room is alive with them. You, your men and young women, when they come out for the night, leave their minds at home. We have come here to enjoy ourselves! they say. So that what they give off is only animal spirits. Like horses.'

She may be right.

There was nothing much about the Kakuk: a small discreetly lighted courtyard, overlooked by a balcony as well-screened—from its single window the occupants could look down into the court-yard without being seen themselves—as any Moorish room, a few tables, the gipsies. And the conversation was not gay, or intelligent. And yet there was in fact gaiety, a smiling movement of the air—those emanations, no doubt.

'He has had a boring day,' Madame F—— K—— said, smiling at her husband. 'He needed to come here.'

His position in a Jewish banking house was, I suspected, a minor one. It was interesting only as a portent. His was the first generation of landowners' sons to go into business.

'The head of my firm is a terrible fellow,' he said to me. 'He drinks coffee. He pulls the saccharine out of his pocket—so—he has diabetes—then stirs it with his pen. Then—excuse me for telling you—he cleans his ear with the pen. Then he says, "Did I put sugar in?" and sticks the pen back in the coffee. Then he wipes it on his sleeve.'

'Look here, Mrs. Before the war people of our class didn't go into trade or banking. Such a thing was unheard of. We left that to the Jews to do for us. But we are learning. In a few months we shall turn every Jew out and run Hungary ourselves. You'll see then!'

F—— K—— burst out laughing. 'You should have stayed here to meet my father. You know, he could bathe in the lake—Lake Balaton—from his own land. But he won't. Why? Because, miles farther on, anyone can bathe, Jews can bathe! So he has a bath filled from a well, and sits in it in his bathing drawers.'

'He is absurd,' Madame F—— K—— said, smiling.

'I daresay, but——'

'But with these hands,' her brother cried merrily, holding them up, 'I am going to strangle every Jew I meet. When the time comes . . .

If you are so fond of Jews in England, why don't you give them Shanghai? Let them fight a little for once.'

'There were many Jews fighting in the war,' I said.

Both young men went off into fits of laughter. 'What did they do? Sell the others their bootlaces?'

I felt savagely angry with myself. Since I hadn't the wit to be able to deal with their unpleasant obsession without incivility, I should not have put myself in this position. I was ashamed.

F—— K—— took from his pocket a photograph of the Nazi leader, Franz Szálasi. Gazing at it with ingenuous devotion, he handed it to me.

'Isn't he in prison?' I asked.

'Yes. But we'll have him out. A few months. And then—well. wait, you wait!'

Jumping up, now perfectly good-humoured, he went over to the gipsies and ordered them to play his favourite song, and conducted them in it with long fine hands. His face was altered and softened by a childlike happiness.

'You must never say *you* to these fellows,' his brother-in-law instructed me. 'Always *thou*. Or they won't respect you. Ah, what do I need more from life than gipsy music and a bottle of wine! No money. The Jews started that filthy habit here.'

Thank God I am leaving tomorrow, I thought. All my pleasure in being here was poisoned by—ah, be honest, I told myself, by your own stupidity and clumsiness.

In the morning, I as near as a touch missed my train. A score of peasants, women, their faces blackened and withered by the sun, close-plaited hair, bare feet, came into the station. I turned to watch them. An elderly man was herding them in front of him like a flock of goats, and their bare feet on the platform made exactly the sound of pattering hooves. One woman had her child with her, a little boy, so skinny, legs like a bird's, and so anxious, that to look at him drained the meaning out of life. What are we worth if only one child is born to know only hunger and fear?

The porter with my luggage had vanished. After a minute's suppressed panic—I was alone on this platform—I saw, two platforms away, a train which looked important enough to be the express from Bucharest, and ran to it across the rails, dodging between two shabbier trains.

My porter was there—and Baneth.

He was staring at the carriages with a blank face. In one hand he held a bunch of pale feathery grasses; they were like something I remembered, something out of childhood. He must, I suppose, have been thinking that I had lied to him. When he caught sight of me his expression changed to one of the liveliest gaiety and affection. He gave me the bunch of grass.

'Why did you come at this hour?' I exclaimed.

'We have frightened ourselves yesterday,' he said softly, 'with the idea that Budapest will be destroyed, or I shall be killed. Thinking of it, I came to say goodbye.'

'Ah, do come to London.'

'I am afraid you will miss your train,' he said, smiling. 'Get in now, please. It leaves suddenly.'

I felt the greatest respect for him—and relief. Only another minute or two, I thought.

As the train moved out he stood, smiling, a hand raised holding the monocle on its black ribbon. Dwindling quickly, he disappeared. I laid the grasses on the rack, meaning to forget them when I got out.

Guy was waiting for me in Basle, with the car, and we drove across France to Talloires, on Lake Annecy. Need I say that I was madly happy? I do not go to France for any other reason than to be happy, and am. And lighthearted and sane. Even when I was writing down, not to forget them, scenes and things said there, the images of Budapest in my brain began to seem unreal; the faces, even Baneth's, became bloodless and spectral, drifting at the back of my mind like the clouds of dead and dying moths I saw a few weeks later on the edge of the Saône at Mâcon, a million slender transparent bodies, visible only as a network of thread-like veins, a dry whisper in the river breath—*Mânes*, the porter at the Hôtel de l'Europe et de l'Angleterre called them: manes, ghosts, spirits of the dead. Well, why not? A river bank is the right place for the dead to collect.

It struck me as I made my notes that Vienna is as far east as an Englishman can go without losing touch completely with a tradition, only partly Christian, which holds in one and the same hand even countries hostile to each other.

Mâcon, Saulieu, Bourges, Troyes, Rheims, St Quentin, Abbeville—so many white stones on a road stretched between the beginning and the end of my life, so many streets seen for the first time, with such delight, with such deep contentment, so many old walls still warm under the hand laid on them.

July 1938: I was happy to be alive . . .

After the war, I tried to find out what had happened to Baneth. In vain—no one could tell me. Many years later, my friend Paul Tabori told me he had been killed in an air raid.

There were many worse ways he could have died in Budapest then.

Chapter 19

What happened at Munich in 1938 is spoken of as a respite for France and England. In effect it was more like a syncope, a failure of the heart which might have ended in the death of both countries. No one word exists to describe the curious taste of those weeks: it was bitter, rough, puckering the mouth like a green fruit, and as indigestible.

Helen Kirkpatrick was in London and I had invited her to lunch with me on the 5th of September. That day *The Times* carried a leader on the benefits of ceding the Sudetenland to Hitler, and started a great fluttering of the stool pigeons. When I walked into the Ivy and saw, at the farther end of the room, her head of a thirteenth-century angel, I wished I were going to have to listen to anyone but an American.

Naturally we talked only of the crisis—back and forth, over bones already picked clean and dry. Is Hitler now absolutely certain that he can have his war without being hindered by France and England (*cluck, cluck, in Parliament* . . .)? What will Russia do? What did a high-ranking French officer say last week? What, who, when? She was as well-informed as anyone, any foreign correspondent, intelligent, very charming. I began to think it had been foolish to dread meeting her.

Towards the end of the meal she said, with a fine ironical smile,

'I think the time has come for your Government to send yet another questionnaire to Berlin. It should run: Now that we have given you Czechoslovakia, how can we help you to (a) Poland (b) anything else you want? Which bit of the Empire would you like first?'

Her irony was completely justified. And since to show my insane rage would give away that I had been stung, I laughed.

That same day or the next I dined with Bjarne Braatoy and a man, a Danish industrialist, whose name I have forgotten. Bjarne this evening was more than ever Peer Gynt at his most excitable and irreverent. As we sat down, I began, 'Do you suppose war——'

He interrupted me with his loud high abrasive laugh. 'There isn't going to be war in this country.'

'Why not?'

'Either Hitler will be intimidated. Or your Government won't fight. Either way there will be no war.'

The Dane, a dry man, with an ironic smile that spread until it twitched his black eyebrows, said,

'You are right, my friend——'

'Of course I'm right!'

'——in Paris yesterday I asked the head of the firm we do business with, a great deal of business, it is a large firm: What about your treaty with the Czechs? He is a nice fellow, but he was ready to spit in my face. He said, "First, that crazy treaty is no longer valid, and second, if it is, no government, not even that *sale coquin* Blum, would dare to ask us to sacrifice another generation. This country is sick to death of war, we must, yes, must save our young men, *je me fous de la Tchécoslovaquie, elle m'emmerde*, Beneš is a crook, he wants to drag us into war and we shan't let him!'

'Neither of your countries is in danger,' I said.

Bjarne looked at me mockingly. 'Don't be too sure that yours is.'

'Why should Hitler take the trouble to invade my country?' the Dane said smiling. 'He has only to come to the front door.'

As the days passed I began to avoid foreigners. Talking about the crisis became as unpleasant as discussing the disgrace of a friend. So much has happened since, to erase the memory of those weeks of fear and sick shame, that it will seem an exaggeration to say that the handing over of the Czechs to Hitler is the worst, most corrosive shock the European mind—is there such a thing?—has suffered. It relegated to the museums the millenial image of European civilization which now, in the sixties, the rest of the world treats with indifference. Or should I say that it began the relegation made final in August 1945?

I worked. I finished James Hill's long novel, *No Victory for the Soldier*. It was a solid lively book, the story of John Knox from the day when, a Busoni of seven, he played in his first concert, to the day when he was killed in the Spanish civil war, and an effort at a portrait of the thirties, with a great many characters and a great many scenes in England and Europe.

After that I wrote rapidly a novel of the greatest ingenuity. *Here Comes a Candle* was a film never, alas, made. When I try to make money I always fail, all my successes of that kind have been accidents.

On the 22nd of September I had the briefest of letters from Jiřina Tůmová, enclosing an appeal signed by Czech writers. I read it, skipping sentences—it was not long—much as one avoids reading carefully the letter a friend has written to reproach us for a mean act.

'To the Conscience of the World

In this fateful moment, when a decision between war and peace is being reached, we, the undersigned Czech authors address this solemn appeal to all those who form the conscience of the world . . . truth . . . freedom . . . spirit' and the rest of it and the rest of it.

It had been sent out on the 14th, exactly a day before Chamberlain flew to Germany, to see how much or little of Jiřina's body would sate Hitler.

Very distinctly I saw her hand, as thin and weak as a child's, serenely folding the single page. Whoever else *took account of realities,* as the leader-writers say, she, when they offended her sense of decency and justice, would not. My poor friend, I thought with anguish, if the Germans invade your country, what will they do to you?

There are people who say that the nearly unbearable tension of the next few days, the distribution of gas-masks, the politicians' deathbed speeches, which sent a number of people, rich enough to pay through the nose for a funk-hole, scurrying out of London, were part of an adroit deception. That at no single moment during the negotiations—if you can use that term of a knock-down argument—was there the least intention on our part of risking war. The precautions were a political comedy.

I do not believe in so accomplished a cynicism. Our old gentlemen were not cynics, not even ironists. Even Chamberlain, fluttering, an elderly dove, between London and the vulture's nest, knew that he was dealing with a ruthless fellow, no compromising fellow Tory. A falling-out among the comedians, and the gas-masks would be needed.

The next day, after the last (near midnight) news on the wireless, I tuned into Prague—the B.B.C. announcer had just said that telephonic communication with Prague had ceased. For a few seconds a strong unhurried voice came into the room from the other side of Europe. I could not understand anything except the word for 'mobilization', which came several times. In a darkened city, lorries crammed with reservists were moving across the bridges, with some old legionary in what might be a French or a Czarist uniform waving them on. We may never hear a voice from Prague again, I thought. Jiřina . . .

I hope that records exist of the speeches made by Hitler and his creatures. Otherwise no one will be able to imagine their obscene energy. (I suppose that the sounds emitted during a lynching might match them, on a small scale.) I listened on Radio Paris to a meeting in the Sportpalast in Berlin—bestial howls from the audience and Hitler screaming like a trumpet and a horse . . . 'Herr Beneš lied . . . this fellow Beneš squatting in Prague . . . *Beneš und ich* . . . the liar and murderer, Beneš . . . Sieg Heil! Sieg Heil! Sieg Heil! . . .'

Divorced from their bodies, his voice and that of Goebbels revealed an odd thing. Even at his most obscene, Hitler did not cease to be a human being: hatred and cruelty are human. The other voice, Goebbels, convinced me that an abstraction, evil, *exists*, and that when the authors of the scriptures speak of the devil entering into a man, they knew what they were writing about.

Against these two energies, a human pitilessness and an inhuman one, what hope had our champion, a vain, obstinate, decent-minded old man? Chamberlain's voice when he broadcast about the Czechs gave away all his distaste for a small democratic people standing between him and his determination to prove that he knew better about the rulers of Germany than those unrealistic persons who babbled about torture, concentration camps, perjury, killings. Allowed, at Godesberg, to see maps prepared showing a dismembered Czechoslovakia, he said nothing about them. Neither his virtues of sincerity and stubbornness, nor his crippling absence of vision, were any use against unscrupulous greedy men who knew exactly what they were going to do as soon as the old gentleman left the room.

At his age, after a prudent life, he could expect that he was safe, that he need fear nothing in this world or the next, that great tragic events had no place in his career of a patient reasonable politician. He was parochial, not sinister. Loving his English parish, he would sacrifice any weaker country to have peace in it. Was it his fault that he had no more imagination than a French peasant unable to see over the top of his splendid dung-hill?

Ambiguous, two-faced, as were my feelings and thoughts during all this time, had I any right to curse him and his fellows? Yes, but *only* for allowing a venomous animal to grow to unmanageable maturity.

'Is it safe to take the children to Pevensey for two weeks?' my sister asked me.

'Yes, why not? After all, it's not the first place they'll bomb.'

She said calmly, 'I would rather be in my own house when a war starts.'

'Well, go. If I hear any certain news I'll telephone to you.'

On the afternoon of the 27th, I went round to her empty house to take in the gas-masks being distributed. The woman handed over three, a small one for Nicholas. I signed for them.

'There's also a four-months-old baby,' I said. 'What have you for her?'

'I'm afraid—nothing. You must wrap a blanket round her and run with her to the nearest gas-shelter.'

'Oh. Where is it?'

That it did not exist was part of the lunacy, no more insane than the rest.

The 9.40 news that evening was frightful. In the middle of it, my sister rang up from Pevensey.

'What does it mean, Dear Dog? Ought we to come home?'

'I don't know what it means. I suppose that Beneš is making up his mind now whether to give in or not.'

I felt absurdly at fault that her holiday was threatened.

Her light voice went on. 'I just thought you might know. I'm sorry for the poor Czechs, but, you know . . .'

'Exactly! In any case, it's not for tomorrow. Stay where you are.'

She rang off, and I went back to the wireless. 'We pray especially for those who bear the heaviest burdens at this time, the Chancellor of the German Reich . . . And we pray for ourselves, for the common people, that is, in every land . . .' A hymn and the benediction, and then, not a breath between them, 'This is the National Programme. A Comedian's Dream.' A salvo of voices bawling *Down at the old*

Bull and Bush and other songs of innocence brought into the room
my mother's strong gay scornful voice ... *As I walked along the
Bois de Boulogne, with an independent air* ... My brother, his small
round body, as hard as a green apple, convulsed with laughter he
could not contain, rolled across the floor between the piano and the
horsehair sofa ... Ah, let me go back, I begged. Nothing got since
is worth a minute of that infinite world, the sharpness and salt air
of its morning, the cold dew scattered by its yellow gorse, the more
than light on its hills, the sea wind, the small curled waves under the
floating gull, the harbour.

I switched the wireless off, so that her voice had it all its own way
in the room ...

After Munich, Jiřina sent out two more documents. Did it never
cross her mind that no one cares to hear from the dead?

The first was short.

'To the Conscience of the World

On this day when, by the decision of four statesmen, our country has
been abandoned and delivered to injustice, with its hands bound, we
remember your declaration of friendship, in the sincerity of which
we believe.' At this point, the writer's real voice failed him. The
trombones took over. 'Even in the difficulties of our present position,
we remain and we shall remain in the forefront of humanity's common struggle for truth and justice. We stand by our President and
without despair we fix our eyes on the tasks of the future and still
remain faithful to the moral and spiritual ideals of our nation.
Sacrificed, but not conquered, we charge you, who for the present
have escaped our lot, to persevere in the common struggle of man-
kind.'

A vast no-man's-land separates truth from the rhetoric composed
in anguish and good faith by people used to handling words. I
could have written the document myself, meaning every syllable
of it, and weighing the effect of each word on its readers.

A Czech who left Prague two or three weeks later told me that
Jewish and German refugees, forced into trains by Czech soldiers,
were being taken to the occupied areas, where they were jailed or
sent off to Dachau. Looking at me coldly, he went on,

'We can't hide them. What else can we do except try to satisfy the
Germans?'

(These appeals to the conscience of the world must be an instinct
with writers, a nervous reflex. The fact that they are addressed to
what obviously does not exist is of no importance. The acid applied,

the nerve twitches. On the 21st of June, 1964, in Oslo, I listened to an elderly Israeli writer reading, to a committee of fellow-writers from I forget how many nations, a statement—he had been refused leave to present it in the form of a resolution—about the employment 'by a neighbouring country' of scientists preparing nuclear weapons for an attack on his people. Trembling, he read it in a low voice. The effort he was making to keep his anguish within bounds almost suffocated him. There was no comment. The briefest possible spatter of applause and, with relief, the committee passed to the next item.)

Jiřina's second document was longer and very bitter. She enclosed with it one of the three letters she wrote during this time to reassure me that, whatever the documents said to the contrary, I, she knew, had not betrayed her and her country.

'. . . no, no, my darling, we need your pen and your strong heart, we are suffering still beyond measure, but there is so much hope in my heart that I can give you part of it . . .'

After the Germans marched into Prague, I had a postcard from her. She had chosen it carefully—a narrow window barred by a grill of Renaissance ironwork; behind it, a single lamp. The first lines were clear—'My darling, thanks for your kind words, they have been a comfort in my illness. It is receding now and I hope to be soon my old courageous self. But you, my love, be careful, your health is so uncertain.' The rest concealed a message I could not, to my grief, decode.

After this, nothing.

Chapter 20

I know one rational human being—one, that is, to whom the term 'man of reason' applies in a sense wholly unlike its meaning when applied, say, to Beneš, whose reasonableness drove him into seeking formula after formula to paper over the most gaping cracks in his policy, or when we mean by it a man temperamentally incapable, as Beneš himself was, of meeting violence by violence.

My one rational human being, one of the most remarkable men I know, Basil Liddell Hart, is governed, or governs himself, by an extreme distaste for the human vices of intolerance and prejudice. This discipline, self-applied by an intelligence at once lucid and solid, would make him inhuman if he were not the most loyal, the friendliest and most humane person in the world, the gayest of pessimists, and the best company.

Lean and tall, he has a head by Goya, tempered by an air of amusement and kindness. I believe he respects the rights even of fools. Certainly he only recognizes two sins—cruelty and intellectual dishonesty.

One of his most disconcerting traits is the mental flexibility which allows him to think an opponent's thoughts for him. The week after Chamberlain returned from Munich he told me that the next crisis would come in March.

'Why March?'

'Six months, not less and probably not much longer, is the time Hitler will need to prepare his next move against the Czechs.'

'Isn't there any hope that he'll be content with what he's got?'

'My dear Storm, no military adventurer could refrain from taking over a defenceless neighbour—we've just made Czechoslovakia completely defenceless and given him notice that we shan't try to stop him. In fact, we can't.'

It would be idiotic not to believe him. I believed that the Czechs—

that is, Jiřina—had until March. I believed at the same time that he was wrong.

A few weeks later, in October or November, he told me that a small group which included Duncan Sandys and himself was meditating a non-party movement—to be called The Hundred Thousand. Its aims: to broaden the government, begin urgent social reforms, put the country on a war footing as rapidly as possible, and stop the catastrophic retreat before Hitler.

As a Yorkshireman, I felt the strongest doubts. Not about him. He was one of the first persons an English nationalist-socialist party, if it turned into that, would silence. I was too diffident to say a word.

Besides, the only thing I wanted to ask him was: Is there going to be war? Afraid to seem naïve, I did not ask outright. I said,

'A war footing? Do you mean conscription?'

'No, certainly not. Militarily it would be useless, and another step towards the Totalitarian State in this country.'

'Then what do you mean?'

One has to listen with desperate attention to hear what he says in his low rapid voice. 'The next crisis may shock our incorrigibly hand-to-mouth government into making promises to the next victim, Poland—an insanely rash thing to do unless we have an alliance with Russia. So far as I know, nothing of the sort is being planned; in the end we shall be forced into one—in the teeth of men who care nothing about the country and only want to keep their power and profits—and the Russians will then be able to impose terms on us. A detestable state of affairs. Almost as unpleasant as the mess our military and civil preparations are in, thanks only in part to the Treasury.' He added with something as close to bitterness as he allowed himself, 'My worst fear is that the government will panic: the War Office and the General Staff would then, by force of habit, swing into the ghastly 1914-18 policy of flinging in masses of men. If they do, half a million young men will be sacrificed before they learn.'

'Do you really think there will be war?' I said.

'I put our chances of avoiding it as almost negligible. It's too late.'

Forgetting to pretend that I was calm and rational, I stammered, 'Because of one vain inhuman old man.'

'No, no, no, Chamberlain is well-meaning. He has no imagination, he doesn't believe that a fellow like Hitler exists. More remarkable, my dear Storm, he doesn't know the most elementary facts of European history.' He looked at me with a kind half mocking smile. 'He's not a pacifist, you know—though he wants their votes and shares some of their illusions.'

That evening, I repeated to my sister what he had said about the near-certainty of war. She sent a slow glance round her room, resting it longest on a Wedgwood bowl and a small old table of which she was proud. So had Anna Jerusalem looked at possessions that were as much part of her as her hands. Neither for my young sister were her things only a table, a chest, a cup. They were a living portion of her life and her children's lives, a promise she had made to the future. If she had cried out, I should not have felt this searing anger against the adventurers who dishonour all these millions of humble promises.

'If I had more of a garden I could grow enough food for Nick and Judy,' she said, scowling.

'You couldn't grow very much here,' I said.

'I know that,' she said sharply. 'I must think.'

I suppose that in the discussions she and her husband had, evening after evening, it was she who decided that they would let this precious house and rent one with enough ground to keep a family alive. In November she told me that they had looked at one in an isolated village some eight miles out of Reading; it was a large shabby Victorian place, standing in three or four acres, with fruit trees and a greenhouse.

'It's far too big for us,' she said, staring at me. 'We can only take it if you and Guy will share it with us.'

The idea of refusing her did not cross my mind.

It will be a bad war, I thought. Worse than the last. We'll go through it as a family.